SUMMARY TABLE

	STATISTICAL TESTS OF INFERENCES				CORRELATIONAL METHODS
e-Sample	Two Samples		K Samples		
	Independent	Related	Independent	Related	
omial test , 115-117 i square . 117-124	Chi square pp. 124-128	Chi square significant changes pp.130-132	Chi square pp.128-130	Chi square significant changes pp.132-134	Contingency coefficient pp. 220-223 Phi coefficient pp. 223-226 Contingent uncertainty pp. 226-230
	Median test pp.137-139 U-test pp. 140-145 Maximum Difference pp.145-150 Runs test pp. 150-153	Sign test pp.153-155 Rank difference test pp. 155-157	Median test p. 139		Spearman's rank coefficient pp. 233-237 Kendall's rank coefficient pp. 237-241 Kendall's coefficient of concordance pp. 241-244 Spearman's partial rank coefficient pp. 245-247 Kendall's partial rank coefficient pp. 247-248
est .161-165	t-test pp.165-176	t-test pp.176-179	Analysis of variance pp.179-197 pp.202-210	Analysis of variance pp.198-202	Pearson's correlation coefficient pp. 251-264 Linear regression pp. 264-279 Correlation ratio pp. 279-286 Partial correlation coefficient pp. 286-287 Multiple correlation pp. 288-293 Point biserial coefficient pp. 294-296 Biserial coefficients pp. 297-300 Tetrachoric coefficient pp. 300-302 Reliability coefficient pp. 311-319
	(See Interval Scale)				*(See* Interval Scale)

A Statistical Analysis
Of Behavior

Merle E. Meyer

University of Florida

A Charles A. Jones Publication

Wadsworth Publishing Company, Inc., Belmont, California

*To the students of the behavioral sciences
and education*

1 2 3 4 5 6 7 8 9 10 / 79 78 77 76

Library of Congress Catalog Card Number: 74-25824

International Standard Book Number: 0-8396-0053-4

Printed in the United States of America

Preface

One of the most fundamental tools for the behavioral sciences and their various technologies is statistics. It plays a role that closely parallels other forms of mathematics as tools for the other sciences. With a background in statistics, the student of behavior will quickly find himself able to read, with full understanding, the experimental literature in his science. Furthermore, with a good working knowledge of statistics, a student will be better able to plan a research study, to analyze the data by statistical methods, and to clearly interpret the findings for future laboratory courses. Statistics is so essential and so relevant in the behavioral sciences that most programs require at least one term of statistics following the introductory course.

The book was written for you, the student of behavior, assuming that this is your first course in statistics. It was designed in such a fashion that regardless of your background you will be able to gain the essential elements of statistics. In a general way, the materials have been programmed so at no time will you need more statistical information than you have already covered in earlier chapters. Each chapter builds upon the previous ones. In all probability you will need to go back for concepts that you missed or forgot. If you slowly work your way chapter by chapter, the materials should be easy for you to learn and to fully comprehend.

You may find the reading and the studying of this material slow going. However, like most research studies and other scientific writing, it just takes time. Hundreds of students have used this book in its prepublication form and enjoyed it. The learning of statistics can be a most rewarding experience.

Acknowledgments

Many individuals contributed to this book during its preparation. Students at Whitman College, Central Washington State College, and Western Washington State College learned portions of their statistics from preliminary drafts. Thanks must be given for their help, suggestions, and encouragement. I am grateful to Gerald Morlock for his critical reading of the final draft, to Joy Dabney for the illustrations, and to the staff of the Department of Psychology at Western who supported much of the clerical work.

I also express my appreciation to the many authors and publishers who permitted me to reproduce materials from their published works. These are acknowledged where the materials appear. In addition, appreciation is extended to the reviewers, Dr. A. R. Starry, Dr. James Walsh, Dr. B. J. Winer, Dr. Robert Wherry, Dr. James Sanders, and graduate student Jan Perney, for their valuable advice.

To the Instructor

In this elementary statistics text, I have used measurement theory as the organizational framework upon which the student can hang his statistical methods and concepts. The theory serves as the basis for the working statistical concepts, and in a general way, the theory functions as a mnemonic that makes statistical methods teachable.

I have attempted to present a variety of methods and to balance the coverage between descriptive, inferential, and correlational procedures. The contents of this text may be more than can be fully covered in one term. It is written for the beginning undergraduate student. Even if all topics are not covered within the time limits of your course, the text can serve as a statistical handbook for the undergraduate student in his later work. As a psychologist, I have drawn examples from my discipline as well as from other behavioral sciences. Each chapter ends with a summary of terms, summary of symbols, and problems. These are designed solely to aid the student in his learning.

Contents

I often say that when you can measure what you are speaking about and express it in numbers, you know something about it; but when you cannot express it in numbers, your knowledge is of a meagre and unsatisfactory kind. . .

Lord Kelvin

Introduction   # Chapter One

Science of Behavior

In general, we may view science as a set of statements that achieve a description and an understanding of nature.

By description we mean the defining, organizing, and classifying of objects, events, or phenomena of nature. By understanding we mean the stating of functional relationships between these objects, events, or phenomena. The science of behavior studies the behavior of living organisms. Therefore, it is concerned with defining and classifying behavior, and with the relationships of behavior to conditions that control it. The primary function of science becomes a search for the lawful relationships between natural events.

A fundamental assumption of science is that nature is lawful as opposed to being spontaneous or random. It is assumed that there are certain functional relationships between events, and that every natural event has a functional relationship associated with some antecedent condition. For example, if y is a function of x, then for every value of x, y would be uniquely determined. It is one of the scientist's tasks to determine what that relationship happens to be. A second assumption, which is in part associated with the assumption of lawfulness, is that every natural event or phenomenon has a limited number of conditions that are functionally related to it. From these assumptions there are two conclusions: that behavior can be predicted, and that behavior can be controlled. If the behavioral scientist has determined a precise relationship between certain antecedent conditions and behavior, then knowing the conditions enables him to predict the behavior and to control it. For the most part, the behavioral technologist in such areas as education, psychotherapy, mental retardation, industrial relations, and business utilizes the obtained functional relationships for prediction and for control of behavior. For example, the educator wants to set the conditions in such a way that children can learn in a more effective manner. Also the clinician wants to modify the patient's behavior in such a way that the individual can lead a better life.

The student of behavior assumes that all behavior is lawful. Upon this basic assumption, he searches for the functional relationships and for the laws and the principles of behavior.

Method of Science

All of science starts with an observation or a question about some object, event, or phenomenon. In the behavioral sciences it starts with an observation or a question about some behavior. As science is a social enterprise, the researcher must describe the behavior in a manner that fully communicates his observations to others. In this way, others may verify his observation. To describe behavior is to define it and the form of scientific description is an operational definition. When we define an object, event, or phenomenon operationally, we define it in terms of measurable and observable operations. The definition would therefore state what operations must be performed, including the measurements that must be made so that another person could observe the behavior that is being defined. It is rather obvious that measurement plays a significant role in science. For if we cannot measure the object, event, or phenomenon, then that observation is not open to science. It is primarily at this definitional level that the behavioral scientist utilizes the techniques of measurement that we will call descriptive statistics. Here the objects or events are measured, described, and classified.

After we have defined the behavior, we would look for the antecedent conditions that are functionally related to it. When these conditions have been established, we have a law or a principle of behavior. In order to determine these functional relationships between variables, the behavioral scientist uses the methods of statistical inference and correlational procedures.

These are the statistical tools that enable the behavioral sciences to verify the functional relationships between variables. In a word, measurement and statistics are essential parts of the modern science of behavior. Measurement and statistics are not science, but rather, tools of science.

An Overview of a Statistical Analysis of Behavior

As measurement is central to the scientific enterprise, we will describe the concept of measurement in the following chapter. We shall see that measurement is the assigning of numerals, according to certain rules, to the objects, events, or phenomena that are under observation. The discussion of measurement is used as an organizational frame of reference for the remainder of the book. The methods of descriptive statistics are set forth in the next four chapters as general procedures for organizing and summarizing our empirical data. The general concept of descriptive statistics may be thought of as a method of data classification which is expressed in numerical form. We may organize the data in pictorial forms with a frequency distribution. However, with measures of central tendency and variability, we can describe that distribution. The measures of individual position describe the position of an individual score in relation to the group from which the measure was drawn. Prior to a discussion of statistical inference, a chapter on research design and a chapter on probability have been included. Three chapters have been devoted to tests of statistical significance. As we will see, statistical inference refers to the procedures of inferring certain statistical characteristics of a population from a randomly selected sample. Perhaps, however, the most important characteristic of inferential statistics is in the testing of hypotheses and in the assessment of differences between organism behaviors as a function of the experimental or treatment conditions. The next three chapters describe various measures or indices of association or correlation and prediction. The correlational methods give a quantitative index to the co-relationship between variables, and from these relations, we can make predictions about behavior. The last chapter is a discussion of errors of measurement and reliability.

Measurement   Chapter Two

Measurement is the procedure of assigning numerals to objects according to specified rules or axioms. By this assignment, the numeral represents the object or some property of the object and becomes amenable to certain statistical analyses. However, in order for such a representation to be meaningful, the axioms that define the relationships between the numerals must correspond to the relationships between the objects or properties that the numerals are to represent.

A numeral is a symbol that has meaning only in its relationship to other symbols. The symbols of 1, 2, 3 may be viewed as numbers when they are appropriately assigned and the operations and rules of arithmetic applied. These symbols can then be manipulated, for example, by addition. On the other hand, these same numerals may have other meanings when they follow the operations and rules of ordering. Thus, 1, 2, 3 become first, second, third. Numerals are, therefore, assigned to represent the specified empirical relationships that exist between the objects to which they are assigned.

With the present development of our methods at least four basic types of scales of measurement can be described. Each scale has certain formal properties (rules or axioms) which provide exact definitions of the scale and certain allowable statistical operations for a given set of numerals. We shall examine the scales of measurements and the operations that are associated with each scale.

The Isomorphic Nominal Scale

Description. The isomorphic nominal scale is measurement at the level of classifying or naming where numerals are assigned to one and only one object. The assignment is isomorphic when a numeral can be assigned to only one object. Numerals, in this case, are used solely to identify objects. Social security numbers, license plates, telephone numbers, numbers on football jerseys are ready examples of an isomorphic nominal scale. No statistical operations are associated with the isomorphic nominal scale and it does not enter into our later statistical discussions.

The Homomorphic Nominal Scale

Description. The homomorphic nominal scale is measurement at the classification or taxonomic level where numerals are assigned to discriminable, mutually exclusive classes of objects or properties of objects. The assignment is homomorphic when one object or property of that object is assigned only one numeral. If we have two or more objects that are discernibly different in the property or characteristic that we are classifying, we assign one numeral to one object and another numeral to the other object. By mutually exclusive, we simply mean that two numerals cannot be assigned to the same property.

Examples. Within this classification system there are numerous illustrations: religious groups—Lutherans, Catholics, Methodists; sex—male and female; diagnostic psychiatric groups—schizophrenia, psychoneurosis; occupations—plumber, teacher, dentist. Generally, any two or more classificatory nouns could be considered measurement on this nominal level.

Formal Properties. Each scale of measurement has formal axioms that provide an exact definition of the scale. Within the homomorphic nominal scale it is assumed that all the entities within one class are equivalent. The determination of equivalence is the first step in all measurement. It is at this taxonomic level that a science begins by cataloging, classifying, and defining the events, objects, and phenomena with which it deals into meaningful classes or categories.

Equivalence, denoted by an equal sign (=), has three axioms that characterize the properties of an equivalent relationship between numerals:

1. Reflexive: $a = a$, for all values of a (equal to, similar to, includes, alike).

2. Symmetrical: If $a = b$, then $b = a$ (equal to, proportional to, spouse of).

3. Transitive: If $a = b$ and $b = c$, then $a = c$ (equal to, proportional to, ancestor of).

Thus all objects or their properties that are equivalent are assigned the same numeral and those that are discernibly different are assigned other numerals.

Transformation. Numerals which have been used to designate each specified class of objects or properties can be transformed or interchanged from one set of numerals to another set of numerals provided that this is done completely and consistently. When this is the case, there is no loss or altering of the meaningfulness of the data. The relationships between the classes remain unchanged with complete identities between these various classes.

A generalized formula for the transformation of a nominal scale may be defined as:

$$X' = a(X) \tag{2.1}$$

where X = the original numeral
X' = the new transformed numeral
$a(\ )$ = direct one-to-one substitution

Thus, if we have two subsets of objects, males ($\male$) and females ($\female$), we can transform or substitute the numerals of 0 for ($\male$) and 1 for ($\female$) provided that we do this consistently and completely for all objects.

The Isomorphic Ordinal Scale

Description. Once we have identified and categorized the objects or their properties on the nominal scales, we may be concerned with the magnitude of ordered relationships of objects or properties of objects. The isomorphic ordinal scale is measurement at the ordering or ranking level where numerals are applied to an ordered or ranked series of objects or their properties. This ordinal relationship is denoted by the carot ($>$), which is read as "greater than." Within the isomorphic ordinal scale the primary empirical relationship is between members of pairs of objects such that one member of the pair is greater than the other. Therefore, the relationship is an asymmetric one and equivalence between members of a pair is not allowed. Numerals are assigned as a series of positive integers based on the empirical relationships of greater than ($>$) or less than ($<$) for all possible pairs.

Example.   Typical ordered relations among classes in our language include such terms as: taller than, heavier than, older than, better than, sweeter than. These terms may be associated with such concepts as intelligence, attitudes, excellence of teaching, or rates of learning.

Formal Properties.   The nominal scale, where the data can be measured by counting, such as eight males and four females, is a discrete or discontinuous scale. However, the ordinal scale, at least in principle, is a continuous one. In theory, a continuous scale is one where there is no limit to the minuteness of the gradations that may be used. The limiting factor is generally the sensitivity of the measuring tool or instrument.

The relationship of greater than ($>$) follows the following three axioms for a series:

1.   Asymmetric: If $a > b$, then $b \not> a$ (greater than, father of, successor to).

2.   Connected: If $a \neq b$, then $a < b$ or $a > b$ (greater than, less than, not equal to).

3.   Transitive: If $a > b$ and $b > c$, then $a > c$ (greater than, ancestor of).

where ($<$) less than, ($\not>$) not greater than, ($\not<$) not less than, and ($\neq$) not equal to.

It is assumed that a and b are different objects or properties and that the assigned numerals are positive integers.

Transformation.   A transformation for the isomorphic ordinal scale may be stated as:

$$X' = 0(X) \qquad\qquad (2.2)$$

where X = the original numeral
X' = the new transformed
numeral
$0(\ )$ = any order preserving
substitution

With this substitution the order or rank is maintained and the numerals show a monotonic function without any loss of information as the relationship between the order of the classes remains unchanged. For example, if in a two-man footrace, one man ran faster and crossed the finish line ahead of the second, we can transform this event to the numerals of 1 and 2 that fully describe the ordered relationships.

If first < second were positive integers and were transformed to 1 < 2 we would have an increasing monotonic function. Any order preserving transformation, that is, monotonic function, fulfills the requirements for the isomorphic scale.

The Homomorphic Ordinal Scale

Description.   The homomorphic ordinal scale is measurement at the ordering or ranking level where numerals are applied to ordered classes of categories or properties. In the homomorphic ordinal case it is assumed that two or more objects are within at least one category. Therefore, the objects within a specified category are judged to be equal and follow the rules of equivalence.

Examples.   We can describe the relationship of families according to socio-economic status, students by grade levels, distribution of grades on a teacher-made test, academic ranks held by professors.

Formal Properties.   Three axioms for the homomorphic ordinal case are:

1.   Irreflexive: If $a = b$, then $a \not> b$ and $b \not> a$.

2.   Connected: If $a \neq b$, then $a > b$ or $b > a$.

3.   Transitive: If $a > b$ and $b > c$, then $a > c$.

It is assumed in the irreflexive axiom that $a = b$ where a and b are different objects or properties but that they are assigned to the same category. In this case, it is the categories that are ranked or ordered and the numeral assigned to that category is associated with the object. For example, all children in the seventh grade are assigned the same numeral.

Transformation. Formula 2.2 holds for monotonic transformations for the homomorphic ordinal scale. In this case, however, where $a = b$, the monotonic function is neither increasing or decreasing. Nevertheless, the order is preserved.

The Interval Scale

Description. The interval scale is measurement where the interval or distance between the numerals is a constant but arbitrary unit of measurement with an arbitrary zero point. At this level of measurement the classes have been identified (nominal), ordered (ordinal), and the equality of intervals between numerals has been established, and the numerals (or numbers) are applied to classes of objects or their properties. The scale can be characterized by a standard and constant unit which is of a standard but arbitrary size assigned to the observations. At this level we have achieved a unit of measurement that corresponds to that of arithmetic and the unit becomes a "quantitative" number.

Example. Most physical units of measurements, such as time, weight, or temperature, are ready examples of the interval scale. Therefore, latency measured by the time it takes an animal to run a maze, the amount of weight gained in an experimental study of aphagia, age at marriage, amplitude of a conditioned response, frequency in cycles per second of a stimulus tone, and income of family all illustrate the interval scale.

Formal Properties. The formal property of the interval scale is equivalence, and the operation is addition. The formal rules of equivalence as seen in the nominal scale are in harmony with the interval scale provided that certain assumptions about addition (+) or the combinations of numerals are admitted. As we have seen, equivalence is characterized by:

1. Reflexive: $a = a$ for all values of a.
2. Symmetrical: If $a = b$, then $b = a$.
3. Transitive: If $a = b$ and $b = c$, then $a = c$.

The operations of addition (+) or combination of properties or elements are assumed to be:

1. Equivalence: $a = b$ implies that $a + e = b + e$ for any constant value of e.
2. Commutative rule: If $a + b = c$, then $b + a = c$. The order in which numerals are added has no effect.
3. Associative rule: $a + (b + c) = (a + b) + c$. The order of operations of addition has no effect.
4. Difference rule: If $a \neq b$, then there would exist an element c, such that if c is an additive constant, then $a + c = b$ and/or $b + c = a$.

These rules hold provided that a, b, and c all belong to the same basic class of elements, that is, they are in the same unit of measurement such as inches, seconds, or grams.

Transformation. The interval scale transformation may be defined as:

$$X' = K + C(X) \tag{2.3}$$

$$\text{where } X = \text{the original score}$$
$$X' = \text{new transformed score}$$
$$K = \text{an additive constant}$$
$$C = \text{a multiplicative constant}$$
$$\text{that is greater than zero}$$

The ordered relationships within the property, as well as the equality of the intervals, are maintained with this transformation which may be described as linear or straight line. A common example of this transformation is that of converting temperature from Fahrenheit to centigrade.

$$F = 32 + 9/5(C)$$
$$F = \text{Fahrenheit value}$$
$$C = \text{centigrade}$$
$$32 = \text{additive constant}$$
$$9/5 = \text{multiplicative constant}$$

The additive constant takes into account the difference between the arbitrary zero points, and the multiplicative constant takes into account the difference in the size of the units.

The Ratio Scale

Description.   Unlike an interval scale, which has an arbitrarily defined zero point, a ratio scale has an absolute zero point. A scale designed to measure mass, for example, can be thought of as a ratio scale because it has an absolute zero point, that is, no mass. Numerals on a ratio scale can be thought of as being multiples of a standard unit from the absolute zero point. A second distinction between interval and ratio scales is that the difference between the numerals can be compared by noting the ratios. It must be noted, however, that no statistical procedures require a real or absolute zero point.

Examples.   The use of expansion ratios to the extrapolated zero is a ratio scale. For example, Kelvin's temperature scale, loudness in zones, weight in grams, are illustrative of the ratio scale.

Formal Properties.   The determination of the equality of ratios is the basic formal property for the ratio scale. In general, the criterion of the interval scale is applied to deviations from an absolute zero point. The properties between ratio numerals are as follows:

1. Multiplicative transitivity: If $a = pb$ and if $b = qc$ for the three classes of a, b, and c and for the two constants, then $a = (pq) c$.
2. Reciprocal asymmetry: If $a = pb$ then $b = (1/p)a$.
3. Unitary reflexivity: $a = la$.
4. Contravariance by division: If $a = pb$ and $b' = db$, then $a = (p/d)b'$.

The last two rules (3 and 4) are basically special cases of the first two. To illustrate, it can be shown that if a yard is equal to 36 inches (a = pb) and a foot is 12 inches (b' = db), then a yard is 3 feet (a = (p/d)b').

Transformation. The ratio scale transformation is defined as:

$$X' = C(X) \qquad\qquad (2.4)$$

where X = the original numeral
 X' = the new transformed
numeral
 C = any constant multiple
or factor greater than
zero

At this level of measurement the transformation results in an unchanged relationship of equality, of multiples, or of ratios. We can thus describe our measurements in terms of multiples, for example, we can say that a is three times greater than b.

Summary of Terms

addition
associative rule
asymmetric
carot
connected

continuous variable
contravariance
commutative rule
difference rule
discrete variable

equivalence
homomorphic nominal
homomorphic ordinal
interval
irreflexive

isomorphic nominal
isomorphic ordinal
measurement
monotonic
multiplicative transitivity

mutually exclusive
numeral
reciprocal asymmetry
reflexive
symmetrical

transformation
transitive
unitary reflexivity

Summary of Symbols

$$= \qquad\qquad \not> \qquad\qquad < \qquad\qquad +$$

$$> \qquad\qquad \not< \qquad\qquad \neq$$

Problems

1. The numerals "one" and "three" have been assigned to represent two hypothetical objects. What can be said about the two objects if it is known that the numerals were assigned to the objects on the basis of

   a. a nominal scale?

   b. an ordinal scale?

   c. an interval scale?

   d. a ratio scale?

2. Assume that, if possible, the use of a ratio scale is most preferred, an interval scale next most preferred, and a nominal scale least preferred. On which level of measurement would a scale designed to measure the following phenomena, events, or objects be based?

   a. Marital status

   b. Time (as measured by a calendar)

   c. "Amount of support given to the government" as measured by the number of tax dollars paid

   d. The "amount of knowledge" possessed by a college graduate as measured by the kind of degree held (B.A., B.S., M.A., M.S., or Ph.D.)

   e. The color of a monochromatic block of plastic

Frequency
Distributions

Chapter Three

The various forms of the frequency distributions organize the raw data into meaningful categories by collecting the like objects, events, or phenomena and treating them as a group rather than as random individuals. The primary value of the frequency distribution is organization, in that it condenses the data and presents them in a readily comprehensible form.

Associated with the frequency distributions are their pictorial or graphic representations. The major consideration for the pictorial representations is the clarity of presentation. The form of the frequency distribution and the graphic representation depends upon the nature of the data and the level of measurement.

Nominal Scale

Bar Graph

Function and Method. The homomorphic nominal scale was described as a set of numerals that are applied to discriminable discrete classes. In the description of this type of data, one of the common forms is a bar graph. The bar graph is a representation in organized pictorial form of the number (N) or frequency (f) within each of the categories.

In the construction of graphs, the horizontal axis (x-axis or abscissa) customarily represents the ordering of the various scores. In the bar graph this would be the representation of the various categories. For the bar graph the ordering of the various categories and the spacing between the bars is completely arbitrary. The meaning derived from the bar graph is not altered by how one chooses to order the categories. The vertical axis (y-axis or ordinate) generally represents the number of cases or frequencies within the various categories. The relative heights of the bars have mathematical meaning and are not arbitrary; therefore, the frequencies begin with a zero point. In this form of organization each bar would represent one category and the length of each bar would represent the frequency of cases within that category. These principles are shown in Figure 3.1 For example, within Category A there are two cases (N_A = 2), within Category B there are three cases (N_B = 3), and C has five cases (N_C = 5).

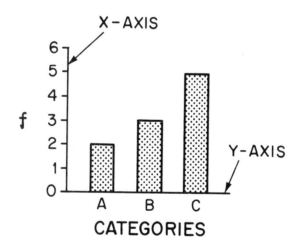

Figure 3.1. Generalized bar graph for nominal data.

After the frequencies for the various discrete classes have been obtained, it is possible to describe the data in terms of percentages and proportions of the frequencies. The proportion values are obtained by taking the frequency of cases in a given category over the total frequency or number of cases.

$$\text{proportion} = f_i/N \tag{3.1}$$

where f_i = frequency of cases within the ith category

and N = total frequency or number of cases

And the percentage values are obtained by:

$$\text{percentage} = (f_i/N)(100) \tag{3.2}$$

For example, in Figure 3.1 we have 2 cases in the A category and the total cases or frequencies are 10; the proportion of cases in the category would be $2/10 = 0.20$ and the percentage would be 20%.

Example. As a part of a study of verbal stereotypes and racial prejudice, the preferential ranking of ten ethnic groups and the types of characteristics attributed to each of these groups were made by 100 students. In Table 3.1 we have the data associated with twelve traits obtained for one of the ten groups. The various categories have been identified and then transformed from word categories to numerals.

Table 3.1.   Twelve traits most frequently assigned to ethnic group D by 100 students.

Category	Assigned Numeral	Frequency
scientific	1	78
industrious	2	65
stolid	3	44
intelligent	4	32
methodical	5	31
nationalistic	6	24
progressive	7	16
efficient	8	16
jovial	9	15
musical	10	13
persistent	11	11
practical	12	11

The data from Table 3.1 are placed in a bar graph as shown in Figure 3.2. The ordering of categories along the abscissa is arbitrary as are the widths of the bars and the spacing between the bars. Only the relative heights of the bars have meaning.

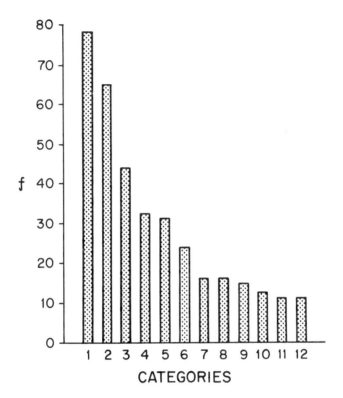

Figure 3.2.   Bar graph of twelve traits most frequently assigned to an ethnic group.

The Isomorphic Ordinal Scale

The isomorphic ordinal scale was described as a set of numerals applied to ranked objects. Thus, objects are not grouped in classes or categories and are not described in terms of frequency distributions.

The Homomorphic Ordinal Scale

Histogram

Function and Method.   The homomorphic ordinal scale was described as a set of numerals that are applied to ordinal categories. At this level of measurement, the data are assumed to be continuous. When the research variable is continuous, the bars on the abscissa for the adjacent categories are contiguous. The resulting bar graph for continuous data is a histogram.

The ordering of the bars is determined by the ordering of the categories, and the bars are contiguous and have no spaces between them. This is because the abscissa represents a continuous variable. As with the bar graph, the height of the bars is determined by the frequencies in the various ordered categories. Therefore, in the histogram, the contiguous order and the heights of the bars have mathematical meaning. At the ordinal level of measurement, however, the widths of the bars along the abscissa are unknown and thus unspecifiable on a graph.

Example. To study some of the conditions under which individuals were most likely to conform to the pressures of a group, an investigator used a procedure which required the subjects to make judgments as to which one of three parallel lines of different lengths was equal to a standard line. A group of confederates had been previously briefed and instructed to give certain incorrect answers on 12 specified trials that were interspersed in the total of 18 trials. The subject was then introduced to the experimental situation, and was obliged to declare himself publicly and to take a stand with or against the group. A control group was given essentially the same task except that no "group pressure" was given to the subjects.

Table 3.2 exhibits the distribution of critical errors (frequency of yielding) for the experimental and control groups. Figure 3.3 is a histogram of this data with the frequency of cases on the ordinate and the number of critical errors plotted on the abscissa. As we can see from the table and the figure, more critical errors were made by the experimental group than by the control group.

In the figure, the bars have equal width; however, the widths of the bars have no mathematical significance at this level of measurement and the equality of widths is just a conventional method of data representation.

Grouped Frequency Distributions. A histogram has a limitation for organization when the number of categories is very large and when there are very few cases within each of the categories. As the order of the categories is contiguous, it is possible to group together the frequencies of various adjacent categories into a new one of a specified range. Generally, the number of new categories of class intervals (i) and the widths of these intervals are arbitrary, and function solely as a method of

Table 3.2. Distribution of errors in experimental and control groups.

Number of critical errors	Experimental group	Control group
	f	*f*
0	13	35
1	4	1
2	5	1
3	6	
4	3	
5	4	
6	1	
7	2	
8	5	
9	3	
10	3	
11	1	
12	0	
	$N = 50$	$N = 37$

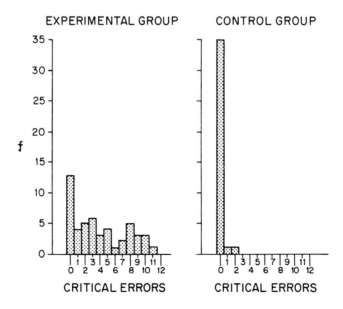

Figure 3.3. Histogram of errors made by the experimental and control groups with an interval width of one.

convenience. However, when the data are placed in large class intervals, we have a slight loss of information since each data point within a given class interval is treated as if it were equal to the midpoint of that interval.

Each class interval is described by stating the *score limits* (class limits or apparent limits). The score limits for a given class interval are the highest and the lowest scores in the class interval. In many experimental procedures, such as in the conformity study, a person receives a score such as 4. This value may look like a discrete value, however, a score of 4.3 is not possible by the measurement technique. Nevertheless, the value 4 is representative of the underlying continuous variable of conformity and encompasses a theoretical range between 3.5 and 4.5. The values of this range are the *real limits* of the class interval for the value of 4. With grouped frequency distributions the class intervals also have real limits which are the upper real limit $(_rU_l)$ of the highest score in that class interval and the lower real limit $(_rL_l)$ of the lowest score in the class interval. These real limits are used when various computations are made from grouped frequency distributions.

Table 3.3. Frequency distribution of scores from 210 subjects.

Score	f	Score	f	Score	f	Score	f	Score	f
8	1	36	6	59	4	79	2	103	2
15	1	38	2	60	1	80	4	104	1
16	2	39	1	61	2	81	3	107	1
17	1	40	2	62	1	82	1	110	1
19	2	41	2	63	1	83	1	112	2
20	2	43	2	64	5	85	1	114	2
21	1	44	5	65	7	86	5	116	2
22	1	45	3	66	5	87	1	130	1
23	2	46	1	67	2	89	1	132	1
24	3	47	2	68	3	90	1	139	1
25	3	48	2	69	3	91	1	145	1
27	2	49	4	70	3	92	1		
29	1	50	4	71	4	94	4		
30	1	51	1	72	1	95	2		
31	2	52	3	73	3	96	1		
32	2	53	2	74	2	97	3		
33	1	54	3	75	4	98	2		
34	1	56	2	76	4	99	1		
35	6	57	3	77	6	101	1		
36	3	58	3	78	6	102	1		

Example. As part of a study in scaling methodology, a researcher gave the 50-item Taylor's Manifest Anxiety Scale to 210 college students. Each item is rated on a five-point scale. Table 3.3 shows the raw data, where a low score represents low anxiety and a high score high anxiety.

The data has been regrouped in Table 3.4 with the width of the interval as 10, starting with the zero score. The class interval 10–19, for example, has as its real limits the values 9.5 and 19.5.

Table 3.4. Frequency distribution with i = 10.

Class interval	f	Interval midpoints
140-149	1	144.5
130-139	3	134.5
120-129	0	124.5
110-119	7	114.5
100-109	6	104.5
90-99	16	94.5
80-89	17	84.5
70-79	35	74.5
60-69	30	64.5
50-59	25	54.5
40-49	23	44.5
30-39	25	34.5
20-29	15	24.5
10-19	6	14.5
0-9	1	4.5
	N = 210	

From the grouped frequency distribution in Table 3.4, we have constructed a histogram as shown in Figure 3.4.

The Frequency Polygon

Function and Method. Data may be presented pictorially by a frequency polygon rather than by a histogram. The frequency polygon is constructed by plotting the midpoints of the various class intervals against the frequency of cases that is associated with each interval, and then connecting the plotted points by a series of straight lines. Generally, the points are extended to one interval below and one interval above the intervals actually used, which brings the lines to the abscissa. As the data are assumed only to be ordinal, the width of the intervals has no mathematical significance.

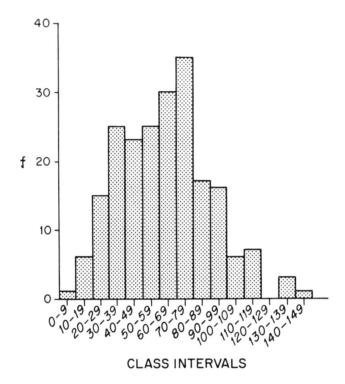

Figure 3.4.   Histogram of anxiety scores with an interval width of ten.

Example.   From the data in Table 3.4, we determine the midpoints for the various class intervals. The midpoint is half of the real limits for each interval. As i is equal to 10 in our example, half of the interval is 5 and this value is added to the real lower limit of each class interval. For example, the class interval 10-19 has as its real lower limit 9.5, and when we add 5 to this value, the midpoint for that class interval is 14.5. These midpoints are given in Table 3.4. If we now plot these midpoints with their respective frequencies and then connect these points by a series of straight lines, we have the frequency polygon for this set of data as shown in Figure 3.5.

Various Cumulative Graphs

Function and Method.   Frequency distributions of ordinal data can also be illustrated by the use of cumulative graphs. One of the most common is the *cumulative frequency graph*. This may be obtained by adding the frequency of cases in each interval to the sum of the frequencies below it. The various cumulative

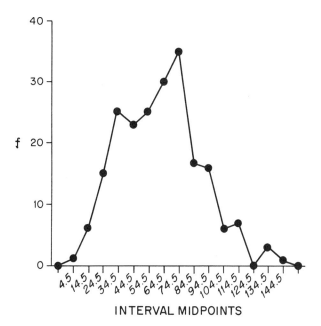

Figure 3.5. Frequency polygon of anxiety scores with an interval width of ten.

frcqucncics (*cf*) arc thcn plotted against thc uppcr rcal limits of the intervals and the plots of the series are then connected by straight lines. This general procedure is used with class interval widths of one ($i = 1$), as well as with class interval widths greater than one ($i > 1$).

In a similar fashion, a *cumulative proportion* and *cumulative percentage graph* (ogive) can be constructed from the cumulative frequency data or graph by transforming the cumulative frequencies into cumulative proportions or percentages. This transformation is made by multiplying the reciprocal of the total number of cases ($1/N$) by each cumulative frequency or

$$(cf)(1/N) = cp \qquad (3.3)$$

By moving the decimal point two places to the right we have the cumulative percentages (*c%*). From these graphs we can make statements about the proportions or the percentage of cases that fall below a given observation.

As with the frequency polygon, the heights and the order of the plots have meaning, but the slope of the lines does not as the horizontal distances between the various plots are arbitrarily selected.

Example. In Table 3.5, we have utilized the data given in Table 3.4. Under the cumulative frequency (*cf*) column we have taken the frequencies of cases in each interval and have added these to the sum of the frequencies below it. In the class interval 0-9 we have one case and none below it. The interval 10-19 has 6 cases plus the sum below that interval, or 1, giving us a *cf* of 7. This general procedure is followed for all the class intervals. The column in Table 3.5 headed *cp* gives the various cumulative proportions. We have multiplied the reciprocal of 1/210 or 0.00476 by each cumulative frequency. And the column *c*% is the cumulative percentage transformed from the cumulative proportion data.

On the left ordinate in Figure 3.6 we show the data plotted for the *cf* from the table, and on the right ordinate are the cumulative percentages.

Table 3.5. Cumulative frequencies, cumulative proportions, cumulative percentages from Table 3.4.

Class interval	*f*	*cf*	*cp*	*c*%
140-149	1	210	.9998	99.98
130-139	3	209	.9950	99.50
120-129	0	206	.9808	98.08
110-119	7	206	.9808	98.08
100-109	6	199	.9474	94.74
90-99	16	193	.9188	91.88
80-89	17	177	.8427	84.27
70-79	35	160	.7618	76.18
60-69	30	125	.5951	59.51
50-59	25	95	.4523	45.23
40-49	23	70	.3333	33.33
30-39	25	47	.2238	22.38
20-29	15	22	.1047	10.47
10-19	6	7	.0333	3.33
0-9	1	1	.0048	.48

$$N = 210$$

Interval and Ratio Scales

Histogram

Function and Method. At the level of measurement on an interval and/or ratio scale it becomes meaningful to describe the shape of the histogram in terms of the height, order, and width of the various bars. With interval and ratio scales, we have equality of the unit of measurement or class size. Therefore, the width of any

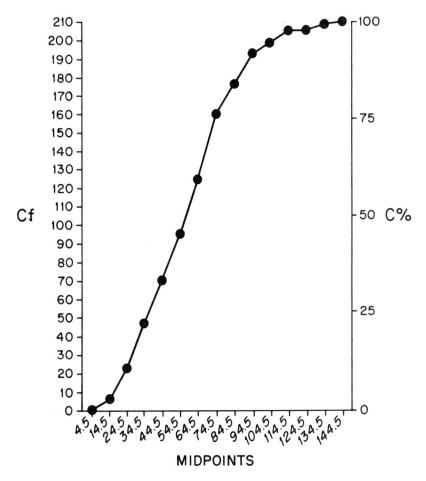

Figure 3.6. Cumulative frequency and cumulative percentile graph of anxiety scores with an interval width of ten.

given bar along the abscissa is equal to the width of any other given bar. Each bar represents a proportion of the total area inside the histogram. Thus, when the width of the bar is equal to one unit of the measurement scale, each bar represents a proportion of all the scores. For example, a bar with height equal to width equal to one unit represents $1/N$ (where N = total number of scores = total area of the histogram). The height of each bar, then, indicates the proportion of cases having the score which the bar represents. In later discussions of various theoretical distributions and curves, this will become an important consideration.

The zero point of the abscissa may be arbitrarily defined for interval data. If the data are ratio, the zero point is predetermined and fixed.

Example. Thirty-nine experimental rats were given a mild electric shock in an escape conditioning study. To escape the shock, an animal ran down a four-foot alley and when it broke a photoelectric beam at the end of the alley the shock was terminated. The response was measured in latencies from the onset to the termination of the shock. For illustrative purposes, the data for the tenth trial, grouped into interval widths of three units, are given in Table 3.6.

Table 3.6. Frequency distributions of latencies in seconds for 39 animals.

Latency	f	Class interval	f
32	2	32-34	2
31	1	29-31	5
30	4	26-28	5
28	2	23-25	6
27	1	20-22	9
26	2	17-19	3
25	3	14-16	4
24	2	11-13	1
23	1	8-10	3
22	1		
21	2		$N = 39$
20	6		
18	3		
16	2		
15	1		
14	1		
12	1		
10	2		
8	1		
	$N = 39$		

These grouped data in Table 3.6 have been plotted in Figure 3.7. As each bar width is made up of a three-second interval, the widths of each bar are mathematically equal.

Frequency Polygon

Function and Method. As the widths of the bars are mathematically equal, the frequency polygon for interval and ratio data can be constructed as before. However, the area under the histogram for interval data is equal to the area under the frequency polygon.

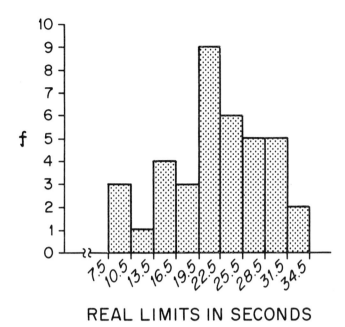

REAL LIMITS IN SECONDS

Figure 3.7. Histogram of latencies grouped in three-second intervals.

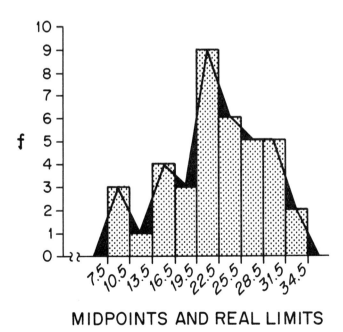

MIDPOINTS AND REAL LIMITS

Figure 3.8. A frequency polygon superimposed on the histogram of latencies grouped in three-second intervals.

Example. From Figure 3.8, it can be seen that the area that has been eliminated is equal to the area that has been added. It must be noted that the plots are the midpoints of the class intervals, therefore, one can correctly read the graph only with the midpoints as representative of the interval and not of the values within that interval; the shape of the lines has meaning in terms of the rate of change.

Various Cumulative Graphs

Function and Method. Various cumulative graphs can be constructed with interval and ratio data in the same manner as with ordinal data. However, as was previously pointed out, since the bar widths are mathematically equal, the area under the lines and the slope of the lines have meanings.

Summary of Terms

abscissa
bar graph
class interval
cumulative frequency
cumulative frequency graph

cumulative percentage
cumulative percentage graph
cumulative proportion
cumulative proportion graph
frequency

frequency polygon
histogram

lower real limit
midpoint of class interval
number

ogive
ordinate

percentage
proportion
reciprocal

score limits
upper real limit

x-axis
y-axis

Summary of Symbols

N % $_rL_l$ CP

f i cf

f_i $_rU_l$ $C\%$

Problems

1. Table 3.1 and Figure 3.2 give the number of students (Frequency) that judged each of the twelve characteristics (Categories) as an accurate description of some ethnic group. Each of the following characteristics make up what proportion of the ethnic group given by the students? What percentage?

    a. Methodical

    b. Musical

    c. Progressive

    d. Scientific

2. Draw two bar graphs (a & b) of the data given in Question 3. Assume

    a. that the data is based on the nominal level of measurement.

    b. that the data is based on the ordinal level of measurement.

3. Given below are the scores (number of correct answers) of 20 third graders on a 100-item spelling test. Using class intervals 5 units wide and following the appropriate conventions, draw and label a frequency polygon and an ogive of the data.

Subjects	Score
1	6
2	9
3	24
4	15
5	13
6	18
7	13
8	17
9	20
10	7
11	14
12	21
13	11
14	7
15	19
16	24
17	14
18	18
19	17
20	16

Measures of
Central Tendency

Chapter Four

The organization of raw data into a frequency distribution or its pictorial representation may be the first step in the overall comprehension of data. However, given a distribution or simply a set of data, we want to be able to further define certain characteristics of it. One such measure is the typical value or the central tendency. The central tendency is a measure which gives a single numerical value that is representative of the given data. The measure of central tendency that is used is primarily a function of the nature of the data and its appropriate level of measurement.

The Homomorphic Nominal Scale

The Mode

Function and Method. The mode is defined as a numeral that is representative of a category of events, objects, or phenomena that occurs with the greatest frequency. For the most part, the mode is determined by visually inspecting a bar graph and noting the category that has the largest number of cases. From the definition, the mode can be used to describe the central tendency for all levels of measurement. However, the principle use of the mode is with nominal data, where the categories are at a classificatory level.

A limitation of the mode occurs in sets of data where all the values have the same frequency of occurrence, or where two categories have the same highest frequency. In this latter case, the data are said to be bimodal. The mode is considerably affected by fluctuations of sampling. For example, if one of the two categories of a bimodal distribution had another case added to it, the mode could greatly change its position. A further limitation of the mode is that it is a terminal statistic in that it is rarely used again in further statistical analysis and is limited primarily to its descriptive function.

Example. In a report on the causes of death, one investigator gives the ten leading causes for a specified year. In Table 4.1 we have part of the data. From this table, we can determine the most frequent or modal cause by observing that category with the highest frequency of cases. The modal cause from this data would be said to be diseases of the heart. In this research we must use the mode as a measure of central tendency, because the reported data are in terms of frequencies of cases in the various categories.

Table 4.1.   The 10 leading causes of death in the United States in 1948.

Causes	Death rate per 100,000 pop.
Diseases of the heart	323
Cancer	135
Cerebral hemorrhage	90
Accidents	67
Nephritis	53
Pneumonia and influenza	39
Tuberculosis	30
Premature birth	27
Diabetes mellitus	26
Arteriosclerosis	19

The Isomorphic Ordinal Scale

The Median

Function and Method.   When the values of the data are in rank order, the appropriate measure of central tendency is the median (*Mdn*). The median is defined as the point on the scale above which and below which 50% of the cases fall. When the total frequency of ranks is odd, the median is the middle-most score. On the other hand, when the total frequency of cases is even, the median is the average of the two middle-most scores.

Example. Let us suppose that we have 9 attitude statements relating to college achievement. These 9 statements are given in all possible pairs of $N(N-1)/2$ or $(9)(8)/2 = 36$ pairs to 100 students. The task is to make comparative judgments for each pair of statements as to which one of the two statements had the most favorable attitude. Assume the scale values given in Table 4.2 for each statement.

The median scale value for this artificial scale of achievement would be the middle-most score or 0.90.

Table 4.2

Statement	Scale Values
1	.00
2	.25
3	.60
4	.85
5	.90 ← Median
6	1.00
7	1.25
8	1.40
9	1.55

The Homomorphic Ordinal Scale

The Median

Function and Method. When the values of the data are in ordered categories, such as a frequency distribution, again the appropriate measure is the median. The median is here similarly defined as the point on the abscissa above which and below which 50% of the cases fall. In the homomorphic case we may have a number of cases in each category of the frequency distribution and the median is obtained by an interpolation procedure. The median is obtained and defined by the general formula:

$$Mdn = {}_r L_1 + \left[\frac{N/2 - \Sigma f_b}{f_w} \right] i \qquad (4.1)$$

where $_rL_l$ = the real lower limit of the interval containing
   the *Mdn*
N = the total number of scores
Σf_b = the sum of frequencies below the interval
   containing the *Mdn*
f_w = the frequency within the interval containing
   the *Mdn*
and i = the width of the interval.

The median may be also defined by a second formula which also
serves as a check to the computations of 4.1, or:

$$Mdn = {_rU_l} - \left[\frac{N/2 - \Sigma f_a}{f_w} \right] i \qquad (4.2)$$

where $_rU_l$ = real upper limit of the interval containing
   the *Mdn*
and Σf_a = the sum of the frequencies above the
   interval containing the *Mdn*

In using the interpolation procedures for the calculations of the
median, certain explicit assumptions must be made about the kind
of data and its distribution. It is assumed that the data values are
from a continuous variable and that the values are ranked. Furthermore, it is assumed that the number of cases within each
interval are equally spaced throughout that interval. A pictorial
representation of the interpolation for finding the median is
shown in Figure 4.1.

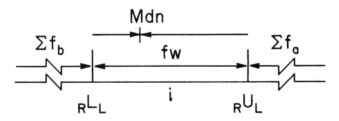

Figure. 4.1.   Interpolation for finding the median with an i width.

Example for $i = 1$.   In a study of the functioning of ex-
pectancies, the investigators trained two groups of rats to run a
simple maze to a feeding platform for food. Upon learning the
task, the experimental group was given a pre-extinction experience

of five 2-minute sessions on the feeding platform without food and the controls had like time sessions on a neutral platform. Table 4.3 gives the results of the extinction trials for the two groups. The data are given in number of trials to reach a criterion of extinction.

Table 4.3. Trials to extinction.

No. of trials	Experimental group f cf_b cf_a			Control group f cf_b cf_a		
25				1	16	1
24						
23				1	15	2
22						
21						
20						
19						
18						
17						
16						
15						
14						
13						
12				1	14	3
11	1	17	1			
10				1	13	4
9				1	12	5
8				2	11	7
7	1	16	2			
6				4	9	11
5	2	15	4	1	5	12
4	1	13	5			
3	3	12	8	1	4	13
2	4	9	12	1	3	14
1	4	5	16	2	2	16
0	1	1	17			
	$N = 17$			$N = 16$		

The procedure to ascertain the median is first to cast the data into cumulative frequencies, *cf.* From Formula 4.1, we then find $N/2$ or $17/2 = 8.5$ for the experimental group and we determine the class interval that contains the 8.5 case. The 8.5 case is in the interval 2 with its real lower limit of 1.5 and real upper limit of 2.5. There are 5 cases below that interval and 4 cases within the interval and i is equal to 1, thus:

$$Mdn = 1.5 + \left[\frac{8.5 - 5}{4}\right] 1$$
$$= 1.5 + [.875] \; 1$$
$$= 2.375$$

We could have determined the median from Formula 4.2, but we shall use it as a check or:

$$Mdn = 2.5 - \left[\frac{8.5 - 8}{4}\right] 1$$
$$= 2.5 - [0.125] \; 1$$
$$= 2.375$$

The median for the controls would be obtained in the same manner, hence:

$$Mdn = 5.5 + \left[\frac{8 - 5}{4}\right] 1$$
$$= 6.25$$

and the check:

$$Mdn = 6.5 - \left[\frac{8 - 7}{4}\right] 1$$
$$= 6.25$$

Example for $i > 1$. For data which has been cast into class intervals with the width greater than one, we use the same general procedure to determine the median. The data in Table 3.5 have been in part repeated in Table 4.4 and the median obtained. As N is equal to 210, $N/2 = 105$, the 105*th* case falls within the interval 60-69, with the real lower limit of 59.5 and we have 95 cases below that interval and 30 cases within it, and the width of i is equal to 10. Therefore, from Formula 4.1 we have:

$$Mdn = 59.5 + \left[\frac{105 - 95}{30}\right] 10$$
$$= 59.5 + 3.33$$
$$= 62.83$$

Table 4.4. Frequency distribution of scores from 210 subjects with i equal to 10.

Class interval	f	cf
140-149	1	210
130-139	3	209
120-129	0	206
110-119	7	206
100-109	6	199
90-99	16	193
80-89	17	177
70-79	35	160
60-69	30	125
50-59	25	95
40-49	23	70
30-39	25	47
20-29	15	22
10-19	6	7
0-9	1	1

$N = 210$

Interval Scale

The Mean

Function and Method. The mean is defined as the sum of (Σ) a series of values of a variable (X), divided by the frequency of cases (N) or:

$$\bar{X} = \frac{\sum\limits_{1}^{N} X}{N} \qquad (4.3)$$

where Σ = sum of

$$\sum\limits_{1}^{N} = \text{sum of 1 to } N$$

$$\sum\limits_{1}^{N} X = (X_1 + X_2 + X_3 + \dots + X_i + \dots + X_n)$$

N = total number of scores, or sum of frequencies
and where X_1 = the first score value

X_i = the general case

X_n = the nth or last case

and ... = a number of other values
in the series

It must be noted that this is the first time the series of values of a variable have been added or summed (Σ). It is assumed that the level of measurement is on an interval scale when the equality of the interval as the unit of measurement has been determined. This being the case, one of the principle features of the mean is that it is amenable to algebraic manipulation. For instance, if we multiply both sides of Formula 4.3 by N, we have:

$$N\bar{X} = \Sigma X \tag{4.4}$$

A further property of the mean states that the mean is that point where the algebraic sum of the deviation of scores from the mean is zero. The deviation of a score from the mean is the value of the difference between the score and the mean or:

$$x = (X - \bar{X}) \tag{4.5}$$

where x = a deviation score

X = a given score value

and $\bar{X}$ = the mean

Summing both sides of Formula 4.5, we have:

$$\Sigma x = \Sigma (X - \bar{X}) \tag{4.6}$$
$$\text{or } \Sigma x = \Sigma X - N\bar{X}$$

If we substitute the $N\bar{X}$ in Formula 4.6 with its identity from Formula 4.4, then:

$$\Sigma x = \Sigma X - \Sigma X$$
$$\text{or } \Sigma x = 0$$

Example. Investigators ran rats for 16 days, one trial a day, in a straight runway with either 3 or 23 hours of food deprivation and 0.2 or 0.8 grams of food at the end of the alley for the incentive. In Table 4.5. we have data on one group at the end of the 16 days measured in terms of seconds to transverse the runway.

Table 4.5.   Runway speed in seconds.

Ss	X	x
1	3.32	−1.68
2	5.22	.22
3	3.48	−1.52
4	3.92	−1.08
5	15.56	10.56
6	2.33	−2.67
7	9.02	4.02
8	2.72	−2.28
9	3.15	−1.85
10	3.08	−1.92
11	3.19	−1.81
12	3.72	−1.28
13	2.64	−2.36
14	3.23	−1.77
15	8.71	3.71
16	6.13	1.13
17	3.08	−1.92
18	4.07	−0.93
19	9.67	4.67
20	3.85	−1.15
	$\Sigma X = 100.09$	$\Sigma x \approx .00$

$$\overline{X} = \frac{100.09}{20}$$

$$= 5.00$$

From the data in Table 4.5, we have summed the X-values and divided by N. In the column of the deviation (x), each X-value has been subtracted from the mean and the sum is approximately equal to zero. The difference from zero is a function of rounding errors.

A Comparison of the Mode, Median, and Mean

Of the three measures of central tendency, the mean is the most stable measure from sample to sample. If we could simply take a set of random values, the mean would vary less than the median, and it less than the mode. To illustrate, suppose we take 9 dice and roll them to obtain the three measures of central tendency, and take three such samples. From the data obtained and shown in Table 4.6 it can be seen that the mean varies less than the other two measures.

Table 4.6.

	Numbers on the die 1 2 3 4 5 6		$\bar{X}$	Mdn	Mode
f of sample 1	4 1 2 — — 2		2.67	2	1
f of sample 2	2 1 2 1 1 2		3.44	3	1,3,6
f of sample 3	1 1 1 2 3 1		3.89	4	5

Ratio Scale

The Geometric Mean

Function and Method. The geometric mean is defined as the *N*th root of the product of *N* values, and is symbolized by:

$$\bar{G} = \sqrt[N]{(X_1)(X_2)\ldots(X_n)} \qquad (4.8)$$

If there are a large number of values, the geometric mean can be more easily computed by the use of logs or:

$$\log \bar{G} = \log X_1 + \log X_2 + \ldots + \log X_n \qquad (4.9)$$

$$= \sum_1^n \log X$$

$$\text{and } \bar{G} = \text{antilog} \left[\frac{\log X_1 + \log X_2 + \ldots + \log X_n}{N} \right]$$

$$= \text{antilog} \frac{\sum \log X}{N}$$

The geometric mean is particularly useful in obtaining an average of a set of ratios, the average of rates of change where the data are assumed to meet the criteria of ratio measurement, and in other statistical formulations.

The geometric mean currently is not utilized very often in psychological literature because this science is not concerned with rates of change. However, in economics, sociology, and education this has been a most useful descriptive tool. For example, if we were interested in annual rates of change for population growth in a segment of schools or grade levels, or if the rate of productivity was of concern, then the geometric mean would be a very important device for describing phenomena.

Example.   In a discussion of the composition of the black population in the United States, a researcher reports the growth of the black population from 1790 to 1950. In Table 4.7 we have the data which have been analyzed in terms of the average rate of growth. The number of persons data are transformed into percentage of population from the previous census data which we will label X, and then the log from Table A is obtained.

Table 4.7.   Black population of the United States - 1790 to 1950.

Year	Number	Percentage of population from previous census data (X)	$\log X$
1950	15,042,286	116.9	2.0679
1940	12,865,518	108.2	2.0342
1930	11,891,143	113.6	2.0556
1920	10,463,131	106.5	2.0274
1910	9,827,763	111.2	2.0461
1900	8,833,994	118.0	2.0719
1890	7,488,676	113.8	2.0561
1880	6,580,793	122.0	2.0864
1870	5,392,172	121.4	2.0842
1860	4,441,830	122.1	2.0867
1850	3,638,808	126.6	2.1025
1840	2,873,648	123.4	2.0913
1830	2,328,642	131.4	2.1186
1820	1,771,656	128.6	2.1093
1810	1,377,808	137.5	2.1383
1800	1,002,037	132.3	2.1216
1790	757,208	. . . . .	
			33.2984

We then sum $\log X$ from 1 to N and divide by N or:

$$\log \bar{G} = \frac{33.2984}{16}$$
$$= 2.08115$$

and antilog $2.08115 = 120.6$

or $\bar{G} = 120.6$

Thus, the average rate of increase over the 16 decades studied is 120.6%.

Summary of Terms

antilog
central tendency
deviation score
geometric mean
identity

interpolation
log
mean
median
mode

sample
sum of
variable
variate

Summary of Symbols

Mdn	ΣX	$\overline{G}$	Σ
Σf_b	X	$\sqrt{}$	
Σf_a	Σx	$\dfrac{N}{\Sigma}$	
f_w	$\overline{X}$	1	

Problems

1. A researcher, employed by a local television station, was assigned the task of discovering the relative popularity of quiz shows: *W, X, Y,* and *Z.* She accomplished this task by making a very rapid door to door survey of the entire town, and counting the number of people viewing each show. She reported that program *W* was the modal quiz show.

    a. What did she mean?

    b. Why didn't the researcher use a geometric mean or at least a median to describe her results?

2. An experimenter was interested in the effect of incentive on maze learning. He taught two groups of mice to run through a maze for food reinforcement. The 10 mice in group 1 received one pellet of food at the end of each trial, and learned the maze in an average of 20 trials. The 12 mice in the second group received three pellets of food at the end of each trial, and learned the maze in an average of 9 trials. What was the mean number of trials for both groups to learn the maze?

3. The mean (25) of ten numbers was subtracted from nine of the numbers. If the sum of these nine deviations from the mean was equal to 7, what was the value of the remaining number?

4. Find the mean, median, and mode of the following distribution of numbers:

2
3
8
4
5
2
6
9
2
4

5. The following frequency distribution is based on the exploration scores of 20 rats exploring a 5-path elevated maze. The rats were placed on a central starting platform and allowed to select one of the 5 paths to explore; when the rat reached the end of the path he was removed, and returned to the starting platform. This procedure was repeated 5 times; thus, the rat had an opportunity to explore all five paths. The exploration score assigned to each rat was based on the order of the paths chosen as well as one the number of different paths chosen.

   a. Find the point in the distribution above which and below which 50% of the cases fall.

   b. Find the point in the distribution above which 25% of the cases fall and below which 75% of the cases fall.

Score	f
41 – 50	1
31 – 40	8
21 – 30	4
11 – 20	4
1 – 10	3

6. Consider the following hypothetical distributions. In which cases is the mean likely to be above the median, and in which cases is the mean likely to be below the median?

a. The distribution of annual incomes in the United States in 1966

b. The distribution of scores on a very difficult exam

c. The distribution of scores on a very easy exam

d. The distribution of the age of death in the United States

7. Find the mean and geometric mean of the following distributions:

a. 4, 9

b. 1, 2, 4

Measures of
Variability

Chapter Five

In descriptive statistics a second numerical index, that of variability, is also required to characterize data. The variability of a set of data is the extent to which various score values are different. The measure of variability or dispersion that we use is a function of the nature of the data and the level of measurement achieved.

Homomorphic Nominal Scale

Uncertainty with Equal Probabilities

Function and Method. The mode was described as the category of objects with the highest frequency of cases. If we wanted to predict from a nominal frequency distribution, our best prediction would be the mode. This prediction, in general, has the highest chance of being correct. However, the chance value varies with the (empirical) distributions. Uncertainty (U) is a measure that describes the nature and extent of this unpredictability. Within the contemporary behavioral sciences such areas as information theory and signal detection theory function essentially with the problems of uncertainty.

Uncertainty is defined as the average minimum number of

binary digits, or bits of information, required to specify a given category, and thus describe its variability. A binary digit is a unit of measurement from the binary or Base 2 system. The system uses only two symbols, 0 and 1, and a single digit specifies a choice from two alternative choices such as yes – no, true – false, on – off. For example, a single flip of a coin has 2^1 or two choices, heads or tails. Flipping it twice has 2^2 or four choices, three times 2^3 or eight choices and so forth. The number of bits is, then, equal to the power to which 2 must be raised to equal the number of choices or:

$$K = 2^U \qquad (5.1)$$

where K = number of equally likely choices

and U = amount of uncertainty, or number of bits

Uncertainty can be expressed as:

$$U = \log_2 K \qquad (5.2)$$

Examples Where the Choices (K) Are Equally Likely.   In game theory we could ask how many guesses it would take to correctly identify the cell on a checker board where the checker is placed. A standard checker board has eight rows and eight columns which make up 64 cells. As each cell is equally likely, the very best one could do is one guess and the very worst is 63 guesses (the 64*th* guess is not needed in that you know if it is not any of the others it must be in the last cell). However, there are some procedures of guessing, or transmission of information, that are better than others. If we ask is the cell in the first 4 columns on the right side of the board, the answer is given as yes or no. This answer gives us one bit of information and we can eliminate half of the cells. The second question asked is, is the cell in the upper 4 rows, and this general procedure would be the same for all following questions. In this fashion, it would take us 6 questions to ascertain the correct cell. From Table B, we can determine the minimum number of questions or bits by entering the column of n that is equal to 64 and its corresponding $\log_2 n$ is 6.000.

As another example, we could ask how many guesses or bits of information it would take to correctly identify a specified card in a standard playing deck. As N is 52 and each card has the same probability, from Table B we determine that on the average 5.700 bits of information are required and hence we would need to ask 5 or 6 questions.

Now let X represent a single variable which can take any value from 1 to K. If each value has an equal probability of occurrence, U is defined as:

$$U_x = \log_2 X \qquad (5.3)$$

The probability of occurrence for any one category of x is the reciprocal of the number of different categories that could occur, thus:

$$U_x = \log_2 \left[1/P_x\right] \qquad (5.4)$$

$$\text{or } U_x = -\log_2 P_x \qquad (5.5)$$

where P_x = the probability of occurrence of x

Where all the categories of a variable have equal probabilities, U_x comes to be the uncertainty of a given outcome, as well as the average uncertainty for all the outcomes. Uncertainty based upon equal probabilities for all categories is defined as *nominal* uncertainty.

Uncertainty with Unequal Probabilities

Function and Method.   When the categories have different probabilities, it becomes necessary to differentiate between the uncertainty for a given category and the average uncertainty for the total distribution. The *average uncertainty* is found by first determining the uncertainty associated with each independent X value and then obtaining a weighted average of these various uncertainties or

$$U_x = -\Sigma P_x \log_2 P_x \qquad (5.6)$$

The data for each category are first converted into the form of a proportion, P, then from Table B the product of the proportion and its log are given as:

$$-P_x \log_2 P_x$$

and the corresponding value is obtained and these values are summed to obtain U_x.

Example. Where the K Choices Are Not Equally Likely. A comprehensive study was made describing various procedures of child rearing. One variable investigated was the extent to which mothers use tangible rewards as a technique of training their children. In Table 5.1 we have the reported data which have been converted into proportions.

Table 5.1. Extent of Use of Tangible Rewards.

	P	$-P \log_2 P$
Mother never uses rewards	.1212	.3671
Rarely uses rewards	.1818	.4453
Sometimes uses rewards	.2121	.4728
Fairly often uses rewards	.2222	.4806
Frequently uses rewards	.1919	.4552
Regularly uses rewards	.0606	.2435
Not ascertained	.0202	.1129
		$U_x = 2.5774$

From Table B, the various $-P\log_2 P$ values are obtained and we have summed over the seven categories. The average uncertainty from these unequal probability categories is 2.5774. This is equal to the average bits of information required to ascertain a given case.

Ordinal Scale

Within this section we will combine both the isomorphic and homomorphic ordinal scales and discuss the various procedures as a unit.

Range

Function and Method. The range is by far the simplest measure of variability and is defined as the difference between the highest and lowest observed values:

$$R = X_h - X_l \tag{5.7}$$

where X_h = highest score value

and X_l = lowest score value

There must be at least an ordinal relationship between these score values if the range is to have any meaning. When describing the range, it is general practice to state the highest and the lowest value, as well as the difference between them, as this procedure conveys the greatest amount of information. If the range is obtained from a grouped frequency distribution, the range becomes the difference between the highest and lowest *score* limits.

The ease of computation and of understanding are, however, offset by the limitation of sampling fluctuation. The range tends to vary greatly from sample to sample. This is due principally to the occurrence of extreme values. To illustrate this, suppose in a given public school the highest score on a group IQ test is 190, the next highest score is 140, and the lowest score is 90. The addition of this one score (190) increases the range by 50 IQ points and accounts for 50 percent of the total range.

The range does not describe where most of the scores fall, hence it does not give a description of the shape of the distribution. The range could be the same for any different distribution shape such as a U shape, J shape, or a symmetrical distribution, whereas other indexes of variability would be quite different.

Interpercentile Ranges

Function and Method.   As a partial solution to the problem of the range, various interpercentile ranges have been constructed to describe the variability of a ranked variable. These various interpercentile ranges delete a specified percentage of cases which fall at the extreme ends of the distribution.

The interquartile range is one of these and is defined as the range between the 25*th* percentile (Q_1) and the 75*th* percentile (Q_3); therefore, this measure of dispersion encompasses the middle 50% of the cases or:

$$\text{Interquartile range} = Q_3 - Q_1 \qquad (5.8)$$

$$\text{where } Q_3 = {_r}\text{L}_l + \left[\frac{3N/4 - \Sigma f_b}{f_w} \right] i \qquad (5.9)$$

and where ${_r}L_l$ = the real lower limit of the interval
containing Q_3

$$\Sigma f_b = \text{the sum of the frequencies below the interval containing } Q_3$$

$$\text{and } f_w = \text{the frequencies within the interval containing } Q_3$$

$$\text{similarly, } Q_1 = {}_rL_l + \left[\frac{N/4 - \Sigma f_b}{f_w}\right] i \qquad (5.10)$$

where ${}_rL_l$ = the real lower limit of the interval containing Q_1

Σf_b = the sum of the frequencies below the interval containing Q_1

and f_w = the frequencies within the interval containing Q_1

Related to the interquartile range is the semi-interquartile range (Q) which is defined as the average of the interquartile range or:

$$Q = \frac{Q_3 - Q_1}{2} \qquad (5.11)$$

When the distribution of scores is a symmetrical one, then the following relationship holds:

$$Q_3 - Mdn = Mdn - Q_1$$

However, if the distribution is positively skewed, or skewed to the right so that the tail of the distribution is towards the right as shown in Figure 5.1, then:

$$Q_3 - Mdn > Mdn - Q_1$$

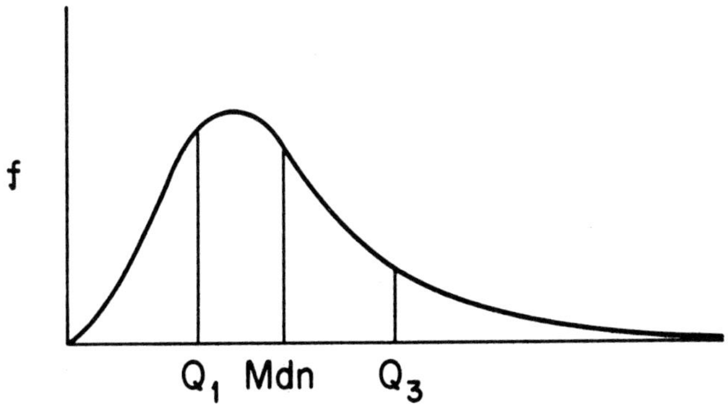

Figure 5.1.   A positive skewed distribution.

On the other hand, if the distribution is skewed to the left, we have a negatively skewed distribution, as shown in Figure 5.2 and the relation is:

$$Q_3 - Mdn < Mdn - Q_1$$

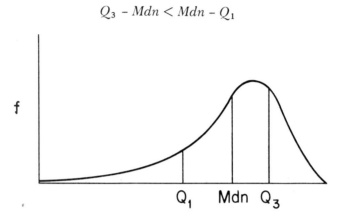

Figure 5.2.   A negative skewed distribution.

Other interpercentile ranges are used as an index of variability where a specified percentage of cases are deleted from the two ends of the frequency distribution, and the remaining values are used to describe the range that is covered. The 10% – 90% range is one such range covering the cases between the first and ninth decile. In practice any specified range may be constructed as a measure of variability.

The interpretation of the various interpercentile ranges for a single sample is based upon the information from an ordinal scale. As the numerals have meaning only for ranking of cases, and widths of the intervals are really unknown, it is not possible to describe the ranges as distances between two points. Rather, the ranges are used to describe the percentile points between which a given percentage of cases fall.

Example.   It has been suggested that there is a tendency for subjects to recall interrupted tasks better than completed tasks when the subjects are not personally or emotionally involved in the tasks. Each subject was assigned a variety of twenty tasks, such as solving arithmetic problems, putting together puzzles, or making clay models, and the subject was interrupted on some of these tasks. In Table 5.2 are the data for the number of remembered tasks under the uncompleted condition. The data have been analyzed for the median and for Q.

Table 5.2. The number of remembered
activities of uncompleted
tasks.

Number of remembered activities	f	cf
19	1	32
18		
17		
16	1	31
15	3	30
14	1	27
13	2	26
12	6	24
11	4	18
10	4	14
9	4	10
8	2	6
7	3	4
6	1	1
	$N = 32$	

$$Q_1 = 8.5 + \left[\frac{32/4 - 6}{4} \right] 1$$

$$= 8.5 + \left[2/4 \right] 1$$

$$= 9.0$$

$$\text{and } Mdn = 10.5 + \left[\frac{32/2 - 14}{4} \right] 1$$

$$= 11$$

$$Q_3 = 11.5 + \left[\frac{\frac{(3)(32)}{4} - 18}{6} \right] 1$$

$$= 11.5 + \left[6/6 \right] 1$$

$$= 12.5$$

$$\text{Hence } Q = \frac{12.5 - 9.0}{2}$$

$$= 1.75$$

The median and Q values suggest that the data are slightly skewed in the positive direction.

Interval Scale

The Variance and the Standard Deviation

Function and Method. In modern statistics the variance (S^2) and the standard deviation (S) have come to be the most used measures of variability or dispersion for data analysis on an interval scale of measurement. The variance is defined as an average sum of squared deviations from the mean:

$$S^2 = \frac{\Sigma (X - \bar{X})^2}{N - 1}$$

$$\text{or } S^2 = \frac{\Sigma x^2}{N - 1} \qquad (5.13)$$

where x^2 = the squared deviation from the mean
Σ = the sum of
and N = total number of cases in the sample

This definitional formula for the variance states that every X score value in the distribution is subtracted from the sample mean, ($X - \bar{X} = x$), each deviation value is squared $(x)^2$, and the squared deviations are summed (Σx^2), and the sum is divided by $N - 1$.

The standard deviation is defined as the square root of the variance or:

$$S = \sqrt{S^2}$$

$$\text{or } S = \sqrt{\frac{\Sigma x^2}{N - 1}} \qquad (5.14)$$

One of the characteristic qualities of the variance and the standard deviation is the sum of squared deviations has been taken from the mean rather than from any other constant. The result is that the sum of squares (Σx^2) will be less than the sum of squares taken from any other constant. Therefore, the value obtained for the variance and the standard deviation will be as small a value as possible, or we say, they will be at a minimum.

The variance and the standard deviation, like the mean, show the greatest amount of stability from sample to sample. Unlike the range and various other percentile ranges, they utilize all the score values in their computations. The result is that they are not open to as wide a fluctuation due to sampling as are some of the other measures of variability.

In order to gain a fuller comprehension of the standard deviation, some description of it in relation to a normal distribution curve is required. A *normal distribution curve,* more simply a *normal curve,* is a *theoretical frequency curve.* It is a symmetrical, bell-shaped curve with continuous scores on the abscissa and frequency of scores on the ordinate. When the distance is measured along the abscissa and is expressed in terms of a standard deviation unit, the area under the curve between the ordinates of the mean and the standard deviation is determined. It may be recalled that for interval data the proportion under the curve has meaning. The standard deviation may thus be thought of as a special range. In Figure 5.3, the areas delineated by the ordinates at the mean and at one standard deviation unit are shown. In the figure, the area from the mean to one standard deviation encompasses 34.13 percent of the total cases, or a proportion of 0.3413. In the range of plus and minus one standard deviation (± 1S), 68.26 percent of the cases fall. If the range is described as (± 2S) as shown in the figure, 95.44 percent of the cases are included. Table C gives the areas and the ordinates of a normal curve, and from it any percentage or proportion value can be determined between the ordinates of the mean and any value expressed in standard deviation units. This table is a theoretical one and hence the interpretation is of a theoretical nature.

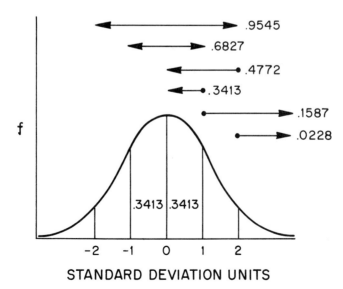

Figure 5.3. The proportions under the normal curve.

In Chapter 4 and also in this chapter, we have been describing data from samples and describing them in terms of various statistics. However, we assume that our sample data are drawn from a well-defined population. A population is all observations of objects or their properties and is described in terms of parameters. It is from a population that samples are drawn and the statistics are estimates of population parameters.

We need to give some indication of why we divide the *sample* sum of squares by N-1 in estimating the population standard deviation (σ) and variance (σ^2) in Formulas 5.13 and 5.14. The population mean (μ) generally is not known and the deviations are from the sample mean $(\bar{X})$. The result is that the estimate of population variance or standard deviation that is defined from the sample, particularly when the sample size is small, is underestimated. The reason for this underestimation is that the sum of squares which we calculate is from the sample mean. Only in the case where the sample mean happens to be identical to the population mean would the sum of squares based upon the sample mean be as large as the sum of squares from the population mean. Regardless of how slightly the sample mean varies from the population mean, any variation at all will give a smaller sum of squared deviations if the deviations are taken from the sample mean rather than from the population mean. Division by N would thus give us an estimate of the population variance which is biased, an estimate which is too small. This bias can be corrected by dividing by $N - 1$ instead of N.

Rather than using the definitional formula for the computation of the sum of squares, a simplified computational procedure can be derived through algebraic manipulation, or:

$$\text{by definition } x = (X - \bar{X})$$

$$\text{squaring } x^2 = (X - \bar{X})^2$$

$$\text{or } x^2 = (X^2 - 2X\bar{X} + \bar{X})$$

$$\text{summing } \Sigma x^2 = \Sigma X^2 - 2\bar{X}\Sigma X + N\bar{X}^2$$

$$\text{substituting an identity } \Sigma x^2 = \Sigma X^2 - 2\left[\frac{\Sigma X}{N}\right]\Sigma X + N\left[\frac{\Sigma X}{N}\right]\left[\frac{\Sigma X}{N}\right]$$

$$\text{or } \Sigma x^2 = \Sigma X^2 - 2\left[\frac{(\Sigma X)^2}{N}\right] + \frac{(\Sigma X)^2}{N}$$

$$\text{or } \Sigma x^2 = \Sigma X^2 - \frac{(\Sigma X)^2}{N} \tag{5.15}$$

This derived and computational formula (5.15) is identical to the definitional one. The major advantage of the derived formula is the ease and the speed of computations. The computational formula for the variance (5.13), therefore becomes:

$$S^2 = \frac{\Sigma X^2 - \dfrac{(\Sigma X)^2}{N}}{N-1} \qquad (5.16)$$

and the computational formula for the standard deviation (5.14) is given as:

$$S = \sqrt{\frac{\Sigma X^2 - \dfrac{(\Sigma X)^2}{N}}{N-1}} \qquad (5.17)$$

Example. In a study of hypothalamic lesions and adiposity in the rat, the experimenters report as part of their findings the maximum weight obtained from the obese rats with hypothalamic lesions and from their controls. In Table 5.3 we have the data for experimental animals only. While these values are large, they are not atypical of the kinds of data obtained in many studies. In the

Table 5.3.   Maximum weight in grams of rats with hypothalmic lesions.

Rat no.	X	x	x^2	X^2
1	447	−3.19	10.1761	199809
2	398	−52.19	2723.7961	158404
3	576	125.81	15828.1561	331776
4	484	33.81	1143.1161	234256
5	447	−3.19	10.1761	199809
6	475	24.81	615.5316	225625
7	339	−111.19	12363.2161	114921
8	387	−63.19	3992.9761	149769
9	460	9.81	96.2361	211600
10	447	−3.19	10.1761	199809
11	521	70.81	5014.0561	271441
12	372	−78.19	6113.6761	138384
13	508	57.81	3341.9961	258064
14	454	3.81	14.5161	206116
15	451	.81	.6561	203401
16	377	−73.19	5356.7761	142129
17	587	136.81	18716.9716	344569
18	437	−13.19	173.9761	190969
19	444	−6.19	38.3161	197136
20	430	−20.19	407.6361	184900
21	413	−37.19	1383.1961	170569
	$\Sigma X = 9454$	$\Sigma x = 0$	$\Sigma x^2 = 77,355.24$	$\Sigma X^2 = 4,333,456$

Therefore $\Sigma x^2 = \Sigma(X-\bar{X})^2$

$$= 77,355.24$$

or $\Sigma x^2 = \Sigma X^2 - \dfrac{(\Sigma X)^2}{N}$

$$= 4,333,456 - \dfrac{(9454)^2}{21}$$

$$= 4,333,456 - 4256100.761$$

$$= 77,355.24$$

then $S^2 = \dfrac{\Sigma x^2}{N-1}$

$$= \dfrac{77,355.24}{20}$$

$$= 3,867.76$$

and $S = \sqrt{S^2}$

$$= 62.2$$

table, we have solved for the sum of squares using the definitional formula as well as the computational one. However, the relative ease of the computational formula is readily apparent with this set of data.

Ratio Scale

Coefficient of Variation

Function and Method. The measures of variability for the interval scale are used for the ratio scale as well. These measures are expressed, however, in terms of the units of measurement from the original scale. If, for example, the unit of measurement is inches, then the mean and the standard deviation are expressed in inches. With the ratio scale it is often desirable to obtain an index of variation which describes the standard deviation in terms of the percentage of the mean and/or to compare variabilities when the unit of measurement differs. Such an index is the coefficient of variation (V), as given in Formula 5.18:

$$V = \frac{100S}{\overline{X}} \qquad (5.18)$$

where S = the obtained sample standard
deviation
and $\overline{X}$ = the obtained sample mean

Example. In addition to measuring the total time in seconds to transverse a runway, the investigators measured the latencies from the raising of the start box door to the leaving of the start box. In Table 5.4 both the total and the goal box latencies are given. It was of interest to compare the variabilities of the two measures and hence the coefficient of variation was utilized. From the two coefficients of variation, we can see that there is almost the same variability in the two measures.

Table 5.4. Goal box and
total latencies.

Goal box latencies	Total latencies
.96	3.32
.16	5.22
.29	3.48
.18	3.92
.30	15.56
.10	2.33
.42	9.02
.53	2.72
.14	3.15
.22	3.08
.33	3.18
.20	3.72
.23	2.64
.22	3.23
.35	8.71
.24	6.13
.17	3.08
.36	4.07
.27	9.67
.41	3.85
$\Sigma X = 6.08$	$\Sigma X = 100.08$

Goal box latencies	Total latencies

$$\bar{X} = \frac{6.08}{20} = .304 \qquad \bar{X} = \frac{100.08}{20} = 5.004$$

$$\Sigma x^2 = .6705 \qquad \Sigma x^2 = 209.7344$$

$$S^2 = .0353 \qquad S^2 = 11.0387$$

$$S = .188 \qquad S = 3.32$$

$$V = \frac{100s}{\bar{X}} \qquad V = \frac{100(3.32)}{5.004}$$

$$V = \frac{100(.188)}{.304} \qquad = \frac{332}{5.004}$$

$$= \frac{18.80}{.304} \qquad = 66.40$$

$$= 61.84$$

Summary of Terms

average uncertainty
binary digit
bits
coefficient of variation
decile

parameter
population
population mean
population standard deviation
positive skew

sum of squared deviations
uncertainty
variance

interpercentile range
interquartile range
negative skew
nominal uncertainty
normal curve

range
sample
semi-interquartile range
standard deviation
statistic

Summary of Symbols

U	R	S^2	σ
K	Q_1	S	μ
U_x	Q_2	Σx^2	$\sqrt{}$
$-\Sigma P_x \log_2 P_x$	Q_3	ΣX^2	σ^2
$-P_x \log_2 P_x$	Q	V	

Problems

1. What is the average uncertainty associated with a bottle containing five black balls, two white balls, and three red balls?

2. Given below, in the form of a frequency distribution, are the results of an introductory psychology test. Find the range and semi-interquartile range. Do you suspect that the students found the test very difficult, very easy, or neither? Why?

Score	f
71 – 80	1
61 – 70	10
51 – 60	20
41 – 50	12
31 – 40	9
21 – 30	5
11 – 20	3
1 – 10	0

3. Find the mean and standard deviation of the following distribution of numbers:

2
6
7
3
4
9
1
4
1
7
6
3
3
2
7
7
6
8
8
2

4. Using Table C, find the proportion of the area under the curve delimited by the following parameters:

    a.   Between $\overline{X}$ and + 1.5 S

    b.   Between $\overline{X}$ and - 0.5 S

    c.   Between ± 1.4 S

    d.   Above + 2.7 S

    e.   Below + 2.4 S

    f.   Above + 1.8 S and below - 2.7 S

5. Assume that you drew 100 numbers at random from a normal distribution of numbers. What proportion of them would be likely to fall

    a.   above the mean?

    b.   above + 1 S from the mean?

    c.   below + 1.96 S from the mean?

Measures of
Individual Position

Chapter Six

Various descriptive measures have been utilized to fully characterize classes of objects, events, or phenomena in terms of their distribution, central tendency, and variability. However, some discussion is needed of the various statistical methods used in the expression of the relationship of a given individual score to group data. A given score value acquires meaning only when it is compared with a well-defined class group. The class group may be a frequency distribution of which a given score value is a member, or the group could be a normative group for a given standardized test. In this latter case, for example, measures of individual position are used with standardized aptitude, achievement, and ability tests, which facilitate the comparison of individual scores to those of a normative group.

The measures of individual position are expressed as various transformed scores that have been derived from raw score data. These allowable transformations depend upon the level of measurement achieved.

Nominal Scale

At the nominal level of measurement no comparison of a given score value to the group is possible. The numeral, it may be recalled, only classifies and therefore does not describe any relationship between a given score value and the group from which it was drawn.

Ordinal Scale

Ranks and Percentile Ranks

Function and Method. Once an ordinal level of measurement has been achieved, a measure of individual position is possible. The transformation of the original scores, where the relationship—greater than—has been established, is into ranks and/or percentile ranks. In general:

$$Z' = O(Z)$$

where Z' = transformed ordinal score
O = any order preserving substitution
Z = the original score

When the original scores have been transformed into equivalent ranks or percentile ranks, the original scores take on a new dimension of meaning. The rank is defined as the number of cases equal to or exceeded by a given score. The percentile rank is a point on the distribution scale.

In the following formula, all of the values are known except for P (the proportion of cases surpassed). We solve for P and multiply the obtained value by 100 for the percentile rank.

$$\text{original score} = {}_rL_l + \left[\frac{PN - \Sigma fb}{fw} \right] i$$

where ${}_rL_l$ = real lower limit of the interval
containing the original score
P = proportion of cases surpassed
N = total number of cases
Σfb = sum of the frequency of cases
below that interval
fw = the number of cases within the
interval
i = interval width
and
%-ile rank = $(P)(100)$ (6.1)

Example. From the data given in Tables 3.3 and 3.5, let's assume that we want to determine the percentile rank of an individual's score of 87. The real lower limit of the interval containing this score is 79.5, there are 160 scores below that interval, 17 scores within the interval, the sample size is 210, and the interval width is 10. Substituting these values we have:

$$87 = 79.5 + \left[\frac{(P)210 - 160}{17} \right] 10$$

$$1479 = 1351.5 + (P)2100 - 1600$$
$$1479 = 1851.5 \, (P)$$
$$0.80 = P$$
$$\% \text{-ile rank} = 80$$

If, on the other hand, the percentile rank is known, an estimate of the original score may be obtained by:

$$\text{score} = {}_r L_l + \left[\frac{(\% \text{-ile})(N) - \Sigma f_b}{f_w} \right] i \qquad (6.2)$$

One of the major values of a cumulative percentage curve, as we previously pointed out in Chapter 3, is that the percentiles as well as the score values may be quickly obtained.

Interval Scale

Standard Scores

Function and Method. In addition to the rank and percentile rank, further measures of individual position may be specified provided that the criteria of the interval scale of measurement have been satisfied. In general, transformed interval data can be described as:

$$Z' = K + C(Z)$$

where Z' = the transformed score
K = an additive constant
C = a multiplicative constant greater than zero
Z = the original score

The basic form of such transformed scores is that of the standard or z-score. A standard score is defined as a transformed score that is expressed in standard deviation units, or:

$$z\text{-score} = \frac{X - \bar{X}}{S} \tag{6.3}$$

and in deviation form:

$$z\text{-score} = \frac{x}{S}$$

Regardless of the obtained values of the mean and standard deviation from a given sample, the means for a transformed z-distribution will always be equal to zero (0.00), and the variance and the standard deviation will always be equal to one (1.00). These properties enable us to directly compare various distributions and to describe the individual positions in them. These properties are shown below. If both sides of Formula 6.3 are summed, then:

$$\Sigma z = \frac{\Sigma(X - \bar{X})}{S}$$

$$= \frac{1}{S} \Sigma(X - \bar{X})$$

and as $\Sigma(X - \bar{X}) = 0$

then $\Sigma z = 0$

and $\bar{z} = \frac{\Sigma z}{N}$

$$= 0$$

And it may be shown that if:

$$S_z^2 = \frac{\Sigma(z - \bar{z})^2}{N - 1}$$

and as $\bar{z} = 0$

then $S_z^2 = \frac{\Sigma z^2}{N - 1}$

by definition $z = \frac{x}{S}$

therefore $S_z^2 = \frac{\Sigma \left(\frac{x}{S}\right)^2}{N - 1}$

$$\text{or } S_z^2 = \frac{\Sigma x^2}{S^2(N-1)}$$

$$\text{however, } S^2(N-1) = \Sigma x^2$$

$$\text{then } S_z^2 = \frac{\Sigma x^2}{\Sigma x^2}$$

$$\text{and } S_z^2 = 1.00$$

$$\text{and } S = 1.00$$

The z-score having been defined in terms of standard deviation units can, therefore, be expressed also as a percentile rank provided that the original frequency distribution of scores is a normal distribution. If the assumption of a normal distribution is met, Table C allows a conversion of z-scores into percentile ranks. From Figure 6.1 the comparisons between z-scores and %-iles may be observed.

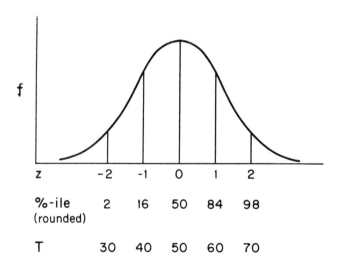

Figure 6.1. The comparison of z-scores, %–iles and T-scores under the normal curve.

It may be recalled that the general interval scale transformation of scores was:

$$Z' = K + C(Z)$$

Therefore, with standard scores the formula may be rewritten as:

$$z = 0 + 1 \left[\frac{X - \bar{X}}{S} \right]$$

where $0 = \bar{z}$

$1 = S_z$

It is theoretically possible to substitute any values for the constants K and C. Irrespective of the values chosen, however, the constant K shall correspond to the mean, and C shall correspond to the standard deviation for the transformed scale. One of the typical variants of the standard score is that of the Z-score or:

$$Z = 50 + 10(z) \tag{6.4}$$

where 50 = mean of the transformed scale
10 = standard deviation of the
transformed scale
z = any z-score

Thus, a person making a score that is one and a half standard deviations below the mean has a Z-score of 35 rather than –1.50. It must be noted, however, that the meaning is exactly the same regardless of the method of expression of standard scores. Generally, the reported values for the standard transformed scores, other than the z-score, are given as rounded values without the decimal point.

A number of methods of expressing standard scores have been developed to report test results on various standardized measures. The College Entrance Examination Board and the Graduate Record Examination both report individual position scores which are expressed with the constants of $K = 500$ and $C = 100$. Similarly, the Wechsler's intelligence full scale uses the constants of $K = 100$ and $C = 15$, rather than raw score data, to express individual scores.

Example.   Let us assume, that as a part of a high school counseling program, the senior men were given a standardized test as part of a battery of tests designed to measure the capacity of the individual to recognize various physical and mechanical relationships. In the manual for this test, one set of norms that was reported was for the freshman engineering students at a given university. The norms given had a mean of 40.58 with the standard deviation of 7.40. Now if a given student made a score of 53, his standard score would be:

$$z\text{-score} = \frac{53 - 40.58}{7.40}$$

$$= \frac{12.42}{7.40}$$

$$= 1.68$$

If the assumption of normality could be met, this z-score would correspond to the $95th$%-ile for the reported norm group.

In many testing programs, it is often highly desirable to compare scores within a given sample. If, for example, a mean of 34.03 and a standard deviation of 9.83 were obtained from the senior sample, then our student's score would now be:

$$z\text{-score} = \frac{53 - 34.03}{9.83}$$

$$= \frac{18.97}{9.83}$$

$$z = 1.93$$

This score would correspond to the $97th$ %-ile of the sample.

Normalized Standard Scores

Function and Method. The transformation of original scores into standard scores does not change the shape of the original frequency distribution. If the original distribution is normal, the standard score distribution is also normal. Similarly, if the original distribution is skewed, the standard score distribution will be skewed. If the assumption of normality cannot be met, a normalized procedure can still be utilized if the variable underlying the original frequency distribution is assumed to be normally distributed. This normalizing procedure can be used any time it is convenient to do so. The most typical normalized standard score is the T-score, and is defined as:

$$T = 50 + 10(z_n) \qquad\qquad (6.5)$$

where 50 = the mean of the transformed
          scale
     10 = the standard deviation of
          the transformed scale
     z_n = normalized z-score

The procedure for the calculation of the normalized T-scores is essentially the same as that used in obtaining ranks and/or percentile ranks. The raw scores are placed in rank order or in cumulative frequency percentages or proportions. The corresponding ranks, percentages, or proportions, are then referred to Table D for ranks and Table E for percentages and proportions, and the corresponding T-scores are determined. Once the T-score values are obtained these in turn may be transformed into other standard scores.

Example. One hundred forty-three college students were given a paper-and-pencil scale which was designed to measure the achievement motive. In Table 6.1 we have the data for these subjects and the scores have been ordered and the cf determined. In the cp column the cumulative proportions were obtained by multiplying the reciprocal $(1/143)$ by each cf. From Table D, the various T-values were obtained from the associated proportions. In this general procedure, data which are basically ordinal in nature can be normalized and placed into interval form. Thus, a person whose score is 152 has a corresponding T-score of 60, or that person's score value is one standard deviation above the mean.

If we could assume that the achievement-need measure was interval scale data, we could also determine the Z-scores without normalizing the data. In Table 6.1 the mean and standard deviation have been calculated.

For the subject with a raw score of 138, his z-score would be:

$$z = \frac{X - \overline{X}}{S}$$

$$= \frac{138 - 131.85}{19.92}$$

$$= 0.308$$

Table 6.1.   Statistics on relative position of Ss' total scale scores.

X	f	cf	cp	T	X	f	cf	cp	T
171	1	143	.999	79	130	6	68	.475	49
170	1	142	.992	74	129	6	62	.433	48
169	1	141	.985	72	128	2	56	.391	47
168	1	140	.978	70	127	3	54	.377	47
167	2	139	.972	69	126	5	51	.356	46
166	1	137	.958	68	125	2	46	.321	45
165	1	136	.951	67	124	1	44	.307	45
160	2	135	.944	66	123	3	43	.300	45
157	2	135	.929	65	122	2	40	.279	44
156	2	131	.915	64	121	2	38	.265	44
155	5	129	.902	63	119	4	36	.251	43
153	1	124	.866	61	118	1	32	.224	42
152	3	123	.860	60	117	3	31	.216	42
151	3	120	.839	60	116	1	28	.196	41
150	1	117	.818	59	115	1	27	.188	41
149	2	116	.811	59	114	2	26	.182	41
148	4	114	.797	58	113	2	24	.167	40
147	1	110	.769	58	112	1	22	.153	40
146	1	109	.755	57	111	4	21	.147	39
145	1	108	.752	57	107	1	17	.118	38
144	4	107	.748	56	106	1	16	.112	38
143	4	103	.719	56	104	2	15	.105	37
142	6	99	.692	55	103	2	13	.091	36
141	1	93	.650	54	101	1	11	.077	35
140	5	92	.643	54	100	2	10	.069	35
139	2	87	.608	53	97	1	8	.056	34
138	1	85	.594	53	96	1	7	.049	33
137	2	84	.587	52	94	1	6	.042	33
136	2	82	.573	52	91	1	5	.035	32
135	3	80	.559	51	84	1	4	.028	31
133	3	77	.538	51	83	1	3	.021	30
132	4	74	.517	50	76	1	2	.014	28
131	2	70	.489	50	69	1	1	.007	25

$$\overline{X} = 131.85 \qquad N = 143$$

$$\Sigma x^2 = 56340$$

$$S^2 = 396.7$$

$$S = 19.92$$

If we assume that the data is normal, this value of z would correspond to the 54.80 %-ile. However, the normalized %-ile is 59.40. These two values are different because the data are not perfectly normal in form. It may be strongly argued that for the best interpretation of individual position on the interval scale level, the data should be normalized.

Summary of Terms

normalized standard score
percentile rank
rank
standard score
transformed score

T-score
z-score

Summary of Symbols

T

z

Z

z_n

Problems

1. An experimenter was interested in the dominance hierarchy of 50 rats. Each rat, after 24 hours of food deprivation, competed with every other rat for a single pellet of food placed between the pair. The experimenter recorded the number of times that each rat won the pellet of food. The results are given below in the form of a frequency distribution.

    a. Which measures of individual position can be used to describe the position of individual rats in the distribution? Why?

    b. What approximate score in this distribution would have a percentile rank value of 40?

    c. What is the approximate percentile rank of a score of 36?

Score	f
45 – 49	2
40 – 44	2
35 – 39	12
30 – 34	8
25 – 29	6
20 – 24	12
15 – 19	0
10 – 14	2
5 - 9	4
0 - 4	2

2. Below is a distribution of test results.

   a. Find the mean and S.

   b. Find the z-scores and percentile ranks for the following scores (assume that the distribution is normal): 25, 20, 15, 10, 5.

   c. Transform the z-scores found in "b" into Z-scores.

   d. Using Formula 6.1 and a group frequency distribution with class intervals five units wide find the percentile rank for each of the scores given in "b."

   e. Using the cumulative proportions associated with the group frequency distribution in "d" and "e" find the approximate normalized standard scores—T—for each of the scores given in "b."

   f. Why are the percentile ranks found in "b" different from those found in "d," and why are the Z-scores found in "c" different than the T-scores found in "e"?

Scores

0	0	12	1
6	5	10	3
2	1	6	16
2	12	2	25
18	10	8	19

Experimental Design

Chapter Seven

In science we conduct research in order to obtain objective answers to various questions. The questions or hypotheses are derived from theories, observations, or even from hunches. However, the conclusions that we make about our hypotheses are based upon objectivity. Within this chapter, we will describe the various objective procedures for decision making.

Some Comments on Theory

A theory is basically defined as a set of summarizing principles, facts, or ideas that can be used for explaining some specified event or phenomenon. When we speak of explanation we generally mean the acccounting of the greatest number of facts with the fewest number of assumptions. A phenomenon is explained if it can be shown to follow a more general principle.

Figure 7.1 exemplifies how the various laws of mechanics and astronomy can be explained by the more general principle of gravity. Theory, therefore, serves the function of integrating knowledge into a more general explanatory system.

A second function of theory is allowance for deductions and predictions of new knowledge. A theory is, in the broadest sense, never directly testable. However, a research hypothesis that is

Figure 7.1.   Newton's Gravitational Principle.

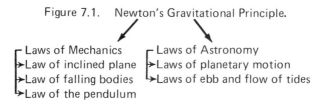

derived or deduced from a theory is open to empirical test. A theory can be evaluated only by empirically testing a number of hypotheses deduced from it. From the statistical analysis of the empirical data we are able to make a probability statement about the acceptance or the rejection of the research hypothesis and the theory from which it was derived.

One of the fundamental assumptions in all sciences is that of determinism. It is assumed that there is lawfulness in nature and that every natural event has a "cause." The deduction follows an if—if—then "causal" pattern, if *a* and if *b,* then *c.* In science we are not able to make such a completely deterministic statement as to the truth of our deductions. This form of complete determinism is not open directly to experimental verification. Rather, in science some probabilistic statement is made, such as, if *a* and if *b,* then there is a high probability that *c* will occur. There is a fundamental relationship between actual research finds and probabilistic determinism. The interpretation of the data analysis is always a probability statement and therefore reflects a probabilistic philosophy. In our scientific probability statement above, no reference was made to causation. Rather, we speak of functional relationships between variables. For example, behavior is a function of the various antecedent conditions.

Many philosophers of science have strongly held that science progresses only by testing of theoretical hypotheses deduced from theories. There is little question that for rapid advancement of science, theory testing is of major importance. Empirical data, resulting from hypothesis testing, contribute both to knowledge and to theory. However, a single study, in and of itself, lacks generality. Typically, theory testing involves the evaluation of a multitude of research hypotheses, each formulated to investigate one or more of the various antecedent conditions. This approach permits a greater degree of generalization than does a single experiment which is not related to other experimental studies or to any theory.

We would make a fundamental error, however, if we insisted that all research be derived from theory. There is a multitude of reasons why we do research besides the evaluation of a theory. Often good hunches, curiosity, or "hypotheses" come from serendipitous findings. These unexpected or side results may lead the researchers to ask new questions. It is through such avenues that we are led to the establishment of a new behavioral phenomenon and the conditions under which it occurs. We must fully recognize that knowledge comes from many directions. Thus, the terms *hypothesis* and *theory* will be used in the broadest scope in the following sections.

Hypothesis Testing

In the statistical analysis of behavior we have an objective decision-making procedure for the evaluation of a set of data. This involves a number of specific procedures which are carried out in advance of data collection.

The Null and Alternative or Research Hypotheses. From a theory a research hypothesis is stated and two statistical hypotheses are formulated. The two statistical hypotheses are in the form of a null hypothesis and an alternative hypothesis. The null hypothesis (H_0) is a statement in regard to the value of a parameter (or values of parameters) that is statistically tested. The alternative hypothesis (H_1) is also a statistical hypothesis and is a logically derived statement from a research hypothesis. The alternative hypothesis is stated in such a manner that if the null hypothesis is rejected, the alternative hypothesis can be accepted. The research or alternative hypothesis in conjunction with the null hypothesis completely describe all possible outcomes of a given experiment.

The statistical hypotheses $(H_0$ and $H_1)$ are stated in non-directional or directional fashion. For example, the null hypothesis is stated: the mean of an experimental group is equal to the mean of the control group. The alternative hypothesis is stated as a difference between the two means but the direction of the difference is not specified.

$$H_0 : \mu_E = \mu_C \qquad \text{or } \mu_E - \mu_C = 0$$

$$H_1 : \mu_E \neq \mu_C \qquad \text{or } \mu_E - \mu_C \neq 0$$

An alternative hypothesis that specifies that two population means are not equal is called a non-directional hypothesis. If the above null hypothesis is false, then the alternative hypothesis must be true, in that there is no other possible relationships between the two population means. Alternative hypotheses that specify which population mean will be the larger are called directional hypotheses. These directional hypotheses are given as:

$$H_0 : \mu_E \leqslant \mu_C \quad \text{or } \mu_E - \mu_C \leqslant 0$$

$$H_1 : \mu_E > \mu_C \quad \text{or } \mu_E - \mu_C > 0$$

or

$$H_0 : \mu_E \geqslant \mu_C \quad \text{or } \mu_E - \mu_C \geqslant 0$$

$$H_1 : \mu_E < \mu_C \quad \text{or } \mu_E - \mu_C < 0$$

If the H_0 that states that μ_E is equal to or less than μ_C is not true, then the H_1 that μ_E is greater than μ_C is true; and if the H_0 that μ_E is equal to or greater than μ_C is false, then the H_1 that μ_E is less than μ_C must be true. Every alternative or research hypothesis has a null hypothesis which is its complement.

Statistical Tests. After the null and alternative hypotheses have been stated, the researcher must choose an appropriate statistical test for the evaluation of the statistical hypotheses. The choice must be based upon the hypotheses to be evaluated. For example, if the statistical hypothesis is the comparison of two means, a statistical test such as t or F should be used. Associated with these tests are various assumptions that must be made. With the present development in the field of statistics, we have many inferential methods, and some of these inferential methods will be described in the following chapters.

Sample Size and Sampling Distributions. A sample of size N is drawn from a specified and well-defined population. In prior chapters we have been describing data from samples and describing them in terms of various statistics. However, a population consists of all possible observations of events, objects, or some phenomena, and it is described in terms of parameters. Our statistical hypotheses (H_0 and H_1) are always stated in terms of population parameters and never about sample statistics. It is from a population that samples are random and the statistics are estimates of population parameters.

The size of the sample is a function of the research design (number of treatment levels and effects), the magnitude of the error variance, and the probability of making Type I and Type II errors. These functions will be described in greater detail later in the chapter.

From the sample size, a set of all possible outcomes that could theoretically occur is determined and the probabilities of each of these outcomes are then obtained. This theoretical distribution is defined as the sampling distribution. It specifies theoretically all the various probabilities for all given outcomes of a sample size of N. As we shall see, there are a number of various sampling distributions that have been theoretically derived for different sample sizes, for various restrictions placed upon the data and types of outcomes, and for various statistical tests.

Level of Significance.   From the theoretical sampling distribution of all possible outcomes, a subset is selected that is associated with some specified probability value. The probability of the occurrence of this subset is the level of significance. The level of significance or alpha (α) is the probability of rejecting the null hypothesis when the null hypothesis is in fact true. In most contemporary behavioral and social science work the probabilities of 0.05 and 0.01 are used as the levels of significance. This means that we run a risk in our decision-making process of rejecting a true null hypothesis, e.g., 5 times out of 100, and accepting a false alternative hypothesis. On the other hand, the probability value of the remaining distribution is the level of confidence and would be 0.95 or 0.99.

Regions of Rejection.   Associated with the levels of significance and confidence are the regions of rejection and acceptance of the null hypothesis. As we have seen, the null and alternative hypotheses can be stated directionally or non-directionally. If, for example, we have non-directional hypotheses such as:

$$H_0 : \mu = 10$$

$$H_1 : \mu \neq 10$$

then to test such hypotheses we would have a two-tailed test. If we specified alpha at the 0.05 level then our sampling distribution would have 0.025 associated with each tail of the distribution as shown in Figure 7.2.

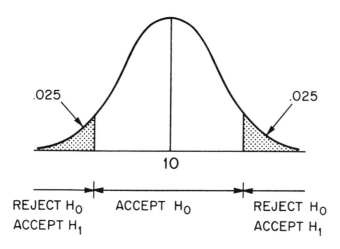

.025 .025

10

REJECT H_0 ACCEPT H_0 REJECT H_0
ACCEPT H_1 ACCEPT H_1

Figure 7.2. Regions of acceptance and of rejection for a two-tailed, non-directional hypothesis that mu is 10, with an alpha of .05.

If, on the other hand, our hypotheses were directional:

$$H_0 : \mu \leqslant 10$$

$$H_1 : \mu > 10$$

then the alpha value would be associated with a one-tailed test as shown in Figure 7.3.

It must be noted that the regions of acceptance and rejection are determined by the statistical hypotheses and that the size of these areas are a function of the value of alpha, and, as we shall later see, of the sample size.

If the data from the research give rise to a probability equal to or less than the predetermined alpha, $P < \alpha$, then the null hypothesis is rejected and the alternative hypothesis is accepted. On the other hand, if the data are associated with a larger probability value than alpha, then the null hypothesis is accepted. In slightly different terms, if the value from the analysis falls within the region of acceptance, then the null hypothesis is not rejected. If that value falls within the region of rejection, the null hypothesis is rejected and the alternative hypothesis is accepted.

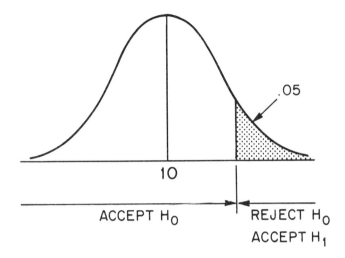

.05

10

ACCEPT H₀ | REJECT H₀
ACCEPT H₁

Figure 7.3.   Regions of acceptance and of rejection for a one-tailed, directional hypothesis that mu is greater than 10 with an alpha of .05.

Errors in Decision Making.   In the decision-making process the researcher runs the risk of making two types of errors. A Type I error is made when we reject a true null hypothesis. The value of alpha is the probability or risk we make in committing this error, P (Type I error) $= \alpha$. Therefore, when the researcher decides what level of significance will be used, the probability of a Type I error is determined. In our decision-making process, the alpha level must be stated before the data are collected. The Type II error is that error made when we accept the null hypothesis when the null hypothesis is in fact false. The probability of a Type II error is given by beta, P (Type II error) $= \beta$, and is a function of sample size, the level of alpha, the "true" values of population parameters, and the specific test used. As we do not know the true values of the parameters, the exact probability of a Type II error is undetermined. However, when the value of beta is high, we have a low probability of committing a Type II error. On the other hand, when the value of beta is low, we have a large chance of committing Type II errors.

Associated with beta is the power of a test of significance. Power is defined as $1 - \beta$ or:

$$\text{power} = 1 - \beta$$

and is the probability of rejecting the null hypothesis when the null hypothesis is in fact false. The power of a test of significance is related to making a correct decision by rejecting the null hypothesis and by accepting the alternative or research hypothesis. Therefore, we should select a test of significance that is the most powerful one appropriate for the level of measurement achieved. Type I and II errors and power are summarized in Table 7.1 below.

Table 7.1

	H_0 true	H_0 false
Decision to reject H_0	Type I error $P = \alpha$	Correct power $= 1 - \beta$
Decision to accept H_0	Correct $P = 1 - \alpha$	Type II error $P = \beta$

Summary. In summary of the decision-making process, we state the null and alternative hypotheses (H_0 and H_1), select a sample size (N) and determine the best statistical test and its sampling distribution under the null hypothesis, state alpha (α), obtain the regions of acceptance and rejection, collect the data and do the statistical analyses, and on the totality, accept or reject the null hypothesis.

Some Comments on Hypothesis Testing

The student of statistical analysis should be made aware that while the above procedure of hypothesis testing is the conventional one, it is not without criticism. This criticism comes from various fronts which you should be aware of and which may help you in being critical of your own and others' statistical analyses.

As was pointed out in the previous section, the power of a statistical test is clearly a function of the sample size, for as you increase the sample size the power also increases. It is therefore possible to select a sample size that is so large that very minute differences which essentially may be of trivial importance may be detected. A word of caution is in order. The researcher, in the interpretation of differences, can develop an attitude of testmanship and, therefore, become the victim of the power of the test. Of critical importance is what the researcher thinks about the information and what is done with the information.

A second line of criticism is that on a solely a priori base, the null hypothesis is already judged to be false and to test a no difference hypothesis is both unreasonable and uninformative. It seems somewhat questionable to assume that if we manipulate an antecedent variable there will be no response difference between means. Rarely does research begin assuming nothing is known about the effects of the antecedent or treatment conditions as it is most unlikely that this is the "initial" study. It has been argued that we should attempt to incorporate as much of the known information as possible from prior studies into our analyses. While this would be desirable, it is difficult with our present development of statistical analyses, to incorporate prior information (known probabilities) in most of our statistical methods.

Research Design for True Experiments

A research hypothesis for a true experiment implies a functional probability relationship between the antecedent variable or independent variable (a given stimulus variable) and the response or dependent variable. Usually, the design of our research is to manipulate the antecedent or independent variable or variables and to measure specific response differences. The one basic principle that we must consider is to design our research in such a fashion that the effects of the manipulation of the antecedent conditions upon the response can be unambiguously evaluated. Thus, we design our problem in advance of the study so that the data are not open to numerous interpretations.

The following research designs should be viewed as examples of or a general outline of various classifications of experimental designs.

Randomized Group Designs

Some Comments on Randomization.   In research involving randomized group designs, a sample of subjects is selected from the population in a specified manner prior to the experimental manipulation. The term population may be defined as all cases that conform to some predetermined criterion. For example, all freshmen in College *A* could be used as the criterion for defining a given, but nonetheless limited, population.

In a true random group design each of the subjects from the

population has the same or equal probability of being selected. Suppose, for example, we have a population of 100 subjects and we wish to have 20 subjects for a given experimental study. If we select at random from the population, the probability of selection would be equal for all subjects. Now, if half of the 20 are to be assigned to an experimental group and half to the control group, the probability of being assigned to the control group must be equal to the probability of being assigned to the experimental group. In the random group design, the logic is simply that differences between groups prior to the treatment conditions on any given subject variable are highly unlikely. Thus, with the randomizing of the subjects, any bias between the groups should be at a minimum and the group differences that might exist before the introduction of the treatment variable are solely a function of chance.

In actual practice, random selection from a population is most often difficult to guarantee. With human subjects, for example, the investigator is always confronted with the availability and recruitment of subjects. The investigator may start with a highly selected group such as volunteers out of a given course in a given college. This sample may be a highly biased one. From this sample there is generally no way of knowing much about the population and it is difficult to generalize about it. Similarly, if the researcher uses animal subjects, he is confronted with the problems of species, sex of the animal, strain differences, age, and practices of the supplier (type of food, cage sizes and animal density, temperature control, and the like). The major point is that great care must be taken in defining the population and sample which was drawn, and that the researcher *must,* at the very least, randomly assign available subjects to the various treatment conditions.

Procedure of Random Assignment. In the actual procedure of random assignment of subjects, we take all potential subjects that may be used and assign a number to each, beginning with 01 to N. When each subject has been assigned a number, we enter the table of random numbers, Table F, where the numbers are equally probable. We may enter the table at any given row or column and read in any direction. Assume for example, that we have randomly selected 30 subjects and these subjects are to be divided into three groups of 10 subjects each. In this case, we assign one number from 01 to 30 to each subject. We then enter the table and read in a given direction. When we match a corresponding number from the table to a subject number, we place that subject in Group I. If we do not have a corresponding subject number, or if that subject had been previously drawn, we simply go on to the next tabled number until we have randomly drawn out 10 subjects for Group I. We would continue in a like fashion for the next 10 subjects for Group II, and, of course, the last 10 subjects become Group III. In this fashion all subjects have the same probability of being selected for a given group.

One Random Sample Design.   In some experimental designs we may have only a single random group. In general, this design is used to test the hypothesis that a particular random sample was drawn from a specified population distribution. Thus this design is referred to as a goodness-of-fit design and enables the researchers to determine if there is a significant difference between the sample and the population. The goodness-of-fit design is illustrated in Figure 7.4.

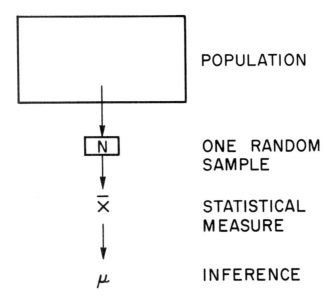

Figure 7.4.   Schematic of a goodness-of-fit design with one random sample drawn from a specified population. From the statistical measure an inference is drawn about the population.

One one-sample design may be used to determine if a particular random sample, after the effects of the treatment condition, differs significantly from some prior value given by a hypothesis. This is shown in Figure 7.5.

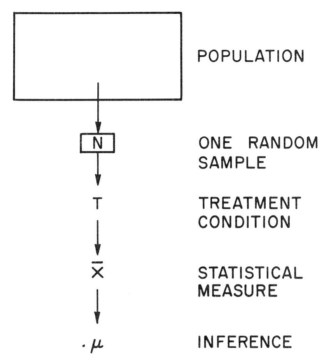

POPULATION

ONE RANDOM
SAMPLE

TREATMENT
CONDITION

STATISTICAL
MEASURE

INFERENCE

Figure 7.5   Schematic of a one-sample design with a single treatment condition. From the statistical measure the effects of the treatment
condition is inferred.

However, usually a control group is used in order that we might
ascertain some meaningful interpretations of the experimental
effects. The major risk of not using a control group is the
possibility that other extraneous factors may confound the results,
and the effects would be attributed to the treatment condition.
When control groups are utilized and when they receive all the
same conditions as the experimental groups, except for the
treatment variable, some functional statement can be specified for
the difference between the two groups. The basic implication is
that the difference between groups is a function of the treatment
conditions.

Two Random Samples Design.   This design is the typical
design in behavioral research. In the design, the subjects are
randomly assigned to the experimental and to the control groups.
The basic operations are to present the treatment condition to the
experimental group and not to the control group and then
measure the behavior.

In some research studies, rather than this traditional control, a yoked control group is utilized. The yoked-control method allows the simultaneous testing of both the experimental and control subjects. For example, in operant conditioning, when the experimental animal performs a given operant behavior, both animals receive the same consequences. The only difference is that this consequence is contingent upon the behavior of the experimental subject and is not contingent for the yoked control.

In general, the design enables us to test a hypothesis about whether the behaviors of two groups differ significantly as a function of the experimental manipulation. This is shown in Figure 7.6.

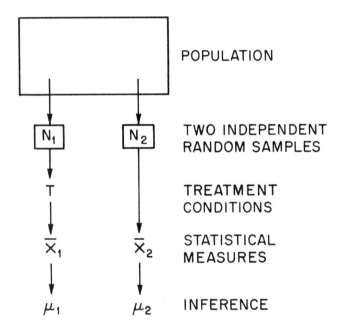

Figure 7.6. Schematic of a two independent random samples design with a treatment condition applied to one group (experimental) and not to the other (control). From the difference between the two statistical measures an inference is drawn in regard to the treatment condition.

In some instances random assignment to the two conditions is not applicable, in that the two groups have already been constituted. The investigator may want to compare two different populations, such as male-female, hospitalized-nonhospitalized, young-old, on some behavioral measure. However, random selection may be used with this distribution, provided that the two groups of subjects have been randomly selected from their respective populations. The research hypothesis would enable the researcher to ascertain if there is a significant difference between the two populations.

K **Random Samples Design.** This research design is a logical expansion of the two random samples design to three or more (*K*) random samples and is illustrated in Figure 7.7.

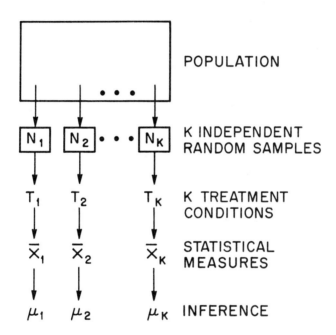

Figure 7.7.   Schematic of a K independent random sample design with various treatment conditions. From the differences among the K statistical measures an inference is drawn in regard to the various conditions.

It enables the investigator to study the effects of a number of different treatment conditions upon a given behavior. For example, we might study the effect of *K* number of drugs upon some performance. However, once we have determined the effects, we might then choose to do a study with a single drug. We could proceed to systematically vary the dosage levels, by giving a specified dosage level to one random group, another dosage level to a second group, and so forth, over the *K* groups. If there is a significant difference between the various groups, it may be argued that the behavior is a function of the dosage level.

Factorial Design.   The factorial design is, similarly, an expansion of the K random samples design. It enables us to design experiments that are concerned with the effects of one variable in combination with another variable, or variables, upon behavior. In a two or more variable or factor study, each factor is varied in two or more ways. Thus, in the simplest case, two factors are both varied in two ways as can be seen in Figure 7.8.

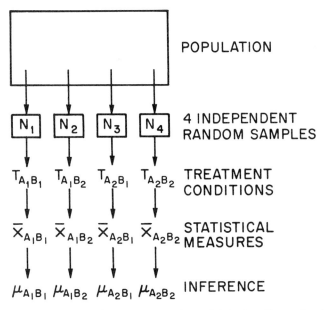

Figure 7.8. Schematic of a two-by-two factorial design. From the differences among the four statistical measures inferences are drawn in regard to the two variables and their interaction or differential effects.

For example, if we were interested in the effects of setting conditions of deprivation, and in the magnitude of the reinforcer upon runway performance, we could vary deprivation in two ways such as 4 hours and 23 hours of food deprivation. Furthermore, we may vary the magnitude of the food reinforcer in two ways, 45 mg and 90 mg. In this design the subjects would be randomly assigned to one of the four treatment groups (4-hour and 45-mg group; 4-hour and 90-mg group; 23-hour and 45-mg group; and 23-hour and 90-mg). It is the combination or interaction between factors or independent variables that gives major significance to this research design.

Related Group Designs

Some Comments on Related Groups.   It is assumed before the experimental and treatment conditions are presented that the sample groups are equal. That is, the experimental group is equal to the control group. This assumption has been made with all the randomized group designs. This same assumption is made with the related group designs. However, with related methods the assumption is measured. In general, we have two procedures for sampling. One is a matching procedure or pairing of subjects; the other is where the subject acts as its own control.

The matching or pairing procedure is used to minimize the subject differences between pairs (or more) on all the relevant variables. The researcher attempts to make each pair as much alike as possible. Thus, the groups before the experimental treatment are more alike than if the subjects had been assigned randomly. Once the pairs of subjects have been matched, the subjects within each of the pairs are then randomly assigned to either the experimental or control groups.

One of the basic problems of the matched group design is that we must match on all the relevant variables. In behavioral research this is often very difficult. More often than not, we simply do not know what these variables might be. A second basic difficulty is that of the ability to generalize from the matched group data to the population. As the groups are not initially selected in a random fashion, often little can be concluded in reference to some specified population or populations.

We must mention the hazards of the matched group design in ex post facto (after the fact) research. Some researchers have utilized this procedure where they measure differences between groups on "all" relevant variables except the treatment condition which was not initially under the control of the investigator. In ex post facto research the experimenter has not had the opportunity to make any random assignment before the fact. We are, therefore, never sure of the effects of the independent variable. The response differences between the groups may be a function of a whole host of uncontrolled factors, and in addition, we may not have matched on the most relevant variable or variables.

Perhaps the most commonly used related group design is where the subject's behavior is measured under the experimental and control conditions or under all the conditions. The problem of matching is in part circumvented in that now we have "identical" matching. However, the results of this experimental design can be confounded by the carry-over effects of the treatment variables. In other words, the effect of one treatment variable may influence or interact with the following treatment condition. This type of confounding may be reduced by a counterbalancing, such as a *A B B A* design, as well as by using a randomly selected control group.

One Related Sample Design.   The most basic one matched sample design has been referred to as a before-after design. In the basic model, this is the measurement of the treatment condition over time, as given in Figure 7.9.

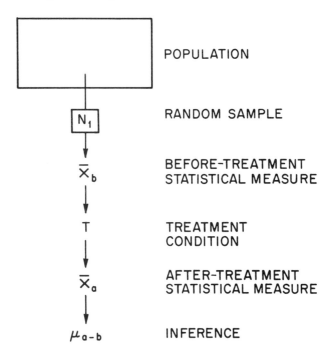

Figure 7.9.   Schematic of a before-after treatment design. From the difference between the before statistical measure and the after measure an inference is drawn as to the effect of the treatment condition.

Each subject's behavior is measured prior to the presentation of the experimental condition, and then is measured following the condition. The rationale is that if the treatment condition has any effect upon behavior it would be reflected in the difference between the before measure and the after-treatment measure.

Two Related Samples Design. Assume that we have matched or paired subjects and have randomly assigned them to the experimental and control groups. Therefore, before the treatment effects, the two groups should be approximately equal and any difference between these groups should be a function of sampling or matching error. If there were no confounding effects occurring over time, we would expect that the differences between the measures for the control groups would be zero. On the other hand, if there are some effects that occur over time these effects would be seen as real differences between the two control groups measures. The differences in the measures for the control group may enable us to draw more meaningful conclusions in regard to the treatment condition. The main research interest is in the differences between the experimental and control groups after the presentation of the treatment conditions. If there are differences they may be attributed to the experimental variable. The two matched or related sample design is illustrated in Figure 7.10 on page 90.

K **Related Samples Design.** An expansion of the before-after design is the repeated measurement design. Some authors refer to it as the treatment-by-subjects design. As in the prior discussion, one group of subjects may be randomly selected from the population, but would, within the present design, receive K treatment conditions. As an illustration, suppose a group of animals learned to perform a task at some stable or asymptotic level. We then present a deprivation level of first 24 hours, followed by another 24 hours, or 48 hours of deprivation, and we measure the performance of the task at each of these levels. If the performance differs between the asymptotic level and 24 hours and 48 hours of deprivation, these differences may be attributed to the treatment conditions. However, for the clearest interpretation we may also want a control group.

Mixed Designs

There are a number of designs that are essentially combinations of the randomized and related group designs and are broadly referred to as mixed designs. These complex experimental designs

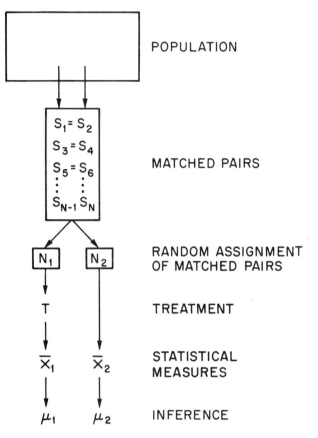

Figure 7.10. Schematic of a two matched or related sample design before the treatment condition.

are beyond the scope of this text. They are introduced in advanced design texts.

Research Design for Correlational Experiments

The research interest may be that of determining whether a relationship or association exists between two variables, and of determining the degree or magnitude and the direction of that relationship. Once the existence of a relationship has been established, then the degree and the direction of the relation has meaning and is described by the correlation coefficient. This numeral index describes the extent that variations in one variable are associated with variations in the second variable.

As with the various tests of statistical inference, we are also concerned here with the testing of various research hypotheses about the association between variables. Science does not go about studying possible relationships in a random fashion, but rather a good articulate theory or a good hunch may suggest what relationships might be of major importance to science, and what variables might be meaningfully associated. The most basic hypothesis is that there is a statistical relationship beyond that expected as a function of random sampling, or that there is a correlation significantly different from zero. If the coefficient differs significantly from zero, it may be argued that there is an association in the population. Furthermore, we may wish to estimate the range of the magnitude of the significant population correlations from the observed sample coefficient, or to test the significant difference between two observed correlation coefficients.

Associated with the bivariate methods are measures of prediction. Frequently the research is not only concerned with relationships but, in addition, with making predictions. When we know that two variables are correlated, then having information about one variable enables us to make predictions of the second variable.

As all science is based upon reliable measurement, a major concern of correlational methods is focused upon various indexes of reliability of measures. All measurement has some element of error. Therefore, it is most important for science to minimize the error and estimate the amount of error in the measurements. For if we cannot make reliable measurements of the phenomenon under investigation, that phenomenon is always open to question.

Summary of Terms

alpha
alternative or research hypothesis
beta
correlation
directional hypothesis

ex post facto
explanation
factorial design
goodness-of-fit
mixed design

non-directional hypothesis
null hypothesis

population
power
randomization

random group design
regions of acceptance
regions of rejection
related or matched group design
sample

statistical hypothesis
theory
Type I and II errors

Summary of Symbols

H_0
H_1
μ
α
β

Probability   Chapter Eight

As probability statements are associated with our functional relationships and our scientific laws, it is imperative that the student of science has a working knowledge of probability theory. All of the various techniques of statistical inference and of correlational methods in the following chapters enable us to make certain decisions based on probability statements.

Some Mathematical Properties of Probability

In general terms, what is meant by the term probability is the theoretical relative frequency or proportion of the time that some specified outcome or event will occur over the long run. For example, if we say that the chances, or likelihood, of the outcome heads on a toss of some idealized coin is the proportion or probability of 1/2 or 50:50, what we are saying, in effect, is that we have some a priori idea of the event that would happen as the number of events approaches infinity (∞). If we toss the coin once the proportion of the event heads is 1/1 or it is 0/1 but not 1/2. If we choose to toss that coin 100 times, the empirical results that might be expected would be close to 50/100; however, we should not be surprised if we got 51/100 or 49/100. As the number of events becomes greater, the relative frequency or proportion of the heads would become close to the theoretical 1/2 probability.

Let N stand for the number of equally possible outcomes of an event. There would be, for example, two possible outcomes of a single toss of a coin, or 52 possible outcomes of a draw from a standard deck of cards, or six possible outcomes from the roll of a die.

Let $n(A)$ stand for the number of some particular class (A) from N. In the above examples, this may be a head, or the ace of spades, or the one on the die. It follows from the general definition that the probability of the outcome A is:

$$P(A) = \frac{n(A)}{N} \tag{8.1}$$

Hence, the $P(A)$ for heads is 1/2, the $P(A)$ for the ace of spades is 1/52, and that for the one spot on a die is 1/6.

As $n(A)$, by definition, is never less than zero nor greater than N, the $P(A)$ is never less than zero nor greater than one. Thus,

$$0 \leqslant P(A) \leqslant 1 \tag{8.2}$$

Let $n(A')$ represent the number of outcomes that are not A, and $Q(A)$ represent the probability of A', then:

$$Q(A) = \frac{n(A')}{N} \tag{8.3}$$

Therefore, the $Q(A)$ for heads is 1/2, the $Q(A)$ for the ace of spades is 51/52, and the $Q(A)$ for the one spot is 5/6.

$$\text{As } n(A) + n(A') = N \tag{8.4}$$

$$\text{and } P(A) = \frac{n(A)}{N} \text{ and } Q(A) = \frac{n(A')}{N}$$

$$\text{then } P(A) + Q(A) = \frac{n(A)}{N} + \frac{n(A')}{N} = 1$$

It therefore holds that:

$$Q(A) = 1 - P(A) \tag{8.5}$$

The Rule of Addition of Probabilities of Mutually Exclusive Outcomes. If events A and B and C and ... and K are all mutually exclusive, then the probability of either A or B or C or ... or K is equal to the sum of their separate probabilities. Thus:

$$P(A + B + C + \ldots + K) = P(A) + P(B) + P(C) + \ldots + P(K) \qquad (8.6)$$

Mutually exclusive outcomes are those outcomes, A and B and C and the generalized K, that cannot occur or happen at the same time. The coin cannot be both heads and tails, the card an ace and a king, or the die a one and a two spot. Applying this additive rule, we have the probability of an ace or a king on a single draw from a 52-card deck:

$$P(\text{ace or king}) = 4/52 + 4/52 = 8/52$$

As we have four aces and four kings in the deck, the probability of not an ace or king is:

$$Q(\text{ace or king}) = 1 - 8/52 = 44/52$$

Now the probability of a head or a tail on the coin throw is:

$$P(\text{heads or tails}) = 1/2 + 1/2 = 1$$

If every possible mutually exclusive outcome is included in one of the classes, as in the coin example where the coin must be heads or tails, we have exhaustive classes. The sum of the probabilities of these exhaustive classes is equal to one.

The Rule of Addition When the Outcomes Are Not Mutually Exclusive. If events A and B are *not* mutually exclusive, then the probability of either A or B is equal to the sum of their separate probabilities *minus* the probability of A and B simultaneously occurring, thus:

$$P(A + B) = P(A) + P(B) - P(AB) \qquad (8.7)$$

When the outcomes are not mutually exclusive, and we want to ascertain the $P(A \text{ or } B)$, four events could occur:

A but not B
B but not A
both A and B
neither A nor B

For example, assume that we want to determine the probability of spades or aces. Spades and aces are not mutually exclusive, as the ace of spades encompasses both of these; therefore, this event could occur with a given probability or $P(AB)$. Hence:

$$P(\text{spades or aces}) = 13/52 + 4/52 - 1/52 = 16/52$$

$$\text{where } 1/52 = \text{probability ace of spades}$$

As we can see, the reason for subtracting out 1/52 is that it has entered the probability twice.

It must be noted here, that if $P(AB)$ is equal to zero, then the events are mutually exclusive. Therefore, we can define mutually exclusive events as those events with a probability of $P(AB)$ equal to zero.

The Multiplication Rule for Independent Outcomes. If events A and B and C and . . . and K are independent events, then the probability of getting A and B and . . . and K is the product of these separate probabilities:

$$P(AB \ldots K) = P(A)\,P(B) \ldots P(K) \qquad (8.8)$$

Events are said to be independent if the probability that they occur is equal to the product of the individual probabilities. Less formally, by independent events we mean that the various events have nothing to do with each other. What happens on event A has no effect upon what happens on event B. For example, if we toss an unbiased coin once, this event has no effect upon the outcome of the second toss of the same or different coin. Thus, the probability of getting two heads on two tosses of a coin would be:

$$P(\text{heads and heads}) = (1/2)\,(1/2) = 1/4$$

The Multiplication Rule for Conditional Probabilities. If events A and B are any two events, then the probability of getting A and B is the product of the probability of the first event and the conditional probability of the second event or:

$$P(AB) = P(A)\,P(B|A)$$

$$P(BA) = P(B)\,P(A|B) \qquad (8.9)$$

The terms $P(A|B)$ and $P(B|A)$ are what we refer to as conditional probabilities. In general, what we mean by a conditional probability is that the probability of event *B* depends upon event *A*. We can ask, for example, what the probability is that we would draw two aces from two draws; as these events are not independent, the first draw will have an effect on the second draw. The *P*(ace) for the first draw is 4/52, but the *P* for the second draw is not the same if we received an ace on the first draw and retained it (did not replace it). Therefore, the *P* for the second draw is 3/51 or the probability for the two aces on the two draws without replacement is:

$$P(\text{ace and ace}) = (4/52)\,(3/51) = 1/221$$

Bayes' Theorem.   Bayes' Theorem is a logical development from the multiplication rules of probability, and the theorem describes the relation among various conditional probabilities. When the initial or a priori probabilities are known or given, and when these probabilities have a simple relative frequency interpretation, this theorem can be well utilized in determining a posteriori conditional probabilities. Of critical importance is the assignment of the prior probabilities. With prior information that is given, the procedure typically results in an increase of the conditional probability of an event, which, in turn, allows us to make better decisions or to draw better conclusions from the data. It is upon these bases that the Bayesian approach to hypothesis testing differs significantly from the conventional model.

As given in 8.9, we have:

$$P(AB) = P(A)\,P(B|A)$$

and

$$= P(B)\,P(A|B)$$

or

$$P(A)\,P(B|A) = P(B)\,P(A|B)$$

In the simplest version, we obtain Bayes' Theorem for two events A and B by rearranging the equation above, or:

$$P(A|B) = P(B)\,\frac{P(A|B)}{P(A)} \qquad (8.10)$$

or

$$P(A|B) = P(A)\,\frac{P(B|A)}{P(B)} \qquad (8.11)$$

Further rearranging and substituting identities in 8.10, we have the more general version of Bayes' Theorem:

$$P(A|B) = \frac{P(B|A)\,P(A)}{P(B|A)\,P(A) + P(B|A')\,P(A')} \qquad (8.12)$$

To illustrate the theorem, suppose a student is considering applying to a given graduate program with very high standards for awarding of the advanced degree and with high but variable admission scores. The published data from the program state that approximately 60 percent of the students admitted to the program actually complete all the degree requirements, and are awarded the degree, or $P(A) = 0.60$ and $P(A') = 0.40$. Furthermore, approximately 80 percent of the students who were awarded the degree were, also, above the admissions standards, or $P(B|A) = 0.80$, and 40 percent of the students who were above the admission standards did not complete the program, or $P(B|A) = 0.40$. If the student assumed that he was a random sample, what are the chances the student, if admitted, will complete the degree requirements, if his admission scores were above the admission standards, or $P(A|B) = ?$ From 8.11, we have:

$$P(A|B) = \frac{(.80)\,(.60)}{(.80)\,(.60) + (.40)\,(.40)}$$

$$= .75$$

In the student's decision process, he now knows that the probability is 0.75 for his being awarded the degree provided that his admission scores are above the admission standards.

Permutations

The multiplication rules for probabilities provide a general method for permutations. The general definition of a permutation states that a permutation of a number of objects, events, or phenomena is any arrangement of these in some specific order. We arrange the objects, events, or phenomena in all possible orders or ways to generate all the possible permutations.

Permutations of *n* Different Things, *n* at a Time.   If we have *n* different things taken all together or *n* at a time, the number of permutations is:

$$_nP_n = n!$$ (8.13)

where $n! = (n)(n - 1)(n - 2)(n - 3) \ldots (1)$

The notation $n!$ is the factorial of n cases and is the product of all the whole numbers from the nth case to 1.

Suppose, for example, we would want to know how many arrangements we could have in the three winners' places in a three-horse race. Let us call the horses X, Y, and Z. The possibilities are shown in a "tree" diagram in Figure 8.1.

First place Second place Third place Possible orders

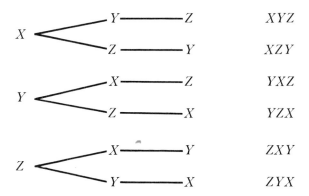

As can be seen from this diagram, the first-place winner could happen to be any of the three, the second-place winner any of the remaining two, and the third-place winner the remaining one. Thus, we have $(3)(2)(1) = 6$. In our example, then, of the three things taken three at a time we have:

$$_3P_3 = 3!$$

$$= (3)(2)(1)$$

$$= 6$$

Permutations of n Different Things, r at a Time. The number of permutations of n things, taken r at a time, where $r < n$, is:

$$_nP_r = \frac{n!}{(n - r)!}$$ (8.14)

The r in this general case is a number of different objects taken from the n objects. If we would now have an eight-horse race, we could ask how many ways we can have three horses from the eight horses arranged in the winners' circle. Now, the first place can be filled by any one of the eight horses, the second place by any of the seven horses, and the third place by any one of the remaining six horses, or $(8)(7)(6)$ or 336 possible orders. Applying Formula 8.14 we have:

$$_8P_3 = \frac{8!}{(8-3)!}$$

$$= \frac{8!}{5!}$$

$$= \frac{(8)(7)(6)(5)(4)(3)(2)(1)}{(5)(4)(3)(2)(1)}$$

$$\text{or} = (8)(7)(6)$$

$$= 336$$

Permutations of n Things That Are Not All Different.   In our previous section, we dealt with the number of possible arrangements of sets of objects that were considered to be different from one another. However, the permutations will be influenced if only part of n things are the same. The number of permutations of n things taken at the same time where n_1 are of one kind, n_2 are of another, and n_k of yet another kind is obtained by:

$$_nP_{n_1 n_2 \ldots n_k} = \frac{n!}{n_1! \, n_2! \ldots n_k!} \tag{8.15}$$

In the problem of the number of permutations we may have when we have two kinds of objects, our general Formula 8.15 becomes:

$$_nP_{n_1 n_2} = \frac{n!}{n_1! \, n_2!} \tag{8.16}$$

$$\text{or} = \frac{n!}{r! \, (n-r)}$$

$$\text{where } n_1 = r$$

$$\text{and } n_2 = n - r$$

If, for example, we have a 10-item true and false test where 5 of the items are true and 5 false, we may ask in how many ways we could get all of the 10 items correctly as a function of chance:

$$_{10}P_{(10)(0)} = \frac{10!}{10!0!} = 1 \text{ way}$$

or 9 correct:

$$_{10}P_{(9)(1)} = \frac{10!}{9!1!} = 10 \text{ ways}$$

Now let us ask how many arrangements can be made from the letters of the word Walla Walla when taken all together. We have $W = 2$, $a = 4$, and $l = 4$ or $n_1 = 2$, $n_2 = 4$, and $n_3 = 4$, and $n = 10$. From Formula 8.15 we have:

$$_{10}P_{(2)(4)(4)} = \frac{10!}{2!4!4!} = 3150 \text{ ways}$$

Combinations

In our previous discussions of permutations we were concerned with the order of events. However, in combinations we are *not* concerned with order; therefore, with combinations, order is ignored. In the three-horse race we considered permutations or orders. If order is ignored, then X, Y, Z, is the same as Z, Y, X, and we would have a combination problem.

Combinations of *n* Things, *r* at a Time. The number of combinations of n things, such that we have r of one kind and $n-r$ of a different kind is:

$$_{n}C_{r} = \binom{n}{r} = \frac{n!}{r!(n-r)!} \qquad (8.17)$$

– where n = number of objects
r = the number of one kind of object
$n-r$ = the number of a different kind of object

If we would apply our Formula 8.17 to a ten-item true and false test, we could ask the number of combinations of ten items (n), eight of which are correct (r) and 2 of which are incorrect $(n-r)$, hence:

$$\binom{10}{8} = \frac{10!}{8!(10-8)!}$$

$$= 45$$

Thus, there are 45 ways we could get 8 items correct and 2 incorrect from the 10 items.

It may be seen that each combination could be ordered in $r!$ ways, and thus could give rise to permutations or:

$$\binom{n}{r}r! = {}_nP_r \tag{8.18}$$

Using the above example, we find:

$$(45)(8) = 360 \text{ permutations or orders}$$

Probability from Combinations.   The probability from combinations can be obtained by:

$$\binom{n}{r}P^r\,Q^{n-r} = \frac{n!}{r!(n-r)!}\,P^r\,Q^{n-r} \tag{8.19}$$

In our 10 item true-false test, if we *assume* that $P = 1/2$ and $Q = 1/2$, then the probability of exactly 8 correct responses is:

$$\binom{10}{8}(1/2)^8\,(1/2)^2 \;=\; \frac{10!}{8!2!}\,(1/2)^8\,(1/2)^2$$

$$= (45)(1/1024)$$

$$= 45/1024$$

$$= 0.044$$

From the rules of addition, when the outcomes are mutually exclusive, we can ascertain the probability of 8 or more correct responses. The probability of 10 correct is equal to 0.001, and 9 correct is 0.010. Therefore eight or more correct responses by the additive rule is:

$$(0.001) + (0.010) + (0.044) = 0.055$$

The Binomial Expansion

An alternative method for finding the probability for all the various combinations is the expansion of the binomial. In the general case the binomial may be written as:

$$(P + Q)^n = \left[\binom{n}{0}P^n\right] + \left[\binom{n}{1}P^{n-1}Q^1\right] + \left[\binom{n}{2}P^{n-2}Q^2\right]$$

$$+ \ldots + \left[\binom{n}{r}P^{n-r}Q^r\right] + \left[\binom{n}{n}Q^n\right] \tag{8.20}$$

As such, the binomial expansion is a theoretical distribution of discrete events.

If we have two mutually exclusive, exhaustive events, the binomial is algebraically determined as:

$$(P + Q)^2 = P^2 + 2PQ + Q^2$$

and with three events we can multiply and:

$$(P + Q)^3 = P^3 + 3P^2Q + 3PQ^2 + Q^3$$

Assume that we toss an unbiased coin three times, thus n is equal to three, and P is $1/2$ and Q is $1/2$ or:

$$(1/2 + 1/2)^3 = (1/2)^3 + 3(1/2)^2(1/2) + 3(1/2)(1/2)^2 + (1/2)^3$$

Each of these four terms in the expansion corresponds to the probability of 3, 2, 1, and 0 heads (or tails) or:

$$(1/2 + 1/2)^3 = 1/8 + 3/8 + 3/8 + 1/8 = 1$$

$$\text{or } 0.125 + 0.375 + 0.375 + 0.125 = 1.000$$

It must be noted here, that the sum of the four terms is equal to unity or 1. In the binomial expansion, $P + Q$ is equal to unity, and thus the sum of all the various probability terms will be equal to unity. Similarly, the binomial can be expanded for any P outcome.

In Formula 8.20, the number in front of each term, or in general the $\binom{n}{r}$ term, is referred to as its binomial coefficient. In our above tossed coin example, 1 (which is not written, but is understood), 3, 3, 1 would be the coefficients for $(P + Q)^3$. In general, the binomial coefficients are simply the number of combinations of n things taken r at a time. Table 8.1, known as Pascal's triangle, gives the binomial coefficients for the values of n from 1 to 10.

Table 8.1.   Binomial coefficients.

N	$\binom{N}{0}$	$\binom{N}{1}$	$\binom{N}{2}$	$\binom{N}{3}$	$\binom{N}{4}$	$\binom{N}{5}$	$\binom{N}{6}$	$\binom{N}{7}$	$\binom{N}{8}$	$\binom{N}{9}$	$\binom{N}{10}$
0	1										
1	1	1									
2	1	2	1								
3	1	3	3	1							
4	1	4	6	4	1						
5	1	5	10	10	5	1					
6	1	6	15	20	15	6	1				
7	1	7	21	35	35	21	7	1			
8	1	8	28	56	70	56	28	8	1		
9	1	9	36	84	126	126	84	36	9	1	
10	1	10	45	120	102	252	210	120	45	10	1

Applying the binomial expansion to our previous example of the 10-item true and false test, we have:

$$(P+Q)^{10} = P^{10} + 10\,P^9\,Q + 45\,P^8\,Q^2 + 120\,P^7\,Q^3 + 210\,P^6\,Q^4 +$$

$$252\,P^5\,Q^5 + 210\,P^4\,Q^6 + 120\,P^3\,Q^7 + 45\,P^2\,Q^8 +$$

$$10\,PQ^9 + Q^{10}$$

As we can see, 8 correct has a coefficient of 45, as has been previously obtained, and the probability can also be determined. The principal advantage of the binomial expansion is that the probabilities associated with the question of equal to or greater than can be determined by using the additive rule.

The Mean and Standard Deviation of the Binomial Distribution.   As we have stated, the binomial distribution is a theoretical distribution, therefore we can determine two theoretical parameters, the mean (μ) or mu and the standard deviation (σ) or sigma. If P is the probability of a given event, then the mean is:

$$\mu = NP \tag{8.21}$$

where μ = theoretical mean
N = number of events
P = probability of the event

The standard deviation is given by:

$$\sigma = \sqrt{NPQ} \tag{8.22}$$

where σ = theoretical standard deviation
N = number of events
P = probability of the event
$Q = 1 - P$

In our example of the 10-item true and false test where $P = Q = 1/2$ then the mean is:

$$\mu = NP$$
$$= (10)(1/2)$$
$$= 5$$

and the standard deviation is:

$$\sigma = \sqrt{NPQ}$$

$$= \sqrt{10(1/2)(1/2)}$$

$$= 1.58$$

The N, P, and Q values in the binomial function are the parameters of a distribution. Therefore, we will have different binomial distributions for different values of these parameters. The knowledge of all the parametric values enables us to describe fully that distribution. For example, binomial distributions can be readily transformed into graphs, such as histograms. However, the shapes of these graphs depend upon two conditions: 1) the fixed value of P, and hence Q, with different numbers of events, N; and 2) a fixed number of events with different values of P.

When we have a fixed probability, P, and increase the number of events, the theoretical mean, μ, moves to the right or increases in value because $\mu = NP$. As the N increases, the heights of the ordinate decrease and the range increases. These general principles are shown in Figure 8.1. As witnessed from the curves by using a

$P = Q = 1/2$, the distributions are symmetrical, and the largest ordinate corresponds to this mean. On the other hand, if we have a

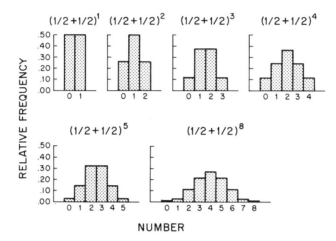

Figure 8.1. Theoretical probability curves with $P=Q= 1/2$ with various N events.

fixed number of events, and vary the P values, the shapes of the distribution are not symmetrical (except where $P + Q = 1/2$) and the mean is not always equal to the point of the highest ordinate. When $P > 0.5$, we will have a positively skewed distribution, and when $P < 0.5$, the distribution will be negatively skewed. If the N events are odd, the mean and the mode (the highest point) will have equal ordinates, and when N is even these two values will not correspond. These events are shown in Figure 8.2.

The Normal Probability Distribution

The binomial distribution, as we have seen, is a theoretical distribution of a discrete variable with a number of events; as the number of events increases, this distribution begins to approximate the normal curve.

The normal curve is a theoretical distribution of a continuous random variable whose possible values range between ± infinity (∞). The general formula for the normal curve is:

$$y = \frac{1}{\sqrt{2\pi}\,\sigma_x}\, e^{-(1/2)\,[(x - \mu_x)/\sigma_x]} \qquad (8.23)$$

where   y = the ordinate of the curve

π = the constant 3.1416 (the ratio of the circumference of a circle to its diameter)

e = the constant 2.7183 (the base of the natural system of logarithms)

As $\mu = 0$ and $\sigma = 1$, then:

$$y = \frac{1}{\sqrt{2\pi}} \, e^{-(1/2)(z^2)}$$

where   z = standard score range of a score from population mean, μ, with a population standard deviation of σ

Table 8.2 gives the coordinates of points on the normal curve for z values between ±3.00 at intervals of 0.25, and Table C is an expansion of this. Now plotting the ordinates for each value and drawing a curve through the plots we would obtain a normal curve as shown in Figure 8.3.

From Figure 8.3, we can see that the normal curve has its maximum highest point at the mean ($z = 0$), where $1/\sqrt{2\pi} = 0.3989$. About this maximum point or the mean, the normal curve is symmetrical and is concave downward between $z = \pm 1$. However, as the z values increase in either direction, the curve approaches

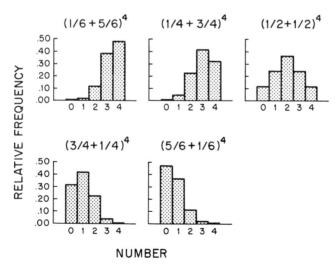

Figure. 8.2.   Theoretical probability curves with *N* events with various *P* and *Q* values.

Table 8.2.   Standardized normal distribution.

z	y
3.00	.0044
2.75	.0091
2.50	.0175
2.25	.0317
2.00	.0540
1.75	.0863
1.50	.1295
1.25	.1826
1.00	.2420
.75	.3011
.50	.3521
.25	.3867
.00	.3989

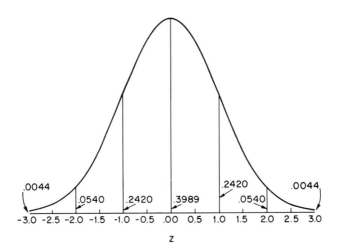

Figure. 8.3.   Theoretical normal curves for various z values and their associative ordinates.

the X-axis or the abscissa but never reaches it, even in the case
of infinity of the X value. From our previous references to the
unit normal curve, we have noted that the total area between the
curve and the abscissa is equal to one. Thus the areas to the right
and to the left of the mean ($z = 0$) are equal.

These properties of the normal curve are involved with the
determination of the probability of a random variable X value
taken between any two points along the X-axis. If we would

construct, for example, two ordinates at any two points, the proportion of the total area under the curve that falls between these points would correspond to the probability that the random X value would fall between these two points, or:

$$P\ (a \leqslant X \leqslant b) \tag{8.24}$$

where a and b = any two points on the abscissa.

To illustrate this, let us take a number of examples. We must keep in mind that the value is continuous and random. We shall also use Table C to find these probabilities.

What is the probability that the score value (here the z value) will fall between 0 and 1, or:

$$P(0 < z < 1)$$

From the table of the unit normal curve we have:

$$P(0 < z < 1) = 0.341$$

Thus approximately 34% of the total values randomly fall between 0 and 1. This example is shown in Figure 8.4.

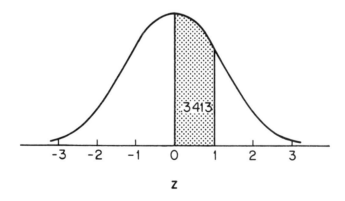

Figure 8.4.   The theoretical probability value or proportion of cases between z of 0 and 1.

As the normal curve is a symmetrical one, the probability that the random value will be between ±1 is:

$$P(-1 < z < 1) = 0.341 + 0.341 = 0.682$$

and the probability that the variable lies between ±2 is:

$$P(-2 < z < 2) = 0.477 + 0.477 = 0.954$$

What is the probability that the value will be greater than 1.00, or:

$$P(z > 1.0) = 0.159$$

This example is illustrated in Figure 8.5.

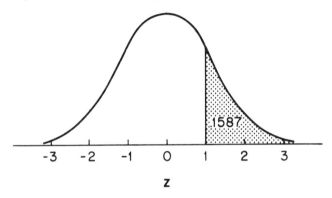

Figure 8.5.   The theoretical probability value or proportion of cases greater than z of 1.

From this example it follows that we can ask,

What is the probability that the value lies between 1.00 and 2.00, or:

$$P(1 \leqslant z \leqslant 2) = 0.159 - 0.023 = 0.136$$

And thus, we can determine the probability of any value within a given range along the abscissa.

The normal probability curve enters our discussions at many levels of statistical analyses. As we have already seen, we can transform many of our observed frequency distributions to fit the normal curve and it gives us ready information in regard to central tendencies and variabilities. From this point forward, most of the methods of statistical inference are based upon the normal probability curve and upon approximations of it.

The Central Limit Theorem

Within probability theory, the central limit theorem has been deduced, and it indicates the conditions under which the normality of a given statistic will occur. The central limit theorem states that for any given random variable, X, regardless of the shape of the underlying distribution, the sampling distribution of randomly drawn independent samples of size N will approach a normal distribution as the sample size increases. The theorem assumes that the population variance, σ_x^2, is finite. This theorem is of importance in that it is the mathematical foundation for various statistics. Its major significance for sampling theory will become more obvious when we discuss the various statistics in the following chapters. For it is on this theorem that the probability distributions or sampling distributions for a specific statistic are derived. As we have seen in the prior chapter, a sampling distribution is a theoretical probability distribution of all theoretical values of that statistic that can be taken from random samples of equal size.

Summary of Terms

additive rules of probability
Bayes' Theorem
binomial distribution
central limit theorem
combinations

conditional probability
normal probability distribution
permutations
sigma
theoretical relative frequency

exhaustive class
independent event
mu
multiplication rules of
probability
mutually exclusive events

Summary of Symbols

$n(A)$	$Q(A)$	$\binom{n}{r}$	σ	π
∞	$_nP_n$	$!$	y	$P(A')$
$P(A)$	$_nC_r$	μ	e	$P(A|B)$

Problems

1. Consider a jar filled with 5 red balls, 3 black balls, and 2 white balls. Assume, unless otherwise stated, that each ball drawn from the jar is replaced before the next draw. Compute the probabilities associated with the following events:

    a. Drawing a white ball

    b. Drawing a non-white ball

    c. Drawing either a red or a black ball

    d. Drawing a red ball on two successive draws

    e. Drawing a red ball on the first draw and a white ball on each of the next two draws

    f. Drawing, and not replacing, a red ball

    g. Drawing, and not replacing, a red ball and then a black ball.

2. Assume that the jar now contains 3 large red balls, 2 small red balls, 3 small green balls, and 2 large green balls. Compute the probabilities associated with the following events. Assume replacement after every draw, unless otherwise stated.

    a. Drawing either a large ball or a green ball

    b. Drawing either a large red ball or a small green ball

    c. Drawing either a small ball, a red ball, or a large green ball

    d. Drawing, without replacement, a small red ball, and on the second draw a large red ball, and on the third draw either a large red ball or a large green ball

3. Consider a group of five chickens numbered one through five.

    a. How many pecking orders are possible?

    b. Assume that the pecking order has been established, and that you want to investigate the pecking order in pairs of chickens placed in new cages, when one member of the pair is placed in the cage 20 minutes before the other member. How many ways are there to pair the chickens such that each chicken will be put in the new cage both before and after every other chicken.

4. A group of ten pennies is shaken in a jar and dumped onto a table top. Compute the number of ways each of the following events could occur:

a.   10 heads

b.   9 heads

c.   8 heads

d.   7 heads

e.   6 heads

f.   5 heads

g.   4 heads

h.   3 heads

i.   2 heads

j.   1 head

k.   0 heads

5.   A group of 9 pennies is shaken in a jar and dumped onto a table top. Compute the probability associated with each of the following events. Assume that the pennies are fair.

a.   4 heads

b.   3 heads

c.   2 heads

d.   1 head

e.   0 heads

f.   Fewer than 4 heads

6.   Five art critics are given the task of picking the original Mona Lisa out of a group of four forgeries plus the real Mona Lisa. Given that the forgeries are so good that each is as likely to be chosen as the original, what is the probability that four or more of the art critics will correctly select the original?

Statistical Tests
for Nominal Data   Chapter Nine

In this chapter we will present various statistical tests that are commonly associated with various research designs and that are appropriate for nominal data. These experimental designs are typically described as random group designs with a single sample, two samples or K samples, or related groups designs. For nominal measurement, it will be recalled, we have measurement at the level of classification and the frequency of cases within the various classification categories.

The One-Sample Case

In Chapter seven, we described the after-treatment design for a one-sample design. In this general case, our research hypothesis is that a particular random sample differs significantly, after the effects of the treatment condition, from some a priori value that is stated by the hypothesis. An analogous hypothesis is that a particular random sample came from a population with a specified distribution. This latter research method is usually described as the goodness-of-fit design, in that it determines how well the sample fits some hypothesis that we have in regard to the population distribution.

Binomial Test

Function and Method.   The binomial test is a procedure in which the observations are assigned to one of two mutually exclusive classes. When the population of objects, events, or phenomena consists of two discrete classes, and when we have a one-sample after-treatment design, or a goodness-of-fit design, we may utilize the binomial test. For example, a coin will be either heads or tails, the answer to a question is correct or not correct; all observations fall into one or the other category. The method is, in general, similar to that of the binomial expansion where the values of P and Q are given by hypothesis. We may consider the binomial expansion as a theoretical or sampling distribution for the sample size of n cases for any P and Q values. The probability of obtaining r objects, events, or phenomena in one category and $n-r$ objects in the other category is given using Formula 8.19, or:

$$\binom{n}{r} P^r Q^{n-r} = \left(\frac{n!}{r!\,(n-r)!} \right) P^r Q^{n-r}$$

Example.   Let us suppose that we have some interest in the behavior of one food-deprived rat in a T-maze; this subject is given 10 trials a day and is reinforced in the right stem of the T. Let us further assume that at the beginning of this study the probability of running right is equal to the probability of running left or that $P(r) = P(1)$. Now, as we know, food acts as a reinforcer, hence, we may hypothesize that $P(r) > P(1)$ after a number of trials. Now that sampling distribution for 10 responses with $P(r) = P(1)$ is:

$$(P + Q)^{10} = P^{10} + 10P^9 Q + 45P^8 Q^2 + \ldots + 10PQ^9 + Q^{10}$$

and the associated probabilities are:

$$0.001 + 0.010 + 0.044 + 0.117 + 0.205 + 0.246 +$$
$$0.205 + 0.117 + 0.044 + 0.010 + 0.001$$

If we found, for example, that the animal made exactly 7 responses to the right, the probability of this event is 0.177. If we continued to run the animal 10 trials a day, a meaningful question would be: When has the subject learned the maze? Now to ask such a question is to state some probability values; that is, to state some alpha level. Generally, we are not interested in an exact number of correct responses, for example, the animal making exactly 7 responses; but rather, we may be interested in that animal making 7 or more correct responses. In stating the problem in such a fashion we utilize the additive rule applied to the binomial. If we set alpha at the 0.05 level, we can see from the summed probabilities of the sample distribution that the subject must make 9 or 10 correct responses to meet the 0.05 criterion. The probability of seven or more correct responses is 0.001 + 0.010 + 0.044 + 0.117 = 0.172.

The Binomial Approximation

When N is large, rather than expanding the binomial, we can approximate the binomial. The binomial approximate test or the z-test is given as:

$$z = \frac{(X \pm 0.5) - \mu}{\sigma} \tag{9.1}$$

$$\text{or} \ = \frac{|X - \mu| \pm 0.5}{\sigma}$$

where X = obtained discrete value
μ = NP or the theoretical mean
σ = $\sqrt{NPQ}$ or the theoretical standard deviation

and where $X < \mu, + 0.5$
or $X > \mu, - 0.5$

In general, when μ or NP is equal to or greater than 5, the binomial distribution is approximately normal. Therefore, the z-test can be applied. In Formula 9.1, we have a correction term ± 0.5; this is because the data of the binomial are discrete and the z assumes a normal distribution for continuous data. This correction is called the correction for continuity; we now assume that the X value has a real upper and lower limit.

In our previous illustration, the subject made 7 or more responses and NP is equal to 5, hence:

$$z = \frac{(7 - 0.5) - (10)(1/2)}{\sqrt{(10)(1/2)(1/2)}}$$

$$= \frac{6.5 - 5.0}{1.58}$$

$$= 0.9495$$

and $P = 0.171$

The probability associated with the obtained z is found in Column 4 of Table C; the area is the smaller portion of the unit normal curve. This obtained probability value by the binomial approximation, or z-test, is approximately equal to that obtained by the binomial expansion.

Example.   Two experimental groups of 10 rats each were trained under thirst motivation and food satiation conditions; they were each given an equal number of trails to food on the side of their least preference, and nothing on the other side in a T-maze. In experimental Group I, secondary reinforcement was minimized, while secondary reinforcements were enhanced for the second experimental group. The 10 control Ss received the same deprivation schedule, but were not trained in the maze. After 12 days of training, the motivation was shifted from water to food. It was hypothesized that there would be no learning in the training series when secondary reinforcement was minimized and that learning would occur when secondary reinforcement was enhanced. Alpha was set at a 0.05 level and each S was given 4 trials a day. The data from the first day of the learning series for the three groups are in Table 9.1. As we can note, only experimental Group II showed a significant difference from the theoretical mean, and hence, statistically speaking, only Group II learned during the training trials. That is, the probability of 27 correct responses from the total of 40 responses could have happened by chance two times out of one hundred. The probabilities associated with the other two groups are greater than the stated alpha and we cannot therefore conclude that they learned the task.

The Chi-Square Test

Function and Method.   The chi-square test, χ^2, is particularly applicable to research situations when the data are given in

Table 9.1

Exp. Gr. I	Exp. Gr. II	Control Gr.
$X = 21 \quad N = 40$	$X = 27 \quad N = 40$	$X = 18 \quad N = 40$
$\mu = (40)(0.5) = 20$	$\mu = (40)(0.5) = 20$	$\mu = (40)(0.5) = 20$
$\sigma = \sqrt{40(0.5)(0.5)}$	$\sigma = \sqrt{40(0.5)(0.5)}$	$\sigma = \sqrt{40(0.5)(0.5)}$
$= 3.16$		
$z = \dfrac{(21 - 0.5) - 20}{3.16}$	$z = \dfrac{(27 - 0.5) - 20}{3.16}$	$z = \dfrac{(18 + 0.5) - 20}{3.16}$
$= \dfrac{0.5}{3.16}$	$= \dfrac{6.5}{3.16}$	$= \dfrac{-1.5}{3.16}$
$= 0.158$	$= 2.057$	$= -0.475$
$P = 0.44$	$P = 0.02$	$P = 0.68$

terms of frequencies of objects, characteristics, or phenomena which fall into two or more mutually exclusive classes. With the chi-square we have theoretical or hypothesized frequencies, proportions, or percentages for each of the categories as well as the obtained frequencies, proportions, or percentages. Our major interest is the departure of observed frequencies in a given sample from the theoretical frequencies that we would expect on the bases of some assumptions derived from a theory. In general, this may be seen as a goodness-of-fit technique. From a theory we determine the frequencies that we expect for each of the various classes. We obtain a random sample of cases of size N and we note the differences between these expected frequencies and the empirical or obtained frequencies. The differences can be assumed to be the result of sampling variation. However, if the differences are too large, we assume that the hypothesis cannot be maintained according to the standards given by the alpha value.

For a one-sample case, the formula of the chi-square, χ^2, is:

$$\chi^2 = \sum_{i=1}^{k} \frac{(o - e)^2}{e} \tag{9.2}$$

where o = observed or obtained frequency for a given category

e = theoretical or expected frequency

$\displaystyle\sum_{i=1}^{k}$ = the sum over all categories from 1 to k

The operations of Formula 9.2 say that we take the differences between the observed and the expected frequencies, we square this difference and divide by its expected frequency. We then sum these ratios over all the categories. If the observed values for the various classes or categories were equal to their expected values, the chi-square would be zero. On the other hand, as the difference between the expected and observed frequencies increases, the chi-square value will increase.

The sampling distribution of chi-square is a function of the number of various classes or degrees of freedom (df) available. Thus, there are sampling distributions of chi-square for different degrees of freedom. Degrees of freedom are parameters that are associated with various theoretical sampling distributions. This concept of degrees of freedom enters our discussion at various stages of statistical inference and is the number of quantities that are free to vary after having placed certain restrictions upon the assignment of the theoretical frequencies by the organization of the data. For the chi-square, it is the number of classes or categories that determines the number of degrees of freedom available. In the one-sample case, the degrees of freedom is $df = k-1$. For example, if we have four classes with a total of 100 cases, then $A + B + C + D = 100$. In this example, we would have an infinite number of solutions for the values of frequencies of the classes. This is because we have four unknowns and one known. If on the other hand, $A = 10$, $B = 20$, and $C = 40$, then the frequency of D is determined or $D = 30$. Since three of the four terms are given and are known, the fourth term is determined, or three of the four terms are free to vary but the fourth term is given and we thus have $df = k-1$ or $df = 3$. Whenever an additional condition or an additional restriction is added or placed upon the data, the number of degrees of freedom is reduced by one. If $50 + A + B + C = 100$, then only two terms are free to vary, or $df = 2$.

Figure 9.1 illustrates an approximation of the chi-square distribution for certain degrees of freedom. As we can see in the figure, the forms of the distributions vary for the degrees of freedom available.

When alpha is set, for example, at the 0.05 level of significance with 4 df, and when we have a two-tailed test or a non-directional difference as stated by the hypothesis, we can evaluate the obtained chi-square from Table H. An obtained chi-square value that is equal to or greater than 9.488 will fall into the region of rejection and is associated with a probability that is equal to or less than 0.05. When the obtained chi-square values are less than 9.488, these values would fall into the region of acceptance of the

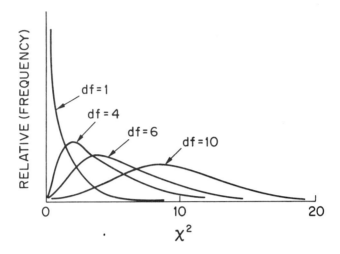

Figure 9.1.   The theoretical sampling distribution of χ^2 for 1, 4, 6, and 10 degrees of freedom.

null hypothesis and would have an associated P value greater than 0.05. These concepts are shown in Figure 9.2. On the other hand, when we have a directional hypothesis, we solve the tabled probabilities for the one-tailed test. Thus the chi-square of 7.779 would be significant at the 0.05 level for a one-tailed test. (See

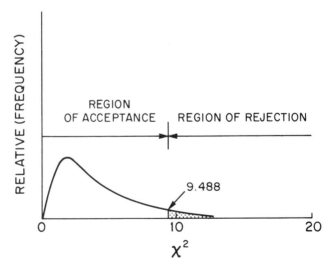

Figure 9.2.   The regions of acceptance and rejection of H_o for a two-tailed χ^2 test with 4 degrees of freedom for alpha at the 0.05 level.

Figure 9.3.) We can conclude from this illustration that the one-tailed test is more powerful against a certain class of hypotheses than the two-tailed test, in that it is more sensitive to differences, and that we more easily reject the null hypothesis and thus accept our research hypothesis.

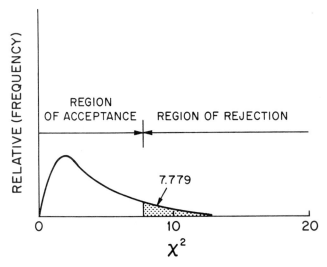

Figure 9.3. The regions of acceptance and rejection of H_o for a one-tailed χ^2 test with 4 degrees of freedom for alpha at the 0.05 level.

The One-Sample Case of Chi-Square for One Degree of Freedom

In our one-sample case, if we have two classes or one degree of freedom, then Formula 9.2 is corrected for continuity:

$$\chi^2 = \sum_{i=1}^{k=2} \frac{(|o - e| - 0.5)^2}{e} \tag{9.3}$$

In this formula we correct for continuity by the subtraction of 0.5 from the absolute difference between the observed and expected frequencies. The rationale for this correction is that when we have one degree of freedom, then:

$$\chi^2 = z^2$$

$$\text{or} \quad \chi^2 = \sum_{i=1}^{k=2} \frac{(|o - e| - 0.5)^2}{e} = z^2 = \frac{(X - \mu - 0.5)^2}{\sigma^2} \tag{9.4}$$

With a single degree of freedom, the correction for continuity is always made; if it were not, we would obtain various probabilities that would be in general smaller than those obtained from the binomial. One further restriction is made: when $k = 2$ or $df = 1$, the expected frequencies should be equal to or greater than 5. With the expected frequencies of 5 or more the observed frequencies can be assumed to be normally distributed about the expected frequencies. With expected frequencies less than 5 it is not possible to make this assumption.

Example: A Priori Hypothesis. The data in the example of the binomial test assumed a 50:50 hypothesis and could be analyzed by the chi-square test as well. If we take the results of the experimental Group II as our illustration, the observed frequency of the responses to the food was 13, with the theoretical expected frequency of 20. The data, in tabular form, is in Table 9.2.

Table 9.2

	To food ·	Not to food	
o	27	13	40
e	20	20	40

$(\|o - e\| - 0.5)$	6.5	6.5
$(o - e - 0.5)^2$	42.25	42.25
$(o - e - 0.5)^2/e$	2.1125	2.1125

$$\sum_{1}^{2} \quad 2.1125 \quad + \quad 2.1125 = 4.225$$

or $\chi^2 = 4.225$ with 1 df
and $P < 0.025$

We must note that the research hypothesis states a given direction and hence, we have a one-tailed test of significance. Thus, as before, the research hypothesis is confirmed at the 0.05 level of significance.

If we note Formula 9.4, we can directly compare the results of the two statistical tests:

$$\chi^2 = 4.225 \quad \text{and} \quad z^2 = (2.057)^2 = 4.230$$

In general, any a priori hypothesis can be tested by these general procedures provided that the hypothesis is stated in terms of some ratio of frequencies and that the restrictions are met.

The One-Sample Case of Chi-Square for More than One Degree of Freedom

From Formula 9.4, the chi-square with one degree of freedom could be logically defined as a normal deviate squared (z^2) drawn randomly and independently from a normal distribution of z-scores. Extending this rationale, the chi-square with N degrees of freedom is the sum of N independent random samples that have been drawn from a normally distributed population, and that are expressed as squared standard scores. Therefore:

$$\chi^2 \text{ with } N \, df = \sum_1^N z^2 \tag{9.5}$$

From Figure 9.1, it can be seen that as the degrees of freedom increase the form of the distribution become more normal. When, in fact, we have more than 30 degrees of freedom for our chi-square, its distribution is approximately normal. As the sampling distribution of chi-square is not given for more than 30 degrees of freedom we can approximate the distribution by:

$$z = \sqrt{2\chi^2} - \sqrt{(2)(df) - 1} \tag{9.6}$$

If we have a single sample of chi-square with more than one degree of freedom, the general Formula 9.2 for chi-square can be used. In this general case, we need not correct for continuity.

Example. An investigation has been made of the various aspects of work and job satisfaction and for illustrative purposes, we have taken only the data from the categories of job satisfaction (liked, no difference, and disliked) for highly repetitive tasks. Without any a priori hypothesis, we assume that the null hypothesis is $fe_1 = fe_2 = fe_3$, or that the expected frequencies are equal and that the observed frequencies are distributed in each category by chance. If we let alpha be given at the 0.05 level and we have a two-tailed test, then, we can make an analysis of the frequency data in Table 9.3. If we assume a two-tailed test of significance, we find the obtained chi-square is associated with a probability less than 0.001 under the null hypothesis. Thus, we

Table 9.3.   Job satisfaction.

	Liked	No difference	Disliked	N
o	13	6	28	47
e	15.667	15.667	15.667	47

$o - e$	-2.667	-9.667	12.333
$(o - e)^2$	7.113	93.451	152.103
$(o - e)^2/e$	0.452	5.965	9.708
$\Sigma(o - e)^2/e$	0.452 +	5.965 +	9.708 = 16.127

$$\chi^2 = 16.127 \text{ with } df = 2$$
$$P < 0.001$$

conclude from this sample, that we have a significant difference in job satisfactions for this type of work.

The Two or More Independent Sample Case

It was previously suggested that our research questions may take one of two various procedural forms. Firstly, a random sample is drawn from each of K populations. When we apply this method to nominal data, our research question is in regard to the frequencies of subjects, characteristics or phenomena that fall into various independent classes or categories. We can use the illustration of the difference in frequencies of cases between class composition (categories defined as upper, middle, and lower socio-economic classes) for eight religious bodies (populations). Secondly, a random sample from a population is drawn, and then random assignments are made to one of $K - 1$) treatment conditions. In general, our research question is whether or not our sample differs in regard to the frequencies of objects, characteristics or phenomena that fall into various independent classes as the result of the treatment conditions. As an example, we have the differences in frequencies of cases for various methods of psychotherapy in regard to their results, categorized as: much improved, improved, slightly improved, and not improved.

Chi-Square Test

Function and Method.   When the hypothesis we have under consideration takes on the form described in the previous section, the chi-square test may be used and the hypothesis tested by:

$$\chi^2 = \sum_{i=1}^{r} \sum_{j=1}^{k} \frac{(o_{ij} - e_{ij})^2}{e_{ij}} \qquad (9.7)$$

where o_{ij} = the observed frequency of cases for the
  cell of the ith row and jth column
  e_{ij} = the expected frequency of cases for the
  cell of the ith row and jth column
  Σ = the sum of all the cells
with the $df = (r - 1)(k - 1)$
  where r = number of rows
  k = number of columns

Generally, we do not have any a priori hypothesis against which to test the observed frequencies. Thus, in order to determine the various expected frequencies, the data are cast into an r x k table, and the two marginal frequencies that are common to the o_{ij} cell are multiplied and the product of these two marginal frequencies is then divided by the total number of cases or N. This general procedure allows us to obtain a common estimate of the population distribution, and we measure the difference for each cell from this estimate. If, for example, we have a 2 by 2 table, the marginal frequencies would be as shown in Table 9.4.

Table 9.4.

	Categories		Total
	a	b	$a + b$
Groups			
	c	d	$c + d$
Total	$a + c$	$b + d$	N

Thus, the e_{11} or the expected frequency for Cell a is $(a + b)(a + c)/N$ and similarly, the e_{12} for Cell b is $(a + b)(b + d)/N$, and so forth for each cell. It follows under the null hypothesis that both the rows and columns are independent; therefore the probability of being in both a given row and a given column follows the multiplicative rule where e_{11} is $(a + b)(a + c)/N$.

As we previously noted, certain restrictions are made upon the chi-square. In addition to the fact that each expected frequency must be equal to or greater than 5, with one degree of freedom, a further restriction is that when we have degrees of freedom greater than one, no more than 20 percent of the cells can have expected frequencies of less than 1. These two restrictions can usually be circumvented by having a large sample size. If, however, we cannot meet these general requirements, the researcher can combine the data of meaningful contiguous categories and thereby increase the expected frequencies sufficiently to meet the stated criteria.

The Two-Sample Case of Chi-Square for One Degree of Freedom

When we have two independent samples, and the frequencies are in two categories, the data are cast into a table such as Table 9.4, for testing the hypothesis. However, for the problem at hand we have $df = (r - 1)(k - 1) = 1$ and we must correct for continuity as in Formula 9.4 or:

$$\chi^2 = \sum_{i=1}^{r=2} \sum_{j=1}^{k=2} \frac{(|o_{ij} - e_{ij}| - 0.5)^2}{e_{ij}} \tag{9.8}$$

Rather than finding the e_{ij} values, we can determine the chi-square by:

$$\chi^2 = \frac{N(|ad - bc| - N/2)^2}{(a + c)(b + d)(a + b)(c + d)} \tag{9.9}$$

$$\text{with } df = (r - 1)(k - 1) = 1$$

This formula is equivalent to Formula 9.8 when we have one degree of freedom and when we have corrected for continuity in both. In Formula 9.9 the correction is made by subtraction of $N/2$. The chief advantage of this procedure is reducing the number of computational sets.

Example. It has been suggested that women are not the dominant figures in matrilineal descent societies although women have more influence within the family structure than in the patrilineal descent societies. As a measure of this observation, an investigator inquired into husband-wife disagreements and the decisions made by the husband or wife for two cultural groups, the Navaho (matrilineal) and the Mormon (patrilineal).

The null hypothesis stated that there is no difference between the two groups in the proportions of decisions made or won. From the theory, the research hypothesis stated that a greater proportion of the decisions are won by the wife in the matrilineal group than is the case in the patrilineal group. We shall let alpha be equal to 0.05 for this one-tailed test. The findings are given in Table 9.5.

Table 9.5.   Decisions made or won.

Cultural group	Husband	Wife	Total
Navaho	34	46	80
Mormon	42	29	71
Total	76	75	151

In order to determine the expected frequencies for the various cells for Formula 9.8, we find the product of the two common marginal frequencies and divide by N. Thus:

$$e_{11} = (76)(80)/151 = 40.2649$$

$$e_{12} = (75)(80)/151 = 39.7351$$

$$e_{21} = (76)(71)/151 = 35.7351$$

$$e_{22} = (75)(71)/151 = 35.2649$$

Applying Formula 9.8, we have:

$$\chi^2 = \frac{(|34 - 40.2649| - 0.5)^2}{40.2649} + \frac{(|46 - 39.7351| - 0.5)^2}{39.7351} +$$

$$\frac{(|42 - 35.7351| - 0.5)^2}{35.7351} + \frac{(|29 - 35.2649| - 0.5)^2}{35.2649}$$

$$= 0.8254 + 0.8364 + 0.9300 + 0.9424$$

$$= 3.534 \text{ with } df = 1$$

From the tabled value of chi-square for one degree of freedom, alpha equal to 0.05, and a one-tailed test, we find that the critical value is 2.706; hence the obtained value exceeds this value and would fall within the region of rejection. We conclude that there is a significant difference in the direction stated by the research hypothesis.

We may apply Formula 9.9 to this same set of data or:

$$\chi^2 = \frac{151 \left(|(34)(29) - (46)(42)| - 151/2\right)^2}{(34 + 42)(46 + 29)(34 + 46)(42 + 29)}$$

$$= 3.54 \text{ with } df = 1$$

and our decision would be the same as above.

The Two or k Sample Case of Chi-Square for More than One Degree of Freedom

Formula 9.8 is utilized when we need to ascertain the significant difference between two or k independent groups, with two or more discrete categories. The procedure is common for both such cases.

Example. As a part of a larger study of the relationship of mass media to reported delinquent behavior, the investigator determined the frequencies of movie attendance for three delinquent scale types for boys. The null hypothesis was that there is no difference in frequencies of movie attendance for the scale types. The research hypothesis was stated as, there is a difference. Thus, we have a two-tailed test for a two by three table and the sampling distribution is for two degrees of freedom. Alpha was given at the 0.05 level: The data are given in Table 9.6.

Table 9.6.   Delinquent scale type.

		High	Intermediate	Low	Total
Frequency of movie attendance	High	87	71	74	232
	Low	28	48	68	144
	Total	115	119	142	376

The expected frequencies are determined from the marginal frequencies or:

$$e_{11} = (115)(232)/376 = 70.9574$$

$$e_{12} = (119)(232)/376 = 73.4255$$

$$e_{13} = (142)(232)/376 = 87.6170$$

$$e_{21} = (115)(144)/376 = 44.0425$$

$$e_{22} = (119)(144)/376 = 45.5745$$

$$e_{23} = (142)(144)/376 = 54,3830$$

Applying Formula 9.8:

$$\chi^2 = (87 - 70.9574)^2/70.9574 + (71 - 73.4255)^2/73.4255 +$$

$$(74 - 87.6170)^2/87.6170 + (28 - 44.0425)^2/44.0425 +$$

$$(48 - 45.5745)^2/45.5745 + (68 - 54.3830)^2/54.3830$$

$$= 3.627 + .081 + 2.116 + 5.844 + .129 + 3.410$$

$$= 15.207 \text{ with } df = 2$$

$$P < 0.001$$

From Table H with $df = 2$ and a two-tailed test, the probability of the obtained chi-square is less than 0.001. Thus, the null hypothesis is rejected and the research hypothesis is accepted and we conclude that there is a significant difference between the three groups and their frequencies of movie attendance.

The Chi-Square Test from Reported Percentage Values

Periodically, in the various fields within the behavioral sciences, a study is reported where the researchers have used percentages in the reporting of research findings without using some statistical inference or analysis. As readers of such reports we may have some hypothesis that we may want to check. Now the chi-square cannot be directly obtained from percentages, however, if N is reported and if a correction term is utilized, the chi-square value can be determined. This correction is:

$$\chi^2 = \chi^2_\% (N/100) \qquad (9.10)$$

where $\chi^2_\%$ = obtained chi-square using
the percentage value
N = total number of cases

Our procedure is to find the chi-square from the percentage figures with the usual methods and then simply apply the correction given in Formula 9.10. For illustrative purposes, we shall compare the chi-square values from the frequency data and from the percent data as shown in Table 9.7.

Table 9.7

	Frequency data Categories		Total			Percentage data Categories		Total
Groups	34	37	71	Groups		17	18.5	35.5
	94	35	129			47	17.5	64.5
Total	128	72	200	Total		64	36	100

$$\chi^2 = \frac{200(|(34)(35) - (37)(94)| - 200/2)^2}{(128)(72)(71)(129)} = 12.40$$

$$\chi^2_\% = \frac{100(|(17)(17.5) - (47)(18.5)| - 100)^2}{(64)(36)(35.5)(64.5)} = 6.2$$

$$\text{and } \chi^2 = 6.2 \, (200/100) = 12.40$$

Thus the two chi-square values are identical when the correction is made.

Two or More Related Sample Case

In our prior discussions of a two-sample design it was assumed the samples were random and were independent statistically. In the two related designs we cannot assume that the obtained values are independent. This is the case in the before-after design, or where the subjects have been matched before presenting the treatment condition.

The Chi-Square Test for Significant Change

Function and Method.   McNemar has described a special use of the chi-square test when we do not have independent measures of behavior. This non-independence or relatedness is a function of the design. For example, we could have one randomly drawn sample from a well-defined population and we then measure the behavior before and then after the treatment condition. The response measure is generally expressed as a dichotomy such as: yes-no, right-wrong, plus-minus, 0-1. These contingencies are expressed in Table 9.8.

Table 9.8

After-treatment

		No	Yes	
Before Treatment	Yes	A	B	$A + B$
	No	C	D	$C + D$
		$A + C$	$B + D$	N

In this 2 by 2 contingency table, Cell A would represent the frequencies of cases that changed from yes to no, B yes to yes, C no to no, and D no to yes. The changes in behavior as the result of the treatment conditions are represented by the cell frequencies of A (yes to no) and in D (no to yes). The frequencies in B and C suggest no behavioral change due to the treatment conditions. This is the chi-square test for significant changes, and our research interests are in Cells A and D.

The frequencies in A and D are the total number of cases of changes in behavior. The null hypothesis states that the frequency of changes between A and D are not different or that $1/2(A + D)$ would be changes from yes to no and $1/2(A + D)$ would be from no to yes, or $fA = fB$. The null hypothesis may be tested by the chi-square with one degree of freedom where the expected frequencies would be $(A + D)/2$. Therefore:

$$\chi^2 = \sum_{A,D} \frac{(|o - e| - 0.5)^2}{e}$$

$$= \frac{\left(\left|A - \frac{A+D}{2}\right| - 0.5\right)^2}{\frac{A+D}{2}} + \frac{\left(\left|D - \frac{A+D}{2}\right| - 0.5\right)^2}{\frac{A+D}{2}}$$

$$= \frac{(|A - D| - 1)^2}{A + D} \quad \text{(with 1 } df\text{)} \tag{9.11}$$

Example. In an analysis of political behavior, the investigators describe the "switching" of votes between two interviews, one in August and the other within the last week in October during a Presidential campaign. For illustrative purposes, the data shown in Table 9.9 describe the changes of responses by Republicans and Democrats between the interviews. Let us assume the null hypothesis that one-half of the changes would be from Republican to Democrat and the other one-half from Democrat to Republican. The research hypothesis is that there is a significant difference at the 0.05 level.

Table 9.9

		October Interview:	
		Democrat	Republican
August Interview:	Republican	17	
	Democrat		6

$$\chi^2 = \frac{(A - D - 1)^2}{A + D}$$

$$= \frac{(17 - 6 - 1)^2}{17 + 6}$$

$$= 100/23$$

$$= 4.348$$

As the obtained chi-square of 4.348 is greater than the tabled chi-square of 3.841 for 0.05 level two-tailed test with 1 df, we conclude that there was a significant change of responses between the two intervals.

The Chi-Square Test for Significant Changes for Three or More Groups

The chi-square test for significant changes has been expanded for K related groups. The method provides for the test of significance between three or more non-independent groups, or for measuring behavioral changes over time.

The data are arranged in an i row and k column table with the responses as a dichotomous measure expressed as 0 or 1. The null hypothesis states that the frequencies of responses in the K columns are equal except for random variation. This null hypothesis may be tested by:

$$\chi^2 = \frac{(K-1)\left[K \sum_{j=1}^{k} T_j^2 - \left(\sum_{j=1}^{k} T_j\right)^2\right]}{K \sum_{i=1}^{N} X_i - \sum_{i=1}^{N} X_i^2} \qquad (9.12)$$

where K = the number of columns
$\quad\quad T_j$ = the total in the j column
$\quad\quad X_i$ = the total in the i row
$\quad\quad N$ = the total cases in the j columns

Cochran (1952) has expressed Formula 9.12 as a Q-test and has shown that it follows approximately the chi-square distribution for $K-1$ degrees of freedom provided that we have $N > 30$.

Example.   An investigator was interested in the changes of attitude toward a given candidate during three stages in the campaign. He selected at random 15 registered voters within a precinct that was judged as a barometer of the political climate. The null hypothesis was that the probability of a favorable response, 1, is the same over all the three intervals and the research hypothesis was that the probability of a favorable response would increase during the campaign. Alpha was set at the 0.01 level. The data are given in Table 9.10.

The tabled value of the chi-square for 2 df and a one-tailed test with alpha at the 0.01 level, is 7.82; the obtained value of 4.33 does not exceed this value, therefore, the research hypothesis would not be supported. We must conclude from this study that there were no significant differences between attitudes reported for the three interviews.

Table 9.10

Subject	Response to Interview 1	Response to Interview 2	Response to Interview 3	X_i	X_i^2
1	0	0	1	1	1
2	0	0	0	0	0
3	0	0	0	0	0
4	1	1	1	3	9
5	0	0	0	0	0
6	0	1	1	2	4
7	1	1	0	2	4
8	1	1	1	3	9
9	0	1	1	2	4
10	1	1	1	3	9
11	0	0	1	1	1
12	0	1	1	2	4
13	1	1	1	3	9
14	1	1	1	3	9
15	1	1	1	3	9

$$T_1 = 7 \quad T_2 = 10 \quad T_3 = 11 \quad \sum_1^{15} X_i = 28 \quad \sum_1^{15} X_i^2 = 72$$

$$\text{or } \chi^2 = \frac{(3-1)\ [3(7^2 + 10^2 + 11^2) - (28)^2]}{3(28) - 72}$$

$$= \frac{(2)\ 3(270) - 784}{12}$$

$$= 52/12$$

$$= 4.33$$

with $(K-1) = 2\, df$

Summary of Terms

binomial test
binomial approximation
correction for continuity
chi-square distribution

chi-square test
degrees of freedom
significant change

Summary of Symbols

z-test	e_{ij}	z^2	o_{ij}
χ^2	df	T_j	

Problems

1. To investigate "wall seeking" behavior in mice, an experimenter built a straight alley 25 cm long. The floor of the straight alley was composed of 5 separate grids, each of which was attached to a timer. The experimenter's research hypothesis was that mice placed individually in the apparatus for a five minute period would spend a greater amount of time on the two end grids than would be expected by chance alone. The amount of time, measured in seconds, that a group of four mice spent on each of the grids was: Grid 1 = 294, Grid 2 = 200, Grid 3 = 196, Grid 4 = 191, Grid 5 = 319.

    a. What is the researcher's null hypothesis?

    b. Using the appropriate statistical test and the 0.05 alpha level, evaluate the null hypothesis and state your conclusion.

2. An investigator hypothesized that highly anxious people would make more freezing responses when facing a conflict situation than would medium anxious people, and that medium anxious people would make more freezing responses than would low anxious people. She tested her hypothesis by presenting people of each anxiety level with the following task, which she cleverly disguised as a reaction time experiment. The subjects were seated in front of a board which had a red and green light on each side and a switch in the middle that could be turned to either side. The subjects were told that one light on each side of the board would be turned on,

and that when this happened they were to immediately turn the switch away from the red light and toward the green light. After six trials the experimenter presented the subjects with the conflict situation by turning on both green lights. If the subject took longer than 1.5 seconds to respond the response was counted as a freezing response. The data are given in Table 9.11. Using the 0.05 alpha level, test the experimenter's hypotheses.

Table 9.11   Response

		Frozen	Not Frozen
	High	17	3
Anxiety	Medium	11	9
Level	Low	9	11

3. A college professor was interested in the effect of attending a concert on attitudes toward classical music. He surveyed the attitudes of his class before and after requiring attendance at a local concert, and hypothesized that more students would change to positive attitudes about classical music than would change to negative attitudes. Ten of the students did change from negative attitudes toward classical music to positive attitudes, but 36 changed from positive to negative attitudes.

   a. What is the value of chi-square associated with this experiment?

   b. Was the professor's research hypothesis supported? Why or why not?

Statistical Tests
for Ordinal Data

Chapter Ten

Various statistical tests have been devised for different types of research designs for ordinal data. These procedures are most appropriate when the classes of objects, events, or phenomena can be ordered and ranked, or when the various assumptions of the statistical tests for interval data cannot be met. With all the following statistical tests for ordinal data, the only assumption is that the data can be logically ordered.

The Two Independent Sample Case

The Median Test for Two Independent Samples

Function and Method. The median test is a procedure for testing for the significant difference between two independent groups by using the median of the combined groups as the statistical basis for dichotomizing the scores. The null hypothesis is that the two groups have the same median, or $Mdn_1 = Mdn_2$. This null hypothesis may be tested by the chi-square test from a 2 by 2 table.

The general procedure is to combine the scores from the two groups and to determine a common median. From the basis of the common median we dichotomize the scores into two frequency categories: those above the median point and those below the median point for the two groups. These contingencies are expressed in Table 10.1.

Table 10.1

	Group I	Group II	
Frequencies above the combined mdn	a	b	$a + b$
Frequencies below the combined mdn	c	d	$c + d$
	$a + c$	$b + d$	N

From this 2 by 2 table, the chi-square test with Formula 9.9 is used provided that the data meets the general assumptions of this test.

$$\chi^2 = \frac{N(|ad - bc| - N/2)^2}{(a + c)(b + d)(a + b)(c + d)}$$

One difficulty could occur when we dichotomize the scores and many of the scores of the two groups fall on the common median. When this occurs we have two choices, drop these median scores and dichotomize those remaining scores into those which are less than or greater than the median, or we could dichotomize the groups in terms of those scores that exceed the common median and those scores that do not.

Example. Thirty-two subjects earned a total of 50 reinforcements on a fixed-interval reinforcement schedule where the reinforcers were points on a counter. One question under investigation was the number of responses related to the verbalized reinforcement contingency (interval or ratio). The null hypothesis was that the two groups—verbalized interval and ratio contingencies—would have the same median number of responses, and the research hypothesis was that they would differ at the 0.05 level. The data are given in Table 10.2.

Table 10.2

Number of responses		Verbalized interval	Verbalized ratio	
	above the median	6	10	16
	below the median	15	1	16
		21	11	32

$$\chi^2 = \frac{32\left(|(6)(1) - (15)(10)| - 32/2\right)^2}{(21)(11)(16)(16)}$$

$$= \frac{524,288}{59,136}$$

$$= 8.866 \text{ with } 1 \ df$$

This obtained value far exceeds the critical value of chi-square for a two-tailed test at the 0.05 level. Thus, we could conclude that the medians differed significantly between the two groups.

The Median Test for K Independent Samples

Function and Method. In general, this is an extension of the median test when we have K independent samples. Our research concern is testing the significance between K groups regarding whether they have been drawn from the same population or from K populations with the same medians. The procedure is identical to the two sample cases in that we combine the K groups and then dichotomize the scores into two frequency sets, one with the frequencies above the common median and one below the median. This procedure leads to a 2 by K table from which we may obtain a chi-square from Formula 9.7. This chi-square value is

$$\chi^2 = \sum_{i=1}^{r} \sum_{j=1}^{k} \frac{(o_{ij} - e_{ij})^2}{e_{ij}}$$

evaluated with $K - 1$ df. In the generalized case we would have Table 10.3.

Table 10.3

	Group I	Group II	...	Group j	...	Group K
Frequencies above combined mdn			...		...	
Frequencies below combined mdn			...		...	

U-Test for Two Independent Samples

Function and Method.   The *U*-test, sometimes referred to as the Mann-Whitney, makes the assumption that we have two independent random samples on at least an ordinal level of measurement. Hence, we must be able to logically rank the obtained data. The primary function of the *U*-test is to ascertain whether two groups have been drawn from two populations with the same central tendencies or whether the two groups have been drawn from the same population. In the latter function, this test would be very appropriate in the experimental-control after-treatment design. The null hypothesis may be stated in a number of forms. In general, it can be said that the sum of the ranks of the first group (R_1) is equal to the sum of the ranks of the second group (R_2), or $H_0 : R_1 = R_2$.

The procedure for obtaining U is dependent upon the number of cases in the two groups, where n_1 is the number of cases in the smaller of the two groups, and n_2 is the number of cases in the larger of the two groups. When we have a small number of cases in n_2, $n_2 < 20$, we can determine the exact probabilities for U. When the number of cases in n_2 is large, $n_2 > 20$, we can approximate the probability values by z.

U-Test for Small Number of Cases, $n_2 < 20$.   The statistical procedure is to combine the obtained scores for both samples and to rank them in order of increasing size. Let n_1 be equal to the number of cases in the smaller of the two groups, and n_2 the number of cases in the larger of the two groups. For each rank score in the n_2 we count the number of rank scores in n_1 which have a greater rank. This procedure is followed for each score in n_2 and we sum the frequencies of the greater-than ranks for each n_1 rank; the result is equal to U. Taking some hypothetical data:

ranks for Group A   1 2 4 5 7 $n_2 = 5$ $R_2 = 19$

ranks for Group B   3 6 8 9 $n_1 = 4$ $R_1 = 26$

let us assume that the data have been ranked and the first rank score in n_1 is 3, and that there are three cases, ranks 4, 5 and 7, having greater ranks in n_2. The second n_1 rank score is 6 and only one case, that of rank 7, is greater. For the following two ranked values of 8 and 9, there are none greater. Thus:

$$U = 3 + 1 + 0 + 0 = 4$$

Now the probabilities of U are given in Table I. With our illustration, where $n_2 = 5$ and $n_1 = 4$ and $U = 4$, the $P = 0.056$. The probabilities in this table are for one-tailed tests of significance and if the research hypothesis specifies a two-tailed test, the tabled values of P are to be doubled, or in the example U has a $P = 0.112$.

When we have a large number of ranks in n_1 and n_2 the method of counting can be simplified by:

$$U = n_1 n_2 + \left[\frac{n_1 (n_1 + 1)}{2}\right] - R_1 \qquad (10.1)$$

where R_1 = sum of the ranks in n_1

Applying Formula 10.1 to our data, we have:

$$U = (4)(5) + \left[\frac{(4)(4 + 1)}{2}\right] - 26$$

$$= 20 + 10 - 26$$

$$= 4$$

which is equivalent to the counting procedure.

If we would have counted the number of ranks in n_2 greater than each of the n_1 ranks, we would have obtained U'. The U' also may be obtained by formula rather than by counting and is written as:

$$U' = n_1 n_2 + \left[\frac{n_2 (n_2 + 1)}{2}\right] - R_2 \qquad (10.2)$$

where R_2 = sum of the ranks in n_2

Thus, from our data applying Formula 10.2 we have:

$$U = (4)(5) + \left[\frac{5(5 + 1)}{2}\right] - 19 = 16$$

If we add U and U' we find that this is equal to the product of n_1 and n_2.

$$U + U' = (n_1)(n_2)$$

$$\text{or } 4 + 16 = (4)(5)$$

This acts as a good check for our computations. However, our statistical interest is in U and not in U'.

Before we look at an example, we need to point out the problem of ties. If we have ties of ranks between two or more cases in the same group, U is not affected. However, when we have ties across the groups, the U is influenced but not significantly so, unless we have a very large proportion of ties. When ties do occur across the groups and when we use the counting method, we take an average of the ranks.

Example. Hull (1951) has suggested that discrimination learning may involve numerous discriminanda in various combinations. The combinations may vary widely regarding the stimuli which are reinforced and those which are not. Hull states in Theorem 14:

> Discrimination learning with three discriminanda in the form – + – is possible, but is more difficult than is comparable discrimination learning with two discriminanda, + –, because in the form – + – the conditioned inhibition $(_SI_R)$ generalizes upon the reinforced reaction potential from both sides, summating at S_1, the slope of this summation gradient being much less steep than would be a single $_SI_R$ gradient from the same maximum (p. 77).

To test the ordinal relationships of the rates of discriminative learning under various combinations of discriminanda, the investigator used six randomly selected groups of rats which were trained in a 2-choice discriminative box under various combinations of discriminanda to the criterion of nine or more correct choices from the ten trials for three continuous days.

The research hypothesis derived from the theory is directional in that group (– +) should learn faster than the (– + –) group. Thus, we have a one-tailed test of significance. The investigator set alpha at the 0.05 level. In Table 10.4 are the numbers of days for the animals to reach the stated criterion for the two groups. The data were, then, transformed into ranks, as shown in the table.

If we center our attention on the (– + –) group, the first ranked value is 10; we have in group (– +) only one rank greater, but we have two ties, thus we have 2 for that ranked score. The rank of 15 is not exceeded by any score in the – + group, thus we have a zero. Continuing in like fashion over all scores, we have:

$$2 + 0 + 0 + 0 + 0 + 0 + 8 + 4.5 = 14.5 = U$$

Table 10.4

(– +) group		(– + –) group	
Days	Ranks	Days	Ranks
10	4.5	15	10
10	4.5	44	15
17	12	33	13
14	8	49	16
9	2	43	14
11	6.5	52	17
15	10	9	2
9	2	11	6.5
15	10	58	18
	$R_2 = 59.5$		$R_1 = 111.5$

From Table I for the *U*-test, we observe that $n_1 = 9$ and $n_2 = 9$ have a critical value for *U* at less than or equal to 21 for alpha at the 0.05 level for a one-tailed test of significance. Thus, our obtained *U* value of 14.5 is much less than the tabled value and we conclude that the two groups differ in the direction stated by the research hypothesis.

If we utilize Formula 10.1 for obtaining *U* we have:

$$U = n_1\, n_2 + \left[\frac{n_1\,(n_1 + 1)}{2}\right] - R_1$$

$$U = (9)(9) + (9)(10)/2 - 111.5$$

$$= 14.5$$

U-Test for Large Number of Cases, $n_2 > 20$. As the number of cases increases, the sampling distribution of *U* approaches the normal curve, and the sampling distribution of *U* can be approximated by:

$$z_u = \frac{U - \mu_u}{\sigma_u}$$

where $\mu_u = (n_1\, n_2)/2$

and $\sigma_u = \sqrt{\frac{(n_1)(n_2)(n_1 + n_2 + 1)}{12}}$ (10.3)

Formula 10.3 becomes a good approximation when n_2 is greater than 20. When n_2 equals or is less than 20, we use the tables to determine the probability values.

Example. As a means of illustration, we will use the data in the previous example for U (when n_2 is small).

$$\text{Thus, } U = n_1\, n_2 + \left[\frac{n_1\,(n_1 + 1)}{2}\right] - R_1$$

$$= (9)(9) + (9)(10)/2 - 111.5 = 14.5$$

$$\text{and } \mu_u = (n_1\, n_2)/2$$

$$= \frac{(9)(9)}{2} = 40.5$$

$$\text{and } \sigma_u = \sqrt{\frac{(n_1)(n_2)(n_1 + n_2 + 1)}{12}}$$

$$= \sqrt{\frac{(9)(9)(9 + 9 + 1)}{12}} = \sqrt{128.25}$$

$$= 11.3$$

$$\text{thus } z_u = \frac{14.5 - 40.5}{11.3} = 2.30$$

From Table C of z we may note that the associated value of P equals 0.011, which is approximately that which we obtained previously from the table of the exact values.

Ties. When we have a very large proportion of ties a correction term may be applied to the estimation of the standard deviation, or:

$$\sigma_u = \sqrt{\left[\frac{n_1 n_2}{N(N-1)}\right]\left[\frac{N^3 - N}{12}\right] - \Sigma T} \qquad (10.4)$$

$$\text{where } N = n_1 + n_2$$

$$T = \frac{t^3 - t}{12}$$

where t = the number of ties in a given rank

As a means of describing the influence of ties upon the data, let's note our example. We have:

3 cases of rank 2

2 cases of rank 4.5

2 cases of rank 6.5

3 cases of rank 10

Thus $\Sigma T = \dfrac{3^3 - 3}{12} + \dfrac{2^3 - 2}{12} + \dfrac{2^3 - 2}{12} + \dfrac{3^3 - 3}{12}$

$$= 2.0 + 0.5 + 0.5 + 2.0 = 5$$

and $\sigma_u = \sqrt{\left[\dfrac{(9)(9)}{18(17)}\right] \left[\dfrac{18^3 - 18}{12}\right] - 5}$

$$= 11.27$$

and $z_u = \dfrac{14.5 - 40.5}{11.27} = 2.307$

When comparing the two z values we can see that the correction for ties has very little influence on the z value. In general, it increases the z value. Siegel recommends that we should correct: a) only if the proportion of ties is very large, b) if we have a very large number of ties in a given rank, and c) if the probability of U without the correction for ties is close to the level of alpha.

The Maximum Difference Test for Two Independent Samples

Function and Method. Kolomogorov and Smirnov have proposed a statistical procedure for measuring the maximum difference between two independent groups. This maximum difference may be between the two measures of central tendency or between the two measures of variability. The major advantage of this procedure is that it may be used in evaluation of research where we find large numbers of cases that are tied or that received a common rank, or where the cases are treated as if they were tied. In research we often find that it is necessary or convenient to conceptualize the variable as a continuous one and to group the data into large ordered categories. We may, for example, categorize persons by socioeconomic status, prestige of occupation, ranks in the military, classifications on aptitude, achievement, and ability scales, and the like.

Basically, the null hypothesis is that two independent random samples have been drawn from the same population, and thus, their cumulative frequency distributions are equal within the limits of random sampling variation. This implies that their central tendencies, variability, and shape are also equal. This null hypothesis is tested by noting the maximum differences between the individual categories for the two cumulative distributions. On the other hand, if the maximum difference is too great to be expected in terms of random sampling variability, then the null hypothesis would be rejected.

The null hypothesis can be tested by one of three procedures which is determined by the size of the samples and by the direction of the research hypothesis.

The Maximum Difference Test for Small Samples

Function and Method. In applying this statistical procedure, for small samples, $n_1 = n_2 \leqslant 40$, we construct a cumulative frequency distribution with the same interval widths for each of the two samples. We then focus on the various differences between the cumulative frequencies for each interval. The statistical test is on the one interval with the largest or maximum difference. When we have a one-tailed test of significance then:

$$D = \text{maximum } (cf_{1i} - cf_{2i}) \qquad (10.5)$$

where cf_i = cumulative frequency of scores for the ith interval

If we have a two-tailed test, then:

$$D = \text{maximum } \left| cf_{1i} - cf_{2i} \right| \qquad (10.6)$$

In the latter case, we are concerned only with the absolute differences between the grouped intervals, whereas in the former case the D is the maximum difference as specified by the direction given by the research hypothesis. The sampling distribution is given in Table J(a) for $n_1 = n_2 \leqslant 40$. In the table, the value of N is the value of n_1 or n_2 as they are equal and D value. Any obtained D value that is equal to or greater than the table value would fall in the region of rejection.

We need to point out the D is influenced by the arbitrary size and number of class intervals. As previously suggested, when we cast the obtained data into wide class intervals we come to treat all the scores in a given interval as if they were the midpoint. Thus, if we use too few close intervals the true maximum difference may not be well defined. In practice it is well to use a rather large number of intervals in order to obtain the best estimate of the maximum difference.

Example.   For illustrative purposes, we shall use the same data that were analyzed by the U-test. The null hypothesis here would state no difference between the two groups, whereas the research hypothesis states the − + group would learn faster than the − + −, and hence, the cumulative frequencies should differ significantly at the 0.05 in one direction. The data have been grouped into class intervals of 5 as shown in Table 10.5.

Table 10.5

	− + Group		− + − Group		
Class intervals	f_1	cf_1	f_2	cf_2	$(cf_1 - cf_2)$
55-59		9	1	9	
50-54		9	1	8	1
45-49		9	1	7	2
40-44		9	2	6	3
35-39		9		4	5
30-34		9	1	4	5
25-29		9		3	6
20-24		9		3	6
15-19	3	9	1	3	6
10-14	4	6	1	2	4
5-9	2	2	1	1	1
0-4					

D = maximum $(9 - 3)$
$D = 6$

As $n_1 = 9$ and $n_2 = 9$, the sampling distribution in Table J(a) gives the critical value of 6 for $N = 9$ (one-tailed test at the 0.05 level of significance). Now as the obtained D of 6 is equal to the critical value, we may conclude that the cumulative frequency distributions differ significantly in the direction stated by the research hypothesis.

The Maximum Difference Test for Large Samples: Two-Tailed Test

When both samples $(n_1$ and $n_2)$ are larger than 40, they need not be of equal size. Table J(b) may be used as the sampling distribution of D provided that we have a two-tailed test of significance. For example, in order to reject the null hypothesis at the 0.05 level, we would need to obtain a D value that was equal to or greater than:

$$1.36 \sqrt{\frac{n_1 + n_2}{n_1 n_2}}$$

In this case, however, D is defined as the absolute maximum difference between the two cumulative proportions, or:

$$D = \text{maximum} \left| \frac{cf_{1i}}{n_1} - \frac{cf_{2i}}{n_2} \right| \qquad (10.7)$$

$$\text{or } D = \text{maximum} \left| cP_{1i} - cP_{2i} \right|$$

Thus we need to transform the cf data into cP data by dividing each by its respective n.

The Maximum Difference Test for Large Samples: One-Tailed Test

Now if both samples are larger than 40, they need not be of equal size, and if we have a stated directional research hypothesis, then D becomes:

$$D = \text{maximum} \left| cP_{1i} - cP_{2i} \right| \qquad (10.8)$$

We may test the null hypothesis by an approximation of the chi-square test where:

$$\chi^2 = 4D^2 \frac{n_1 n_2}{n_1 + n_2} \qquad (10.9)$$

This sampling distribution is approximated by the chi-square distribution for 2 *df.*
This same approximation can be used when we have $n_1 \neq n_2$ with smaller sample sizes than 40. However, Goodman reports that his approximation gives us a conservative test, in that if the null hypothesis is rejected with small samples, it is always in the direction of confidence about the decision.

Example.   The researcher reported cumulative frequency distributions of anxiety, as measured on an anxiety scale, for two independent samples: patients in a mental hospital and normals. For illustrative purposes, let's suppose that he did not specify a directional hypothesis, and he stated alpha at the 0.05 level.

In Table 10.5 the class interval width is 3. The frequency data are just transformed into cumulative frequencies and then transformed into cumulative proportions. As we have no directional hypothesis, we would note the absolute maximum differences between the two groups.

Table 10.5

	f_1	cf_1	cp_1	f_2	cf_2	cP_2	$cP_2 - cP_1$
48-50	3	100	1.00			1.00	.00
45-47	10	97	.97			1.00	.03
42-44	8	87	.87			1.00	.13
39-41	10	79	.79			1.00	.21
36-38	13	69	.69	2	100	1.00	.31
33-35	12	56	.56	3	98	.98	.42
30-32	9	44	.44	2	95	.95	.51
27-29	5	35	.35	6	93	.93	.58
24-26	5	30	.30	5	87	.87	.57
21-23	8	25	.25	5	82	.82	.57
18-20	5	17	.17	5	77	.77	.60
15-17	3	12	.12	14	72	.72	.60
12-14	3	9	.09	10	58	.58	.49
9-11	4	6	.06	17	48	.48	.42
6-8	1	2	.02	15	31	.31	.29
3-5	1	1	.01	14	16	.16	.15
0-2			.00	2	2	.02	.02
	$n_1 = 100$			$n_2 = 100$			

In this example $D = 0.60$. From Table J(b) we may calculate the critical value.

$$1.36 \sqrt{\frac{n_1 + n_2}{n_1 n_2}}$$

$$\text{or}\ \ 1.36 \sqrt{\frac{100 + 100}{(100)(100)}}$$

$$\text{or}\ \ 0.192$$

Now as the obtained D of 0.60 is very much larger we would conclude that the two groups differ significantly at the 0.05 level of significance.

If on the other hand we would have had a directional hypothesis that the patients would have a higher cumulative proportion than the normals, then we may use the approximation of the chi-square. Thus:

$$\chi^2 = 4D^2 \ \frac{n_1 n_2}{n_1 + n_2}$$

$$= 4(0.60)^2 \ \frac{(100)(100)}{100 + 100}$$

$$= 72.00 \text{ with } 2 \ df$$

When evaluated from the chi-square sampling distribution, the obtained value is highly significant as well. Thus we would conclude that the patients have a significantly higher anxiety than normals as measured by the manifest anxiety scale and as evaluated by the maximum difference test.

The Runs Test for Two Independent Samples

Function and Method.   The runs test has been suggested by Wald and Wolfowitz to test for significant differences between two independent samples for any null hypothesis. The only assumptions that are required are that the two groups are independent and that the level of measurement is at least on an ordinal scale. The runs test measures all possible differences simultaneously. However, if our research interest is basically that of differences between central tendencies, other statistical procedures may be more powerful.

In applying the runs test, we take the combined data from both samples and we rank these combined scores in order of increasing size, and determine from this ordered series the number of runs or sequence of scores for the same sample. Now if the null hypothesis that there are no differences between groups is true, then the sequences of scores in runs for the two independent groups should be random. When the null hypothesis is false, then in general the number of runs shall be small. For example, suppose that the two groups had the same central tendency, variability, and shape, then we would expect that the runs would be random and that the number of runs would be fairly large. On the other hand, if the two groups had the same variability and shape but differed in central tendencies, we would now expect that we would find a long run at the lower end of the sample with the smallest central tendency and, also, a long run at the upper end of the sample with the larger central tendency. Thus, we would observe a smaller number of runs. Similarly, if the two samples had the same central tendency but differed greatly in either their shape or variability, we would again anticipate a smaller number of runs than if the two samples were random.

Small-Sample Case for the Runs Test. When n_1 and $n_2 \leqslant 20$, the exact sampling distribution of the number of runs is given in Table K. These tabled values are significant at the 0.05 level, hence the number of runs that is equal to or less than this value would fall within the region of rejection. Any value greater than the tabled value would be in the acceptance region.

Example. The operant behavior of 40, 24-hour-old chicks was investigated as a function of two light onset durations of a sensory reinforcer within a simple visual environment. One group of 20 animals was given a one-second duration of a dim light, and the second group a three-second duration each time they performed the operant of breaking a photo-electric beam. The null hypothesis states that there was no difference in the runs or sequences of scores between the two groups. The research hypothesis was that there would be a difference at the 0.05 level of significance. In Table 10.6 the data have been cast into runs which have been underscored and numbered.

Table 10.6

response	2	15	33	49	105	131	149	171	189	194	206	226
duration	1	1	1	3	3	3	3	1	3	3	3	3
		1			2			3		4		

response	227	236	247	250	253	260	282	299	300	311
duration	1	1	1	1	1	1	1	1	1	1
					5					

response	333	338	348	354	362	402	404	417	452	477
duration	3	3	3	1	3	3	3	3	3	3
		6		7			8			

response	488	406	515	553	648	657	676	841
duration	1	1	3	1	3	1	3	1
		9	10	11	12	13	14	15

$r = 15$

From Table K when n_1 and n_2 both equal 20, the critical run value is 14 or less at the 0.05 level. Hence, we must conclude that there is no significant difference in runs between the two duration groups.

Large-Sample Case for the Runs Test.   Where n_1 or $n_2 \geqslant 20$ the sampling distribution for the runs test is approximately normal and is estimated by the approximation:

$$z_r = \frac{r - \mu_r}{\sigma_r} \tag{10.10}$$

where r = number of runs

$$\text{and } \mu_r = \frac{2n_1 n_2}{n_1 + n_2} + 1$$

$$\text{and } \sigma_r = \sqrt{\frac{(2n_1 n_2)(2n_1 n_2 - n_1 n_2)}{(n_1 + n^2)^2 (n_1 + n_2 - 1)}}$$

$$\text{Therefore } z_r = \frac{r - \left[\dfrac{2n_1 n_2}{n_1 + n_2} + 1\right]}{\sqrt{\dfrac{(2n_1 n_2)(2n_1 n_2 - n_1 - n_2)}{(n_1 + n_2)^2 (n_1 + n_2 - 1)}}}$$

Now if n_1 and n_2 are small, but $r \geqslant 5$, we can utilize Formula 10.10, provided that we correct for continuity. Thus:

$$z_r = \frac{|r - \mu_r| - 0.5}{\sigma_r} \tag{10.11}$$

Example.   If we would utilize the same data as above and apply Formula 10.10, then:

$$zr = \frac{15 - \dfrac{2(20)(20)}{20 + 20} + 1}{\sqrt{\dfrac{[2(20)(20)][2(20)(20) - 20 - 20]}{(20 + 20)^2 (20 + 20 - 1)}}}$$

$$= -1.94$$

The obtained z_r value approaches the significant -1.96 level of z for a two-tailed test at the 0.05 level. However, the obtained value falls within the region of acceptance for the null hypothesis. We would thus conclude, as before, that there is no significant difference between the two groups.

Ties. With the assumption of continuity, theoretically, we should not have any ties. But as our methods of measurement may not allow us to make finer measures of the behavioral phenomena, we often find tied scores. Now if ties do occur and do so *within* the same sample group, the number of runs would not be influenced. However, the basic problem arises when ties occur *between* groups. There are, however, some common procedures used in breaking the ties. The most satisfactory method is to compute all various combinations of ways of breaking up the ties. If this procedure leads to the same decision in terms of acceptance or rejection of the null hypothesis then we have no real problem. The basic difficulty comes when some decisions are to reject and others to accept the null hypothesis. Probably the most satisfactory approach would be to find the probability values. If we have a large number of such ties the use of the runs test is inappropriate and we might use such a statistical test as the maximum difference test.

The Sign Test for Two Related Sample Case

Function and Method. When the investigator has matched the pairs of objects between the two groups (for example, where the subject acts as his own control, as in a before-after design), the sign test could be utilized. The sign test is particularly appropriate when we wish to determine whether two related groups differ under conditions where we are not justified in assuming that we can obtain quantitative measurements. However, it must be possible to differentiate between the two members of each and every pair on the behavioral variable such that $X_A > X_B$ (greater than pair) or $X_A < X_B$ (less than pair). When $X_A > X_B$ we assign a positive sign (+), and when $X_A < X_B$, a negative sign (−). Essentially, the null hypothesis states that the probability of a pair being a greater than pair is equal to the probability of it being a less than pair, or:

$$H_0 : P(X_A > X_B) = P(X_A < X_B)$$

$$: P(+) = P(-)$$

The null hypothesis can be evaluated by the binomial distribution when we assumed that $P = 1/2$ and $Q = 1/2$ where $N =$ the number of pairs. As with the binomial test when $NP > 5$ we can approximate the sampling distribution, thus:

$$z_{sign} = \frac{(X \pm 0.5) - \mu}{\sigma} \tag{10.12}$$

where $X =$ number of the positive or negative signs

$\mu = NP$

$\sigma = \sqrt{NPQ}$

and $N =$ total number of pairs

Example.   An investigator has examined the frequency of familiar verbal recalls of neurotic patients and observed that it is a function of the behavior of the therapist as well as that of the subject. He suggested that the therapist selectively reinforces certain desired verbal behaviors. Thus, he suggests a directional hypothesis. Let alpha be set at the 0.05 level of significance for this one-tailed test. In Table 10.7 we have a portion of his data. The data are for the frequency of memories of the operant period (base line) and the change of response frequency during the reinforcement period. For the sign test we shall note only the change in rate between the two conditions where the subject acts as his own control.

We shall be concerned with the frequency of changes that are +, and we have 13 such changes in the table.

$$z_{sign} = \frac{(13 - 0.5) - (16)(0.5)}{\sqrt{(16)(0.5)(0.5)}}$$

$$= \frac{12.5 - 8}{2}$$

$$= 2.25$$

From Table C for the unit normal curve we find that the obtained value falls into the region of significance and that the associated probability for a $z = 2.25$ is $P = 0.012$. We conclude that the selective verbal reinforcements that the therapist uses highly influence the subjects' behaviors.

Table 10.7

S	Operant	Reinforcement	Change
1	.30	.43	+
2	.39	.41	+
3	.37	.29	−
4	.40	.48	+
5	.25	.12	−
6	.55	.58	+
7	.50	.56	+
8	.06	.26	+
9	.60	.70	+
10	.50	.46	−
11	.50	.62	+
12	.33	.47	+
13	.53	.62	+
14	.53	.70	+
15	.38	.43	+
16	.33	.48	+

The Rank-Sign Test for Two Related Samples

Function and Method.   The rank-sign test is an expansion of the sign test under conditions where we are able to rank the differences between each of the related pairs. The sign of the differences within pairs specifies the direction between the subjects and the rank specifies the magnitude among the pairs of subjects. The general procedure for this test is to obtain a difference score for each pair, and then these difference scores are ranked according to the absolute difference values. Having obtained the ranks, we then go back and assign a + when $X_A > X_B$ and a − when $X_A < X_B$ and we sum the ranks of the + differences and also we sum the ranks of the − differences. The null hypothesis states that the probability of the sum of + ranks is equal to the probability of the sum of the − ranks, or:

$$H_0 : P\left(\Sigma + \text{ranks}\right) = P\left(\Sigma - \text{ranks}\right)$$

Thus, we would expect, on the basis of random sampling, that the sum of the + ranks would be approximately equal to the sum of the − ranks: however, if the two sums are very different the null hypothesis would be rejected.

The Rank-Sign Test for Small Number of Pairs ($N < 25$).   Let us define T as the smaller of the sums of the two ranks with N equal to the number of pairs. Table L gives the critical T values; thus any obtained value that is equal to or less than the tabled values would fall within the region of rejection. For a one-tailed test of significance the direction of the smaller sum of ranks would be predicted in advance of the data collection.

Example. For comparative purposes, we shall utilize the example from the sign test. However, now we shall note the magnitude of the changes as well as their directions (see Table 10.8).

Table 10.8

S	Operant	Reinforcement	Difference	Rank	Rank with less frequent sign
1	.30	.43	+.13	+11.5	
2	.39	.41	+.02	+1	
3	.37	.29	−.08	−6.5	6.5
4	.40	.48	+.08	+6.5	
5	.25	.12	−.13	−11.5	11.5
6	.55	.58	+.03	+2	
7	.50	.56	+.06	+5	
8	.06	.26	+.20	+16	
9	.60	.70	+.10	+9	
10	.50	.46	−.04	−3	3.0
11	.50	.62	+.12	+10	
12	.33	.47	+.14	+13	
13	.53	.62	+.09	+8	
14	.53	.70	+.17	+15	
15	.38	.43	+.05	+4	
16	.33	.48	+.15	+14	
					$T = 21.0$

From Table L for the critical values of T for our one-tailed test we find that a $T = 21$ for $N = 16$ is less than the tabled value and we must conclude as before that there is a significant difference between the operant and reinforcement periods. For the $T = 21$ the $P < 0.01$ and > 0.005.

The Rank Sign Test for Large Number of Pairs ($N > 25$). When Table L is no longer appropriate the null hypothesis can be tested by the z approximation as the sampling distribution is approximately normal. Thus:

$$z_{\text{sign-rank}} = \frac{T - \mu_T}{\sigma_T} \qquad (10.13)$$

where T = smaller sum of the two ranks

$$\mu_T = \frac{N(N+1)}{4}$$

$$\sigma_T = \sqrt{\frac{N(N+1)(2N+1)}{24}}$$

where N = number of pairs

This general approximation can be used with small samples as we have exact tables for small samples. Using the same illustration as with the small number of pairs:

$$z_{\text{sign-rank}} = \frac{T - \mu_T}{\sigma_T}$$

$$= \frac{21 - \dfrac{16(16+1)}{4}}{\sqrt{\dfrac{(16)(16+1)[(2)(16)+1]}{24}}}$$

$$= \frac{21 - 68}{\sqrt{374}}$$

$$= 2.43$$

The associated probability from Table C for this value of Z is $P = 0.007$. Thus approximately the same statistical results are obtained with the two methods.

Some Comments on Further Designs.   Within this chapter those statistical methods most commonly used in the research literature have been described. However, there are a number of other procedures that have been developed. For a coverage of other "distribution-free" or "non-parametic" techniques which utilize nominal and ordinal data, the student is advised to see such texts as Fraser (1957), Noether (1967), Siegel (1956), and Walsh (1962, 1965). These books also describe the procedures in greater mathematical depth.

Summary of Terms

maximum difference test   *U*-test
median test
rank-sign test
runs test
sign test

Summary of Symbols

χ^2	R_1	μ_u	z_r	z_{sign}	μ_T
U	R_2	σ_u	μ_r	T	σ_T
U^1	z_u	D	σ_r	$z_{sign\text{-}rank}$	

Problems

1. An animal trainer hypothesized that one 16-oz. steak, two 8-oz. steaks, and four 4-oz. steaks would have differential reinforcing effects on a lion's hoop jumping behavior. She randomly assigned 8 lions to each of three groups, and reinforced the lions for each hoop jump in a 45-minute period. The resulting data are given in Table 10.9. Using the appropriate statistical procedure and the 0.05 alpha level, test her hypothesis and state your conclusions.

Table 10.9.   Number of Hoop Jumps.

1 16-oz steak	2 8-oz steaks	4 4-oz steaks
2	3	7
4	5	5
3	3	5
4	6	6
1	3	8
1	4	8
4	3	5
1	5	7

2. It was predicted that one year of college would change the effect of written affective statements on the attitudes of college freshmen towards a fictitious person. Students in fall and spring introductory psychology classes read a paragraph describing a fictitious person—the paragraph was preceded by a positive affective statement—and then completed a questionnaire. A high score on the questionnaire indicated a positive attitude towards the fictitious person. The data are given below. Using the *U* test and the 0.05 alpha level, determine whether or not the above research hypothesis can be maintained.

Fall data	Spring data
40	26
39	33
39	11
10	8
17	27
17	27
11	28
26	27
25	14
26	15
24	10
38	6
18	10
26	26
36	13
15	25
16	27
35	35
13	25
12	35
27	2
31	32
19	
38	

3. Use the maximum difference test, the 0.01 alpha level, and a class interval 5 units wide to determine if the following two samples were drawn from the same population of random numbers.

A	B
17	9
3	14
25	23
24	11
18	13
15	21
13	8
6	20
7	4
18	16
4	3
3	22
18	16
9	5
9	7
18	2
15	3
22	3
23	2
21	15

4. An experimenter was interested in the effect of sensory deprivation on free looking time. He measured the amount of time that college students spent looking at equivalent slides before and after spending one hour in a dark, sound-shielded room. His research hypothesis was that the subjects would spend more time looking at the slide after the sensory deprivation period than before the sensory deprivation period. The data are given below. Using the simplest appropriate test and the 0.05 alpha level, evaluate his research hypothesis.

Before	After
8	28
5	19
17	21
8	10
12	27
11	10
1	12
3	21
7	4
6	7
18	12

Statistical Tests for Interval and Ratio Data

Chapter Eleven

We will describe, within this chapter, two tests of inference for measurement on the interval scale, the t-test, and the analysis of variance (anova). These two are the most powerful of all the tests of inference for the rejection of the null hypothesis when that hypothesis is false. But in addition, these tests also require the strongest assumptions. We must assume, for example, that the level of measurement is on the interval scale, that the variable being measured is from a normally distributed population, that the effects of treatment conditions are additive, and that the variances from the two (or more) populations are equal or homogeneous.

One-Sample Case

The t-test for the One Random Sample Case.

Function and Method. One of the functions of the one-sample case is that of a goodness-of-fit design for testing the hypothesis that the one random sample was drawn from some specified population with known parameters. However, a more common function of the t-test for one random sample is for the testing of a hypothesis concerning the magnitude of a simple population mean. The t-test may be applied to such problems when we have interval data.

Assume that we have a continuous variable X which is normally distributed in the population. If we would draw a large number of random samples each of size N from this population, it is assumed that the mean of these sample means will be an estimate of the population mean, μ. If the population standard deviation is known and the population mean or μ is stated by the null hypothesis, rather than drawing a large number of samples from the population, we draw a single random sample. The hypothesis is evaluated by:

$$z = \frac{\overline{X} - \mu}{\sigma_{\overline{x}}} \tag{11.1}$$

where $\overline{X}$ = sample mean
    μ = population mean given from H_0.
    $\sigma_{\overline{x}} = \sigma/\sqrt{N}$ = standard error of the mean
and where σ = given population standard deviation
    N = sample size

If random samples of z were drawn from a normal population then they would be distributed as a normal curve, provided that the sample sizes remained constant. This being the case, the denominator, or the standard error of the mean, $\sigma_{\overline{x}}$, will be a constant, and only the numerator will vary as a function of sampling fluctuation.

In testing a hypothesis concerning the mean, we are generally confronted with the problem in Formula 11.1, of knowing the population standard deviation. If the population standard deviation is not known, we can estimate it from the sample standard deviation. However, when we estimate the standard deviation, the denominator will vary as well as the numerator for each sample. Rather than testing the hypothesis by the z-test we commonly use the t-test or t-ratio, which is given in Formula 11.2:

$$t = \frac{\overline{X} - \mu}{S_{\overline{x}}} \tag{11.2}$$

where $\overline{X}$ = sample mean

    μ = population mean given from H_0

    $S_{\overline{x}}$ = estimate of the standard error
        of the mean

The standard error of the mean in Formula 11.2 becomes:

$$S_{\bar{x}} = \frac{S}{\sqrt{N}} \qquad (11.3)$$

where S = sample standard deviation

N = number of cases

Whereas the z distribution with a mean of zero and a variance of one will be a normal curve distribution, the t distribution will not. The t distribution is influenced by both the sample size and the variability of the sample standard deviation. We can assume, as with the z distribution, that the distribution of sample means will be normal; however, the shape of the distribution will be a function of the standard error of the mean.

For the t there is more than one sampling distribution, each associated with the degrees of freedom upon which the standard errors are based, rather than a single distribution as with z. The distribution of t is not a normal distribution but it is a symmetrical one. The shape of the t distribution is a function of the sample size and $N - 1$ degrees of freedom available. The function of the shape of this distribution is given in Formula 11.4 in terms of the ordinate of the curve.

$$y = \frac{N-1}{S\sqrt{2\pi}}\ e^{-x^2/2S^2} \qquad (11.4)$$

When N reaches infinity, the t distribution is equal to the z or normal curve distribution and with 30 degrees of freedom the t distribution closely approximates the normal curve.

The t for a single mean has $N - 1$ degrees of freedom, where N is the number of scores. The mean may be thought of as a constant with $N - 1$ scores that are free to vary; the last score is, thus, determined. In evaluation of a t, it is always necessary to determine the degrees of freedom available. In Figure 11.1, we have illustrated curves for various sampling distributions. As we can see from this figure, the curves for various t distributions do not approach the abscissa as quickly as does the curve for the normal distribution. Thus, more of the total area under the curve is in the two tails of the t distribution. In order to determine some

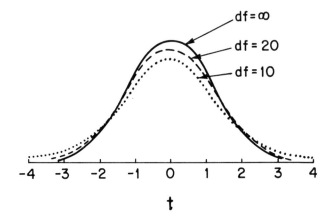

Figure 11.1. Theoretical sampling distributions of *t* for 10, 20, and ∞
degrees of freedom.

critical value of *t*, we must have more extreme values than for the
normal curve. Table M gives the critical *t* values for various degrees
of freedom for both the one- and two-tailed tests with various
alpha levels.

Example. Assume that we are interested in testing the
hypothesis that the population mean is 50, when the population is
normally distributed with a population standard deviation of 10.
Suppose that a researcher took a random sample of 25 cases and
obtained a mean of 53. The hypothesis states that the population
mean is 50 and so let us assume that we have a nondirectional
hypothesis and a two-tailed test with alpha at 0.05. As the
population standard deviation is given, the best choice of our
statistical tests would be the *z*-test, thus from Formula 11.1 we
have:

$$z = \frac{\overline{X} - \mu}{\sigma/\sqrt{N}}$$

where $\overline{X} = 53$
$\mu = 50$
$\sigma = 10$
$N = 25$

therefore:
$$z = \frac{53 - 50}{10/\sqrt{25}}$$

$$= \frac{3}{10/5}$$

$$= 1.50$$

To evaluate this z value of 1.50, we enter the table of the unit normal curve, Table C. With a two-tailed test the critical z value at 0.05 is tabled as ±1.96. As our obtained z value is less than the tabled value, we would conclude that our sample mean does not differ significantly from the population mean of 50. The exact probability that is associated with our obtained z value is 0.0668 + 0.0668 or 0.1336, and as this probability value is greater than the stated alpha, our conclusions in regard to the hypothesis would be the same.

The *t*-test for Two Independent Samples with Homogeneous Variances.

Function and Method. In addition to functions of the t-test as seen with the one-sample case, the t-test is also a procedure for testing whether two groups differ in central tendencies. More precisely, the t-test will give us information about whether it is probable that the two groups have been drawn from a common population with a value of μ, or from two populations with the same central tendency, such that $\mu_1 = \mu_2$, or $\mu_1 - \mu_2 = 0$.

In our two independent sample case, we have two sample means and our procedure is testing the difference between the two means $\overline{X}_1 - \overline{X}_2$. It holds that if the two independent distributions are both normally distributed, then the differences between two means will also be normally distributed.

In addition to the assumption that the differences between means are normally distributed and that the two groups are at least on an interval scale, it is further assumed that the two sample variances are equal. In the evaluation of the differences between the two means by use of the t-test, it is implicity stated as a part of the hypothesis being tested that the population variances from which the samples were drawn are equal or that:

$$\sigma_1^2 = \sigma_2^2$$

As the standard deviations and the variances of the populations are not known, the standard error must be estimated. This standard error is based on the standard deviations and variances obtained from the two samples. As with the t-test for the one-sample case, the degrees of freedom must be specified.

In experimental research the determination of whether an observed difference between two sample means is of such a magnitude that it cannot be attributed to chance factors is often our major interest. We may find, for example, that a random group of subjects tested under one set of experimental conditions has a larger mean value than a comparable control group tested under a different set of experimental conditions. If the observed difference between the means is so great that the probability of this difference by chance is less than some specified value of alpha, then we may infer that the difference is a function of the experimental or treatment conditions.

The null hypothesis is that the two means are equal or that:

$$\mu_1 = \mu_2$$

$$\text{or} \quad \mu_1 - \mu_2 = 0$$

and that our research or alternative hypothesis is:

$$\mu_1 \neq \mu_2$$

$$\text{or} \quad \mu_1 > \mu_2$$

$$\text{or} \quad \mu_1 < \mu_2$$

The null hypothesis is tested by Formula 11.5:

$$t = \frac{\overline{X}_1 - \overline{X}_2}{S_{\overline{x}_1 - \overline{x}_2}} \tag{11.5}$$

where $\overline{X}_1$ = sample mean of the first group
$\overline{X}_2$ = sample mean of the second group
and $S_{\overline{x}_1 - \overline{x}_2}$ = standard error of the difference between two means

The estimate of the standard error of the difference between the two means is given as:

$$S_{\overline{x}_1 - \overline{x}_2} = \sqrt{S_{\overline{x}_1}^2 + S_{\overline{x}_2}^2} \tag{11.6}$$

$$\text{where} \quad S_{\overline{x}_1}^2 = \frac{S_1^2}{N_1}$$

$$\text{and} \quad S_{\overline{x}_2}^2 = \frac{S_2^2}{N_2}$$

If we can make the assumption that the two variances are equal within the limits of random sampling, we can pool the sum of squares and the degrees of freedom from our two samples in order to obtain an estimate of the common variance. Hence:

$$S^2 = \frac{\Sigma x_1^2 + \Sigma x_2^2}{N_1 + N_2 - 2} \tag{11.7}$$

or computationally,

$$S^2 = \frac{\Sigma X_1^2 - \dfrac{(\Sigma X_1)^2}{N_1} + \Sigma X_2^2 - \dfrac{(\Sigma X_2)^2}{N_2}}{N_1 + N_2 - 2} \tag{11.7a}$$

Now if we substitute this common variance in Formula 11.6 we have:

$$S_{\bar{x}_1 - \bar{x}_2} = \sqrt{\frac{\dfrac{\Sigma x_1^2 + \Sigma x_2^2}{N_1 + N_2 - 2}}{N_1} + \frac{\dfrac{\Sigma x_1^2 + \Sigma x_2^2}{N_1 + N_2 - 2}}{N_2}} \tag{11.8}$$

and if we collect and rearrange these terms:

$$S_{\bar{x}_1 - \bar{x}_2} = \sqrt{\left(\frac{\Sigma x_1^2 + \Sigma x_2^2}{N_1 + N_2 - 2}\right)\left(\frac{1}{N_1} + \frac{1}{N_2}\right)} \tag{11.9}$$

$$\text{or} = \sqrt{S^2 \left(\frac{1}{N_1} + \frac{1}{N_2}\right)}$$

$$\text{or} = S \sqrt{\frac{1}{N_1} + \frac{1}{N_2}} \tag{11.10}$$

The general definitional formula for the *t*-test when we have homogeneity of variances then becomes:

$$t = \frac{\bar{X}_1 - \bar{X}_2}{\sqrt{\left[\dfrac{\Sigma x_1^2 + \Sigma x_2^2}{N_1 + N_2 - 2}\right]\left[\dfrac{1}{N_1} + \dfrac{1}{N_2}\right]}} \tag{11.11}$$

$$\text{where } \Sigma x_1^2 = \Sigma X_1^2 - \frac{(\Sigma X_1)^2}{N_1}$$

$$\text{and } \Sigma x_2^2 = \Sigma X_2^2 - \frac{(\Sigma X_2)^2}{N_2}$$

The computational formula therefore becomes:

$$t = \frac{\overline{X}_1 - \overline{X}_2}{\sqrt{\left\{\frac{\left[\Sigma X_1^2 - \frac{(\Sigma X_1)^2}{N_1}\right] + \left[\Sigma X_2^2 - \frac{(\Sigma X_2)^2}{N_2}\right]}{N_1 + N_2 - 2}\right\} \left\{\frac{1}{N_1} + \frac{1}{N_2}\right\}}} \tag{11.11a}$$

When $N_1 = N_2$, then Formula 11.11 can be written as:

$$t = \frac{\overline{X}_1 - \overline{X}_2}{\sqrt{\frac{\Sigma x_1^2 + \Sigma x_2^2}{N(N-1)}}} \tag{11.11b}$$

or computationally:

$$t = \frac{\overline{X}_1 - \overline{X}_2}{\sqrt{\frac{\left[\Sigma X_1^2 - \frac{(\Sigma X_1)^2}{N_1}\right] + \left[\Sigma X_2^2 - \frac{(\Sigma X_2)^2}{N_2}\right]}{N(N-1)}}} \tag{11.11c}$$

When we have two independent random samples with homogeneous variances, the sampling distributions of t (Table M) are distributed with the degrees of freedom that are equal to $N_1 + N_2 - 2$.

The Homogeneity of Two Variances. The null hypothesis, the hypothesis of no difference between means, is rejected if the absolute value of the obtained t is equal to or greater than the appropriate tabled theoretical value of t associated with an alpha level of significance. In the evaluation of the difference between the two means by the t-test, we have stated the assumption that

the two variances are equal. This assumption can be tested by the
F-test, or:

$$F\text{-test} = \frac{S_1^2}{S_2^2} \text{ or } \frac{S_2^2}{S_1^2} \qquad (11.12)$$

$$\text{such that} \quad F \geqslant 1$$

The sampling distribution of F is given in Table N. The tabled
values correspond to various probabilities with $N_1\text{-}1/N_2\text{-}1$ or
$N_2\text{-}1/N_1\text{-}1$ degrees of freedom. In the entering of the table, the
column df corresponds to the $N-1$ for the numerator, and $N-1$
for the denominator corresponds to the row df, or:

$$df \text{ for } F = \frac{\text{column}}{\text{row}} \qquad (11.13)$$

If the observed F value is equal to or greater than the tabled value
of F associated with a level of alpha, then the assumption of
homogeneity of variance is rejected. On the other hand, if the
observed F is less than the tabled value, the assumption of
homogeneity of variance can be accepted.

In Figure 11.2 we have illustrated three statistical situations. In
A we have the two means differ and the variances are equal. If $\bar{X}_1$
is the mean of the control group and the $\bar{X}_2$ the mean of the
experimental group, then the effect of the treatment condition
was to increase the mean value but the treatment condition had no
effect upon the variances. The B shows the two means to be equal
but the variances differ. The effect of the treatment condition had
no effect upon the mean but increased the variability. In C both
the means and the variances differ. Thus the effect of the
treatment condition was to increase both the mean and the
variance of the experimental group in comparison to the control
group.

Example. To investigate the effects of bilateral frontal
ablations upon response inhibition, ten food-deprived rats were
trained on a 15-sec drl reinforcement schedule. The differential
reinforcement of the low rate (drl) should be particularly sensitive
to impairment of response inhibition in that a pause of 15 seconds
or longer must occur after the last response before the food
reinforcer is given. Five rats were given a bilateral frontal ablation
and five served as sham controls. The measure was in time to reach
the criterion of 50% reinforced responses. The null hypothesis was
stated as no difference between the mean of the two groups, and

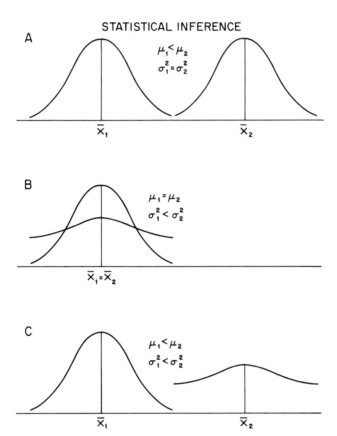

Figure 11.2.   Schematic of various statistical inferences for t.   A. The two
mu values differ significantly with equal variances.   B. The
means are equal with heterogeneity of variances.   C. Both
the means and variances differ.

the research hypothesis stated that there is a difference. Alpha was
set at the 0.05 level for this two-tailed test. The data are given in
Table 11.1.

Table 11.1

Sham Controls	Frontals
76	52
42	18
11	29
18	11
10	32

$\Sigma X_1 = 157$ $\Sigma X_2 = 142$

$\Sigma X_1^2 = 8085$ $\Sigma X_2^2 = 5014$

$\overline{X}_1 = 31.40$ $\overline{X}_2 = 28.40$

$\Sigma x_1^2 = 3155.2$ $\Sigma x_2^2 = 981.2$

$S_1^2 = 788.8$ $S_2^2 = 245.3$

In general, we test the assumption of homogeneity of variances first, hence:

$$F\text{-test} = \frac{788.8}{245.3}$$

$$= 3.216 \text{ with 4 and 4 } df$$

From Table N for F at the 0.05 level for a two-tailed test and with 4 and 4 degrees of freedom is given as 6.39. Any obtained value that is equal to, or greater than this sampling distribution value would be significant at the 0.05 level. Our obtained F value of 3.216 is less than the theoretical value and thus, we would assume that our variances are homogeneous.

Having met this assumption we can pool our obtained sums of squares and the degrees of freedom for the estimate of the standard error of the difference between the two means as the denominator of the t formula (11.11):

$$t = \frac{31.40 - 28.40}{\sqrt{\left(\frac{3155.2 + 981.2}{5 + 5 - 2}\right)\left(\frac{1}{5} + \frac{1}{5}\right)}}$$

$$= 0.20 \text{ with } 5 + 5 - 2df$$

As we have equal N's we could also use Formula 11.11b, or:

$$t = \frac{31.40 - 28.40}{\sqrt{\frac{3155.2 + 981.2}{5(5 - 1)}}}$$

$$= 0.20$$

The tabled t value for 8 degrees of freedom at the 0.05 level is 2.306. Any obtained t that is equal to or greater than this value would fall within the region of rejection. Therefore, our obtained t of 0.20 is well within the region of acceptance and we must conclude that there is no significant difference between the two means and that the treatment conditions had no effect upon the behavior.

The t-test for Two Independent Samples with Heterogeneous Variances.

Function and Method.   Let us suppose that a significant value of F has been obtained and the experimenter concludes that the variances are not equal, or that they are heterogeneous. In general, the primary research interest is in the difference between the two means, and not in the variances. However, one of the major assumptions of the t is that of equal variances between the two groups. Snedecor and others have suggested several approximations for testing the hypothesis of differences between means when the variances are not equal.

The Unequal N Case.   If our research hypothesis is non-directional, $H_1 : \mu_1 \neq \mu_2$, and if the two variances are found to be not equal, $\sigma_1^2 \neq \sigma_2^2$, and if the number of cases in the two groups differ, $N_1 \neq N_2$, then instead of pooling the sums of squares and the degrees of freedom as we did in Formula 11.11, we compute the variances of each mean separately and utilize Formula 11.6 for the standard error of the difference between the two means. The computational formula for t thus becomes:

$$t = \frac{\overline{X}_1 - \overline{X}_2}{\sqrt{\dfrac{S_1^2}{N_1} + \dfrac{S_2^2}{N_2}}} \qquad (11.14)$$

In order to determine whether the obtained t is significant at some predetermined value of alpha we may use an approximation of the sampling distribution. This approximation must be determined as we have not been able to pool sums of squares and the degrees of freedom. An approximation is given by Cochran and Cox as:

$$t_{\text{alpha}} = \frac{(S_{\overline{x}_1}^2)(t_1) + (S_{\overline{x}_2}^2)(t_2)}{S_{\overline{x}_1}^2 + S_{\overline{x}_2}^2} \qquad (11.15)$$

where t_1 = sampling distribution value for
the stated alpha with N_1-1 *df*
for a two-tailed test

t_2 = sampling distribution value for
the stated alpha with N_2-1 *df*
for a two-tailed test

$$S^2_{\bar{x}_1} = \frac{S^2_1}{N_1}$$

and $$S^2_{\bar{x}_2} = \frac{S^2_2}{N_2}$$

Now if the obtained value of t, as found by using Formula 11.14, is greater than the t approximation value from Formula 11.15, then the obtained t would fall in the region of rejection and the null hypothesis would be rejected in favor of the research hypothesis. If, on the other hand, the obtained t value is less than the t approximation, it would fall in the region of acceptance and the null hypothesis would be accepted.

It should be pointed out, that if both the t-and the F-tests give significant differences, the evidence would point to the inter-pretation that both variances and means differ significantly. If the two samples were drawn from two populations, the researcher must conclude that the populations differ in both respects. Or, if we were concerned with the treatment and control group differences, the treatment effect had a differential effect as seen by the differences between the variances, as well as by the differ-ences between the mean values.

The conclusions, however, are made only for a nondirectional hypothesis for there is little reason to believe that we would be in error. If on the other hand, we had a directional hypothesis, a significant difference in variances may lead us to commit Type II errors. Therefore, when the research hypothesis is directional it is suggested that some other statistical technique, such as U-test, is warranted. As we may recall, the U-test makes no assumptions in regard to the shape of the distributions.

Example.   Let us suppose that we have latency measures for two groups of animals. One group of 10 animals had a history of a simple visual environment and the second group of 20 animals, a history of a complex visual environment. The task was simply a visual discrimination one, and we shall concern ourselves only with the total latencies in seconds for ten discrimination trials. We shall assume a non-directional research hypothesis and shall set alpha at the 0.05 level. The data are given in Table 11.2:

Table 11.2.

Simple Visual Group   Complex Visual Group

$\bar{X}_1 = 22.3$ $\bar{X}_2 = 13.2$

$S_1^2 = 29.82$ $S_2^2 = 5.42$

$N_1 = 10$ $N_2 = 20$

Testing for the homogeneity of variance between the two groups, we have:

$$F\text{-test} = 29.82/5.42$$

$$= 5.502 \text{ with 9 and 19 } df$$

The sampling distribution of F with 9 and 19 df at the 0.05 level is 2.43. Because the obtained value exceeds the critical value, we must reject the assumption of homogeneity of variance and we must then conclude that the variances differ significantly.

Now utilizing Formula 11.14 to test for the significant difference between means, we have:

$$t = \frac{22.2 - 13.2}{\sqrt{\frac{29.82}{10} + \frac{5.42}{20}}}$$

$$= 4.989$$

This obtained t value is now evaluated by the approximation of the sampling distribution as given by Formula 11.15:

$$t_{.05} = \frac{\left(\frac{29.82}{10}\right)(2.262) + \left(\frac{5.42}{20}\right)(2.0930)}{\left(\frac{29.82}{10}\right) + \left(\frac{5.42}{20}\right)}$$

$$t_{.05} = \frac{7.312}{3.253}$$

$$= 2.248$$

As the obtained t of 4.989 is greater than the approximation of the theoretical or critical value of 2.248, we would conclude that the treatment conditions affected the means as well as the variances.

The Equal N Case. If our research hypothesis, again, is non-directional, $H_1 : \mu_1 \neq \mu_2$, and we find heterogeneity of variances, $\sigma_1^2 \neq \sigma_2^2$, but the N's are equal, $N_1 = N_2$, then we have two alternative approaches available to us. The standard error of the difference between the two means may be based upon Formula 11.10, where the sum of squares and degrees of freedom are pooled, or it may be based upon Formula 11.8. With exactly equal N's these two formulas are algebraically identical. The value of t which would be regarded as significant as obtained by the Cochran and Cox approximation, will under this condition be the tabled value of the t sampling distribution for N-1 df or $1/2(N_1 + N_2 - 2)$. If the obtained $t >$ the tabled value of N-1, the null hypothesis would be rejected and if the obtained $t <$ the tabled value, the null hypothesis would be accepted.

Some Comments on Heterogeneity of Variances. There are basically three sources that may give rise to the heterogeneity of variance. One source is that which rises solely as a function of random sampling. We would anticipate some heterogenity of variances based upon the level of alpha that we use, hence, for example, 5 out of 100 significant F-tests would occur solely as a function of chance.

A second source is the assignment of subjects. In general, when we randomly assign subjects to the various groups, we attempt to insure that the individual differences that may affect the treatment conditions are not systematically assigned to any one group. However, if we are interested in significant differences between the well-defined populations, randomization is impossible. Therefore, if the population variances differ, this factor may give rise to a significant F value.

A third major source may be the function of the treatment condition. Each X_i score, in a distribution of scores measured on the interval level, can be theoretically thought of as a function of two or more parts. One part is a constant, for example the mean of a distribution. A second part is the individual difference or the variability of the score value from its respective mean. Therefore:

$$X_i = \mu_i \pm \epsilon_i$$

where X_i = individual score
μ_i = a population mean
ϵ_i = individual difference

When we add a constant as a function of a single treatment condition then:

$$X_i = (\mu_i \pm \epsilon_i) + T_j$$

where T_j = additive constant effect from

the jth treatment condition

It is generally assumed that the treatment condition functions as an additive constant for the experimental groups. When one adds (or subtracts) a constant to (or from) each X score within the distribution, the addition has its effect only upon the mean of that distribution and *not* upon the variance, the within group variability. However, if, for example, the treatment condition functions as a multiplicative constant, then both the mean and the variance would be influenced and hence, would give rise to heterogeneity of variances. Therefore, when we have heterogeneity any one of the three possibilities is open to question.

Two Related Sample Cases

The *t*-test for Two Related Groups.

Function and Method.   The t-test is also a suitable statistical method when the two groups are related. This may be by matching or by having each subject act as his own control. It is assumed again, that the data are interval in nature and the variances between the two groups are homogeneous. If we cannot meet this latter assumption the Wilcoxon test can be used. The null hypothesis of no difference between the two related means can be tested by Formula 11.5:

$$t = \frac{\overline{X}_1 - \overline{X}_2}{S_{\overline{x}_1 - \overline{x}_2}}$$

where $S_{\bar{x}_1 - \bar{x}_2} = \sqrt{S^2_{\bar{x}_1} + S^2_{\bar{x}_2} - 2r_{x_1 x_2} S_{\bar{x}_1} S_{\bar{x}_2}}$ (11.16)

r = correlation coefficient between
the pairs of observations

The obtained t value is evaluated as before from the sampling distribution of t. However, the degrees of freedom that are available are equal to $N - 1$, where N is the number of pairs of observations. When we have related groups we lose one-half the total degrees of freedom when compared to the random groups design. However, this loss of degrees of freedom can be overcome by the subtractive term of $2r_{x_1 x_2} S_{\bar{x}_1} S_{\bar{x}_2}$. Now if the correlation coefficient of $r_{x_1 x_2}$ were zero then the standard error of the difference between the two means would be equal to the same term if we did not have related groups. On the other hand, if the correlation was negative the term would be increased. Thus, for an efficient use of the matching design, the correlation must be positive and large enough to overcome the loss of the degrees of freedom. The related group design can be a very valuable one when the correlation is high and positive, as it substantially reduces the standard error of the difference between the two means. For a fuller treatment of correlation, see Chapters 12, 13, and 14.

The standard error of the difference between two related means can be determined by the difference magnitude (D) between each related pair rather than from the correlational method. Or:

$$S_{\bar{x}_1 - \bar{x}_2} = \frac{S_d}{\sqrt{N}}$$ (11.17)

where $S_d = \sqrt{\dfrac{\Sigma d^2}{N - 1}}$

and where $\Sigma d^2 = \Sigma D^2 - \dfrac{(\Sigma D)^2}{N}$

where $D = X_1 - X_2$ = difference between a related pair

Formula 11.17 can be reduced to:

(11.18)

$$S_{\bar{x}_1 - \bar{x}_2} = \sqrt{\frac{\Sigma d^2}{N(N - 1)}}$$

$$\text{or} \quad = \sqrt{\frac{\Sigma D^2 - \frac{(\Sigma D)^2}{N}}{N(N-1)}}$$

Thus, a computational formula for t when we have two related groups becomes:

$$t = \frac{\overline{X}_1 - \overline{X}_2}{\sqrt{\frac{\Sigma D^2 - \frac{(\Sigma D)^2}{N}}{N(N-1)}}} \tag{11.19}$$

with $df = N - 1$ where N is the number of pairs

Example.   It has been theorized that a reinforcing stimulus in addition to increasing the probability of an operant response, also activates the organism. Twenty experimental chicks were reinforced by a 3-second light onset in performing an operant and 20 yoked control birds received the same stimulus consequence except that the presentation of the stimulus was not contingent upon their behavior. We shall here assume that the rate of response, number of responses, is interval data. The null hypothesis is that there is no significant difference between means for the experimental and yoked control animals and the research hypothesis is that the mean rate shall be significantly greater at the 0.05 level than the mean for the yoked controls. The theory suggests that there is a positive correlation between the two groups. The data are given in Table 11.3.

From Formula 11.18 we have:

$$\Sigma d^2 = 822{,}029 - \frac{(3277)^2}{20}$$
$$= 285{,}092.55$$
$$S_{\overline{x}_1 - \overline{x}_2} = \sqrt{\frac{285{,}092.55}{20(19)}}$$
$$= 27.39$$

And from Formula 11.19:

$$t = \frac{331.20 - 167.35}{27.39}$$
$$t = 5.982 \text{ with } 19 \text{ } df$$

Table 11.3

Exp. Gr.	Yoked Control Gr.	D	D^2
648	360	288	82944
226	54	172	29584
515	128	387	149769
676	220	456	207936
404	222	182	33124
402	152	250	62500
206	90	116	13456
338	216	122	14884
49	39	10	100
194	57	137	18769
105	74	31	961
477	210	267	71289
417	243	174	30276
348	247	101	10201
189	202	-13	169
149	0	149	22201
131	126	5	25
336	203	133	17689
452	361	91	8281
362	143	219	47961

$\Sigma X_1 = 6624$ $\Sigma X_2 = 3347$ $\Sigma D = 3277$ $\Sigma D^2 = 822029$

$\Sigma x_1^2 = 577,723$ $\Sigma x_2^2 = 187,387$

$r = 0.729$

If we had treated the experimental and the yoked control groups as two independent groups, the obtained t would be equal to 3.649 and with 38 degrees of freedom, the probability associated with the obtained t value would be less than the 0.0005 level. With 19 degrees of freedom the obtained t of 5.982 with the two related samples is even more highly significant.

From the data, we must conclude that light as a sensory reinforcer is highly effective, as the two means differ significantly beyond the stated 0.05 alpha level. In addition, there is a positive correlation between the two measures which more than offsets the loss of degrees of freedom related to the matching procedure.

The Analysis of Variance for K Independent Random Groups.

Function and Method.   In the prior sections on the t-test, it was suggested that our research interest is with the mean difference between the experimental and the control groups. As science advances, research comes to be centered on the generalization of a phenomenon at more than two points along the research variable continuum; therefore, we may have a number of treatment conditions. The analysis of variance is a procedure to test the significant differences between K random means simultaneously.

In general, the null hypothesis is stated as:

$$H_0 : \mu_1 = \mu_2 = \mu_3 = \cdots = \mu_K$$

This null hypothesis states that three or more population means are equal. As with the t distribution, it is assumed that our K random samples are from normally distributed populations and that the population variances are equal:

$$\sigma_1^2 = \sigma_2^2 = \sigma_3^2 = \cdots = \sigma_K^2$$

On the other hand, the research or alternate hypothesis is given as:

$$H_1 : \mu_1 \neq \mu_2 \text{ and/or} \neq \mu_3 \text{ and/or} \neq \ldots \text{ and/or } \mu_K$$

and in the general case:

$$H_1 : \mu_i \neq \mu_{K-1}$$

The alternate hypothesis simply states that at least two population means are not equal. Therefore, we have a two-tailed test.

The F statistic enables us to evaluate our hypothesis. This statistic is based upon a ratio of two independent estimates of the population variance, hence the name, the analysis of variance. The general rationale for the analysis of variance is that the total variance can be logically divided into meaningful parts, each with an independent and specific source of variance. With the K independent sample design, the total variance can be divided into two independent sources. The first source of variance is between the K group means from the total mean and is the variance or mean square between groups. This estimate of variance is simply the variability among our K group means around a total mean. If the null hypothesis were true then the differences observed among the K means could be simply a function of sampling variability. On the other hand, if the null hypothesis were false at least one mean will differ from the others. The second independent source of variance is the variability of scores about their own individual group means. If we can meet the assumption that the independent population variances are equal, the individual group variances can be pooled to give us an estimate of the population variance. This second source is the variance or mean square within groups. The within variance is a function of the population variability, and it is analogous to the standard error for the t.

The null hypothesis for K independent random groups is tested by the F ratio between the two sources of the variance.

$$F = \frac{\Sigma x^2 \text{ between groups}/K - 1df}{\Sigma x^2 \text{ within groups}/K(n_i - 1)\, df} \qquad (11.20)$$

$$\text{or} \quad F = \frac{\text{mean square between groups}}{\text{mean square within groups}} \qquad (11.21)$$

The mean square between groups is the sum of squares associated with the between groups divided by $K - 1$ degrees of freedom and similarly, the mean square within groups is the sum of squares within groups divided by $K(n_i - 1)$ degrees of freedom. For the F ratio the mean square between groups is always the numerator and the mean square within groups is always the denominator irrespective of the obtained F values.

Alternative forms can be stated for both the null and alternative hypotheses. The null hypothesis is given as:

H_0 : mean square between groups = mean square within groups

and the alternative hypothesis as:

H_1 : mean square between groups > mean square within groups

The null is always evaluated from the F distribution with $K - 1$ and $K(n_i - 1)$ degrees of freedom.

In the case where the null hypothesis is true, and in the special case where all the means for the K groups are equal, $\overline{X}_1 = \overline{X}_2 = \overline{X}_3 \ldots = \overline{X}_K$, then the sum of squares between groups will be zero and the sum of squares within groups will be equal to the total sum of squares. However, as the K mean values differ, then the sum of squares between the K groups takes a specified value. As the differences between the K means increase in a marked way, the sum of squares between groups will be larger than the sum of squares within groups, and the value of F will increase. A significant F is interpreted as evidence that the K means are not equal and the null hypothesis is rejected in favor of the research hypothesis. However, if the null hypothesis is true, then the differences between the K means is assumed to be the result of random sampling.

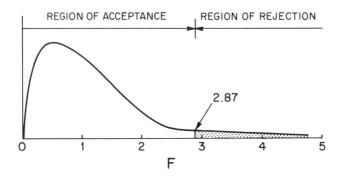

Figure 11.3. Theoretical sampling distribution of F for 4 and 20 degrees of freedom with a critical F value for alpha at 0.05.

The sampling distribution for the analysis of variance is given in Table N for various $K - 1$ and $K(n_i - 1)$ degrees of freedom. Figure 11.3 is illustrative of the F sampling distribution. In this case we have 4 and 20 degrees of freedom. The curves of the various sampling distributions are of different forms for each F distribution with $K - 1$ and $K(n_i - 1)$ degrees of freedom. The large F values occur in the right side of the F sampling distribution. From Table N with 4 and 20 degrees of freedom and alpha = 0.05, the critical value of F is 2.87. Any obtained F value with 4 and 20 degrees of freedom that is equal to or greater than 2.87 will fall within the region of rejection and similarly, any obtained F value with 4 and 20 degrees of freedom that is less than 2.87 will fall within the region of acceptance of the null hypothesis. The F distribution is a function of two parameters, the degrees of freedom associated with the numerator and also the denominator of the F ratio. The F can be defined as a ratio of two independent chi-squares with each chi-square divided by its appropriate degrees of freedom:

$$F = \frac{\chi_1^2 / df}{\chi_2^2 / df} \qquad (11.22)$$

As we can see from Figure 11.3, the F distribution is not symmetrical. However, it approaches the normal curve for large degrees of freedom associated with both variances. In addition, it can be seen that the F distribution ranges from zero to positive values. This is because of the ratio of two independent chi-squares over the appropriate degrees of freedom; therefore, negative F values are not possible.

The general definitional formula for partitioning the total sum of squares into the within and the between groups sum of squares is:

$$\sum_{1}^{N} (X - \bar{\bar{X}})^2 = \sum_{1}^{K} \left[\sum_{1}^{n_i} (X - \bar{X}_i)^2 \right] + \sum_{1}^{K} \left[n_i (\bar{X}_i - \bar{\bar{X}})^2 \right] \quad (11.23)$$

Total sum of squares = Within sum of squares + Between sum of squares,

where $\bar{\bar{X}}$ = mean for the total scores
$\bar{X}_i$ = mean of the ith group
N = total number of scores
n_i = number of scores in the ith group
K = number of groups or columns

From this definitional formula, we can determine a general computational formula for the analysis of variance given in Formula 11.23. Considering first the total sum of squares:

$$\text{Total sum of squares} = \sum_{1}^{N} (X - \bar{\bar{X}})^2$$

$$\text{or computationally,} = \sum_{1}^{N} X^2 - \frac{(\sum_{1}^{N} X)^2}{N} \quad (11.24)$$

Here we simply treat the data from all K groups as one set. The N over the Σ says to sum over all N observations. Computationally, we sum the values, square each value, and sum the squared scores over all N cases.

Determining the sum of squares within groups, we have:

$$\text{Within sum of squares} = \sum_{1}^{K} \left[\sum_{1}^{n_i} (X - \bar{X}_i)^2 \right]$$

$$\text{or computationally,} = \sum_{1}^{K} \left[\sum_{1}^{n_i} X^2 - \frac{(\sum_{1}^{n_i} X)^2}{n_i} \right] \quad (11.25)$$

To find the within sum of squares, we consider each ith group separately, or:

$$\sum_{1}^{n_i} (X - \bar{X}_i)^2 = \sum_{1}^{n_i} X^2 - \frac{(\sum_{1}^{n_i} X)^2}{n_i}$$

The n_i is the size of the sample of the specified group. The sample sizes are not necessarily the same. If we have unequal N's, those samples with larger size are weighted and therefore count more in the determination of the within sum of squares. From Formula 11.25, we obtain the sum of squared deviations from the mean (X_i) for each ith group, and we then sum over the K groups, $\sum_{1}^{K}$, the sum of squares of the independent groups.

For the between sum of squares, the definitional formula can be used, or:

$$\text{Between sum of squares} = \sum_{1}^{K} \left[n_i(\bar{X}_i - \bar{X})^2 \right]$$

Again the n_i is the size of a given group. The squared deviation of a given sample mean and the total mean is based upon the sample size of that group, and is, therefore, weighed by the number of subjects in the sample, n_i. If the sample size varies over groups, the samples that are larger are thus weighed more in the determination of the between sum of squares. We then sum over the K groups. However, the sum of squares between groups can be obtained by another procedure which does not involve the utilization of the various means but rather the sums:

$$\text{Between sum of squares} = \sum_{1}^{K} \frac{\left(\sum_{1}^{n_i} X\right)^2}{n_i} - \frac{\left(\sum_{1}^{N} X\right)^2}{N} \qquad (11.26)$$

In summary, the computational formula for partitioning the sum of squares is:

$$\sum_{1}^{N} X^2 - \frac{(\sum_{1}^{N} X)^2}{N} = \sum_{1}^{K} \left[\sum_{1}^{n_i} X^2 - \frac{(\sum_{1}^{n_i} X)^2}{n_i} \right] + \sum_{1}^{K} \left[\frac{\left(\sum_{1}^{n_i} X\right)^2}{n_i} - \frac{\left(\sum_{1}^{N} X\right)^2}{N} \right]$$

Total sum of squares = Within sum of squares + Between sum of squares

Associated with this partition of the sum of squares is the partition of the degrees of freedom. The total degrees of freedom in the K independent random group design is $N - 1$, where N is the total number of observations. The total degrees of freedom are similarly partitioned. For the degrees of freedom associated within groups, each ith group has $(n_i - 1)$ degrees of freedom available and over all K groups there are $K(n_i - 1)$ degrees of freedom. The number of degrees of freedom for the between groups is $K - 1$. Therefore:

$$\text{total } df = \text{within } df + \text{between } df$$

$$N - 1 = K(n_i - 1) + (K - 1)$$

In order to make an unbiased estimate of the population variance (the mean square, M.S.) for the numerator of the F ratios we have:

$$\text{Mean square between groups} = \frac{\sum\limits_{1}^{K} \dfrac{\left(\sum\limits_{1}^{n_i} X\right)^2}{n_i} - \dfrac{\left(\sum\limits_{1}^{N} X\right)^2}{N}}{K - 1}$$

Our second estimate of the population for the denominator is:

$$\text{Mean square within groups} = \frac{\sum\limits_{1}^{K}\left[\sum\limits_{1}^{n_i} X^2 - \dfrac{\left(\sum\limits_{1}^{n_i} X\right)^2}{n_i}\right]}{K(n_i - 1)}$$

and the computational formula for the F ratio in 11.20 becomes:

$$F = \frac{\left[\sum\limits_{1}^{K} \dfrac{\left(\sum\limits_{1}^{n_i} X\right)^2}{n_i} - \dfrac{\left(\sum\limits_{1}^{N} X\right)^2}{N}\right] / (K - 1)}{\sum\limits_{1}^{K}\left[\sum\limits_{1}^{n_i} X^2 - \dfrac{\left(\sum\limits_{1}^{n_i} X\right)^2}{n_i}\right] / K(n_i - 1)} \qquad (11.27)$$

Example. A study was carried out to determine the behavioral effects of various exposures to an electric shock upon acquisition of one-way avoidance conditioning. Group 1 was given

30 unavoidable shocks of a three-second duration each on the "start" side of a "Miller" box. A second group was given 30 unavoidable shocks on the "stop" side and Group III was given no shock. The avoidance training consisted of running from the start side to the stop side. A delayed conditioning procedure was used with a 10-second *CS-US* interval. If the rat responded by running from the start side to the stop side during the 10-second interval, the *CS* (a tone) was terminated and the *US* (an electric shock) was avoided. In Table 11.4 are the results of the latency of the first avoidance response measured in seconds.

Table 11.4

Group I	Group II	Group III
.7	.5	9.0
1.2	3.7	1.5
9.8	5.7	3.9
8.2	2.6	.4
4.5	9.5	4.8
2.6	4.3	1.2
5.9	2.1	3.1
4.2	6.8	1.3
3.8	1.6	.8
4.3	7.6	.5

$$\Sigma X_1 = 45.2 \qquad \Sigma X_2 = 44.4 \qquad \Sigma X_3 = 26.5 \qquad \sum_{1}^{K} \sum_{1}^{n_i} X = 116.1$$

$$\Sigma X_1^2 = 227.60 \quad \Sigma X_2^2 = 272.90 \quad \Sigma X_3^2 = 135.29 \quad \sum_{1}^{K} \sum_{1}^{n_i} X^2 = 635.79$$

The total sums of squares from Formula 11.24 for the 30 scores is:

$$\sum_{1}^{N} x^2 = (.7)^2 + (1.2)^2 + (9.8)^2 + \ldots + (.5)^2 - \frac{(116.1)^2}{30}$$

$$= 635.79 - \frac{(116.1)^2}{30}$$

$$= 186.48$$

For the within sums of squares, we shall consider the sums of squares for each group separately and then from Formula 11.25, sum over the three groups:

$$\Sigma x_1^2 = (.7)^2 + (1.2)^2 + (9.8)^2 + \ldots + (4.3)^2 - \frac{(45.2)^2}{10}$$

$$= 227.60 - \frac{(45.2)^2}{10}$$

$$= 23.30$$

$$\Sigma x_2^2 = (.5)^2 + (3.7)^2 + (5.7)^2 + \ldots + (7.6)^2 - \frac{(44.4)^2}{10}$$

$$= 272.90 - \frac{(44.4)^2}{10}$$

$$= 75.76$$

$$\Sigma x_3^2 = (9.0)^2 + (1.5)^2 + (3.9)^2 + \ldots + (0.5)^2 - \frac{(26.5)^2}{10}$$

$$= 135.29 - \frac{(26.5)^2}{10}$$

$$= 65.06$$

$$\sum_1^K \sum_1^{n_i} x_i^2 = 23.30 + 75.76 + 65.06$$

$$\Sigma x_{within}^2 = 164.12$$

The sum of squares between groups as given in Formula 11.26 becomes:

$$\frac{(45.2)^2}{10} + \frac{(44.4)^2}{10} + \frac{(26.5)^2}{10} - \frac{(116.1)^2}{30}$$

$$\text{or } \Sigma x_{between}^2 \quad = 204.30 + 197.14 + 70.23 - 449.31$$

$$= 22.36$$

In Table 11.5 we have the analysis of variance for the three random groups with their independent source of variation, their associated sum of squares and degrees of freedom, and the mean squares and the F ratio (Formula 11.27).

Table 11.5

Source of Variation	Σx^2	df	M.S.	F
Between Groups	22.36	2	11.18	1.806
Within Groups	164.12	27	6.19	
Total	186.48	29		

From the sampling distribution given in Table N for 2 and 27 degrees of freedom, we have 3.35 as the critical value at the 0.05 level of significance. As our obtained F value of 1.806 is less than tabled or 3.35, we must conclude that there are no significant differences among the three treatment conditions.

Analysis between the K Groups: Multiple Comparison Procedures.

When we obtain a significant F value, we know that at least two of the means of our treatment groups are significantly different. However, the analysis of variance does not describe where the difference is, only that there is a difference. It is of fundamental importance, therefore, that we perform subsequent analyses in order to determine where the significant differences between means are present. For example, in Figure 11.4, the means of groups one and two may not be statistically different, but they both may differ statistically from the third mean. It is this general type of statistical question that we would need to answer. The primary function of the procedures of multiple comparisons is, then, to determine which pairs of means differ significantly and are responsible for the rejection of the null hypothesis of no difference in the analysis of variance.

At present there are several available procedures for multiple comparisons. These are described and compared in many of the advanced statistical design texts (eg., Edwards, 1960; Hopkins and Chadbourn, 1967; Winer, 1971). However, it must be pointed out that there is not complete agreement regarding the most useful procedures for making multiple comparisons. The various procedures have different criteria that are utilized for the rejection of the null hypothesis at various alpha levels.

Multiple comparison procedures have been designed to make certain a priori comparisons before the data analysis *or* they are a posteriori comparisons, designed to be used after the rejection of the null hypothesis in the analysis of variance. In the a priori comparisons, during the design phase, the researcher will state that he is interested in making only certain comparisons which he believes to be critical to his research problem. Logically, these a priori comparisons can be made even though the treatment mean square from the analysis of variance is not significant. On the other hand, the a posteriori comparisons are made only after the rejection of the null hypothesis and the research interest is to determine which comparison or comparisons of means differ significantly.

For the purpose of introducing multiple comparisons, we will describe three procedures that are commonly used for a priori and a posteriori comparisons.

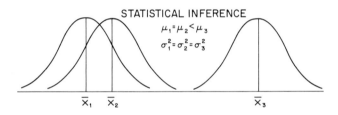

Figure 11.4.   Schematic of a statistical inferences from multiple comparisons.

Multiple *t*-Tests.   The multiple *t*-tests can be used as an appropriate procedure for making multiple a priori comparisons. The *t*-test was originally designed for determining the significance of the difference between two random samples as stated in the hypotheses. If the researcher follows the same logic in stating which independent group comparisons he plans to make before the analysis of the data, he may not violate the statistical methodology. However, the utilization of the multiple *t*-tests always increases the probability of a Type I error. On the other hand, if the multiple *t*-tests are made a posteriori, the use of multiple *t*-tests are invalid from probability theory. For example, if we chose (after the fact) to compare the largest and the smallest of all the obtained means, we have not taken into account the number of means. It is, therefore, probable that we will find a "significant difference" a larger proportion of the time than that specified by alpha. Thus, if that is the case, we are committing a Type I error.

Assuming we have multiple a priori comparisons to be determined from a hypothesis, we can compute a general critical difference with Formula 11.28:

$$\text{critical difference} = (t_{\text{alpha}}) \left(\sqrt{\frac{2 \ M.S. \ \text{within}}{N}} \right) \qquad (11.28)$$

where t_{alpha} = tabled t value (Table M) for a given alpha
with the $M.S.$ within degrees of freedom

$M.S.$ within = mean square within groups

and $\bar{N} = \dfrac{(\text{number of groups})}{\dfrac{1}{n_1} + \dfrac{1}{n_2} + \dfrac{1}{n_3} + \ldots + \dfrac{1}{n_k}}$

The $\bar{N}$ in Formula 11.28, however, is not unbiased in respect to any two particular groups with different sample sizes.

The obtained critical difference value is used for testing all of the a priori hypotheses. When the difference between the two means is larger than the obtained critical difference value, then the difference between the means would be statistically significant and we would reject the a priori null hypothesis in favor of the research hypothesis.

Example. From the previous example of the analysis of variance, assume that the researcher was, during the design of the study, interested in the difference between Group 1 and Group 3 (two-tailed test). The summary of the analysis of variance is repeated below.

Source of variation	Σx^2	df	$M.S.$	F
Between groups	22.36	2	11.18	1.806
Within groups	164.12	27	6.19	

Even though the F was not significant, we could test our a priori hypothesis. The means of the three groups are:

$$\bar{X}_1 = 4.52$$
$$\bar{X}_2 = 4.44$$
$$\bar{X}_3 = 2.65$$

From Formula 11.28 with alpha at the 0.05 level and 27 df, we have:

$$\text{critical difference} = [2.052] \left[\sqrt{\frac{(2)(6.19)}{3/\left(\frac{1}{10} + \frac{1}{10} + \frac{1}{10}\right)}} \right]$$

$$= 2.283$$

The difference between $\overline{X}_1$ and $\overline{X}_2$ is:

$$4.52 - 2.65 = 1.87$$

As the critical difference is greater than the obtained difference between the two means, we would conclude that the two means were not significantly different.

The Studentized Range Test. The studentized range statistic has been designed to be used after the null hypothesis has been rejected. As an a posteriori model it allows us to make multiple comparisons of each obtained mean with every other obtained mean. As a procedure of multiple comparisons, this statistic is theoretically a more stringent test than the multiple t. That is, in using this statistic, we will make fewer Type I errors.

The Neuman-Keuls test $(N - K)$ is one of several studentized ranges tests, and it is defined by:

$$N - K = \frac{\overline{X}_{max} - \overline{X}_{min}}{\sqrt{M.S. \text{ error}/N}} \tag{11.29}$$

where $\overline{X}_{max}$ = largest sample mean
$\overline{X}_{min}$ = smallest sample mean
N = number of cases that each mean is based upon
$M.S.$ error = error variance

The error variance for the K independent sample case would be the mean square within groups, hence:

$$N - K = \frac{\overline{X}_{max} - \overline{X}_{min}}{\sqrt{M.S. \text{ within}/N}}$$

where $M.S.$ within = within group variance for all K groups

The sampling distribution of the studentized range is approximated by the number of steps between the ordered means and the degrees of freedom that are associated for the mean square within groups. The obtained K means are ranked or ordered and the parameter of r is the number of steps between these ordered means. For example, if we had five ordered means of $\overline{A}, \overline{B}, \overline{C}, \overline{D}, \overline{E}$, then the r between $\overline{A}$ and $\overline{B}$ would be two, between $\overline{A}$ and $\overline{C}$ is three, $\overline{A}$ and $\overline{D}$ four, $\overline{A}$ and $\overline{E}$ five, $\overline{B}$ and $\overline{C}$ two, and so forth. The critical values for the studentized range are given in Table O for various values of r and degrees of freedom with alpha that is equal to 0.05 and 0.01. If the obtained value of $(N - K)$ exceeds the tabled value, the null hypothesis of equal means would be rejected.

Example. The means for the three groups in the previous example have been rank ordered, or:

$$(\text{Gr. 1}) \; 4.52, (\text{Gr. 2}) \; 4.44, (\text{Gr. 3}) \; 2.65$$

We can make all possible comparisons using Formula 11.29, or:

$$\text{Gr. 1 and 2} \quad N - K = \frac{4.52 - 4.44}{\sqrt{6.19/10}}$$

$$= <1$$

With $r = 2$ and $df = 27$, the critical value is 2.90.

$$\text{Gr. 1 and 3} \quad N - K = \frac{4.52 - 2.65}{\sqrt{6.19/10}}$$

$$= 2.37$$

With $r = 3$ and $df = 27$, the critical value is 3.51.

$$\text{Gr. 2 and 3} \quad N - K = \frac{44.4 - 2.65}{\sqrt{6.19/10}}$$

$$= 2.27$$

With $r = 2$ and $df = 27$, as before the critical value is 2.90, and with $r = 3$ and $df = 27$ the critical value is 3.51. As all the values are less than the tabled critical values, we conclude that there are no significant differences among the various combinations of the three mean values.

Scheffé's Test for Multiple Comparisons. Once the null hypothesis in the analysis of variance has been rejected at a given alpha level of significance, we can make any and all subsequent comparisons between two means or combinations of means that may be of interest to us by using Scheffé's procedure. The Scheffé test is one of the most useful methods for multiple comparisons. Of all the procedures for subsequent comparisons, this test has the most rigorous criterion in regard to the Type I errors. For any comparison that we make, the probability of making a Type I error (rejecting the null hypothesis when it is true) will not be greater than the stated alpha level. The application of the Scheffé results in relatively few significant differences and as such it is the most conservative of the various techniques. This test is easy to apply to all situations in that it uses the data from F.

The general formula for Scheffé's test for multiple comparisons is:

$$F = \frac{C_1 \overline{X}_1 + C_2 \overline{X}_2 + \ldots + C_K \overline{X}_K}{\sqrt{M.S. \text{ within } \left(\frac{C_1^2}{n_1} + \frac{C_2^2}{n_2} + \ldots + \frac{C_K^2}{n_K} \right)}} \qquad (11.30)$$

where $\overline{X}_1$ = mean of group one

$\overline{X}_K$ = mean of the Kth group

$M.S.$ within = the appropriate error term

C = positive and negative numbers that sum to zero

n_1 = number of cases in group one

n_k = number of cases in the Kth group

The C's are constants which are related to the various comparisons that are made. This relationship for a $K = 3$ case can be shown as in Table 11.6.

To evaluate the obtained F value in Formula 11.30, we compare the obtained F to F', where F' is:

$$F' = \sqrt{(K - 1) F_{(t)}} \qquad (11.31)$$

where F' = standard to which the obtained
F values are evaluated

K = number of groups

$F_{(t)}$ = theoretical tabled value of F
for a specified alpha level with
$(K - 1)$ and $K(n_i - 1)$ degrees of
freedom

For any difference to be statistically significant, the obtained F
from 11.30 must be larger than or equal to F' as given in Formula
11.31.

Table 11.6.

Values of C

Comparisons	C_1	C_2	C_3	Σ
$\bar{X}_1 - \bar{X}_2$	1	-1	0	0
$\bar{X}_1 - \bar{X}_3$	1	0	-1	0
$\bar{X}_2 - \bar{X}_3$	0	1	-1	0
$\bar{X}_1 - \left(\dfrac{\bar{X}_2 + \bar{X}_3}{2}\right)$	1	$-1/2$	$-1/2$	0
$\bar{X}_2 - \left(\dfrac{\bar{X}_1 + \bar{X}_3}{2}\right)$	$-1/2$	1	$-1/2$	0
$\bar{X}_3 - \left(\dfrac{\bar{X}_1 + \bar{X}_2}{2}\right)$	$-1/2$	$-1/2$	1	0

Example.   From a four independent group experiment, the
data appear below.

$$\bar{X}_1 = 13.8 \qquad \mu_1 = 20$$

$$\bar{X}_2 = 10.3 \qquad \mu_2 = 10$$

$$\bar{X}_3 = 9.8 \qquad \mu_3 = 10$$

$$\bar{X}_4 = 6.7 \qquad \mu_4 = 20$$

$$M.S. \text{ within} = 7.7$$

In the analysis of these data, a significant F value was obtained at less than the 0.05 level. With an obtained significant F, the Scheffé test could be used to determine which groups or combination of groups contributed to the significant F value. For illustrative purposes, however, we will make only two comparisons.

Comparisons	C_1	C_2	C_3	C_4
$\bar{X}_1 - \bar{X}_4$	1	0	0	-1
$\bar{X}_1 - \left(\dfrac{\bar{X}_2 + \bar{X}_3}{2}\right)$	1	-1/2	-1/2	0

For $\bar{X}_1 - \bar{X}_4$:

$$F = \frac{(1)\ 13.8 + (0)\ 10.3 + (0)\ 9.8 + (-1)\ 6.7}{\sqrt{7.7 \left[\dfrac{(1)^2}{20} + \dfrac{(0)^2}{10} + \dfrac{(0)^2}{10} + \dfrac{(-1)^2}{20}\right]}}$$

$$= \frac{13.8 - 6.7}{\sqrt{7.7 \left(\dfrac{2}{20}\right)}}$$

$$= 8.11$$

For $\bar{X}_1 - \left(\dfrac{\bar{X}_2 + \bar{X}_3}{2}\right)$:

$$F = \frac{(1)13.8 + (-1/2)10.3 + (-1/2)9.8 + (0)6.7}{\sqrt{7.7 \left[\dfrac{(1)^2}{20} + \dfrac{(-1/2)^2}{10} + \dfrac{(-1/2)^2}{10} + \dfrac{(0)^2}{20}\right]}}$$

$$= \frac{13.8 - 10.05}{\sqrt{7.7 \left(\dfrac{1}{20} + \dfrac{1}{40} + \dfrac{1}{40}\right)}}$$

$$= 4.25$$

To evaluate the above obtained F values, we find F' from Formula 11.31 where:

$$K = 4$$

$$N = 60$$

$$F_{3\ \&\ 56} = 2.78 \text{ with } \alpha = 0.05$$

$$\text{then} \quad F' = \sqrt{(4-1)(2.78)}$$

$$= 2.86$$

As our obtained F values are greater than 2.86 we would conclude that there is a significant difference between our comparisons where alpha is equal to 0.05. This F' value would be used to evaluate any or all additional comparisons that we could make.

Homogeneity of K within Variances.   As with the t-test, one of the major assumptions of the analysis of variance is that the variances within each group that makes up the mean square within groups are equal within the limits of random sampling. Therefore, we have the homogeneity of variances within the K groups, or:

$$\sigma_1^2 = \sigma_2^2 = \ldots = \sigma_k^2$$

The test for the homogeneity of K within variances can be approximated by F_{max}-test. If we find the within variance for each of the independent groups, or:

$$S_i^2 = \frac{\sum\limits_{1}^{n_i} x_i^2}{n_i - 1}$$

and take the two extreme values, then the F_{max}-test becomes:

$$F_{max} = \frac{\text{largest } K \text{ treatment variance}}{\text{smallest } K \text{ treatment variance}} \qquad (11.31)$$

If the obtained F value exceeds the tabled F_{max} value (Table P) that is associated with K and $(n_i - 1)$ degrees of freedom with a given alpha level, the hypothesis of homogeneity of the within variances would be rejected. Formula 11.31 assumes that all the K within variances are based upon the same sample size or n_i.

A somewhat analogous test for homogeneity of variances, proposed by Cochran (1947), utilizes the total K treatment variances and the largest treatment variance, or:

$$C\text{-test} = \frac{\text{largest of the } K \text{ treatment variances}}{\text{sum of the } K \text{ treatment variances}} \quad (11.32)$$

The sample distribution of the C-test is given in Table Q with K and $N - 1$ degrees of freedom for alpha at the 0.05 and 0.01 levels of significance. If the obtained C value is equal to or greater than the critical tabled C value, this would be evidence for heterogeneity of variances. On the other hand, if the obtained value of C was less than the critical value, we would conclude that there was evidence for homogeneity of variances.

Example. If we would select the highest and lowest variances from our previous sample on page 187, then:

$$S_1^2 = \frac{23.30}{10 - 1} = 2.589$$

$$\text{and } S_2^2 = \frac{75.76}{10 - 1} = 8.418$$

The F_{max} for this example is:

$$F_{max} = \frac{8.418}{2.589}$$

$$= 3.251$$

The critical value of F with 2 and 9 degrees of freedom at the 0.05 level is 4.03. As our obtained value of F_{max} is less than the tabled value, we conclude that the variances do not differ significantly.
Utilizing the same data the C-test is:

$$C\text{-test} = \frac{8.418}{11.180} = .753$$

This ratio is evaluated with $K = 3$ and $n - 1 = 9$ degrees of freedom. The critical tabled value of C with 3 and 9 degrees of freedom is equal to 0.8010 for alpha at the 0.05 level, and as our obtained value of 0.753 is less than 0.801 we will conclude, as with the F_{max}-test that the variances are homogeneous.

The Analysis of Variance for *K* Related Groups

Function and Method.   The analysis of variance can be used when the *K* groups are related. The *K* group design may be utilized for two general research designs. In one design the subjects in the *K* groups have been matched on the relevant variable or variables in order to minimize the subject differences between the *K* groups before each group receives the specified treatment condition. As an illustration, suppose the experimenter is interested in the effects of various dosages of a drug upon the rate of an operant response. However, the effect of the drug may be dependent upon the initial weight of the animal. Therefore, in order to determine the influence of the various dosages of the drug, the various subjects are matched according to weight across the various *K* groups. A second design for eliminating the differences between subjects is the experimental design where each of the several subjects received the various treatment conditions. If the researcher was interested in the effects of a given dosage over time, a major advantage would be to compare the changes over time in the same organism, where various time intervals would make up the *K* groups.

In the discussion of the *t*-test, we saw that it was possible to subtract out, from the standard error of the difference between means, the variability that was attributable to the matching or the relating of subjects. For the analysis of variance with *K* related groups, the variability that pertains to the *K* related groups procedure can logically be subtracted from the total variability.

The null hypothesis for *K* related groups is:

$$H_0 : \mu_1 = \mu_2 = \mu_3 = \ldots = \mu_k$$

or H_0 : Mean square between groups =
mean square residual

and the alternative hypothesis is stated in the general case as:

$$H_1 : \mu_i \neq \mu_{k-1}$$

or H_1 : Mean square between groups >
mean square residual

The null hypothesis is tested by:

$$F = \frac{M.S. \text{ between groups}}{M.S. \text{ residual}} \qquad (11.33)$$

with $K - 1$ and $(k - 1)(r - 1)$ df

The sum of squares of the residual is the difference between the total sum of squares, less the sum of squares between the K groups (columns) and less the sum of squares between the rows (subjects), thus:

Σx^2 residual $= \Sigma x^2$ total $- \Sigma x^2$ between columns $- \Sigma x^2$ between rows

The computation of the sum of squares between the rows is written as:

$$\Sigma x^2 \text{ between rows} = \overset{r}{\underset{1}{\Sigma}} \left[\frac{\left(\overset{n}{\underset{1}{\Sigma}} X_j \right)^2}{n_j} \right] - \frac{\left(\overset{N}{\underset{1}{\Sigma}} X \right)^2}{N} \qquad (11.34)$$

where $\overset{n}{\underset{1}{\Sigma}} X_j$ = sum across the jth row

n_j = number of scores in the jth row

$\overset{r}{\underset{1}{\Sigma}}$ = sum of the r rows

r = number of rows

The total and between columns sum of squares are found as before.

The mean square residual becomes:

$$M.S. \text{ residual} = \frac{\Sigma x^2 \text{ residual}}{(K - 1)(r - 1)} \qquad (11.35)$$

It is possible to test the significance between the row's means. While this is not of research interest, if we obtain a significant difference between the rows, this difference suggests that there is a high positive relationship between the K groups. The mean square residual is dependent upon this relationship. If there is a high positive relationship between the K groups, the mean square residual will be smaller than if the relationship is zero. In this latter case the mean square residual is equal to the mean square within groups. Therefore, for an efficient use of matching, as with the *t*-test, the relationship must be positive and high to offset the loss in degrees of freedom. In the K independent group design we have $K(n - 1)$ degrees of freedom but in the K related group design there are $(K - 1)(r - 1)$ degrees of freedom. In general, we lose $(r - 1)$ degrees of freedom in the denominator for the evaluation of the null hypothesis.

Example.   As part of a larger study, the investigator examines the size of daily water ration upon food intake over days, using rats as subjects. The data in Table 11.7 indicate the food intake in grams over 5 four-day periods for one size of water ration.

Table 11.7

Ss	Day 1	Day 5	Day 9	Day 13	Day 17	Over days
1	21	18	19	14	12	84
2	27	22	22	16	13	100
3	24	20	19	16	13	92
4	20	18	18	13	11	80
5	25	21	20	17	13	96
6	23	19	20	14	10	86
7	24	20	19	13	10	86
8	28	24	22	17	15	106
9	23	18	19	14	12	86
10	25	20	22	16	11	94
$\Sigma x =$	240	200	200	150	120	910
$\Sigma x^2 =$	5814	4034	4020	2272	1462	

These data may be analyzed as follows:

$$\text{Total } \Sigma x^2 = (21)^2 + (27)^2 + (24)^2 + \ldots + (11)^2 - \frac{(910)^2}{50}$$

$$= 17602 - \frac{(910)^2}{50}$$

$$= 1040$$

Between treatments or columns:

$$\Sigma x^2 = \frac{(240)^2}{10} + \frac{(200)^2}{10} + \frac{(200)^2}{10} + \frac{(150)^2}{10} + \frac{(120)^2}{10} - \frac{(910)^2}{50}$$

$$= 5760 + 4000 + 4000 + 2250 + 1440 - 16562$$

$$= 17450 - 16562$$

$$= 888$$

Between rows:

$$\Sigma x^2 = \frac{(84)^2}{5} + \frac{(100)^2}{5} + \frac{(92)^2}{5} + \ldots + \frac{(94)^2}{5} - \frac{(910)^2}{50}$$

$$= 1411.2 + 2000 + 1692.8 + 1280 + 1843.2 + 1479.2$$

$$+ 1479.2 + 2247.2 + 1479.2 + 1767.2 - 16562$$

$$= 117.20$$

$$\text{Residual } \Sigma x^2 = 34.80$$

The analysis is summarized in Table 11.8

Table 11.8

Source of Variation	Σx^2	df	M.S.	F
Between treatments (days)	888	4	222	229.57
Between rows (Ss)	117.2	9	13.02	13.46
Residual	34.8	36	0.967	
	1040	49		

From the table of F (Table N) for 4 and 36 degrees of freedom, the critical value for alpha at the 0.05 level is 2.63. As the obtained F value exceeds the theoretical sampling distribution, we would conclude that the treatment conditions differ significantly. From the null and alternative hypotheses, our main research interest was in the treatment conditions (days). Typically, the significance between rows is not of major research interest. This obtained difference simply shows that there is a significant difference among animals in their mean amount of food consumed. We, at this point, could utilize one of the methods for subsequent analysis between the various treatment groups in order to further ascertain which treatment conditions differ significantly.

Factorial Design

Function and Method.   A factorial design is an expansion of the analysis of variance where the research design has two or more independent variables or factors, and each factor is varied in two or more independent ways. In the simplest factorial design, factor A is varied in two ways and factor B is also varied in two ways and we have equal n's for each treatment condition. This design is shown on page 86.

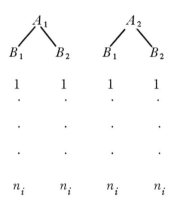

| Treatment groups | $A_1 B_1$ | $A_1 B_2$ | $A_2 B_1$ | $A_2 B_2$ |

In this 2 by 2 factorial design, there are, as seen in the above illustration, four treatment groups: $A_1 B_1, A_1 B_2, A_2 B_1$, and $A_2 B_2$. The subjects are randomly selected for each of these four groups. Therefore, the treatment groups are independent.

The general rationale of the factorial design is that the total variance can be divided into two component parts, the mean square between groups and the mean square within groups, and the mean square between groups can be further broken down into meaningful component parts. There are, in the illustration, as many parts as there are degrees of freedom for the between groups. With $K = 4$, there are $(K - 1)$ or three degrees of freedom and therefore three meaningful parts. One comparison is between the main A effect, one between the main B effect, and the third is the A by B interaction.

The mean square for the A effect compares the differences between the two means of A, that is, averaged over the two levels of the B factor. If the mean square of A is statistically significant, it is concluded that the two means of A are not equal. Similarly, the mean square for the B effect compares the difference between the two means of B when averaged over the two levels of the A factor. The interaction effect $(A \times B)$ is a statistical measure of the differential influence of the factors upon each other. If there is no differential effect, then the difference between $\bar{A}_1$ and $\bar{A}_2$ for the level of B_1 is not statistically different from the difference between $\bar{A}_1$ and $\bar{A}_2$ for the B_2 level, or:

$$B_1 : \bar{A}_1 - \bar{A}_2 = B_2 : \bar{A}_1 - \bar{A}_2$$

or an equivalence:

$$A_1 : \bar{B}_1 - \bar{B}_2 = A_2 : \bar{B}_1 - \bar{B}_2$$

If there is a significant differential effect, then:

$$B_1 : \bar{A}_1 - \bar{A}_2 \neq B_2 : \bar{A}_1 - \bar{A}_2$$

or:

$$A_1 : \bar{B}_1 - \bar{B}_2 \neq A_2 : \bar{B}_1 - \bar{B}_2$$

It is the analysis for this differential or interaction effect that is the major advantage of the factorial design. As science develops, we have increasing interests about the interaction of variables upon behavior. In the following discussion we will concern ourselves with a random-group design. However, this model could be further expanded to different research designs.

In the 2×2 factorial design with random and independent groups, there are three major research components which are each associated with a given null and alternative hypothesis. The null hypotheses are stated as:

$$H_0 : \bar{A}_1 = \bar{A}_2$$

$$\bar{B}_1 = \bar{B}_2$$

$$B_1 : \bar{A}_1 - \bar{A}_2 = B_2 : \bar{A}_1 - \bar{A}_2 \text{ or } \bar{A}_1 : \bar{B}_1 - \bar{B}_2 = A_2 : \bar{B}_1 - \bar{B}_2$$

or   M.S. between A groups = M.S. within groups

M.S. between B groups = M.S. within groups

M.S. between $A \times B$ = M.S. within groups

The research or alternative hypotheses for the three effects are:

$H_1 : \overline{A}_1 \neq \overline{A}_2$

$\overline{B}_1 \neq \overline{B}_2$

$B_1 : \overline{A}_1 - \overline{A}_2 \neq B_2 : \overline{A}_1 - \overline{A}_2$ or $A_1 : \overline{B}_1 - \overline{B}_2 \neq A_2 : \overline{B}_1 - \overline{B}_2$

or   M.S. between A groups $\neq$ M.S. within groups

M.S. between B groups $\neq$ M.S. within groups

M.S. between $A \times B$ $\neq$ M.S. within groups

These null hypotheses are tested by:

$F = \dfrac{M.S. \text{ of } A}{M.S. \text{ within}}$ with $K_a - 1$ and $K(n_i - 1)\ df$

$F = \dfrac{M.S. \text{ of } B}{M.S. \text{ within}}$ with $K_b - 1$ and $K(n_i - 1)\ df$

$F = \dfrac{M.S. \text{ of } A \times B}{M.S. \text{ within}}$ with $(K_a - 1)(K_b - 1)$ and $K(n_i - 1)\ df$

In order to determine the sum of squares between the two levels of the A factor we can use the computational formula (11.36):

$$\Sigma x_A^2 = \frac{\left(\overset{n}{\underset{1}{\Sigma}} X_{A_1}\right)^2}{n_{A_1}} + \frac{\left(\overset{n}{\underset{1}{\Sigma}} X_{A_2}\right)^2}{n_{A_2}} - \frac{\left(\overset{N}{\underset{1}{\Sigma}} X\right)^2}{N} \qquad (11.36)$$

where $\sum\limits_{1}^{n} X_{A_1}$ = sum of all A_1 scores

$\sum\limits_{1}^{n} X_{A_2}$ = sum of all A_2 scores

$\sum\limits_{1}^{N} X$ = sum of all scores

n_{A_1} = number of A_1 scores

n_{A_2} = number of A_2 scores

N = total number of scores

If there are more than two levels of A, Formula 11.36 can be expanded into a generalized formula:

$$\sum x_A^2 = \frac{\left(\sum\limits_{1}^{n} X_{A_1}\right)^2}{n_{A_1}} + \frac{\left(\sum\limits_{1}^{n} X_{A_2}\right)^2}{n_{A_2}} + \ldots + \frac{\left(\sum\limits_{1}^{n} X_{A_K}\right)^2}{n_{A_K}} - \frac{\left(\sum\limits_{1}^{N} X\right)^2}{N}$$

$$(11.37)$$

In order to obtain an estimate of the population variance for the A effect, we divide the sum of squares that are associated with A by $K_A - 1$ degrees of freedom, where K is the number of ways that factor A varies. In our 2×2 design, factor A varies in two ways, A_1 and A_2, therefore, we would have one degree of freedom associated with A. The computational mean square for the general case would be:

$$\text{M.S. of } A = \frac{\left[\dfrac{\left(\sum\limits_{1}^{n} X_{A_1}\right)^2}{n_{A_1}} + \dfrac{\left(\sum\limits_{1}^{N} X_{A_2}\right)^2}{n_{A_2}} + \ldots + \dfrac{\left(\sum\limits_{1}^{n} X_{A_K}\right)^2}{n_{A_K}} - \dfrac{\left(\sum\limits_{1}^{n} X\right)^2}{N}\right]}{K_A - 1}$$

$$(11.38)$$

The mean square between the levels of the B factor is obtained in a similar procedure, except that we sum the B values. In the general case for B:

$$\text{M.S. of } B = \frac{\left[\frac{\left(\sum\limits_{1}^{n} X_{B_1}\right)^2}{n_{B_1}} + \frac{\left(\sum\limits_{1}^{n} X_{B_2}\right)^2}{n_{B_2}} + \ldots + \frac{\left(\sum\limits_{1}^{n} X_{B_K}\right)^2}{n_{B_K}} - \frac{\left(\sum\limits_{1}^{N} X\right)^2}{N}\right]}{K_B - 1}$$

$$(11.39)$$

The sum of squares that are associated with the $A \times B$ interaction can be obtained directly by subtraction of the sum of squares of the A factor and also the B factor from the between groups sum of squares. The remainder sum of squares is attributable to the interaction effect, or:

$$\Sigma x^2_{AXB} = \Sigma x^2_{\text{between}} - \Sigma x^2_A - \Sigma x^2_B$$

For the 2×2 factorial design we can compute the interaction sum of squares directly:

$$\Sigma x^2_{AXB} = \frac{\left[\left(\sum\limits_{1}^{n} X_{A_1 B_1} + \sum\limits_{1}^{n} X_{A_2 B_2}\right) - \left(\sum\limits_{1}^{n} X_{A_1 B_2} + \sum\limits_{1}^{n} X_{A_2 B_1}\right)\right]^2}{(K)(n)} \quad (11.40)$$

The mean square for the $A \times B$ interaction is the interaction sum of squares divided by the degrees of freedom associated with the interaction. The degrees of freedom is a product of the degrees of freedom associated with the factors involved. In the illustration, we would have $(K_A - 1)(K_B - 1)$ degrees of freedom. The mean square for the $A \times B$ interaction would be given as:

$$\text{M.S. of } A \times B = \frac{\dfrac{\left[\left(\sum\limits_{1}^{n} X_{A_1 B_1} + \sum\limits_{1}^{n} X_{A_2 B_2}\right) - \left(\sum\limits_{1}^{n} X_{A_1 B_2} + \sum\limits_{1}^{n} X_{A_2 B_1}\right)\right]^2}{(K)(n)}}{(K_A - 1)(K_B - 1)}$$

$$(11.41)$$

Example. Response contingencies of dim light onset and offset in a complex environment have been investigated. It has been hypothesized that animals receiving light offset in a complex environment will have a lower response rate than those receiving light offset in a visually simple environment, whereas, animals receiving light onset in a complex environment will have a higher rate than those receiving light onset in a simple environment. In Table 11.9, we have the data for the number of stimulus changes for this 2 by 2 experiment.

Table 11.9

	Complex		Simple	
Onset	Offset	Onset	Offset
354	128	82	123
249	169	104	143
215	85	147	140
185	118	81	126
325	146	37	125
183	90	166	241
252	186	245	184
239	196	87	116
296	119	85	171
169	149	294	195
188	81	241	166
238	0	160	189
212	17	195	161
282	118	218	167
349	154	226	131
304	180	199	188
256	214	95	117
149	171	159	147
298	148	167	190
208	177	276	139
$\Sigma X = 4951$	2646	3264	3159

$\Sigma X^2 = 1,293,489$ 410,044   634,168   519,649

Total $\Sigma X^2 = (354)^2 + (249)^2 + (215)^2 + \ldots + (139)^2 - \dfrac{(14020)^2}{80}$

$\qquad = 400,345$

Between groups $\Sigma x^2 = \dfrac{(4951)^2}{20} + \dfrac{(2646)^2}{20} + \dfrac{(3264)^2}{20} + \dfrac{(3159)^2}{20} - \dfrac{(14020)^2}{80}$

$\qquad = 150,330$

and breaking the between sum of squares down into their logical parts we have:

complex-simple $\Sigma x^2 = \dfrac{(4951 + 2646)^2}{40} + \dfrac{(3264 + 3159)^2}{40} - \dfrac{(14020)^2}{80}$

$\qquad = 17,228$

$$\text{onset-offset } \Sigma x^2 = \frac{(4951 + 3264)^2}{40} + \frac{(2646 + 3159)^2}{40} - \frac{(14020)^2}{80}$$

$$= 72{,}602$$

$$\text{interaction } \Sigma x^2 = \frac{(4951 + 3159) - (2646 + 3264)^2}{4(20)}$$

$$= 60{,}500$$

The within sum of squares may be directly calculated or obtained by subtraction, or:

$$\text{within } \Sigma x^2 = 400{,}345 - 150{,}330 = 250{,}015$$

The statistical summary is in Table 11.10.

Table 11.10

Source of variation	Σx^2	df	$M.S.$	F
Complex-Simple	17,228	1	17,228	5.236
Onset-Offset	72,602	1	72,602	22.067
Interaction	60,500	1	60,015	18.389
Within	250,015	76	3,290	
Total	400,345	79		

The tabled value of F with 1 and 76 degrees of freedom with alpha at the 0.05 level is 3.97. As all obtained F values are greater than the critical value, we would conclude that all three F values differed significantly from chance.

The mean stimulus changes for this two-variable factorial design are given in Table 11.11. If we first consider the onset-offset variable, we find that the sum of the two combined means (complex and simple) for onset is 410.8 and for offset 290.2. From the obtained significant F we know that we have a significant main effect between onset and offset with the largest number of stimulus changes occurring within the onset condition. The other main effect, the complex-simple environment, was also statistically different. Summing for the complex condition we have 379.9 and for the simple condition 321.1 with the largest

Table 11.11

	light onset	light offset	
complex	247.6	132.3	379.9
simple	1 63.2	157.9	321.1
Σ	410.8	290.2	

number of changes occurring within the complex situation. Furthermore, our obtained F value revealed a significant interaction effect between onset and offset within the simple or complex environment. This differential effect can be seen if we consider the difference between onset: complex-simple or 124.4 and offset: complex-simple or -45.6. From the null hypothesis for the interaction, these two different scores are equal. With a significant interaction, we reject our null and accept our alternative hypothesis.

As we have only two ways that the stimulus changes, onset or offset, and only two ways that the environments are different, simple or complex, we do not need to make any further comparisons. We know that onset differs from offset and that complex differs from simple. However, with a significant interaction effect further comparisons can be made from a further breakdown of the variances by using, for example, the Neuman-Keuls test. We will not show here all the computations, but only report the statistics. Under the onset condition, significantly more stimulus changes occurred in the complex condition as compared to the simple one ($N - K = 8.97, p < 0.01$). Similarly, there was a significant difference under the complex condition between the light onset and offset groups ($N - K = 6.56, p < 0.01$). However, nonsignificant results were obtained between the complex and simple conditions for offset ($N - K = 1.99, p > 0.05$). and between onset and offset within the simple environment ($N - K = 0.41, p > 0.05$).

The interpretation of the significant main effects is a function of the significant interaction effect. Consider first the obtained significant effect between light onset and light offset. The significant interaction suggests that there may be varying differences between these two conditions as related to the environment. From the subsequent analysis the number of light onsets is not significantly different from the number of light offsets. However, within the complex environment a significant difference does occur between the two groups. Furthermore, the significant interaction suggests that there may be differences between the two environments as a function of the two conditions of light onset and light offset. Under the light offset condition there is no significant difference between the two environments, but within the light onset condition there is a difference between the two environments. These results support the theory from which they were derived.

Graphing the Interaction. Previously our graphs have consisted of only two variables with the dependent variable plotted along the ordinate, and the independent variable plotted along the abscissa. It is possible to graph the results of an experiment having two independent variables and one dependent variable. In such a graph, the dependent variable and one of the independent variables are plotted on the ordinate, and the other independent variable on the abscissa.

Figure 11.5 is a graph of a 2 × 2 factorial. The first independent variable, A has been plotted on the abscissa. The second independent variable, B, has been plotted on the ordinate, but its level label has been placed on the right side of the graphs. While the level labels of 1 and 2 for variable A are graphed on the abscissa, each of the lines of 1 and 2 for variable B corresponds to its mutual values on the dependent variable. Each line on the graph corresponds to a different level of B, and the dot at the end of each line represents one of the treatment combination means of a 2 × 2 factorial.

From a graph it is possible to visually examine each of the main effects and the interaction. The main effect of variable A can be seen by comparing the means of $(A_1 B_1)$ and $(A_1 B_2)$ to the means of $(A_2 B_1)$ and $(A_2 B_2)$. Similarly, the main effect of the B variable can be seen by comparing the means of $(A_1 B_1)$ and $(A_2 B_1)$ to the means of $(A_1 B_2)$ and $(A_2 B_2)$. The interaction effect can be examined by comparing the difference between $(A_1 B_1)$ and $(A_1 B_2)$ to the difference between $(A_2 B_1)$ and $(A_2 B_2)$. In Part A of Figure 11.5 the differential effects for the interaction are zero, therefore, there is no interaction effect. On the other hand, there is an A effect and a B effect. Part B shows an A effect, B effect, and an $A \times B$ interaction effect. In Part C, there is no effect for A or B, but there is an $A \times B$ interaction.

Some Comments on Further Designs. With the K independent random samples design, the related K model, and the factorial design, most of the experimental literature which utilizes the analysis of variance should be comprehensible to the student of behavior. From these three basic designs, you should be able to

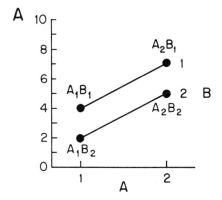

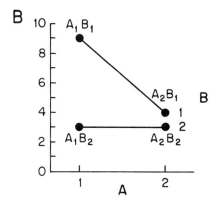

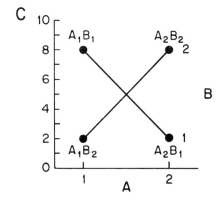

Figure 11.5.   Schematic of various two by two interaction effects.

generalize in your reading of the literature to most other models of the analysis of variance. The most logical extension of these designs is to what we refer to as mixed designs. For example, we can design a study where we have two independent random groups and where we take repeated measures on each subject (related K model). In this example we are mixing two designs, and it should be evident that there are numerous other mixed designs. For these more complex designs, you can consult advanced experimental design texts.

Without going into the details of the analysis, we have included an example below of a two independent random samples with three repeated measures experiment. Try to work it through and interpret the findings.

Example. The results of several experiments investigating the general locomotor activity of rodents have indicated that rodents sometimes use activity as a means of maintaining arousal

Table 11.12

Period	Experimental group				Control group			
	1-4	5-8	9-12	ΣX	1-4	5-8	9-12	ΣX
	41	44	12	97	132	53	62	247
	51	7	40	98	112	89	98	299
	103	62	0	165	112	105	94	311
	117	56	52	225	30	34	0	64
	77	141	79	297	372	294	212	878
	103	25	16	144	99	87	55	241
	42	16	13	71	83	78	79	240
	42	41	14	97	83	59	56	198
	49	12	8	69	95	81	60	236
	66	41	33	140	52	94	71	217
	37	19	7	63	142	187	235	564
	68	12	26	106	107	92	55	254
	188	75	80	343	129	110	98	337
	82	166	109	357	73	66	53	192
	105	49	100	254	107	90	92	289
	43	19	21	83	43	41	29	113

ΣX = 1214   785   610   2609   1771   1560   1349   4680

ΣX^2 = 116,338 69,681 41,910 576,327 283,985 211,548 168,239 1,909,116

$\overline{X}$ = 75.875 49.062 38.125 163.062 110.687 97.50 84.312 292.50

$$\frac{(\Sigma X)^2}{N} = \frac{(7289)^2}{96} = 553,432.5104 \quad \Sigma X^2 = 891,701.0$$

at an optimal level. Thus, it was hypothesized that rodents having a high level of arousal would be less active than rodents which had low levels of arousal. In order to test this hypothesis, the arousal levels of rats in the experimental group were increased by exposing the rats to complex-novel stimuli, while rats in the control group were not exposed to complex-novel stimuli prior to the activity test. Activity was measured for a 12-minute period in an open field, which was divided in half by an infra-red photo beam. The number of photo-beam disruptions served as the measure of general locomotor activity. For purposes of data analysis, the activity period was divided into three successive 4-minute test periods. The resulting design was a 2 × 3 mixed analysis of variance, with the three successive 4-minute test periods serving as the repeated measures variable. The data are given in Table 11.12, and the summary in Table 11.13.

Table 11.13

Source	Σx^2	df	M.S.	F	p
Between groups	275048.4896	31			
(Exp/Cont)	44677.5104	1	44677.5104	5.8181	$p < 0.05$
Error$_b$	230370.9792	30	7679.0326		
Within groups	63220.0000	64			
Periods	16784.0835	2	8392.0417	11.0464	$p < 0.05$
(Periods × Exp/Cont)	853.5832	2	426.7916	0.5617	$p > 0.05$
Error$_w$	45582.3333	60	759.7055		
Total	338268.4896	95			

Summary of Terms

analysis of variance
C-test
correlation coefficient
critical difference
degrees of freedom

differential effect
F_{max}-test
F ratio
F-test
factorial design

heterogeneity of variance
homogeneity of variance
interaction effect
mean square between groups
mean square within groups

mixed design
multiple comparison
Neuman-Keuls test
residual mean square
Scheffé's test

standard error of the difference   t distribution
standard error of the mean   *t*-test
sum of squares between groups   total sum of squares
sum of squares within groups

Summary of Symbols

μ	$\overline{X}$	t_α	Σx_b^2	$M.S._e$	$A \times B$
$\sigma_{\overline{x}}$	$S_{x_1 - x_2}$	r	Σx_w^2	C^2	$M.S._{A \times B}$
$S_{\overline{x}}$	$S_{\overline{x}}^2$	Σd^2	Σx_t^2	F'	
σ	F	S_d	$M.S._b$	F_{max}	
σ^2	df	K	$M.S._w$	$M.S._{res.}$	

Problems

1.   In order to find out if rats avoid strangers, an experimenter
     gave 20 rats 5 trials each on an elevated 5-path maze. The
     stranger sat next to Path Number I, with Path Number V
     being the furthest away from him. The number of the path
     chosen by each rat on each trial was recorded, and the mean
     of the five trials given each rat is given below. Answer the
     experimenter's question by analyzing the data as a one-sample
     t-test. Use the 0.01 alpha level.

                         3.2
                         4.2
                         4.2
                         3.8
                         2.6
                         3.6
                         3.8
                         3.8
                         3.4
                         4.8
                         4.2
                         2.8
                         4.0
                         4.2

3.4
4.0
4.4
3.4
3.2
4.0

2. The experimenter in the first problem also collected data on the behavior of another 20 rats, which were each given 5 exploration trials on the elevated maze in the absence of the stranger. The mean of the path numbers chosen by each of these rats is given below. Use the appropriate statistical analysis to compare the mean of this group to the mean of the path numbers chosen by the rats tested in the presence of a stranger. Use a two-tailed test and the 0.05 alpha level.

1.2
2.6
3.8
3.0
3.4
3.0
3.6
5.0
3.0
2.4
3.0
3.4
3.8
3.4
2.2
2.8
2.0
3.8
3.0
3.8

3. A lab instructor used the mirror-tracing experiment to demonstrate bilateral transfer. Ten students were given a pretest using their preferred hands, then 10 practice trials using their nonpreferred hands, and finally a posttest using their preferred hands. The lab instructor predicted that there would be fewer errors on the posttest than on the pretest.

Evaluate her hypothesis at the 0.05 alpha level. Regard the variances as being homogeneous.

Pretest	Posttest
77	51
51	7
99	42
85	58
84	73
56	45
65	47
59	49
65	23
91	77

4. In order to investigate the effect of light intensity on the activity of male rats, an experimenter measured the activity of 8 different mice under each of three intensity levels: low, medium, and high. The data, the number of photo-beam disruptions, are given below. Begin by using the F_{max}-test to test for homogeneity of variances, then use the appropriate analysis of variance. If subsequent analyses are indicated, use the Studentized Range Test. Use the 0.05 alpha level throughout.

Low	Medium	High
180	72	124
141	68	132
155	97	99
134	87	88
85	95	78
99	142	63
163	117	58
100	137	36

5. The operant rate, the rate at which an animal makes some response before any reinforcement has been made contingent upon that response, has been typically regarded as a stable base rate determined primarily by chance. Herman Swift-science, however, hypothesized that the operant bar pressing rate of a rat was a decreasing function of the rat's exposure to the bar. Herman tested his hypothesis by recording the number of bar presses made by each of 8 rats on each of 4

successive days in a Skinner box. Assuming that Herman's data meet the assumption of homogeneity of variance, evaluate his data at the 0.05 alpha level.

Day 1	Day 2	Day 3	Day 4
211	309	236	149
117	71	45	63
238	163	158	154
135	95	205	90
162	68	75	92
137	77	33	40
200	92	60	47
296	267	157	72

6. An advertising firm wanted to know if ads containing pictures were more effective than ads not containing pictures. They decided to investigate this problem by placing two ads, one with a picture and one without a picture, in two magazines. Each ad directed the reader to make a toll-free telephone call for more information. The number of telephone calls on each day of a ten-day period served as the dependent variable. Assume homogeneity of variance, and evaluate the data of this 2 × 2 factorial design at the 0.001 alpha level.

Magazine A		Magazine B	
No Picture	With Picture	No Picture	With Picture
11	48	75	50
25	58	84	64
2	60	80	87
18	54	85	60
20	50	84	57
23	55	83	55
13	27	91	50
16	69	90	47
16	48	87	69
21	59	78	50

Correlational Methods for the Nominal Scale

Chapter Twelve

Introduction to Correlational Methods

Our research interest may be determining whether a relationship or an association exists between variables and determining the degree or the magnitude and the direction of that association. The correlation coefficient is a numerical index that describes the extent that variations in one variable are associated with variations in the second variable. Just as a mean of a sample is descriptive of the sample of scores, so too, the correlation coefficient is descriptive of the association between two variables.

As with various tests of statistical inference, we are also concerned here with the testing of various research hypotheses about the association between variables. Science does not go about studying possible relationships in a random fashion. A good articulate theory or a good hunch may suggest what relationships might be of major importance to the science and what variables might be meaningfully associated. Once the existence of the relationship has been established then the degree and the direction of that relationship has meaning. Associated with correlational methods are various tests of statistical inference. These statistical tests enable the researcher to ascertain the probability associated with a sample correlation coefficient under the null hypothesis. The null hypothesis is basically a hypothesis of no difference or a hypothesis that the relationship between two variables in the population is zero, or:

$$H_0 : \rho = 0$$

where ρ = population correlation

Whereas the research or alternate hypothesis states:

$$H_1 : \rho \neq 0$$

or $H_1 : \rho < 0$

or $H_1 : \rho > 0$

If the obtained coefficient differs significantly from zero, it can be argued that there is an association in the population. Furthermore, we may wish to estimate the range of the magnitude of the significant population correlation from the observed sample coefficient or to test the significant difference between two observed correlation coefficients.

Associated with the correlation methods are measures of prediction. Frequently, the research is not only concerned with relationships but also with making predictions. When we know that two variables are correlated, then having information about one variable enables us to make predictions of the second variable.

As all science is based upon reliable measurement, a major concern of correlational methods is focused upon various indexes of reliability of measures. All measurement has some element of error. Therefore, it is most important for science to minimize the error and to estimate the amount of error in its measurements. For, if we cannot make reliable measurements of the phenomenon under investigation, that phenomenon is always open to question.

There are various correlational procedures and associated statistical tests which differ in terms of assumptions and rules of measurement. This chapter will be devoted to the discussion of measures of correlation and hypothesis testing for the nominal scale.

The Contingency Coefficient

Function and Method.   The contingency coefficient, C, is a measure of association between two or more variables when the frequency data fall into mutually exclusive classes. In these cases the categories for the variables need not have any meaningful order relations. Therefore, the contingency coefficient makes no assumption of continuity for the underlying variables and is applied to nominal level variables. The contingency coefficient can be obtained from any unordered $k \times r$ contingency table. The magnitude or the degree of association for the contingency coefficient can be obtained by:

$$C = \sqrt{\frac{\chi^2}{N + \chi^2}} \tag{12.1}$$

$$\text{where} \quad \chi^2 = \sum_{i=1}^{r} \sum_{j=1}^{k} \frac{(o_{ij} - e_{ij})^2}{e_{ij}}$$

N = number of cases

Thus, in order to find the contingency coefficient, the chi-square is first obtained. The chi-square enables us to determine if there was a significant difference between variables and it is the contingency coefficient that describes the magnitude of that relationship. In order to obtain a contingency coefficient, the assumptions of chi-square must be met.

The magnitude of the contingency coefficient may vary from 0.00 to < 1.00. If the chi-square is zero, the contingency coefficient will be zero. The maximum upper limit of the coefficient is a function of the number of k and r categories. For example, when $k = r$ the maximum value for the contingency coefficient is given by:

$$\sqrt{\frac{k-1}{k}} \tag{12.2}$$

and thus:

$$2 \times 2 = \sqrt{1/2} = 0.707$$

$$4 \times 4 = \sqrt{3/4} = 0.866$$

$$6 \times 6 = \sqrt{5/6} = 0.913$$

$$8 \times 8 = \sqrt{7/8} = 0.935$$

$$10 \times 10 = \sqrt{9/10} = 0.949$$

$$\infty \times \infty = 0.999$$

In order to compare two contingency coefficients, the values must come from the same size contingency tables as the size determines the maximum value. One further aspect of the C is that it is not directly comparable to any other measures of relationship. Hence, only contingency coefficients from the same size table can be compared.

Significance of C. Once we have obtained a coefficient from our sample which is assumed to be representative of the population, we can determine if our sample value is the result of random or chance sampling, or whether the association exists in the population. The null hypothesis for measures of association states that the population correlation (ρ) is zero. Thus:

$$H_0 : \rho = 0$$

For the contingency coefficient to be zero, the difference between the observed frequencies (o_{ij}) and expected frequencies (e_{ij}) must be zero. However, if $\rho = 0$ we would expect from random sampling some obtained differences, but these would be small, as would the coefficient.

The null hypothesis for the contingency coefficient states that:

$$C = 0.00$$

and the research hypothesis is given as:

$$C > 0.00$$

The null hypothesis of the contingency coefficient is tested by chi-square with $(k-1)(r-1)$ degrees of freedom. If the probability is equal to or less than the previously stated level of alpha, then the null hypothesis is rejected in favor of the research hypothesis, and we conclude that the contingency coefficient is significantly greater than zero. On the other hand, if the probability is greater than alpha, the null hypothesis is accepted and we assume that the obtained coefficient is a function of random sampling.

Example. In the study described in Chapter 9 of the difference between three delinquent scale types for boys and the frequency of movie attendance, the investigators reported a chi-square value of 15.207. They concluded that there was a significant difference. We can now determine the magnitude of the significant relationship between these two variables, delinquent scale type and frequency of movie attendance, by using the contingency coefficient where:

$$\chi^2 = 15.207 \text{ and } N = 376$$

$$C = \sqrt{\frac{15.207}{376 + 15.207}}$$

$$= \sqrt{0.03887}$$

$$= 0.197$$

As we have previously seen, the probability that is associated with a chi-square value of 15.207 and two degrees of freedom is less than 0.001. Therefore, the obtained contingency coefficient differs significantly from zero.

The Phi Coefficient

Function and Method. The phi coefficient, ϕ, is used to describe the strength and the direction of the relationship between two variables that are both truly dichotomous or binary. When we have a genuine or real dichotomous variable, the frequency of cases fall into one of two discrete classes. For example, we may have: male-female, living-dead, yes-no, right-wrong. The phi coefficient is thus computed from a 2×2 contingency table where the numerals could be transformed into two categories, or 0 or 1, or into a binary system. The 0 represents one trait, and 1 the other trait.

$$
\begin{array}{ccc}
 & X & \\
 & 0 \quad 1 & \\
0 & \boxed{a \;\; b} & a + b \\
Y & & \\
1 & \boxed{c \;\; d} & c + d \\
 & a + c \quad b + d &
\end{array}
$$

In the contingency table above a is the frequency of cases that have the 0 traits on both X and Y, b is the frequency of cases that have the 1 trait on X and 0 on Y, etc.; $a + b$ is the marginal frequencies for one row, $c + d$ the marginal frequencies for the second row, and $a + c$ is the marginal frequencies for one column and $b + d$ for the other column.

The strength and the direction of the relationship is obtained by:

$$\phi = \sqrt{\frac{\chi^2}{N}} \tag{12.3}$$

$$\text{where } \chi^2 = \frac{N(|ad - bc| - N/2)^2}{(a + c)(b + d)(a + b)(c + d)}$$

$$N = \text{number of cases}$$

and where the assumptions of the chi-square are met. An equivalent formula for the phi coefficient is:

$$\phi = \frac{ad - bc}{\sqrt{(a + b)(c + d)(a + c)(b + d)}} \tag{12.4}$$

and is computed from the frequencies in a 2 × 2 table.

The direction of the coefficient depends upon how the 2 × 2 table is arranged. To have a positive coefficient the table is constructed so that cells *a* and *d* represent the frequencies of cases that both have the trait, or neither have the trait. On the other hand, if *a* and *d* represent the frequencies that possess one trait and not the other, the numerator of the formula should be *bc - ad*. This relation is shown in Table 12.1.

Table 12.1

	0	1				0	1		
0	100	0	100		1	0	100	100	
				or					= +1.00
1	0	100	100		0	100	0	100	
	100	100				100	100		

	0	1				0	1		
0	0	100	100		1	100	0	100	
				or					= -1.00
1	100	0	100		0	0	100	100	
	100	100				100	100		

The magnitude of the phi coefficient can vary from -1.00 to 0.00 to 1.00 but only under the condition where $a + b = b + d$. The size of the phi coefficient becomes restricted when these marginal frequencies differ in a marked way.

A major advantage of the phi coefficient is that it is directly comparable to other phi coefficients and in addition, it is a special case of the Pearson product moment coefficient. This relationship will be discussed in Chapter 14.

Significance of ϕ.   The null hypothesis states that $\phi = 0.00$ and the research hypothesis that $\phi \neq 0.00$, < 0.00, or > 0.00. The null hypothesis is evaluated by chi-square with one degree of freedom where:

$$\chi^2 = N \phi^2 \tag{12.5}$$

As with the contingency coefficient, if the probability associated with the chi-square is equal to or less than alpha, then the null hypothesis is rejected in favor of the research hypothesis. When the research hypothesis states that $\phi \neq 0.00$, we have a two-tailed test of significance, and where $\phi <$ or > 0.00 a one-tailed test is used. As shown before, the direction of phi coefficient is dependent upon how the 2 X 2 contingency table is organized.

Example.   It has been suggested that when our motivations come into conflict, one possible consequence is that we change our perceptions in order to bring them in line with our motivations. To test such a hypothesis, assume that an investigator asked two groups of college subjects, smokers and non-smokers, if they believed that the relationship between smoking and lung cancer had been proven. The responses were either yes or no. Assume that the research hypothesis stated that there would be a significant relationship or correlation at the 0.05 level of significance. Table 12.2 contains the hypothetical data.

Table 12.2

	Not Proven	Proven	Total
Smokers	46(a)	34(b)	80
Non-smokers	29(c)	42(d)	71
Total	75	76	151

To determine the magnitude of this association we may use Formula 12.4:

$$\phi = \frac{(46)(42) - (29)(34)}{\sqrt{(80)(71)(75)(76)}}$$

$$= 0.153$$

and to test the research hypothesis that the relationship is different from zero, we use Formula 12.5:

$$\chi^2 = (151)(0.153)^2$$

$$= 3.54$$

The critical chi-square value for one degree of freedom with a directional hypothesis is 2.71. As our obtained chi-square value is greater than the critical value, we would conclude that the magnitude of our phi coefficient differs significantly from zero.

Contingent Uncertainty

Function and Method. The contingent uncertainty, U_{xy}, is a measure of the amount of reduction of uncertainty in one variable from the knowledge of another variable. It is in a very general sense a special measure of relatedness or association between frequency distributions; and it may utilize the data from any contingency table. Unlike the other measures of association, the contingent uncertainty does not measure the magnitude of the coefficient, but rather it measures the amount of the association. The obtained value of this measure is always expressed in terms of bits. The amount is always positive, and as such it does not state the direction of the association. The contingent uncertainty may range from zero; however, its upper limit is a function of the uncertainty in the variable that is being predicted. Thus, the values can be greater than one.

For a two-variable case we may express our measure of contingent uncertainty as:

$$U_{xy} = U_y - U_{(x|y)} \tag{12.6}$$

$$\text{or} \qquad U_x - U_{(y|x)}$$

where U_y or U_x = original uncertainty in the y or x variable

$U_{(x|y)}$ or $U_{(y|x)}$ = residual uncertainty when y or x is constant

The terms $U_{(x \mid y)}$ and $U_{(y \mid x)}$ express conditional uncertainty and are the average amount of uncertainty in one variable, while the other variable is held constant. The conditional uncertainty in Formula 12.6 is given as conditional probability in Formulas 12.7 and 12.7a:

$$U_{(x \mid y)} = - \Sigma_x P(x) \Sigma_y P_x(y) \log P_x(y) \qquad (12.7)$$

$$\text{or} \quad U_{(y \mid x)} = - \Sigma_y P(y) \Sigma_x P_y(x) \log P_y(x) \qquad (12.7a)$$

In general, it may be seen that contingent uncertainty is equal to the difference between uncertainty and conditional uncertainty or that uncertainty is made of two parts. One part is from contingent uncertainty and the other part from conditional uncertainty:

$$U_y = U_{xy} + U_{(x \mid y)} \qquad (12.8)$$

$$\text{and} \quad U_x = U_{xy} + U_{(y \mid x)} \qquad (12.9)$$

The partitioning in Formula 12.8 is analogous to partitioning in the analysis of variance. Therefore, we can express the amount of contingent uncertainty as a proportion of the reduction. (see Formula 12.10).

$$\frac{U_{xy}}{U_y} = \frac{U_y - U_{(x \mid y)}}{U_y} = 1 - \frac{U_{(x \mid y)}}{U_y} \qquad (12.10)$$

Test of Significance of Contingent Uncertainty. We can determine the significance of the contingent uncertainty by the chi-square where:

$$\chi^2 = 2(\log 2)\, nU_{xy} \qquad (12.11)$$

$$\text{or} \quad = 1.3863\, nU_{xy}$$

where n = number of cases

U_{xy} = value of the obtained contingent uncertainty

with $(r-1)(k-1)$ degrees of freedom. If we obtain a significant chi-square, we would conclude that there is a significant amount of relationship between the variables, or that we have significantly reduced unpredictability or uncertainty.

Example.   Suppose we have two properties, such as hue (X) and brightness (Y), of a visual stimulus, and that each of these variables has four categories. We would in this example then, have 16 joint categories or cells. Assume that Table 12.3 is our obtained bivariate frequency distribution where each X category has been presented randomly 50 times. From this information the subject has responded with one of the Y categories.

Table 12.3

		1	2	3	4	Y_i
				X		
	1	14	8			22
	2	36	32	4		72
Y	3		10	28	22	60
	4			18	28	46
	X_i	50	50	50	50	200

To determine our contingent uncertainty, we shall first obtain the uncertainty of Y and then the associated conditional uncertainty.

The uncertainty of Y is obtained from the sums of the four Y categories, or:

P_{yi}	$-P_{(y)}\log_2 P_{(y)}$
Y_1 22/200 = 0.11	0.3503
Y_2 72/200 = 0.36	0.5306
Y_3 60/200 = 0.30	0.5211
Y_4 46/200 = 0.23	0.4877

$$P_y = 1.00 \quad -P_{(y)}\log_2 P_{(y)} = 1.8897 = U_y$$

Therefore the uncertainty of Y, U_y, is 1.8897 bits.

To determine the conditional uncertainty, we shall first transform the frequencies within each category into P_i or 14/50 = 0.28, 36/50 = 0.72, etc. (see Table 12.4).

Table 12.4

		1	2	3	4
	1	.28	.16		
	2	.72	.64	.08	
Y	3		.20	.56	.44
	4			.36	.56
$P_{xi} =$		1.00	1.00	1.00	1.00

The associated $-P_i \log_2 P_i$ values are then determined and are shown in Table 12.5.

Table 12.5

		1	2	3	4
	1	.5142	.4320		
	2	.3412	.4121	.2915	
Y	3		.4644	.4684	.5211
	4			.5306	.4684
		.8554	1.2995	1.2905	.9895
		$U_{(1\mid y)}$	$U_{(2\mid y)}$	$U_{(3\mid y)}$	$U_{(4\mid y)}$

The sum of the $-P_i \log_2 P_i$ within each category is the conditional uncertainty for that category. To determine the conditional uncertainty from Formula 12.6 we need to find $_x P_{(x)}$, or the P value for each X category. In our example $X_i = 50$ in each of the four categories, or $P_{xi} = 50/200 = 0.25$. Therefore we would have:

$$(0.25)(0.8554) = 0.2138$$

$$(0.25)(1.2995) = 0.3248$$

$$(0.25)(1.2905) = 0.3226$$

$$(0.25)(0.9895) = \underline{0.2474}$$

$$U_{(x\mid y)} = 1.1087 \text{ in bits}$$

or with equal P_i

$$U_{(x \,|\, y)} = 1/4\,(0.8554 + 1.2995 + 1.2905 + 0.9895)$$

$$= 1.1087 \text{ in bits}$$

We need to note that the P_x values need not be equal as in our example, however the $P_{(x)}$ is always equal to 1.00.

From the calculations from the above data, we can now find the contingent uncertainty (Formula 12.8):

$$U_{xy} = 1.8897 - 1.1087$$
$$= 0.7810 \text{ in bits}$$

This obtained value is the amount of association between the two variables. The amount of uncertainty has been reduced by 0.7810 as the amount of uncertainty in bits of the Y variable which can be predicted from our information of the X variable. As a proportion of the total uncertainty (Formula 12.10), we would have 0.4133.

To test the significance of this reduction of uncertainty, we use Formula 12.11, or:

$$\chi^2 = (1.3863)(200)(0.7810)$$

$$= 216.54$$

With $(k - 1)\,(r - 1)$ degrees of freedom or 9 degrees of freedom. This obtained chi-square is associated with a probability of less than 0.001. We would thus conclude that there has been a highly significant reduction of uncertainty, or that the amount of association is greater than can be attributed to chance.

Summary of Terms

bit
chi-square
contingency coefficient
contingent uncertainty
correlational methods

phi coefficient
population correlation

Summary of Symbols

C

ϕ

ρ

U_{xy}

Problems

1. A political science major at a large university was interested in the degree of association, if any, between the number of speeches given by a candidate for a student government office and the number of votes received. Over a three-year period he collected the following data. Compute the contingency coefficient, and test its significance at the 0.01 alpha level.

		Number of Speeches Given	
		Under 5 Speeches	Over 5 Speeches
Number of Votes Received	Under 500 Votes	51	69
	Over 500 Votes	96	16

2. "Old Wives Tales" suggest that males do better than females in math classes. Herman decided to investigate this hypothesis by using the phi coefficient. The data, collected from an introductory math class that was graded on a pass/fail basis, are presented below. Help Herman by analyzing his data at the 0.05 alpha level, and stating the conclusion that he should reach.

		Student's Grade		
		Pass	Fail	Total
Student's Sex	Male	37	78	115
	Female	76	35	111
	Total	113	113	

3. A physiological psychologist, having developed a new general anesthesia, tried to determine the dosages at which the anesthesia would have (1) no effect, (2) a successful effect, or (3) a fatal effect. She administered one of four doses to each of 10 animals. The data are given below. Compute the contingent uncertainty, and test its significance at the 0.001 alpha level.

		Dosage				
		5mg/kg	10mg/kg	15mg/kg	20mg/kg	Total
	No Effect	8	2	0	0	10
Effect	Successful Effect	2	6	6	2	16
	Fatal Effect	0	2	4	8	14

Correlational Methods
for the
Ordinal Scale   Chapter Thirteen

This chapter will cover the measures of correlation that have been developed to describe the relationships between sets of rank-ordered data. These measures of rank-order correlations describe the functional relationship for a hypothesis about orders.

Spearman's Rank Difference Correlation Coefficient

Function and Method. The Spearman rank difference correlation coefficient, r_s, or rho, is a measure of covariation between two variables, each of which is ordered or ranked in a series. Therefore, rho requires that both variables be measured on at least the ordinal scale of measurement. This procedure is of major importance in research when it is not feasible to measure the attributes on an interval scale, but when they can be ranked along a continuous dimension. When there are no tied ranks, the Spearman coefficient is equal to and a special case of the Pearson coefficient. This latter coefficient is discussed in Chapter 14. One of the assumptions of the Pearson coefficient is that of linearity, thus we assume linearity for rho as well.

The formula for computing the Spearman coefficient is:

$$r_s = 1 - \frac{6 \sum\limits_{i=1}^{N} d_i^2}{N^3 - N} \qquad (13.1)$$

where N = number of subjects ranked

$d_i = X_{Ri} - Y_{Ri}$, the difference for the ith case between the ranked score of variable $X(X_{Ri})$ and the ranked score of variable $Y(Y_{Ri})$

In the computation of rho, each subject or object has two scores and the rank is determined for the X variable and then for the Y variable. The differences in ranks are obtained, and then squared and summed over the N cases. This value is then entered into the formula.

When two or more persons receive the same score on a variable, each person is assigned the average of the associated ranks that would have otherwise occurred. The effect of this upon the magnitude of rho is minimal.

The direction and the size of the coefficient is determined by the differences in ranks. When $\sum_{i=1}^{N} d_i^2$ is zero, then r_s will be 1.00. On the other hand, when $\sum_{i=1}^{N} d_i^2$ is at the maximum the coefficient will be –1.00. Table 13.1 illustrates these cases.

Table 13.1

X_R	Y_R	d	d^2	X_R	Y_R	d	d^2
1	1	0	0	1	5	-4	16
2	2	0	0	2	4	-2	4
3	3	0	0	3	3	0	0
4	4	0	0	4	2	2	4
5	5	0	0	5	1	4	16

$d = 0 \quad d^2 = 0 \qquad\qquad d = 0 \quad d^2 = 40$

$$r_s = 1 - \frac{6(0)}{5^3 - 5} \qquad\qquad r_s = 1 - \frac{6(40)}{5^3 - 5}$$

$$= 1.00 \qquad\qquad\qquad = -1.00$$

Significance of r_s. The significance of rho may be tested against the null hypothesis that population correlation is equal to zero, where the research hypothesis is $\neq$, $<$, or $>$. The null hypothesis is evaluated from Table R with $N - 2$ degrees of freedom, or by Formula 13.2:

$$t = r_s \sqrt{\frac{N-2}{1-r_s^2}} \tag{13.2}$$

with $N - 2$ degrees of freedom, when $N < 30$. In Table R, critical values corresponding to alpha levels of 0.05 and 0.01 are given for one- and two-tailed tests with various degrees of freedom. When $N \geqslant 30$, the sampling distribution of r_s with the null hypothesis that the population correlation is zero is evaluated by Formula 13.3:

$$z = r_s \sqrt{N - 1} \qquad (13.3)$$

and we enter the table of the normal curve (Table C) to determine if the null hypothesis is tenable.

If, for example, we had set $\alpha = 0.05$ to test a $H_1 : \rho \neq 0.00$ and the sample size was 25, we enter the table for a two-tailed test for 23 *df*. The tabled value for r_s is 0.396. This is interpreted as: in 5 cases in 100 correlation observations, rho as large as ±0.396 or larger would occur by chance if the population correlation was zero. If, as shown in Figure 13.1, the obtained magnitude of rho was equal to or greater than this tabled value, regardless of sign, then the rho would fall in the region of rejection of the null hypothesis, and we would conclude that the population correlation was not zero. From the same information, but for the one-tailed test or a directional research hypothesis, we enter the table for the one-tailed test for 23 *df*. The critical tabled value is

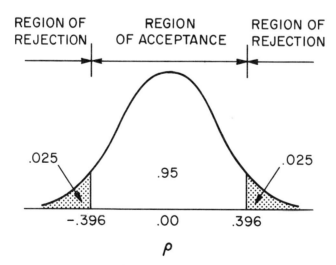

Figure 13.1.   Regions of acceptance and rejection of two-tailed hypothesis for the rank-order correlation coefficients with 23 degrees of freedom for alpha at the .05 level.

0.337 if the hypothesis states a positive association and is also
–0.337 if the hypothesis is given in terms of the negative
relationship.

Example.   It has been suggested that there is a significant
positive relationship between the visual complexity of a stimulus
object and the amount of time subjects will take looking at the
stimulus. In order to test such a hypothesis, the investigators asked
a number of judges to rank order a set of twelve visual stimuli
from the least complex to the most complex. Medians were
obtained for the twelve stimuli and were used as the ranks. The
stimuli were then randomly presented to fifty subjects with the
instruction that they could look at the stimulus as briefly or as
long as they wanted. When they had finished looking at the
stimulus they pressed a button which shut off that stimulus and
presented the next one. Mean "looking time" was determined for
each stimulus and the means of the stimuli were ranked. The
associated median complexity score and the mean looking time
values are given in Table 13.2.

Table 13.2

Stimulus	Complexity Score	Looking-Time Score
A	6.1	10.9
B	6.8	5.8
C	9.2	14.2
D	4.6	9.2
E	13.8	12.3
F	2.4	4.7
G	16.3	13.7
H	7.6	7.7
I	3.9	6.8
J	8.6	9.0
K	12.5	14.9
L	17.4	15.8

These two sets of scores were then averaged into two sets of ranks,
with the low-complexity stimulus receiving Rank 1 and the shortest
looking time also Rank 1. These rankings, along with the d_i and d_i^2,
are given in Table 13.3.

Table 13.3

Stimulus	Complexity Rank	Looking-Time Rank	d_i	d_i^2
A	4	7	-3	9
B	5	2	3	9
C	8	10	-2	4
D	3	6	-3	9
E	10	8	2	4
F	1	1	0	
G	11	9	2	4
H	6	4	2	4
I	2	3	-1	1
J	7	5	2	4
K	9	11	-2	4
L	12	12	0	—

$$\Sigma d_i^2 = 52$$

By applying Formula 13.1 to these data, we have:

$$r_s = 1 - \frac{6(52)}{1716}$$

$$= 0.82$$

In testing the hypothesis that this positive magnitude of rho differs significantly from zero, we utilize Table R for our one-tailed test, and let us assume alpha at the 0.05 level. With 10 degrees of freedom, alpha at the 0.05 level, and the one-tailed test, we observe a critical value for rho that is equal to 0.564. Thus, as the obtained magnitude of 0.82 is greater than the critical value, we would reject the null hypothesis and hence accept the research hypothesis. The conclusion that we would draw is that there is a significant positive association between visual complexity and "looking time," as measured in this study.

Kendall's Coefficient of Rank Correlation

Function and Method. Kendall's rank correlation coefficient, τ (tau) is, like rho, a measure of correlation where both X and Y variables are measured on at least an ordinal scale, and where the two variables have been ranked. While tau and rho both utilize the same data, they will not give identical coefficients. Nevertheless, both measures detect the existence of the association in the population. The greatest limitation of tau is that we cannot compare tau to other correlational methods. However, it can be pointed out that tau is approximately equivalent to rho squared. With this relationship between tau and rho, tau may be more nearly seen as a coefficient of determination than as a correlation measure. The concept of the coefficient of determination is fully discussed in Chapter 14.

Tau is defined as a ratio of the obtained value of S to the maximum S, or:

$$\tau = \frac{S_o}{S_{max}} \qquad (13.4)$$

The obtained S is derived by arranging the X ranks in their natural order $(1, 2, 3, \ldots, N)$ and then determining the degree of correspondence with the Y ranks. Each rank on the Y variable is compared with every other rank in its natural order of $N(N-1)/2$ comparisons of pairs.

We determine how many such pairs of the Y variable are in their natural order. When a pair is in its natural order a +1 value is assigned to it. If the order is reversed or the ranks are not in their natural order, a -1 value is given. The S_o is the sum of negative (–) and positive (+) values for all the $N(N-1)/2$ pairs. The S_{max} will be $N(N-1)/2$ comparisons. Therefore tau is:

$$\tau = \frac{S_o}{1/2 \; N(N-1)} \qquad (13.5)$$

The degree and the direction of the coefficient is determined by the sign and size of the ratio of the S_o to the S_{max}. When the S_o is positive, then the Y ranks show a correspondence with the X ranks, and the Y ranks are generally in their natural order. We can have a +1.00 coefficient only when all the Y pairs are in their natural order. When the S_o is negative the ranks are generally inversed, and the Y ranks are not in natural order. A –1.00 value occurs where all the Y pairs are not in their natural order. When tied scores occur, they are assigned the average of the ranks they would have been assigned if there had been no ties.

Significance of Tau. Kendall has given the exact sampling distribution for S_o when N is from 4 to 10. This sampling distribution is obtained by noting the $N!$ orders of the Y ranks when X are in their natural order. The $1/N!$ values form the probability of occurence under the null hypothesis. The sampling distributions are symmetrical with the – and + maximum values in the tails of the distribution.

For example, if $N = 4$ then $N!$ is (4) (3) (2) (1) or 24 possible orders of the Y ranks. Furthermore the obtained values of τ could only be -1.00, -0.67, -0.33, 0.00, 0.33, 0.67, 1.00. Now, the value of -1.00 could be obtained only in one way and the probability of this event under the null hypothesis is 1/24 or P = 0.042; the value of -0.67 could be obtained in 3 ways or 3/24 or P = 0.125; -0.33 in 5 ways or 5/24 or P = 0.208; 0.00 in 6 ways or 6/24 or P = 0.25; 0.33 in 5 ways or 5/24 or P = 0.208; and so forth.

When $N > 10$ the sampling distribution of tau under the null hypothesis can be approximated by the normal curve:

$$z = \frac{\tau - \mu_\tau}{\sigma_\tau} \tag{13.6}$$

$$\text{where } \mu_\tau = 0 \tag{13.7}$$

$$\text{and } \sigma_\tau = \sqrt{\frac{2(2N + 5)}{9N(N - 1)}} \tag{13.8}$$

Therefore, the probabilities for any observed tau can be determined, and the significance of tau can be made for the various research hypotheses with a stated level of alpha.

Example. As tau and rho can be utilized for the same data, we shall use the same example for tau as was used for rho (see Table 13.4).

Table 13.4

Stimulus	Complexity	"Looking Time"
A	4	7
B	5	2
C	8	10
D	3	6
E	10	8
F	1	1
G	11	9
H	6	4
I	2	3
J	7	5
K	9	11
L	12	12

Now we arrange the complexity ranks in their natural order as shown in Table 13.5.

Table 13.5

Stimulus	Complexity	"Looking Time"
F	1	1
I	2	3
D	3	6
A	4	7
B	5	2
H	6	4
J	7	5
C	8	10
K	9	11
E	10	8
G	11	9
L	12	12

The value of S_o is now determined for the degree of correspondence with the ranks on "looking time," or:

$$S_o = (11 - 0) + (9 - 1) + (6 - 3) + (5 - 3) + (7 - 0) + (6 - 0) + (5 - 0) + (2 - 2) + (1 - 2) + (2 - 0) + (1 - 0)$$
$$= 44$$

From Formula 13.5 we have:

$$\tau = \frac{44}{1/2 \ (12)(11)}$$

$$= 0.67$$

As with rho, this obtained value of tau represents the correspondence in rankings between the complexity and the "looking-time" variables.

As the sample size is greater than 10, we shall use Formula 13.6 to determine the significance of the obtained value of tau, or:

$$z = \frac{0.67}{\sqrt{\dfrac{2[(2)(12) + 5]}{(9)(12)(11)}}}$$

$$= 3.03$$

This obtained z value falls well beyond the criterial z value of 1.645 for a one-tailed test. Therefore, we would conclude that there is a significant positive association between the two variables of this research.

As we have previously pointed out, and shown here, rho and tau will not give the same coefficient. However the obtained tau is approximately equal to the previously obtained rho squared or:

$$0.67 \approx (0.82)^2 \approx 0.6764$$

Both methods with the same data will detect if the magnitude of the association differs significantly from a null hypothesis.

Kendall's Coefficient of Concordance

Function and Method. Kendall's coefficient of concordance, W, is an index of the relationship between three or more sets of ranks. The coefficient of concordance serves two major functions in statistical analysis. In the first place, it can be used as a measure of association among three or more variables, each of which has been ranked. As rho and tau measure the degree of association between two ranked variables, the coefficient of concordance is used when we need to determine a relationship between K variables. Secondly, the coefficient can be utilized to ascertain the reliability or agreement among judges about N objects when there are no other objective procedures readily available.

The coefficient of concordance is defined as a ratio between the observed sum of squares of the deviations of the K sum of ranks from their common mean (S_o), and the sum of squares which would occur if there were perfect agreement or disagreement among the K rankings (S_{pa}), or:

$$W = \frac{S_o}{S_{pa}} \tag{13.9}$$

$$\text{where } S_o = \sum_{1}^{N}\sum_{1}^{K} R_i^2 - \frac{\left(\sum_{1}^{N}\sum_{1}^{K} R_i\right)^2}{N} \tag{13.10}$$

$$\text{and } S_{pa} = \frac{K^2(N^3 - N)}{12} \tag{13.11}$$

and where K = the number of ranked sets (variables or judges)

N = number of ranked objects in the sets

In order to determine the value of S_o, we sum the assigned ranks by the K judges for each subject or object, or:

$$\sum_1^N R_i = X_{R_i} + \ldots + Z_{R_i} \tag{13.12}$$

X_{R_i} = the rank for the ith case on variable X or by judge X

Formula 13.10 tells us then to sum over the N cases, and also to square each sum and then to sum over all N cases.

The magnitude of W can vary between 0.00 and 1.00. When we have complete agreement between the K ranks the coefficient is 1.00. The coefficient becomes 0.00 when we observe maximum disagreement. The W cannot have a negative coefficient as we cannot have complete disagreement. For example, if A disagrees with B and also C, then B and C must agree.

It is possible to find a rho coefficient between all possible combinations of K ranked variables or $K(K-1)/2$ coefficients. The average of these coefficients is related to W in that:

$$\bar{r}_s = \frac{KW - 1}{(K - 1)} \tag{13.14}$$

From this average, $\bar{r}_s$, we can determine an estimate of the reliability of the combined judges by utilizing the Spearman-Brown Formula (15.11), page 313:

$$r_{xx} = \frac{K\bar{r}_s}{1 + (K - 1)\,\bar{r}_s} \tag{13.15}$$

Formula 13.15 can be utilized as a statistical procedure to determine the common agreement among judges about objects or statements where we do not have other objective procedures. For a further discussion of reliability see Chapter 15.

Significance of *W*.   When *N* is from 3 to 7 and *K* is 3 to 20, then Table S can be used to determine the critical values of *W* for alpha at the 5- and 1-percent levels. If the obtained coefficient is equal to or greater than the tabled value, the null hypothesis is rejected and the research hypothesis, that there is agreement, is accepted.

For cases where *N* is greater than 7 and *K* is greater than 20, the probability that is associated with the null hypothesis of a zero relation for the coefficient of concordance can be determined by the chi-square or:

$$\chi^2 = K(N - 1)W \qquad (13.16)$$
$$\text{with } N - 1 \ df$$

If the obtained χ^2 value is equal to or greater than the tabled value for $N - 1$ degrees of freedom and a predetermined alpha, the null hypothesis that the *K* rankings are not related can be rejected.

Example.   As part of a project on the evaluation of teaching, ten professional judges observed the teaching performance of fifteen professors over a period of days. At the end of their observations, the judges evaluated each instructor by making a separate judgment on a five-item scale, and a composite score was determined. These scores are given in Table 13.6. A low score was associated with a high evaluation.

Table 13.6

Instructors

Judges	1	2	3	4	5	6	7	8	9	10	11	12	13	14	15
A	2.1	4.6	1.9	3.3	1.3	2.3	1.7	4.1	4.7	2.4	5.7	4.9	1.4	3.7	3.2
B	1.3	4.1	1.7	3.1	1.6	3.3	1.4	4.9	4.2	1.8	5.2	5.0	1.9	3.7	3.2
C	2.1	4.5	1.9	3.1	2.0	2.4	1.7	4.9	5.6	2.3	5.5	5.1	1.8	3.2	3.8
D	1.4	4.3	1.9	3.8	1.2	2.9	1.1	4.5	5.2	2.8	5.7	4.4	1.3	3.2	3.9
E	1.3	4.1	1.1	3.7	1.7	3.0	2.3	4.8	4.7	2.4	4.4	4.5	1.8	3.5	3.4
F	1.8	3.8	1.7	4.2	2.7	3.2	1.9	4.5	4.4	3.6	4.3	4.6	1.3	3.4	3.9
G	2.3	3.0	1.2	4.0	1.3	2.1	2.6	5.4	5.6	2.8	5.8	5.3	2.0	3.6	4.2
H	2.2	3.6	1.0	3.1	2.0	2.8	2.5	4.8	5.7	3.0	5.5	4.2	1.8	4.1	3.9
I	2.2	4.5	1.5	3.6	1.6	2.3	1.8	3.7	5.2	3.2	5.3	4.8	1.4	3.1	3.9
J	2.5	3.1	1.3	4.1	1.6	2.9	1.8	4.7	5.4	2.6	4.7	4.6	1.2	3.6	3.4

These scores were then transformed into ranking.

Instructors

Judges	1	2	3	4	5	6	7	8	9	10	11	12	13	14	15
A	5	12	4	9	1	6	3	11	13	7	15	14	2	10	8
B	1	11	4	7	3	9	2	13	12	5	15	14	6	10	8
C	5	11	3	8	4	7	1	12	15	6	14	13	2	9	10
D	4	11	5	9	2	7	1	13	14	6	15	12	3	8	10
E	2	11	1	10	3	7	5	15	12	6	13	14	4	9	8
F	3	9	2	11	5	6	4	14	13	8	12	15	1	7	10
G	5	8	1	10	2	4	6	13	14	7	15	12	3	9	11
H	4	9	1	8	3	6	5	13	15	7	14	12	2	11	10
I	5	12	2	9	3	6	4	10	14	8	15	13	1	7	11
J	5	8	2	11	3	7	4	12	15	6	14	13	1	10	9
R_i	39	102	25	92	29	65	35	126	137	66	142	132	25	90	95

$\Sigma R_i = 1200$

$\Sigma R_i^2 = 121644$

$N = 15$

$K = 12$

$$W = \frac{121644 - \dfrac{(1200)^2}{15}}{1/12 \ (10)^2 \ [15^3 - 15]}$$

$\quad = 0.9159$

The coefficient of concordance was computed where the mean of ranks is 80, the sum of squares of the deviations is 25,644, 10 judges (or K) and 15 instructors (or N). The obtained coefficient of 0.9159 is the degree of agreement among the judges on the composite scores assigned to the various instructors.

To test the hypothesis that the judges agree beyond the 0.01 level of significance, we shall apply Formula 13.16:

$$\chi^2 = 10(15 - 1)(0.9159)$$

$$= 128.225$$

The probability of occurance of this event under the null hypothesis is less than 0.001. Therefore, we conclude that there is a significant high agreement among the judges.

Spearman's Partial-Rank Correlation

Function and Method. The various sections on correlational method that have been described are basically applied to a simple two-variable study. In much of correlation research, we often have a number of variables and have interests in all possible combinations of pairs of variables. The magnitude of the coefficient between any two variables may be highly misleading in that the obtained value can reflect a common influence from another variable or variables. When this common effect is removed there may be relatively little or no association between a particular pair of variables because both are highly correlated with other variables. The partial correlation is a measure of correlation of the residual relationship between two variables where the common effects of the other variables have been partialed out. Both tau and rho can be used to determine a partial correlation coefficient when the variables have been ordered or ranked, or when we cannot meet the assumptions of an interval scale.

The formula for a Spearman three-variable, partial-rank correlation is comparable to that used with the partial correlation of the Pearson correlation coefficient (Formula 14.39), and is stated as:

$$ r_{s\,12\cdot3} = \frac{r_{s\,12} - r_{s\,13} - r_{s\,23}}{\sqrt{(1 - r_{s\,13}^2)(1 - r_{s\,23}^2)}} \tag{13.17} $$

where $r_{s\,12}$ = rho between variables 1 and 2

$r_{s\,13}$ = rho between variables 1 and 3

$r_{s\,23}$ = rho between variables 2 and 3

Formula 13.17 shows the partial correlation between variables 1 and 2 where we partialed out the interrelations with variable 3. The statistical operations in Formula 13.17 imply that we determine the coefficients for all combinations of variables. If we subtract out the estimates of r_{s13} and r_{s23}, we have two sets of residuals or of errors. The partial correlation coefficient, in general, is between these two sets of residuals.

Test of Significance for Spearman's Partial Rank Correlation.
The sampling distribution for $r_{s12\cdot3}$ with the null hypothesis that
the population correlation is zero, is evaluated by the t-test with
$N - 3$ degrees of freedom or from Table R. The formula is given as:

$$t = \frac{r_{s12\cdot3}}{\sqrt{(1 - r^2_{s12\cdot3})/N - 3)}} \qquad (13.18)$$

Example. Suppose a researcher was interested in the relationship between an attitude toward war, and a measure of
aggressive personality in men. However, he may be concerned that
these two variables are intercorrelated with age, a variable which
he wants to partial out. Assume that he takes a random sample of
25 men over ages, and rank orders these individuals on the basis of
the three variables. The data may appear as shown in Table 13.7.

Table 13.7

Subject	Rank (attitude)	Rank (personality)	Rank (age)
1	1	2	3
2	2	5	2
3	3	1	1
.	.	.	.
.	.	.	.
.	.	.	.
N	N	$N - 4$	$N - 6$

We further assume that he then obtained all possible combinations
of Spearman's rank coefficients as given in Table 13.8.

Table 13.8

	(1) Attitude	(2) Personality	(3) Age
(1)	——	.58	.48
(2)		——	.36
(3)			——

Computing the Spearman partial-rank correlation coefficient between 1 and 2, and partialing out 3, we have, from Formula
13.17:

$$r_{s12.3} = \frac{.58 - (.48)(.36)}{\sqrt{[1 - (.48)^2][1 - (.36)^2]}}$$

$$= .519$$

With 22 degrees of freedom and a two-tailed test of significance, the obtained coefficient is larger than the tabled critical value at the 0.05 level of significance of 0.428. Thus, we would conclude that the obtained coefficient differs significantly from zero. Furthermore, we can observe that the influence of age is relatively small, 0.519 from 0.58, when we partialed it from the other two variables.

Kendall's Partial-Rank Correlation

Function and Method.   Kendall's partial rank correlation is comparable to both the Spearman and the Pearson partial correlational methods in function and procedure. However, the coefficients in the computational formula are all taus and are stated as:

$$\tau_{12.3} = \frac{\tau_{12} - \tau_{13}\tau_{23}}{\sqrt{(1 - \tau_{13}^2)(1 - \tau_{23}^2)}} \qquad (13.19)$$

where τ_{12} = tau between variables 1 and 2

τ_{13} = tau between variables 1 and 3

τ_{23} = tau between variables 2 and 3

Formula 13.19 shows the partial correlation between variables 1 and 2 where we partialed out the interrelations with variable 3.

Test of Significance for Kendall's Partial Rank Correlation. No test of significance of $\tau_{12.3}$ can be made in that the sampling distribution for the partial tau is unknown.

Summary of Terms

Kendall's coefficient of concordance
Kendall's partial-rank correlation
Kendall's rank-order coefficient
rank difference
rho

Spearman's rank difference correlation coefficient
Spearman's partial-rank correlation
tau

Summary of Symbols

r_s μ_τ r_{xx}

d_i σ_τ $r_{s12 \cdot 3}$

τ W $\tau_{12 \cdot 3}$

S_o S_{pa}

S_{max} $\bar{r}_s$

Problems

1. Herman Swiftscience once hypothesized that maze explora-
    tion and maze learning are positively related. In other words
    he believed that animals that explored more than other
    animals would also learn mazes faster than other animals.
    Herman tested his hypothesis by measuring both maze
    exploration and maze learning on the same group of 20 rats.
    (See data on page 249.) Compute both rho and tau, and
    test their significance at the .05 alpha level. Be sure to notice
    that high exploration scores indicate a greater amount of
    exploration than low exploration scores, but that low maze-
    learning scores indicate more rapid maze learning (number of
    days to criterion) than high maze-learning scores.

Exp. Score	Learning Score
2	40
3	18
20	58
20	15
20	21
20	42
20	38
20	37
21	38
21	19
22	43
22	15
24	25
24	41
37	36
37	25
38	53
38	31
46	21
48	31

2. A psychologist, while preparing slides of various complexity for a looking-time experiment, asked 5 judges to independently rank his slides from least to most complex. The rankings of the 5 judges are given below. Compute the coefficient of concordance between the 5 judges, and test its significance at the 0.01 alpha level.

Slides

Judges	1	2	3	4	5	6	7	8	9	10
A	2	5	3	1	6	8	4	10	7	9
B	4	2	3	5	6	7	1	9	8	10
C	2	4	1	3	5	7	6	9	8	10
D	4	1	3	5	10	6	2	8	9	7
E	1	6	4	2	5	7	3	9	8	10

3. An experimenter hypothesized that social dominance in chicks was related to general locomotor activity. She did find a high degree of association as measured by tau, however, she became concerned that this might be due to a high degree of

association between each of the variables and the weight of the birds. The necessary taus are given below. What is the degree of association between social dominance and general locomotor activity when the effect of the birds' weight is partialed out?

	Dominance	Activity	Weight
Dominance		.66	.38
Activity			.20
Weight			

Correlational Methods for the Interval and Ratio Scales Chapter Fourteen

This chapter will present the various measures of correlation, and statistical tests of significance, that are associated with the interval scale of measurement. In addition, portions of the chapter are devoted to methods of prediction, and to discussions of some special methods of correlation.

Pearson Product-Moment Correlation Coefficient

Function and Method. The Pearson product-moment correlation coefficient, or r, is the principle measure of correlation between two variables, each of which is measured on an interval scale. The Pearson r is the most general measure of association for interval scales; we must make the assumptions that both the X and Y variables are continuous and each has an underlying standard unit of measurement, and that the trend of the relationship between X and Y is linear.

The Pearson r can be defined in numerous ways. One of the most common definitions states that r is the mean of cross products of z-scores:

$$r = \frac{\sum\limits_{i=1}^{N} (z_{xi})(z_{yi})}{N} \tag{14.1}$$

where $z_{xi} = \dfrac{X_i - \overline{X}}{S_x}$

$$z_{yi} = \dfrac{Y_i - \overline{Y}}{S_y}$$

N = number of X and Y pairs

From Formula 14.1, each N_i subject or object would have a z-score on the X variable and also on the Y variable. The cross product of each z-score is:

$$(z_{xi})\,(z_{yi})$$

and the sum of the cross products of z-scores would be:

$$\sum_{i=1}^{N} (z_{xi})(z_{yi})$$

In Figure 14.1 we have illustrated a single bivariate point in relation to the two means. The x, in the figure, is the deviation of

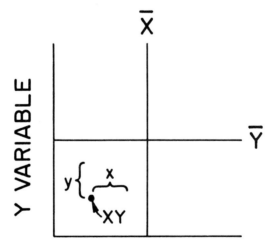

Figure 14.1. Plot of a single bivariate point (X and Y value) and the deviations from the two means.

X from the mean of X and the y the deviation from $\overline{Y}$. As the X value is less than $\overline{X}$, the obtained z-score would have a negative value, and similarly, the z value is less than $\overline{Y}$ and its z-score would also be negative. Therefore, the product for the two z-scores would be positive. It is the sign of the cross products as shown in Figure 14.2 that determines the direction of the correlation, and the magnitude of the product that describes the value of r. The r can range from -1.00 to +1.00.

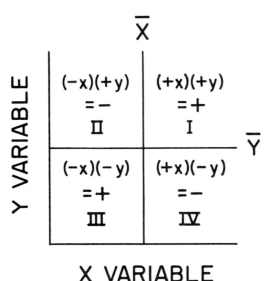

Figure 14.2.   Schematic representation of the sign of the cross products of deviation scores.

An equivalent formula for 14.1 is given as:

$$r = \frac{\Sigma xy}{\sqrt{\Sigma x^2 \, \Sigma y^2}} \qquad (14.2)$$

where Σxy = sum of cross products

Σx^2 = sum of squares of the X variable

Σy^2 = sum of squares of the Y variable

and where $\Sigma xy = \Sigma [(X - \overline{X})(Y - \overline{Y})]$

The Σxy is the sum of cross products of the deviation of the bivariate points from the two means. We would find the product of deviations, or $xy = (X - \overline{X})(Y - \overline{Y})$, and sum over all cases, or $\Sigma xy = \Sigma[(X - \overline{X})(Y - \overline{Y})]$. However, rather than using the definitional formula, we can use an equivalent computational formula for the sum of cross products:

$$\Sigma xy = \Sigma XY - \frac{(\Sigma X)(\Sigma Y)}{N}$$

and the computational formula for r becomes:

$$r = \frac{\Sigma XY - \frac{(\Sigma X)(\Sigma Y)}{N}}{\sqrt{\left[\Sigma X^2 - \frac{(\Sigma X)^2}{N}\right]\left[\Sigma Y^2 - \frac{(\Sigma Y)^2}{N}\right]}} \quad (14.3)$$

Computationally, Formula 14.3 saves finding the means, standard deviations and z-scores, and it reduces a large number of computational sets in comparison to Formula 14.1. Both Formula 14.1 and Formula 14.3 state that r is a ratio between the sum of cross products, and the geometric mean of the sum of squares of the two variables X and Y.

A Comparison of Pearson's *r*, Spearman's *r*, and the Phi Coefficients

In the previous chapters, we stated that both the Phi and Spearman coefficients were special cases of the Pearson product-moment correlation coefficient.

From Formula 14.3, if we substitute the following symbols:

$$b = \Sigma XY$$

$$b + d = \Sigma X$$

$$b + d = \Sigma X^2$$

$$a + b = \Sigma Y$$

$$a + b = \Sigma Y^2$$

and $a + b + c + d = N$

Then:

$$\phi = \frac{b - \frac{(b + d)(a + b)}{a + b + c + d}}{\sqrt{\left[(b + d) - \frac{(b + d)^2}{a + b + c + d}\right]\left[(a + b) - \frac{(a + b)^2}{a + b + c + d}\right]}}$$

$$= \frac{bc - ad}{\sqrt{(a + b)(c + d)(a + c)(b + d)}} \tag{12.3}$$

Therefore, the ϕ with two true dichotomous variables is equivalent to r.

Similarly, the Spearman coefficient is the product-moment correlation coefficient applied to a set of untied ranks. When the X and Y values are ranks then it can be shown that:

$$\Sigma X = \frac{N(N + 1)}{2}$$

$$\text{and} \quad \Sigma X^2 = \frac{N(N + 1)(2N + 1)}{6}$$

$$\text{therefore} \quad \Sigma x^2 = \frac{N(N + 1)(2N + 1)}{6} - \frac{[N(N + 1)/2]^2}{N}$$

$$= (N^3 - N)/12$$

$$\text{and} \quad \Sigma y^2 = (N^3 - N)/12$$

Now, as given:

$$d = x - y$$

$$\Sigma d^2 = \Sigma x^2 + \Sigma y^2 - 2r\sqrt{\Sigma x^2 \Sigma y^2}$$

We can then write: $r = \dfrac{\Sigma x^2 + \Sigma y^2 - \Sigma d^2}{2\sqrt{\Sigma x^2 \Sigma y^2}}$

Substituting: $r_s = \dfrac{\dfrac{N^3 - N}{12} + \dfrac{N^3 - N}{12} - \Sigma d^2}{2\sqrt{\left(\dfrac{N^3 - N}{12}\right)\left(\dfrac{N^3 - N}{12}\right)}}$

$$= \frac{2\left(\frac{N^3 - N}{12}\right) - \Sigma d^2}{2\left(\frac{N^3 - N}{12}\right)}$$

$$= 1 - \frac{6\Sigma d^2}{N^3 - N}$$

and as $d = x - y$

$$= (X - \bar{X}) - (Y - \bar{Y})$$

with X and Y as ranks, $\bar{X} = \bar{Y}$

therefore $d = X - Y = D$

or $r_s = 1 - \frac{6\Sigma D^2}{N^3 - N}$

and $r_s = r$

Significance of r.   As with the other measures of association, we want to determine whether the obtained correlation coefficient from our sample of two bivariate attributes is indicative of a non-zero correlation in the population. Our null hypothesis is:

$$H_0 : \rho = 0.00$$

and $H_1 : \rho \neq 0.00$

or $H_0 : \rho \leqslant 0.00$

$$H_1 : \rho > 0.00$$

or $H_0 : \rho \geqslant 0.00$

$$H_1 : \rho < 0.00$$

To test for the significance of r, we must assume that the scores are from a bivariate normal distribution.

Assuming that our obtained coefficient is a function of chance, we test this null hypothesis by the t-distribution:

$$t = r \frac{N-2}{1-r^2} \tag{14.4}$$

We have $N-2$ degrees of freedom, where N is the number of pairs in our sample. Table T gives the critical values for one- and two-tailed tests with alpha levels of 0.05 and 0.01. For example, from Table T we see that for 10 df the criterial r value for 10 df with alpha at 0.05 is $\pm$ 0.576 for a two-tailed test. This is shown in Figure 14.3.

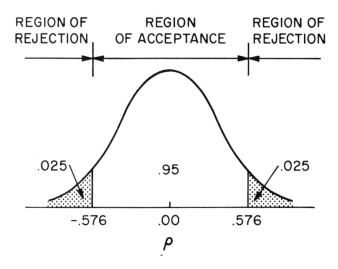

Figure 14.3   Regions of acceptance and rejection for a two-tailed test for 10 degrees of freedom with alpha at .05 for r.

If the observed coefficient, r, falls in the region of acceptance, we conclude that the coefficient was a function of chance or sampling variation where the population correlation is zero. On the other hand, if the obtained coefficient falls in the region of rejection, we reject the null hypothesis that population correlation is zero and conclude that the relationship between the two variables in the population differs significantly from zero.

On the other hand, if the alternative hypothesis states that the correlation is positive, with 10 df for this one-tailed test with alpha at 0.05, the critical value is 0.497 and is shown in Figure 14.4.

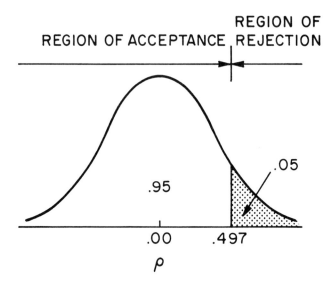

Figure 14.4.   Regions of acceptance and rejection for a hypothesis that the *r* is positive for 10 degrees of freedom with alpha at .05.

Or, if the alternative hypothesis states a negative relationship, then the region of rejection is in the left side of the curve as seen in Figure 14.5.

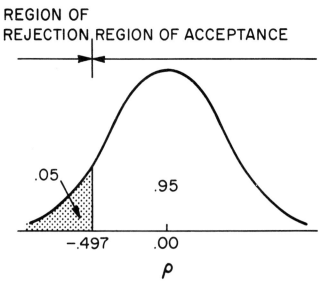

Figure 14.5.   Regions of acceptance and rejection for a hypothesis that *r* is negative for 10 degrees of freedom with alpha at .05.

Example.   During the past two decades, there has been a quest for short forms of various well-known psychological tests. In general, the rationale of a short form is to save time and effort in psychodiagnosis. However, the assumption is that the short form is highly correlated with the original longer form. For illustrative purposes, we shall use a small sample, which would create some methodological problems in terms of later decisions, but the data here are only hypothetical.

Let us assume that an investigator was interested in the development of a short form for an intelligence scale for children, and that he has drawn a random sample of 20 boys from the population. In order to counter-balance the tests he randomized the order in which he gave the two forms.

Table 14.1 gives each of the 20 subjects' scores on the two scales.

Table 14.1

Subjects	Original Scale	Short Form Scale
A	90	87
B	66	75
C	96	106
D	122	114
E	142	138
F	91	93
G	101	98
H	116	119
I	106	102
J	120	114
K	105	97
L	99	90
M	81	88
N	108	104
O	97	95
P	109	112
Q	95	98
R	85	83
S	97	91
T	88	86

In order to compute the Pearson correlation coefficient we may apply Formula 14.3, or:

$$\Sigma X = 2014$$

$$\Sigma X^2 = 208038$$

$$\Sigma Y = 1990$$

$$\Sigma Y^2 = 202092$$

$$\Sigma XY = 204755$$

$$N = 20$$

$$r = \frac{204755 - \dfrac{(2014)(1990)}{20}}{\sqrt{\left[208038 - \dfrac{(2014)^2}{20}\right]\left[202092 - \dfrac{(1990)^2}{20}\right]}}$$

$$= \frac{4362}{\sqrt{(5228.2)(4087)}}$$

$$= \frac{4362}{4622.5}$$

$$= 0.9436$$

The $r = 0.94$ represents the magnitude of relation between the two scales as shown for the 20 subjects.

Table T shows that a correlation coefficient as large as this for a one-tailed test of significance and 18 degrees of freedom is associated with a probability at less than the 0.01 level. Therefore, we would reject the null hypothesis that the correlation is zero, and could conclude that the two scales are significantly correlated at less than the 0.01 level of significance.

Goodness of Fit of *r*. A research hypothesis could state that the correlation coefficient between two variables from the population is of a given value that differs from zero. The purpose of such research would be to test the goodness of fit of the obtained correlation coefficient (r) to the theoretical population correlation (ρ), or:

$$r = \rho$$

where $\rho \neq .00$

If the population correlation is, in fact, different from zero, then the sampling distribution from this population may be skewed. This skewness is due primarily to the limitations placed upon the range of the coefficient (–1.00 to +1.00) and of the sample size. If the sample size is small and the magnitude of the population coefficient is large, then the sampling distribution could be skewed in a very marked fashion. However, if the sample size is large and if the magnitude of the population correlation is not great, the sampling distribution could be considered to be fairly normal.

Fisher has developed a statistical transformation of r which has the distinct advantages of testing various hypotheses when the sample size is small and when the size of the population coefficient is large. This transformation is written as:

$$z'_r = 1/2 \left(\log_e (1 + r) - \log_e (1 - r) \right) \qquad (14.5)$$

Table U gives the transformations derived from this formula from r to z'_r and z'_r to r.

The standard error of this distribution of transformed r is based on the size of the sample of r:

$$S'_z = \frac{1}{\sqrt{N - 3}} \qquad (14.6)$$

where N = number of pairs in the sample

We can test the null hypothesis by z where:

$$z = \frac{z'_r - z'_\rho}{S'_z} \qquad (14.7)$$

where z'_r = transformed value of r

z'_ρ = transformed value of ρ

S'_z = standard error of r

The obtained z value is evaluated from Table C, in the usual fashion with the areas of acceptance and rejection dependent upon the nature of the research hypothesis. But, in general, our research hypothesis is simply a difference hypothesis that calls for a two-tailed test.

Example. In our illustration of the Pearson correlation we obtained a $r = 0.94$ between an original scale of intelligence and a short form of the same scale. If we assume that the reliability of the original scale was 0.96, we may ask if our obtained correlation coefficient is equal to this reliability. We can test this goodness of fit by Formula 14.7. In Table C we have the z' transformation of r, and hence:

$$r = 0.9436 \qquad\qquad z'_r = 1.783$$

$$\rho = 0.96 \qquad\qquad z'_\rho = 1.946$$

$$z = \frac{1.783 - 1.946}{1/\sqrt{20 - 3}}$$

$$= \frac{-0.163}{0.2425}$$

$$= -0.672$$

If we assume a two-tailed test of significance, a z-value of $+1.96$ at the 0.05 level would be required to reject the null hypothesis. As our obtained value of -0.672 falls in the region of acceptance, we conclude that there is no significant difference between our obtained r and the population r as estimated by the reliability coefficient of the original scale.

Significance Between Two Independent Correlation Coefficients. A frequent problem in research is the testing of the significance between two independent correlation coefficients. We may wish to determine if two independent sets of observations on the same population are different, or if two independent population's coefficients differ. To test the hypothesis that two independent correlations differ significantly, the null hypothesis is stated as:

$$H_0 : \rho_1 = \rho_2$$

$$\text{or} \quad : \rho_1 - \rho_2 = 0$$

$$\text{and } H_1 : \rho_1 \neq \rho_2$$

$$: \rho_1 > \rho_2$$

$$: \rho_1 < \rho_2$$

The null hypothesis is evaluated by:

$$z = \frac{z'_{r_1} - z'_{r_2}}{S_{z'_1 - z'_2}} \qquad (14.8)$$

where z'_{r_1} = transformed value of r_1

z'_{r_2} = transformed value of r_2

$S_{z'_1 - z'_2}$ = the standard error of the difference between two independent values of z'

In Formula 14.6 we had the standard error of r for a single sample and in Formula 14.8 we have the standard error of the difference between two independent values of z', or:

$$S_{z'_1 - z'_2} = \sqrt{\frac{1}{N_1 - 3} + \frac{1}{N_2 - 3}} \qquad (14.9)$$

where N_1 = number of pairs for r_1

N_2 = number of pairs for r_2

Thus, to compare two independent correlations we do not have to have equal numbers of pairs to test our hypothesis.

The general procedure for evaluating the obtained z value is comparable to that in the previous section. From the sampling distribution in Table C, and with the predetermined level of alpha and research hypothesis, the significance of z can be determined.

Example. Let us assume in our prior example that the investigator also obtained a sample of 20 girls from the population and determined the relationship between an original intelligence scale and the short form. Assuming this coefficient to be 0.8972, we can ask the question, is there a significant difference between these two samples from two different populations. Let alpha be equal to 0.05 for this two-tailed test and we shall utilize Formula 14.8 for this example.

Boys	Girls
$r = 0.9436$	$r = 0.8972$
$z'_r = 1.783$	$z'_r = 1.447$
$N = 20$	$N = 20$

$$z = \frac{1.783 - 1.447}{\sqrt{\dfrac{1}{20 - 3} + \dfrac{1}{20 - 3}}}$$

$$= \frac{0.336}{\sqrt{\dfrac{2}{17}}}$$

$$= \frac{0.336}{0.343}$$

$$= 0.980$$

This obtained $z = 0.980$ would fall within the region of acceptance and we would conclude that these two independent correlations do not differ significantly from each other.

Linear Regression

Function and Method. Our major research interest is generally in the magnitude and direction of a relationship between two variables. However, a second major interest is prediction.

Regression is the method of prediction of one variable from a knowledge of the values of a second variable. In general, if we determine that the relationship between X and Y is zero, where there is no systematic relationship between the two variables, then knowing a value of X would not help us in predicting Y. Our best prediction in this case would simply be the mean of Y. Similarly, if we had no knowledge of a correlation between two variables, our best prediction of a variable would be the mean of that variable. However, as the coefficient between the two values differs from zero, and there is some systematic relationship, then when we know the value of X, we can predict the value of Y. As the magnitude of the relationship increases, the better the predictions—to the point of perfect prediction, when the coefficient is unity.

If we had a perfect linear relationship when we plotted the X values against the Y values on a graph, all the plotted points would fall on a straight line. The method for prediction is the determination of values for the equation of a straight line:

$$Y = a + bX \tag{14.10}$$

where Y = the predicted Y value

X = the known X value

a = the intercept of the line

b = the slope of the line

The nature of the additive constant, or a, is shown in Figure 14.6. The intercept of the line is that value of Y when the value of X is equal to zero. Therefore, when X is equal to zero, then Y is equal to a.

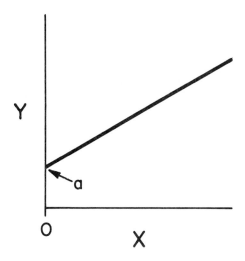

Figure 14.6. Schematic representation of a, intercept of the line Y, when X is equal to zero.

The multiplicative constant, or b, is the slope of the line, or the rate of change. This constant describes the rate at which Y changes with changes in X. The slope of any straight line is the ratio of the distance in a vertical direction to the horizontal distance, or:

$$b = \frac{A - C}{B - C}$$

This relation is shown in Figure 14.7.

The Linear Regression of Y on X. Generally, the relationship between X and Y is not perfect, in that all the bivariate points

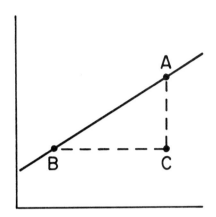

Figure 14.7.   Schematic representation of *b,* slope of the regression line. See text for explanation.

do not fall on the line, but rather, vary about some straight line. We can determine a line that best fits the data when we wish to predict *Y,* knowing *X.* This line of best fit is one which makes the variability about the line as small as possible. This line is the regression line of *Y* on *X,* and is given by:

$$\tilde{Y}_x = a_{yx} + b_{yx}X \qquad (14.11)$$

The $\tilde{Y}$ is the predicted value for an observed *Y* and does not necessarily equal the observed *Y.* As *Y* does not equal $\tilde{Y}$, we shall have some errors of prediction of $Y - \tilde{Y}$, as shown in Figure 14.8.

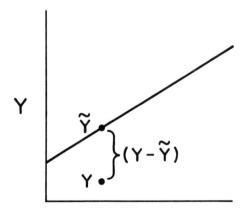

Figure 14.8.   Schematic of the observed and predicted *Y* values and its error of prediction.

The line that is determined from Formula 14.11 has the property that the sums of squares of all these vertical deviations, or those parallel to the Y axis, will be at a minimum, or:

$$\Sigma(Y - \tilde{Y})^2 = \text{minimum}$$

This is the property of least squares.

The least squares for the regression line of Y on X is given by the two constants of a_{yx} and b_{yx}. The slope of the line, b_{yx} or the regression coefficient is determined by:

$$b_{yx} = \frac{\Sigma xy}{\Sigma x^2} \tag{14.12}$$

$$= \frac{\Sigma(X - \bar{X})(Y - \bar{Y})}{\Sigma(X - \bar{X})^2}$$

$$= \frac{\Sigma XY - \frac{(\Sigma X)(\Sigma Y)}{N}}{\Sigma X^2 - \frac{(\Sigma X)^2}{N}}$$

When the rate of change is positive, the rate of increase in Y is associated with an increase in X, and a decrease in Y is accompanied by a decrease in X. From Figure 14.2 it can be seen that the sum of cross products would be positive when the majority of the points would fall in Quadrants I and III. If the rate of change is negative, then the relationship is best described as an increase in X, associated with a decrease in Y, and a decrease of X with an increase in Y. The sums of cross products would be negative when the majority of the points would fall in Quadrants II and IV.

The a_{yx} is computed by:

$$a_{yx} = \bar{Y} - b_{yx}\bar{X} \tag{14.13}$$

and the computational formula for the linear regression of Y on X becomes:

$$\tilde{Y} = a_{yx} + b_{yx}X$$

$$\tilde{Y} = (\bar{Y} - b_{yx}\bar{X}) + \left[\frac{\Sigma xy}{\Sigma x^2}\right]X \tag{14.14}$$

The Linear Regression of X on Y.   Just as we can predict Y from X, we can also predict X from Y. Thus, we need a different regression equation. This is the regression line of X on Y. The regression line also has the property of least squares for the deviations, in that they are horizontal or parallel to the X axis.

The equation for the regression line of X on Y is given as:

$$\widetilde{X} = a_{xy} + b_{xy} Y \tag{14.15}$$

$$\text{where } b_{xy} = \frac{\Sigma xy}{\Sigma y^2} \tag{14.16}$$

$$\text{and } a_{xy} = \overline{X} - b_{xy} \overline{Y} \tag{14.17}$$

Example.   We shall utilize the same data as given in the illustration for the Pearson correlation. These data are summarized in Table 14.2.

Table 14.2

$\Sigma X = 2014$

$\Sigma X^2 = 208038$

$\Sigma Y = 1990$

$\Sigma Y^2 = 202092$

$\Sigma XY = 204755$

$N = 20$

thus,

$$\overline{X} = \frac{\Sigma X}{N} = \frac{2014}{20} = 100.7$$

$$\Sigma x^2 = \Sigma X^2 - \frac{(\Sigma X)^2}{N} = 208038 - \frac{(2014)^2}{20} = 5528.2$$

$$\overline{Y} = \frac{\Sigma Y}{N} = \frac{1990}{20} = 99.5$$

$$\Sigma y^2 = \Sigma y^2 - \frac{(\Sigma Y)^2}{N} = 202092 - \frac{(1990)^2}{20} = 4087$$

and

$$\Sigma xy = \Sigma XY - \frac{(\Sigma X)(\Sigma Y)}{N} = 204755 - \frac{(2014)(1990)}{20} = 4362$$

From these data we shall compute the regression equations of Y on X and X on Y. Hence:

$$Y \text{ on } X$$

$$\widetilde{Y}_x = a_{yx} + b_{yx} X \tag{14.11}$$

$$\text{where } b_{yx} = \frac{\Sigma xy}{\Sigma x^2} \tag{14.12}$$

$$b_{yx} = \frac{4362}{5228.2} = 0.8343$$

$$\text{and } a_{yx} = \overline{Y} - b_{yx} \overline{X} \tag{14.13}$$

$$= 99.5 - 0.8343(100.7) = 15.486$$

$$\widetilde{Y} = 15.486 + 0.8343 \, (X)$$

$$X \text{ on } Y$$

$$\widetilde{X}_y = a_{xy} + b_{xy} Y \tag{14.14}$$

$$\text{where } b_{xy} = \frac{\Sigma xy}{\Sigma Y^2} \tag{14.15}$$

$$b_{xy} = \frac{4362}{4087} = 1.0673$$

$$\text{and } a_{xy} = \overline{X} - b_{xy} \overline{Y} \tag{14.16}$$

$$= 100.7 - 1.0673(99.5) - 5.496$$

$$\text{or } \widetilde{X}_y = -5.496 + 1.0673(Y)$$

Now for any known X value we can predict an associated $\widetilde{Y}$ value. If $X = 70$, then:

$$\widetilde{Y} = 15.486 + .8343(70) = 73.887$$

and similarly for any Y value, we could predict $\widetilde{X}$. As a good check on our computations, if we take the mean of X as the X value, the predicted Y would be the mean of Y, or:

$$\bar{X} = 100.7$$

thus $$\widetilde{Y} = 15.486 + .8343(100.7)$$

$$= 99.5 = \bar{Y}$$

The Relation Between Regression and Correlation Coefficient. In general we have two regression lines, one for Y on X, and one X on Y. When there is no relationship between X and Y, the b_{yx} is zero, and a_{yx} is the mean of Y or any $\widetilde{Y} = \bar{Y}$. Similarly, then $b_{xy} = 0$ and $\widetilde{X} = \bar{X}$. Then we have a perfect relationship when the two regression lines are superimposed upon one another. The relations of correlation and regression are shown in Figure 14.9.

In general, the magnitude of the relationship between X and Y can be expressed as the angle of separation between the two regression lines. When the correlation between X and Y is zero, the two regression lines are at right angles, and as the angle decreases, the magnitude of the correlation coefficient increases.

There is a very simple, but very meaningful, relationship between the slopes of the two regression lines and the correlation coefficient:

$$b_{yx} = \frac{\Sigma xy}{\Sigma x^2} \quad \text{and} \quad b_{xy} = \frac{\Sigma xy}{\Sigma y^2}$$

substituting an identity:

$$b_{yx} = \frac{\Sigma xy}{(N-1)\,S_x^2} \qquad b_{xy} = \frac{\Sigma xy}{(N-1)\,S_y^2}$$

now r is:

$$r = \frac{\Sigma xy}{\sqrt{\Sigma x^2 \, \Sigma y^2}}$$

or $$r = \frac{\Sigma xy}{\sqrt{[(N-1)(S_x^2\ )]\,[(N-1)(S_y^2\ )]}}$$

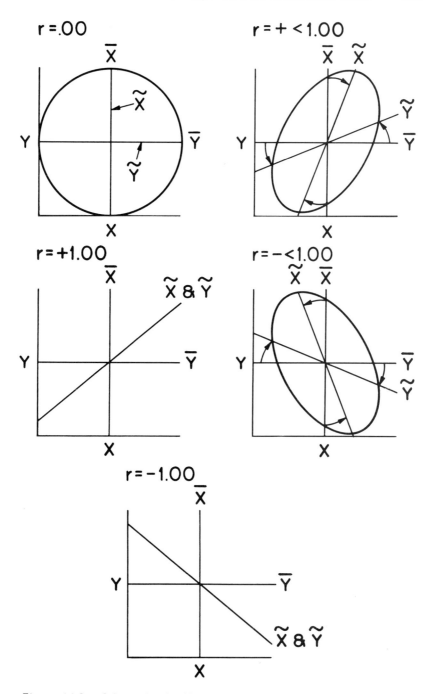

Figure 14.9. Schematic of different values of correlation coefficients and their relations to the two regression lines.

$$\text{or} \quad r = \frac{\Sigma xy}{(N-1)\, S_x\, S_y}$$

$$\text{therefore,} \quad b_{yx} = r\frac{S_y}{S_x} \quad \text{and} \quad b_{xy} = r\frac{S_x}{S_y}$$

If we now multiply, we obtain:

$$(b_{yx})(b_{xy}) = \left(r\frac{S_y}{S_x}\right)\left(r\frac{S_x}{S_y}\right)$$

$$\text{or} \quad (b_{yx})(b_{xy}) = r^2$$

$$\text{and} \quad \pm r = \pm\sqrt{(b_{yx})(b_{xy})} \tag{14.18}$$

Thus, the correlation coefficient is the geometric mean of the two regression coefficients. In our previous example, $b_{yx} = 0.8343$, and $b_{xy} = 1.0673$, we have:

$$r^2 = (0.8343)(1.0673) = 0.8904$$

$$\text{and} \quad r = \sqrt{0.8904}$$

$$= 0.944$$

This obtained value of the correlation coefficient is equal to that found for Formula 14.3.

The Residual Errors about the Regression of Y on X.   It was stated that the regression line is a line of best fit where the sum of squares, or the difference between the observed value and the predicted value from the regression line, is at a minimum. The residual sum of squares is a statistic that describes this sum of squares about the regression line. It is assumed that the variability about the regression line is equally distributed within the range of random sampling. The definitional formula for this residual sum of squares about the regression line of Y on X is:

$$\Sigma(Y - \tilde{Y})^2 = \Sigma[Y - (a_{yx} + b_{yx}X)]^2 \tag{14.19}$$

This definitional formula is very cumbersome for computational purposes. If we use a deviation form we have:

$$\Sigma(Y - \widetilde{Y})^2 = \Sigma(y - \widetilde{y})^2$$

$y = Y - \overline{Y}$, the true deviation

$\widetilde{y} = \widetilde{Y} - \overline{Y}$, the predicted deviation

and the residual sum of squares can be written as:

$$\Sigma(y - \widetilde{y})^2 = \Sigma y^2 - \frac{(\Sigma xy)^2}{\Sigma x^2} \qquad (14.20)$$

When the two variables of X and Y are unrelated and $\overline{Y} = Y$, then the $\Sigma xy = 0$, and the residual sum of squares is equal to sum of squares of Y:

$$\Sigma(y - \widetilde{y})^2 = \Sigma y^2 - \frac{(\Sigma xy)^2}{\Sigma x^2}$$

$$\text{when} \quad \Sigma xy = 0$$

$$\text{then} \quad \Sigma(y - \widetilde{y})^2 = \Sigma y^2$$

In this case we have not improved our prediction. On the other hand, when we have a perfect relationship between X and Y, where all the bivariate points fall on the regression line, then the quantity is:

$$\frac{(\Sigma xy)^2}{\Sigma x^2} = \Sigma y^2$$

and the $\Sigma(y - \widetilde{y})^2 = 0$. It is clearly the term $(\Sigma xy)^2 / \Sigma x^2$ that measures the improvement of prediction. We can make more accurate predictions when the $\Sigma(y - \widetilde{y})^2$ becomes small.

The residual variance is another index of the variability about the regression, and is equal to:

$$S_{yx}^2 = \frac{\Sigma(y - \widetilde{y})^2}{N - 2} \qquad (14.21)$$

We have $N - 2$ df that are associated with the residual sum of squares. One df is lost as the observations have been obtained from the mean, and the second df lost is related to the deviation about the regression line.

The square root of the residual variance is the standard error of estimate, and for the regression of Y on X becomes:

$$S_{yx} = \sqrt{\frac{\Sigma(y - \tilde{y})^2}{N - 2}} = \sqrt{S_{yx}^2} \qquad (14.22)$$

and is shown in Figure 14.10.

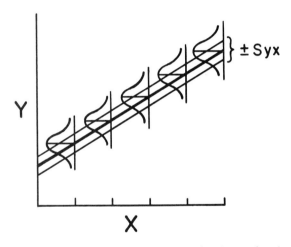

Figure 14.10.   Schematic of the standard error of estimate for the regression line of Y on X.

The standard error of estimate is an estimate of a standard deviation of the bivariate points about the specified regression line. We would therefore expect that approximately 68% of these points would fall between $\pm 1 S_{yx}$. Theoretically it is assumed that the variability of the bivariate points from the regression line is approximately equal among the various distributions. Figure 14.10 illustrates this relationship of S_{yx} about the regression line of Y on X with homogeneous variances.

If we have a zero relationship between X and Y, the standard error estimate of Y on X is approximately equal to the standard deviation of Y. The difference is accounted for by the fact that the first case has $N - 2$ degrees of freedom and the second has $N - 1$ degrees of freedom.

When there is some relationship between X and Y we predict the regression and the measure of errors of our prediction by the standard error of estimate. As the magnitude of the relationship becomes larger, the standard error of estimate becomes smaller, and with perfect relationship the standard error of estimate is zero.

The Residual Errors about the Regression of X on Y.   Just as we have two regression equations, we also have two residual sums of squares, two residual variances, and two standard error of estimates.

When our concern is the prediction of X from Y, the residual sum of squares is:

$$\Sigma(x - \tilde{x})^2 = \Sigma x^2 - \frac{(\Sigma xy)^2}{\Sigma y^2} \qquad (14.23)$$

and the residual variance becomes:

$$S^2_{xy} = \frac{\Sigma(x - \tilde{x})^2}{N - 2} \qquad (14.24)$$

and the standard error of estimate is written as:

$$S_{xy} = \sqrt{\frac{\Sigma(x - \tilde{x})^2}{N - 2}} = \sqrt{S^2_{xy}} \qquad (14.25)$$

and a comparable illustration of Figure 14.10 is shown in Figure 14.11.

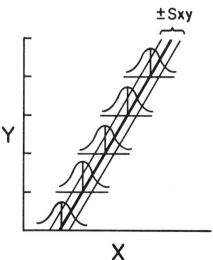

Figure 14.11.   Schematic of the standard error of estimate for the regression line of X on Y.

Example.   For completeness, we shall use the data in the prior example to compute the standard errors of estimate for Y on X and X on Y.

Standard error of estimate of Y on X:

$$\Sigma(y - \tilde{y})^2 = \Sigma y^2 - \frac{(\Sigma xy)^2}{\Sigma x^2} \qquad\qquad 14.20$$

$$= 4087 - \frac{(4362)^2}{5228.2}$$

$$= 447.69$$

$$S^2_{yx} = \frac{\Sigma(y - \tilde{y})^2}{N - 2} \qquad\qquad 14.21$$

$$= \frac{447.69}{18} = 24.8717$$

$$S_{yx} = \sqrt{S^2_{yx}} \qquad\qquad 14.22$$

$$= \sqrt{24.8717} = 4.987$$

Standard deviation of Y:

$$S^2_y = \frac{\Sigma y^2}{N - 1}$$

$$= \frac{4087}{19} = 215.105$$

$$S_y = \sqrt{S^2_y}$$

$$= \sqrt{215.105} = 14.667$$

Standard error of estimate of X on Y:

$$\Sigma(x - \tilde{x})^2 = \Sigma x^2 - \frac{(\Sigma xy)^2}{\Sigma y^2} \qquad\qquad 14.23$$

$$= 5228.2 - \frac{(4362)^2}{4087}$$

$$= 572.70$$

$$S^2_{xy} = \frac{\Sigma(x - \widetilde{x})^2}{N - 2} \qquad\qquad 14.24$$

$$= \frac{572.70}{18} = 31.8167$$

$$S_{xy} = \sqrt{S^2_{xy}} \qquad\qquad 14.25$$

$$= \sqrt{31.8167} = 5.641$$

Standard deviation of X:

$$S^2_x = \frac{\Sigma x^2}{N - 1}$$

$$= \frac{5228.2}{19} = 275.168$$

$$S_x = \sqrt{S^2_x}$$

$$= \sqrt{275.168} = 16.588$$

As we have seen in our prior section, with a significant correlation between two variables, we are able to improve our predictions by predicting Y or X rather than their respective means. This observation may be more clearly seen if we view the deviation terms as errors in our prediction. If we had no relationship between X and Y, or if we had no measure of such a correlation, then our best prediction of a variable would be the mean of that variable, and the errors of this prediction would be measured by the standard deviation. In the prior calculations we can observe that the standard deviation of the Y variable is 14.667. However, if we know the relationship between X and Y, and if we know X, then we can predict Y, and the extent of our error could be measured by the standard error of estimate, or 4.987. Thus, we are able to make far better predictions in the sense that the range of our error will be greatly reduced.

The Coefficients of Determination and Nondetermination.

Function and Method. The coefficient of determination, r^2, measures the proportion of the variance of one variable that has been accounted for by the variance of the second variable. On the other hand, the coefficient of nondetermination or $1 - r^2$, is that proportion of the variance that is not accounted for by the variance of the second variable.

In the analysis of variance we saw that the variance could be viewed as comprising two additive component parts. A similar case holds here as well. The total variance of the Y (or X) variable, S_y^2, is made up of two parts; one part is associated with the predicted variance of Y from X, or the values on the regression line $S_{\tilde{y}}^2$, and the second part is the residual variance, S_{yx}^2 :

$$S_y^2 = S_{\tilde{y}}^2 + S_{yx}^2 \qquad (14.26)$$

Dividing Formula 14.26 by S_y^2 will give us the proportion:

$$\frac{S_y^2}{S_y^2} = \frac{S_{\tilde{y}}^2}{S_y^2} + \frac{S_{yx}^2}{S_y^2}$$

$$1.00 = \frac{S_{\tilde{y}}^2}{S_y^2} + \frac{S_{yx}^2}{S_y^2} \qquad (14.27)$$

$$\text{where } \frac{S_{\tilde{y}}^2}{S_y^2} = r^2 \qquad (14.28)$$

$$\text{and } \frac{S_y^2}{S_y^2} = 1 - r^2 \qquad (14.29)$$

therefore, $1.00 = (r^2) + (1 - r^2)$

The $S_{\tilde{y}}^2$ is the part of the total variance of Y that is accounted for by the variance in X; therefore, the first term on the right in Formula 14.26 is that proportion of the total variance that is associated with the variance in X. The second term in Formula 14.27, S_{yx}^2 / S_y^2, is the proportion of the original variance which is yet unaccounted for by the relationship with X.

The concept of the coefficient of determination gives the correlation coefficient a new meaning. If $r = 0.83$, then $r^2 = 0.69$ or 69%. The r^2 is an index of how much of the total variance of predictability we have accounted for, from one variable with its relationship to a second variable. Figure 14.12 describes r^2 and $1 - r^2$ for r values from 0.00 to 1.00.

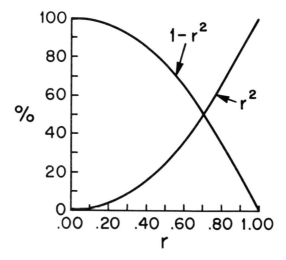

Figure 14.12.   The relationship between the coefficient of determination and the coefficient of nondetermination.

Example. With our obtained correlation coefficient of 0.944 between the original scale and the short form, it may be of considerable interest to determine the amount of common variance between the two scales. The coefficient of determination for the coefficient of 0.944 would be 0.89 or 89%. Thus, 11% of the variance between the two variables is unaccounted. The magnitude of the coefficient of nondetermination is small in this example and may be the result of many factors. In many psychological tests the errors associated with the reliability of the instrument are often greater than this.

The Correlation Ratio

Function and Method. Two major functions are served by the correlation ratio, E or eta. One of the major assumptions of the Pearson correlation is that the two variables are linearly related. The correlation ratio is, on the other hand, a coefficient of curvilinear or nonlinear correlation. It may be described as an index of association between two variables whose bivariate distribution is nonlinear. In these cases, it is generally assumed that the two variables are measured on at least an interval scale, as is the correlation coefficient, but we cannot meet the assumption of linearity. The problem of nonlinearity is circumvented in the correlation ratio by treating one of the variables as a noncontinuous nominal variable. The arranging or rearranging of the order within the variable has no effect upon the correlation ratio but a major effect upon the correlation coefficient, *r*. Thus, a second function of the correlation ratio is the relationship between interval and nominal variables.

The general formula for eta is derived from the general model of the analysis of variance. The correlation ratio is defined as the square root of a ratio between the sum of squares between groups (rows or columns) and the total sum of squares:

$$E_{yx} = \sqrt{\frac{\Sigma y_b^2}{\Sigma y_t^2}} \qquad (14.30)$$

$$\text{or} \quad E_{yx} = \sqrt{1 - \frac{\Sigma y_w^2}{\Sigma y_t^2}} \qquad (14.31)$$

where Σy_t^2 = total sum of squares, or $\sum_{1}^{N}(Y - \bar{Y})^2$

Σy_b^2 = between columns sum of squares, or

$$\sum_{1}^{K} n_i (\bar{Y}_i - \bar{Y})^2$$

Σy_w^2 = within columns sum of squares, or

$$\sum_{1}^{K}\sum_{1}^{n_i} (Y_i - \bar{Y}_i)^2$$

$\sum_{1}^{K}$ = sum over the number of columns

In designs of the analysis of variance more complex than those given within this book, it can be shown that the Pearson *r* is a special case of eta when the regression lines are linear. If the between sum of squares are, in fact, linear, then eta and Pearson's *r* will be equal.

These formulas for E_{yx} are based upon the procedure for the prediction of *Y* from *X*. The *Y* variable is taken as the continuous interval scale, and *X* as the discrete nominal variable. If the procedure was to predict *X* from *Y*, the E_{xy} becomes:

$$E_{xy} = \sqrt{\frac{\Sigma x_b^2}{\Sigma x_t^2}} \qquad (14.32)$$

$$\text{or} \quad E_{xy} = \sqrt{1 - \frac{\Sigma x_w^2}{\Sigma x_t^2}} \qquad (14.33)$$

where $\Sigma x_t^2 = $ total sum of squares, or $\overset{N}{\underset{1}{\Sigma}} (X - \bar{X})^2$

Σx_b^2 = between rows sum of squares, or

$$\overset{r}{\underset{1}{\Sigma}} n_i (\bar{X}_i - \bar{X})^2$$

Σx_w^2 = within rows sum of squares, or

$$\overset{r}{\underset{1}{\Sigma}} \overset{n_i}{\underset{i}{\Sigma}} (X_i - \bar{X}_i)^2$$

$\overset{r}{\underset{1}{\Sigma}}$ = sum over the number of rows

Thus, for the same data we have two coefficients, E_{yx} and E_{xy}. In the usual case, the magnitude of these two coefficients will differ.

The E is a ratio whose coefficients may range between 0.00 and 1.00. It therefore measures the magnitude of the association between two variables but not the direction of the relationship. From the various formulas we can observe how the magnitude of the coefficients is determined by the variances. For example, if Σy_b^2 is zero, where $\bar{Y}_1 = \bar{Y}_2 = \bar{Y}_i = \bar{Y}_t$, then E_{yx} is zero. On the other hand, if Σy_w^2 is zero, then $\Sigma y_b^2 = \Sigma y_t^2$, and the coefficient is unity. It should be emphasized that the magnitude of E is greatly affected when there are only a few cases within each group. In the limited case, if we had, for example, a single value within each column, the E_{yx} would be unity. It becomes obvious that we need an adequate sampling from the population to circumvent this problem.

As we were with the r, we are concerned with prediction, but rather than predicting from the regression as we do with r, we predict for any X the mean of its corresponding Y value, or $\bar{Y}_i$. Similarly, if we wish to predict X from a known Y value, we would predict the mean of its corresponding X values or $\bar{X}_i$.

Standard Error of Estimate of E.   The errors of our predictions of the mean values for the correlation ratio are measured by the standard error of estimate of E. As we have two correlation ratios, we also have two standard errors of estimate, one for the prediction for Y from X, and one for X from Y. The standard error of estimate of E_{yx} is:

$$S_{w \cdot y} = \sqrt{\frac{\Sigma y_w^2}{N - K}} \qquad (14.34)$$

where $S_{w \cdot y}$ = standard error of estimate of E_{yx}, or the square root of the within mean square

Σy_w^2 = within columns sums of squares

K = number of columns

N = total number of pairs

The Σy^2 is sum of squares within each column about their individual column means, and we have pooled these sums of squares over the K columns to give an estimate of the common error term. When we pool these sums of squares, we must assume homogeneity of variances within groups. For the standard error of estimate of E_{xy} we have:

$$S_{w \cdot x} = \sqrt{\frac{\Sigma x_w^2}{N - r}} \qquad (14.35)$$

and $S_{w \cdot x}$ = standard error of estimate of E_{xy}

Σx_w^2 = within rows sum of squares

r = number of rows

Test of Significance for Eta.   The null hypothesis states that the population correlation ratio, η, is zero and the research hypothesis is that the population correlation ratio is significantly greater than zero:

$$H_0 : \eta = 0$$

$$H_1 : \eta > 0$$

This null hypothesis is tested by the F-test, or:

$$F = \frac{E_{yx}^2/(K-1)}{(1 - E_{yx}^2)/(N-K)} \quad \text{or} \quad F = \frac{E_{xy}^2/(r-1)}{(1 - E_{xy}^2)/(N-r)} \quad (14.36)$$

depending upon which E is determined, with $K - 1$ and $N - K$ degrees of freedom or $r - 1$ and $N - r$ degrees of freedom. A comparable formula for the F-test is:

$$F = \frac{\Sigma y_b^2/(K-1)}{\Sigma y_x^2/(N-K)} \quad \text{or} \quad F = \frac{\Sigma x_b^2/(r-1)}{\Sigma x_w^2/(N-r)} \quad (14.37)$$

The first of these latter two formulas is identical to those used with a two part analysis of variance when we test for the difference between groups (columns).

Example. There are evidences based upon the behavior of the mouse, the rat, and the chick that suggest a curvilinear relationship between the intensity of the stimulus and activity of the animals. It has been hypothesized that a stimulus change to low intensity would result in greater activity, while a change to high intensity would lead to a marked decrease of the response. The animals were randomly assigned to one of seven intensities of the stimulus for a single session. The results are given in an analysis of variance table (Table 14.3) and are shown in Figure 14.13.

Table 14.3

Source of variation	Sum of squares	df	Mean square	F
Between groups	367,397	6	61,233	6.304
Within groups	1,291,881	133	9,713	
Total	1,659,278	139		

This analysis of variance yielded a significant difference in mean responses among the seven experimental groups as a function of intensity of the stimulus ($F = 6.304$, $df = 6/133$, $p < 0.001$). This obtained significant F value represents a significant curvilinear function and the magnitude is given by eta.

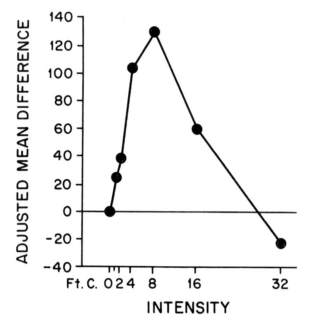

Figure. 14.13.   The adjusted mean number of responses for the seven intensities.

$$E^2_{yx} = \frac{367,397}{1,659,278}$$

$$E^2_{yx} = 0.2214$$

$$E_{yx} = 0.471$$

It should be pointed out here that the treatment conditions accounted for 22 percent of the variance of E^2_{yx}, and that 78 percent of the total variability occurred within the individual treatment groups.

If we wish now to predict the behavior of a given organism, our best prediction would be the mean of the responses for a given intensity level, and the errors of our predictions would be given by the standard error of estimate of E, or:

$$S_{w \cdot y} = \sqrt{\frac{\Sigma y^2_w}{N - K}}$$

$$= \sqrt{\frac{1,291,881}{133}}$$

$$= \sqrt{9,713}$$

$$= 98.6$$

Test for Linearity. The test of the linearity of regression is a goodness-of-fit type. It states that $\eta_{yx} = \eta_{xy} = \rho$; this would be the case when we have perfect linearity. However, because of sampling error, r is rarely equal to E. In general, with the same data, $E > r$; the difference between the two coefficients is used as an index of linearity. The greater the similarity between the two coefficients, the greater the linearity, and conversely, the greater the discrepancy, the greater the nonlinearity. The goodness-of-fit test for linearity is found with Formula 14.38:

$$F = \frac{(E^2_{yx} - r^2_{xy})/K - 2}{(1 - E^2_{yx})/N - K} \quad \text{or} \quad F = \frac{(E^2_{xy} - r^2_{xy})/r - 2}{(1 - E^2_{xy})/N - r} \quad (14.38)$$

where E_{yx} = eta of Y and X

r_{xy} = correlation coefficient

E_{xy} = eta of X and Y

K = columns

r = rows

with $K - 2$ and $N - K$ or $r - 2$ and $N - r$ degrees of freedom. If the obtained value of F were equal to or greater than the tabled value of F for the given degrees of freedom and the previously stated alpha level, we would conclude that the relationship between the two variables differed significantly in their linearity. On the other hand, if the obtained F were less than the tabled value, we would conclude that the two variables were linearly related and that any discrepancy was due to random sampling error.

Partial Correlation Coefficient

Function and Method.   The partial correlation is a measure of the residual relationship between two variables, where the common effects of other variables have been partialed out. The formula for a three-variable partial correlation is:

$$r_{12 \cdot 3} = \frac{r_{12} - r_{13} - r_{23}}{\sqrt{(1 - r_{13}^2)(1 - r_{23}^2)}} \tag{14.39}$$

where $r_{12 \cdot 3}$ = correlation between variables 1 and 2, partialing out 3

$\qquad r_{12}$ = correlation between 1 and 2

$\qquad r_{13}$ = correlation between 1 and 3

$\qquad r_{23}$ = correlation between 2 and 3

This formula implies that the partial correlation coefficient is between variables 1 and 2, with variable 3 partialed out. The operation also implies that we correlate variables 1 and 3, as well as variables 2 and 3, and if we subtract these estimates we have two sets of residuals or errors. It is the correlation between these two sets of residuals that defines the partial correlation. It is generally assumed that these correlation coefficients are Pearson coefficients, or are estimates of it.

The partial correlation between two variables may be influenced by any number of variables. However, beyond the three-variable partial correlation, the data become very difficult to interpret. For the K-variable partial correlational method, the student should consult an advanced text.

Test of Significance for a Partial Correlation.   The null hypothesis, that the population correlation is equal to zero, will be tested by the t-test with $N - 3$ degrees of freedom or from Table M. The t-test formula is written as:

$$t = \frac{r_{12 \cdot 3}}{\sqrt{(1 - r_{12 \cdot 3}^2)/N - 3}} \tag{14.40}$$

Example. Suppose we have a research interest in the relationship between children's verbal abilities and psychomotor skills, and, in addition, assume that the research interest is across ages 2 to 7. This correlation between the two variables of verbal abilities and psychomotor skills, however, may be in part a function of the ages of the subjects. Therefore, we may wish to partial out the influence of the age variable.

To illustrate the use of the three-variable partial correlation coefficient, we shall assume we have scores on the three different variables for each child in a random sample of 100. Furthermore, assume that we have obtained correlation coefficients for all combinations of the three variables. These intercorrelations are given in Table 14.4:

Table 14.4

	X	Y	Z
X	—	.45	.77
Y		—	.52
Z			—

where X = verbal abilities

Y = psychomotor skills

Z = age

Using these intercorrelations, we calculate the partial coefficient:

$$r_{xy \cdot z} = \frac{.45 - (.77)(.52)}{\sqrt{[1 - (.77)^2][1 - (.52)^2]}}$$

$$= \frac{0.05}{0.54} = 0.093$$

Our obtained partial correlation coefficient between verbal abilities and psychomotor skills is greatly reduced when we have partialed out the influence of age. With 97 degrees of freedom and a one-tailed test, the coefficient would not differ significantly from zero. We would conclude from our sample and measuring techniques, or tests, that there is no correlation between the two variables.

Multiple Correlation and Regression

Function and Method. In the previous sections of this chapter, we have seen the relationship between the Pearson correlation and linear regression when we predict X from Y or Y from X. In much of our research, predictions from bivariate data lead to an improvement in our predictions; however, we often have considerable variance that remains unaccounted for. The multiple correlation methods are concerned with this variance. The task of the method is to increase the size of the correlation coefficient, thus increasing the size of the coefficient of determination, or accounting for more of the variance in order to make better predictions.

The multiple correlation, $r_{1 \cdot 23 \ldots k}$, is a correlation between a criterion variable and a weighted sum of two or more predictor variables. With the multiple correlation we are interested in the prediction of the $X_{1 \cdot 23}$, or the criterion variable, from two or more predictor variables. The formula for the multiple correlation of the single criterion variable with two predictor variables is given as:

$$r_{1 \cdot 23} = \sqrt{\frac{r_{12}^2 + r_{13}^2 - 2r_{12}\,r_{13}\,r_{23}}{1 - r_{23}^2}} \qquad (14.41)$$

where r_{12} = correlation between criterion (X_1) and predictor (X_2)

r_{13} = correlation between criterion (X_1) and predictor (X_3)

r_{23} = correlation between predictors (X_2) and (X_3)

It is assumed that each correlation coefficient meets the assumptions that are associated with this method. In general, we use the Pearson correlation coefficients in the computation of the multiple correlation coefficient.

As we take the square root in Formula 14.41, the multiple correlation coefficients are always positive in their direction. However, the magnitude of this coefficient can be interpreted as a

Pearson coefficient, and therefore, the coefficients of determination and nondetermination can be obtained. The coefficient of multiple determination describes the proportion of the variance of the criterion variable that is accounted for by the weighted sum of the predictor variables. On the other hand, the coefficient of multiple nondetermination is the amount of the variance of the criterion variable that remains to be accounted for from our predictors. The magnitude of the multiple coefficient is determined by the relationship between the predictor variables. In general, the magnitude of the multiple coefficient will be large if the magnitude of the correlations between predictor variables is small, and r's between predictors and the criterion are high. On the other hand, if there are high correlations between the predictor variables, the size of the multiple correlation will be small.

Test of Significance for the Multiple Correlation.   The null hypothesis that the correlation is equal to zero may be tested by the F-test where:

$$F = \left[\frac{r_{1 \cdot 23 \ldots K}^2}{1 - r_{1 \cdot 23 \ldots K}^2} \right] \left[\frac{N - K - 1}{K} \right] \tag{14.42}$$

where $r_{1 \cdot 23 \ldots K}$ = multiple correlation coefficient

N = number of cases

K = number of predictors

with K and $(N - K - 1)$ degrees of freedom. If the obtained F value exceeds the tabled value of F for some predetermined alpha value, we would conclude that the multiple coefficient differed significantly from zero.

Multiple Regression Equation

In multiple regression we have a single equation, in that our research interest is in the prediction of the criterion variable. This equation is, as is Formula 14.11, an equation of best fit where the variability is at the minimum. The multiple regression equation for a criterion variable and two predictor variables is given in Formula 14.43.

$$\tilde{X}_1 = a_{1 \cdot 23} + b_{12 \cdot 3} \, X_2 + b_{13 \cdot 2} \, X_3 \qquad (14.43)$$

where $\quad b_{12 \cdot 3} = \dfrac{S_1}{S_2} (\beta_{12 \cdot 3}) \qquad (14.44)$

where $\quad \beta_{12 \cdot 3} = \dfrac{r_{12} - r_{13} \, r_{23}}{1 - r_{23}^2} \qquad (14.45)$

and where $\quad b_{13 \cdot 2} = \dfrac{S_1}{S_3} (\beta_{13 \cdot 2}) \qquad (14.46)$

where $\quad \beta_{13 \cdot 2} = \dfrac{r_{13} - r_{12} \, r_{23}}{1 - r_{23}^2} \qquad (14.47)$

and $\quad a_{1 \cdot 23} = \overline{X}_1 - [(b_{12 \cdot 3})(\overline{X}_2)] - [(b_{13 \cdot 2})(\overline{X}_3)] \quad (14.48)$

In Formulas 14.44 and 14.45, the *b*'s are partial regression coefficients, in that the common influence of the correlations have been partialed out by the beta coefficients (β). The partial regression coefficients, thus, may be seen as multiplicative constants, or weights that are given to a predictor variable when the effects of the other predictor variable or variables have been partialed out. They have essentially the same meaning as the regression coefficients in linear regression, in that they represent the rate of change between the criterion variables and the predictor variable with other variables held constant.

The Standard Error of Multiple Estimate. As we have a single regression equation for multiple prediction, we have a single standard error of estimate as well. The standard error of multiple estimate is given as:

$$S_{1 \cdot 23} = S_1 \sqrt{1 - r_{1 \cdot 23}^2} \qquad (14.49)$$

where S_1 = standard deviation of the criterion variable

$r_{12 \cdot 3}$ = multiple correlation

This standard error of estimate has the same meaning as before, or as a special case of the standard deviation, except that here the deviation is around the multiple regression line.

Example. To illustrate the use of the multiple correlation and regression, let us assume the intercorrelations of the variables as given in Table 14.5, with X_1 as the criterion, and X_2 and X_3 as the predictors.

Table 14.5

Variable	X_1	X_2	X_3	
X_1	—	.46	.52	
X_2		—	.17	
X_3			—	$N = 50$
$\bar{X}_x$	34.19	68.40	19.35	
S_x	9.24	21.17	3.61	

$$r_{1 \cdot 2 3} = \sqrt{\frac{.46^2 + .52^2 - 2(.46)(.52)(.17)}{1 - (.17)^2}}$$

$$= \sqrt{\frac{.21 + .27 - 2(.04)}{1 - .03}}$$

$$= \sqrt{.4124}$$

$$= .64$$

As we can see, the weighted sum of the two predictors has increased the size of the multiple coefficient, and from the coefficient of multiple determination we have accounted for approximatcly 41 percent of the variance of the criterion variable. Thus we have increased our predictability of the criterion as well, in that we have accounted for more of the variance than with either of the two predictor variables.

To determine the significance of the null hypothesis that the multiple coefficient is zero, we shall use Formula 14.42.

$$F = \left(\frac{.64^2}{1 - .64^2}\right)\left(\frac{50 - 2 - 1}{2}\right) = 16.33$$

With 2 and 47 degrees of freedom, the probability of this obtained F value is less than 0.001. We therefore would conclude that the multiple coefficient of 0.64 is significantly greater than zero.

Assuming now that we wish to predict X, knowing the X_2 and X_3 values, we would have to determine the constants in the multiple regression equation (Formula 14.43). Using the various formulas we would have the following:

$$\beta_{12\cdot3} = \frac{.46 - (.52)(.17)}{1 - (.17)^2} \qquad 14.45$$

$$= .383$$

$$\text{therefore } b_{12\cdot3} = \left(\frac{9.24}{21.17}\right)(.383) \qquad 14.44$$

$$= .167$$

$$\text{and } \beta_{13\cdot2} = \frac{.52 - (.46)(.17)}{1 - (.17)^2} \qquad 14.47$$

$$= .455$$

$$\text{therefore } b_{13\cdot2} = \left(\frac{9.24}{3.61}\right)(.455) \qquad 14.47$$

$$= 1.165$$

$$\text{and } a_{1\cdot23} = 34.19 - (.167)(68.40) -$$

$$(1.165)(19.35) \qquad 14.48$$

$$= .224$$

$$\text{thus } \widetilde{X}_1 \text{ becomes } \widetilde{X}_1 = 0.225 + (.167)X_2 + (1.165)X_3 \quad 14.43$$

If we know that a given individual had a score of 86 for X_2, and 24 for X_3, we could now predict his criterion score:

$$\widetilde{X}_1 = 0.224 + (.167)(86) + (1.165)(24)$$

$$= 42.546$$

The standard error of multiple estimate, Formula 14.49, for our data can now be determined:

$$S_{1 \cdot 23} = 9.24\sqrt{1 - 0.64^2}$$

$$= (9.24)\sqrt{(.59)}$$

$$= (9.24)(.768)$$

$$= 7.10$$

Therefore, we could predict a given X score and state that the standard error of estimate will be ± 7.10.

The Relationship Between the Beta Coefficients and the Multiple Correlation.   If the beta coefficients and their associated correlation coefficients have been obtained, we can find the multiple correlation coefficient. Formula 14.50 indicates the multiple correlation with two beta coefficients and the three intercorrelations.

$$r_{1 \cdot 23} = \sqrt{(\beta_{12 \cdot 3})(r_{12}) + (\beta_{13 \cdot 2})(r_{13})} \qquad (14.50)$$

From our data in the prior example, we would have:

$$r_{1 \cdot 23} = \sqrt{(.383)(.46) + (.455)(.52)}$$

$$= \sqrt{.176 + .237}$$

$$= \sqrt{.413}$$

$$= .64$$

In Formula 14.50, we can see that the multiple correlation is the sum of two products. Each product is, in a way, an estimate of the amount of the variability that may be accounted for from the criterion variable. Thus, X_2 can be said to account for 18 percent of the variance, while X_3 accounts for approximately 24 percent of the total variance of the criterion.

The Point Biserial Correlation Coefficient

Function and Method.   The point biserial correlation coefficient, r_{pb}, is a special case of the Pearson correlation coefficient, and is used for measuring the relationship between a dichotomous variable and a continuous one. The dichotomous variable, the X variable, may be a genuine one or the variable may be treated as if it were truly dichotomous, so that the values can be expressed in binary form: 0 or 1. The assignment of 0 or 1 to the two categories is, in general, arbitrary. No assumption is made as to the form of the dichotomous variable. However, the point biserial correlation assumes that the two distributions from the continuous variable (the distribution of Y scores with a corresponding X score of 0 and the distribution of Y scores with a corresponding X score of 1) are normally distributed within each of the dichotomous categories, and that these two distributions have equal variances.

The formula for the point biserial correlation can be expressed in a number of forms. The most simple and common form is expressed in terms of means, standard deviation, and proportions as:

$$r_{pb} = \left(\frac{\overline{Y}_1 - \overline{Y}_0}{S_t} \right) \sqrt{pq} \qquad (14.51)$$

where $\overline{Y}_1$ = mean of the continuous
variable with the corresponding
dichotomous score of 1

$\overline{Y}_0$ = mean of the continuous
variable with the corresponding
dichotomous score of 0

S_t = standard deviation for the
total Y distribution

p = proportion of cases scored as 1

q = proportion of cases scored as 0

The magnitude and the direction of the point biserial correlation is, in part, a function of the two proportions and of the differences between the two means. When the two proportions are equal, the range of this coefficient can reach unity. However, when the two proportions differ, the range is restricted. If the difference between the two means is zero, the point biserial coefficient shall be zero. On the other hand, if the difference is positive, that is, if the $\bar{X}_p$ is greater than $\bar{X}_q$, then the direction is positive, and if the difference is negative ($\bar{X}_p$ is less than $\bar{X}_q$) the relationship is negative. Thus, the direction depends on the mean values and on the rationale for assigning scores of 0 and 1. Similarly, the magnitude of r_{pb} is related to the difference between the two means. In general, the larger the difference, the greater the absolute size of the coefficient.

Test of Significance for the Point Biserial Correlation. To test the null hypothesis, that the population point biserial correlation coefficient is zero, we may use the t distribution, as we did with r:

$$H_0 : \rho_{pb} = 0$$

$$t = r_{pb} \sqrt{\frac{N-2}{1-r_{pb}^2}} \qquad (14.52)$$

We use $N-2$ degrees of freedom, where N equals the number of pairs. Similarly, Table M may be utilized to test the significance of the point biserial correlation.

Example. Consider a situation where a researcher has college entrance examination scores on a group of students, and he wishes to determine if there is a relationship between these scores and graduation at the end of a normal four year program. The graduation variable is measured in a binary system: graduate (1), or non-graduate (0). For illustrative purposes we shall work with a small number of cases (see Table 14.6).

Table 14.6

Student	Entrance Scores (Y)	Category
1	46	0
2	53	1
3	68	1
4	35	0
5	49	0
6	62	1
7	66	1
8	54	0
9	59	1
10	55	1
10	547	

$$\overline{Y}_0 = Y_0/N_0 = 184/4 = 46$$

$$\overline{Y}_1 = Y_1/N_1 = 363/6 = 60.5$$

$$p = 6/10 = .60$$

$$q = 4/10 = .40$$

$$S_t = \sqrt{\frac{\Sigma y^2}{N-1}} = \sqrt{\frac{30797 - \frac{(547)^2}{10}}{9}}$$

$$= \sqrt{97.34}$$

$$= 9.866$$

Calculating for the point biserial coefficient (Formula 14.51) using these data we have:

$$r_{pb} = \left(\frac{60.5 - 46.0}{9.866}\right)\left(\sqrt{(.60)(.40)}\right)$$

$$= 0.72$$

If we assume a one-tailed test of significance the obtained coefficient is associated with a probability of less than 0.01. We would conclude that this obtainĕd coefficient differs significantly from zero, and that the two variables are significantly related.

Biserial Correlation Coefficient

Function and Method. The biserial correlation coefficient, r_b, is a measure of relationship between two variables, both of which are assumed to be continuous and normally distributed, and both of which meet the assumptions of the interval scale of measurement. For the biserial correlation, however, one of the variables has been artificially dichotomized at some given position or point along the continuum of this variable. The scores that are greater than that point are assigned a value of 1 and those values that are less are assigned 0. The dichotomization may be logically made at any point along the continuum. However, like the point biserial correlation, the difference between the proportions on each side of the point (P and Q) can influence the magnitude of the coefficient. Typically, therefore, this variable is dichotomized at the mean or median.

The general formula for the biserial correlation is expressed as:

$$r_b = \left(\frac{\overline{Y}_1 - \overline{Y}_0}{S_t} \right) \left(\frac{(PQ)}{y} \right) \tag{14.53}$$

where $\overline{Y}_1$ = mean of the continuous variable
with the corresponding dichotomous score of 1

$\overline{Y}_0$ = mean of the continuous variable
with the corresponding dichotomous score of 0

S_t = standard deviation of the total Y
distribution

P = proportion of cases scored as 1

Q = proportion of cases scored as 0

y = ordinate of the normal curve
distribution at the point
between P and Q

The direction and the magnitude or size of the biserial coefficient is a function of the difference between the two means. If $\overline{Y}_1$ is greater than $\overline{Y}_0$, then we have a positive coefficient. On the other hand, if $\overline{Y}_0$ is larger, the coefficient is negative. If there is no difference between the means, the coefficient will be zero. As the difference between the means becomes greater, the coefficient becomes larger.

The values of P, Q, and y directly imply the normal distribution. When the dichotomous variable departs from the assumption of normality, for example—a very skewed Y sampling distribution, the biserial correlation coefficient becomes an erroneous estimate of an association in that the magnitude of the coefficient may actually exceed unity.

The biserial correlation is not a special case of the Pearson correlation, as is the point biserial correlation, but is an estimate of it when N is very large and when the dichotomy is made at or near the median. The biserial coefficient is a good estimation when the population coefficient is low, but when the magnitude of the population coefficient is very high and reaches unity, the biserial correlation leads to an erroneously high coefficient.

An alternative formula for 14.53 is:

$$r_b = r_{pb} \frac{\sqrt{PQ}}{y} \tag{14.54}$$

The formula describes the relationship between the biserial correlation as an estimate of the Pearson correlation, and the point biserial correlation as a special case of the Pearson coefficient. If we compute both the biserial and point biserial coefficients, the magnitude of the point biserial will be smaller than the biserial. This is particularly the case when the value of the population coefficient is large.

Test of Significance of the Biserial Correlation Coefficient.

At present the exact sampling distribution of the biserial correlation is unknown. Thus, no test of significance is possible. A number of attempts at approximation have been cited in the literature; however, for the most part they are all open to question, in that they must make certain untested assumptions about the data. These tests of significance, if used, must be used with extreme caution. The student may consult advanced texts for further discussion of these approximations.

Example.   Assume that we have a research interest in the association between intellectual abilities and conformity, and that we have artificially dichotomized the latter variable into those individuals above (1) and below (0) the mean value. For illustrative purposes we shall use a small sample of 12 cases (see Table 14.7).

Table 14.7

Subjects	Abilities (Y)	Conformity
1	127	1
2	99	0
3	81	1
4	108	1
5	97	0
6	99	1
7	93	0
8	117	0
9	111	1
10	101	1
11	90	0
12	103	1
12	1226	

From the data we have the following calculations:

$$\overline{Y}_1 = 104.28$$

$$\overline{Y}_0 = 99.20$$

$$S_t = 12.35$$

$$P = .583$$

$$Q = .417$$

$$y = .3902$$

$$r_b = \left[\frac{104.28 - 99.20}{12.35} \right] \left[\frac{(.583)(.417)}{.3902} \right] \qquad 14.53$$

$$= (.4113)(.6230)$$

$$= 0.256$$

If we determined the point biserial coefficient from Formula 14.51, we would have:

$$r_{pb} = \left[\frac{104.28 - 99.20}{12.35}\right]\left[\sqrt{(.583)(.417)}\right]$$

$$= (.411)(.493)$$

$$= .203$$

This obtained point biserial coefficient does not differ significantly from zero with a two-tailed test with 10 degrees of freedom and alpha at the 0.05 level.

If we had determined the point biserial coefficient, we could obtain the biserial coefficient from Formula 14.54.

$$r_b = 0.203 \frac{\sqrt{(0.583)(0.417)}}{0.3902}$$

$$= (0.203)(1.263)$$

$$= 0.256$$

Tetrachoric Correlation

Function and Method. The tetrachoric correlation coefficient, r_t, like the biserial correlation, is an estimate of the Pearson product-moment correlation coefficient. The tetrachoric correlation is developed from the general assumptions that both variables are based on continuous, interval data, and their distributions are normal. However, both variables have been artificially dichotomized. Thus, when the data for the two variables of tetrachoric coefficient have been collapsed, all that is known is the frequency, and proportion of cases in each cell of a 2 × 2 contingency table. The r_t is therefore similar to ϕ in that both coefficients are computed from a 2 × 2 table, however, the assumptions upon which these two coefficients are based differ in marked ways.

The computational formulas for the tetrachoric coefficient are complex. However, when the two variables have been dichotomized at approximately the median, and when the number of cases is large, we can estimate it from Table V by determining the K ratio so that $K > 1$.

$$K = \frac{BC}{AD} \quad \text{or} \quad \frac{AD}{BC} \qquad (14.55)$$

where A, B, C, and D are the cell entries

Significance of r_t.   As with biserial correlation, the sampling distributions of the tetrachoric coefficients are open to question. It has been recommended that it be evaluated as a 2 × 2 contingency coefficient by means of the chi-square test. Using the chi-square test, however, violates the assumption of independent measures in each cell.

Example.   Assume that we would like to determine the homogeneity of items in a 50 item scale. The response on an equal appearing interval scale is from 1 (low) to 7 (high). For an index of association between items we may use the tetrachoric method and split the responses at the median point for each item. For the association between Items 1 and 2, assume the data in Table 14.8 with N equal to 100.

Table 14.8

Item 1

Median	above	below	total
above	(A) 26	(B) 32	58
below	(C) 34	(D) 8	42
total	60	40	100

$$AD = 208$$
$$BC = 1088$$

therefore:

$$\frac{BC}{AD} = \frac{1088}{208} = 5.23$$

From Table V with 5.23, we have the estimation of the tetrachoric coefficient of 0.58:

$$r_t = .58$$

From this example one can observe the relative ease in estimating the coefficients. When we are interested in only an estimate, the tetrachoric method may be a suitable procedure for obtaining the association between two truly continuous variables.

Summary of Terms

beta coefficient
biserial correlation
bivariant point
coefficient of determination
coefficient of nondetermination

Pearson's correlation coefficient
point biserial correlation
popluation correlation
regression coefficient
residual error

correlation ratio
cross product
curvilinear
intercept
least squares

residual variance
slope
standard error of estimate
standard error of r
sum of cross products

linear regression
linearity
multiple correlation
multiple regression
partial correlation

tetrachoric correlation

Summary of Symbols

r	S_z'	$\widetilde{X}_y$	$\Sigma(x - \widetilde{x})^2$
Σxy	a_{yx}	a_{xy}	S_{yx}^2
ρ	b_{yx}	b_{xy}	S_{yx}
z_r'	$\widetilde{Y}_x$	$\Sigma(X - \widetilde{X})^2$	S_{xy}^2
z_ρ'	$\Sigma(Y - \widetilde{Y})^2$	$\Sigma(y - \widetilde{y})^2$	S_{xy}
r^2	$r_{1\cdot 23}$	r_t	
$1 - r^2$	$b_{12\cdot 3}$		
E_{yx}	$\beta_{12\cdot 3}$		
η	r_{pb}		
$r_{12\cdot 3}$	r_b		

Problems

1. In order to investigate the relationship between age and motor skill, Herman randomly selected 15 children and measured the number of seconds out of a one-minute period that each child could successfully perform a rotor pursuit task. The data are given below. Using the Pearson product-moment correlation, determine the score and the 68% confidence interval around that score that a 50-month-old child would make on the rotor pursuit task.

(X)	(Y)
Age in Months	Rotor Pursuit Score
31	49
23	38
22	41
27	48
30	44
26	38
19	37
10	22
33	58
35	59
29	53
26	45
31	44
26	51
17	34

2. Habituation to a novel environment is likely to be a function of the amount of time spent in that environment. It has been postulated that the amount of habituation to a novel environment during a "pre-exposure" period can be measured by the amount of time taken by an animal to begin drinking during a subsequent drinking test in the novel environment. The results of such an experiment, in which the length of the "pre-exposure" period was varied, are given below. Compute eta as a measure of the degree of association, and test to see if the relationship is linear or curvilinear.

Source	SS	df	MS	F	p
Pre-Exposure	2604.0000	4	651.0000	6.3800	<.05
Within	7142.6320	70	102.0376		
Total	9746.6320	74			

$r = +.1907$

3. Assume a research interest in predicting marital success, that is the number of years that a couple will stay married, on the basis of average income and the number of relatives living in the same town. On the basis of the data given below, predict the number of years of successful marriage for a couple having 15 relatives living in the same town and having an average income of 25 thousand dollars per year. What is the 99% confidence interval for your prediction?

Number of Relatives	Average Income (in thousands)	Years of Marriage
10	13.5	23
2	12	42
8	8	16
35	4	5
12	7	45
4	16	66
3	10	10
7	11	24
2	17.9	34
1	15	22

4. As part of a program designed to evaluate the usefulness of an A, B, C, D, E grading system, a psychologist became interested in the relationship between grade point average (GPA) and success (1) or failure (0) in acquiring a job upon graduation from college. On the basis of the data given below, compute the degree of association between GPA and success or failure in acquiring a job upon graduation, and test its significance at the 0.05 alpha level.

GPA

(1)	(0)
3.89	2.24
2.87	1.83
1.87	3.68
2.39	3.25
2.15	3.09
2.26	1.21
1.21	2.41
2.61	2.18
1.71	2.86
2.44	1.53

5. Using the data given in Problem 4, determine the value of the biserial correlation coefficient. What does the discrepancy between the point biserial correlation coefficient obtained in Problem 4 and the biserial correlation coefficient obtained in this problem indicate?

6. Why is the assumption of independent cell measures violated when a chi-square test is used to evaluate the significance of r_t?

Errors of Measurement and Reliability Chapter Fifteen

Some General Comments

All sciences attempt to discover and to describe reproducible phenomena. Therefore science is based upon the assumption of the reproducibility or reliability of measurement. For without reliability, the phenomena under investigation are always open to question. Within the behavioral sciences, when we have measured the response, our fundamental concern is always the reliability of our measure, for we are always confronted with the problem of errors that can distort our response measurement. In general, the scientist tries to determine the reliability and reproducibility of his measures by reducing or minimizing errors and the sources of errors, as well as by estimating the amount of errors in his measurements.

The reliability of measurement is logically concerned with the problem of random variability. Assume, for example, that we present the same antecedent or stimulus condition a number of times to a given organism and we measure some specific response. If we had perfect reliability we would obtain the same response measure each time. However, what we generally obtain is not the same measure, but some variant of the measure.

Variability can be a function of both random and systematic errors. With the systematic errors, the errors are constants and result in either an over *or* an underestimation of true measure. On the other hand, if random errors are truly random in nature, they result in both an over *and* an underestimation of the true value. In general, the researcher attempts to eliminate the systematic errors and to reduce the random ones. It is basically the random errors that enter our discussion of reliability of measurements.

Sources of Errors.   The researcher in the sciences should be fully aware of the sources of variability and errors. At this point, we will briefly consider some of the sources of errors that may give rise to the unreliability of measurement within the study of behavior.

Within the behavioral sciences we are always concerned with errors from subject variability. We can assume variability between subjects as a function of individual differences. However, the problem arises in the variability within subjects. If we would give a subject a standardized behavioral test and then give the person the test again at a later time, we might observe that we have obtained a different measure associated with his behavior. The unreliability of the measure is not a function of the test, as the test is constant, but is perhaps a function of such variables as memory, learning, or experience. Fluctuations within the measures may be from many unknown conditions such as the subject's attitudes, or his general health. With animals as our subjects we may obtain unreliable measures associated with changes in cycles of behavior, motivational and emotional variables, learning, and a whole host of other variables.

Closely related to subject variability are the influences of environment upon the measure. If we have changes in the laboratory such as fluctuations in temperature, lighting, humidity, noise, plus many other variables, these can produce both random and systematic errors.

A further source of errors may be associated with the variability of the measuring instruments. This is not a significant source of errors for most psychological and educational tests, because these tests have typically been carefully edited and produced. However, it can be a source of errors with other types of measuring equipment. Within the laboratory setting we may find differences between comparable pieces of apparatus, or with a single apparatus over time. These sources of error become problems of maintenance and of calibration.

Lastly, we have experimenter or examiner error. Science is logically a science of the individual, for in the last analysis, it is the individual that reads the dial, observes the color, measures the records, etc., and then records the values. This source of error is of major importance in psychological and educational testing where the responses are not confined to discrete categories. In these cases, the researcher or examiner must be the measuring instrument in that he is required to judge, to evaluate, and to give numerical value to the responses. We find these problems, for example, in evaluating essay exams, projective measures, and individual intelligence tests. The sources of these errors, however, are not confined to behavioral testing. A researcher can inadvertently clue or coach the subject, differentially handle the experimental animal, misread the dial and the like. Hence, many experimental studies are run "blind" or "double-blind" to eliminate the "experimenter effects."

The Influence of Systematic and Random Errors. Systematic errors are directional or constant errors in that the error is added or subtracted from the true score. Therefore, the observed score is made up of two parts, the true value and the constant error. If we assume an additive constant, then:

$$X = X_t + X_k \tag{15.1}$$

where X = observed measure

X_t = true measure

X_k = constant error

If all the observed measures have the same systematic error then the observed mean will be influenced by the additive constant, or:

$$\bar{X} = \bar{X}_t + K \tag{15.2}$$

On the other hand, the observed variance is uninfluenced by the addition or subtraction of a constant, or:

$$S^2 = S_t^2 \tag{15.3}$$

The systematic errors are not associated with reliability, because the obtained and true variance from systematic errors are equal. However, systematic errors are of concern whenever the differences between means, for example, is under investigation, such with the t-test and the analysis of variance.

With random errors we also assume that the observed measure is made up of two parts, the true measure and the random error. We assume, however, that the sum of random errors is zero. Then:

$$X = X_t + X_e \qquad (15.4)$$

where X = observed measure

X_t = true measure

X_e = random error measure

As the sum of random errors is zero, the obtained mean is equal to the true mean.

$$\overline{X} = \overline{X}_t + \overline{X}_e$$

where $\Sigma X_e = 0$ and $\overline{X}_e = 0$

$$\text{or } \overline{X} = \overline{X}_t \qquad (15.5)$$

While random errors have no effect upon the mean, random errors influence the variance. If we transpose the observed measure into a deviation, then:

$$x = x_t + x_e \qquad (15.6)$$

where x = deviation of observed measure from the mean

x_t = deviation of true measure from the mean

x_e = deviation of random error

if we square and sum, then:

$$\Sigma x^2 = \Sigma x_t^2 + 2\Sigma x_t x_e + \Sigma x_e^2 \qquad (15.7)$$

However, if we assume the errors and true scores are uncorrelated, then the sum of the errors is zero, and:

$$\Sigma x^2 = \Sigma x_t^2 + \Sigma x_e^2 \tag{15.8}$$

These random errors are of concern in many of our tests of inferences and correlational procedures. For example, with the *t*-test, while random errors do not influence the means, they influence the standard error of the difference between two means by increasing this error term, hence reducing the obtained *t* value. Similarly, these errors will not influence the sum of cross products in the correlation coefficient but will enlarge the denominator and will thus reduce the obtained value of the correlation coefficient. In every case, the random errors increase the measures of variability and reduce the value of the procedures that utilize variance terms.

Reliability Coefficient. In measurement theory the reliability of a set of measurements is defined as the proportion of the total obtained variance that is true variance. From this definition the reliability coefficient (r_{xx}) becomes:

$$r_{xx} = \frac{S_t^2}{S^2} \tag{15.9}$$

or its equivalent form:

$$r_{xx} = 1 - \frac{S_e^2}{S^2} \tag{15.10}$$

Thus the reliability coefficient is a ratio of the true variance to the total observed variance (Formula 15.9), or one minus the ratio of error variance to the total obtained variance (Formula 15.10). If the random error variance were zero in Formula 15.10, then the reliability coefficient would be 1.00. On the other hand, if random error variance were equal to the total obtained variance then our coefficient would be zero.

Methods of Estimating Reliability. In actual practice we do not directly know the error component for a given score and hence it is not possible to determine the true and the error variances. This being the case, it logically follows that the reliability of a set of measures cannot be directly determined.

Nevertheless, we can estimate the reliability by one of four procedures. For the most part, these methods have been centered about the estimation of reliability for psychological and educational tests. However, these procedures are related to other types of measurement, and can be considered general techniques.

As an estimate of reliability, a reliability coefficient is a special use of the correlation methods. In a general way, the coefficient of determination gives us an estimate of the proportion of the true variance; and the coefficient of nondetermination, an estimate of the error variance. The reliability coefficient can be obtained from the various correlational procedures that are related to certain given assumptions.

One form of estimating reliability is the retesting procedure. With this method we can obtain an estimation of the reliability by retesting the same sample of subjects with the same measuring instrument. Therefore we would have two measures for each subject, and we could obtain an appropriate correlation coefficient. If the same instrument is used in estimating the reliability of our measures, we are confronted with the problem of the time interval separating the two measures. This time interval can influence the correlation. If the interval is short we may have spuriously high correlations as a function of memory, learning, practice effects, and other variables that can influence the reliability. On the other hand, if the interval is long we could have maturational changes and new learning that give rise to error. In a reliability study that utilizes the retest procedure, one must describe the test-retest time interval.

A second method of estimating reliability is a parts method. This procedure is appropriate if we have a number of measures from a single administration. A common method is to divide the measures in equal parts such as first half-second half or odd-even; this results in two values or scores. Equal parts, however, are not mandatory. We could, for example, compare the first third with the last two thirds. The split-half reliability procedure assumes that the two halves are equivalent and that the subject has responded to all the items of the test. The odd-even estimate of reliability makes the same assumptions. This procedure has the distinct advantage that the conditions for responding to a set of items are comparable.

The reliability of a test is in part a function of the number of items in the test. For, in general, we have a higher estimate of reliability with tests that have a large number of items. With the parts method, either the split-half or odd-even procedure, we in effect reduce the number of items by one-half, and thus, lower the magnitude of the reliability coefficient. Given the reliability coefficient obtained from one of the parts procedures, we can estimate the reliability of the total measures from the Spearman-Brown Formula (15.11).

$$r_{xx} = \frac{(K/n)(r_{x_1 x_2})}{1 + (K/n - 1)r_{x_1 x_2}} \qquad (15.11)$$

where r_{xx} = estimated reliability with K items

K/n = ratio of test length

$r_{x_1 x_2}$ = the obtained reliability coefficient

Formula 15.11 is the general formula and can be used with unequal parts. In the special case where the total test has been divided into two equal parts or K/n is equal to 2, the estimated reliability is:

$$r_{xx} = \frac{2r_{x_1 x_2}}{1 + r_{x_1 x_2}} \qquad (15.12)$$

For example, if the $r_{x_1 x_2}$ was 0.70 then r_{xx} would be 0.82 or

$$r_{xx} = \frac{2(0.70)}{1 + 0.70} = 0.82$$

Thus, we would estimate the total test reliability to be 0.82. Formula 15.12 can be used to determine what the reliability would be if we would double the length of the test; and 15.11 if we would increase the test by some proportion. This assumes that we hold everything else constant except the length or number of items of the test.

The parallel-forms estimate of reliability is highly associated with psychological and educational testing. This estimate is an index of association between two forms of a test, and describes the correlation between the forms. The general procedure is to administer one form, and at a later time to give the parallel form to the same sample of subjects; then, correlate the two sets of scores. This estimation of reliability overcomes the problem of the subject recalling specific items, which is a common problem with the test-retest method. The greatest difficulty is meeting the criterion of parallelism which is required. Two forms are parallel if they sample the same behavior and are statistically equal in means, variances, and inter-item correlations. The error between the measures of the two forms may be a function of the differences in measures as well as other fluctuations associated with the time interval between testing. One procedure of reducing errors due to learning is to counter-balance the presentations of the two forms. We may give Form A and then B to one subject, and to the second subject Form B, and later A. However, the determination of the source of error is not always possible, and it is difficult to say that error is solely a function of the differences between the two forms.

The last procedure for estimating reliability we shall describe is internal-consistency reliability. This method measures the internal consistency or homogeneity of the behavior. Basically, internal consistency or homogeneity is the extent that all the items of a given test measure the same behavior. To use this method we must make this assumption, for if we are measuring heterogeneity, this estimate of reliability shall be low. We can have a psychological test that has very high retest reliability but very low internal-consistency reliability. This is because the items of the test measure different behaviors. Like the parts method, the internal-consistency procedure has the major advantage of a single measuring session.

For estimating the reliability of measures based on the assumption of homogeneity, we have the Kuder-Richardson formulas. These are a number of derived formulas based on certain assumptions. However, we shall discuss only the general formulas.

$$r_{xx} = \left(\frac{N}{N-1}\right)\left(\frac{S^2 - \sum\limits_{i=1}^{N} P_i Q_i}{S^2}\right) \tag{15.13}$$

where N = number of measured behaviors

S^2 = total variance

$P_i Q_i$ = product of the proportion of P (pass) and Q (fail) on the ith measure, where $P + Q = 1$

$\sum\limits_{i=1}^{N}$ = sum of the products over all n measures

Formula 15.13 is generally referred to as the K-R 20. If we deal with a homogeneous test, then n would be the number of items in the total test; P_i, the proportion of individuals passing the ith item; and Q_i, the proportion failing that item. If all the item inter-correlations, as measured in this case by the phi coefficient, were unity, the estimate of reliability would be one. This event would occur only where every item in the test had the same measured level of difficulty. On the other hand, if the inter-correlation coefficients were zero, the reliability coefficient would be zero. Assume we have a six-item scale and that we have obtained the P and Q values as well as the variance and the mean. This data is given in Table 15.1.

Table 15.1

Item	P	Q	PQ
1	.9	.1	.09
2	.6	.4	.24
3	.3	.6	.18
4	.2	.8	.16
5	.7	.3	.21
6	.5	.5	.25
			$\Sigma 1.13$

$$S^2 = 2$$

$$\overline{X} = 3.2$$

$$r_{xx} = \left(\frac{6}{5}\right) \frac{(2 - 1.13)}{2}$$

$$= .52$$

The K-R 20 formula can be applied not only to situations where the measures are binary but also where the response measure has more than two categories. The response measure, in such a case, is given a stated weight, such as 0, 1, 2, 3, and we would find the proportions of subjects responding to the various categories of an item. We must assume, however, that we can combine weights. This procedure could be used in such measuring instruments as personality and attitude scales.

A simplified formula for the K-R 20 can be used when we have a binary system such as 0-1, pass-fail, right-wrong. This formula is referred to as K-R 21.

$$r_{xx} = \left[\frac{N}{N-1}\right] \frac{(S^2 - NPQ)}{S^2} \tag{15.14}$$

where P = average proportion passing each item

Q = average proportion failing each item

The K-R 21 is a special case of the K-R 20 when we have binary values. This estimate, however, utilizes less information, and we must assume that all measures have the same level of difficulty. For further discussions of the K-R formulas, the student should consult an advanced text in measurement and testing theory.

Spearman's Correction of Attenuation. If our research interest is in obtaining a correlation between two variables, the effect of error of measurement is to reduce the magnitude of the coefficient. We thus say that the correlation coefficient has been attenuated. We may be very interested in estimating the relationship between two variables when the reliabilities of these two measures are unity, or when no random errors are present. Formula 15.15 gives us such an estimation.

$$r_{x'y'} = \frac{r_{xy}}{\sqrt{r_{xx} r_{yy}}} \tag{15.15}$$

where $r_{x'y'}$ = estimated coefficient

r_{xy} = obtained coefficient

r_{xx} = reliability of the X measures

r_{yy} = reliability of the Y measures

To illustrate the correction for attenuation, assume the following data:

$$r_{xy} = 0.40 \qquad r_{xx} = 0.80 \qquad r_{yy} = 0.90$$

$$\text{therefore} \quad r_{x'y'} = \frac{0.40}{\sqrt{(0.80)(0.90)}}$$

$$= \frac{0.40}{\sqrt{0.72}}$$

$$= 0.471$$

Thus, the estimated correlation between the variables would be 0.471, and the correlation has been attenuated from 0.471 to 0.40.

Rearranging Formula 15.15, we can observe that the obtained correlation is a function of the product of the true or estimated correlation and the geometric mean of the two reliabilities, or:

$$r_{xy} = \sqrt{r_{x'y'} r_{xx} r_{yy}} \qquad (15.16)$$

If the two reliability coefficients in Formula 15.15 or 15.16 were unity, then the observed correlation coefficient would be equal to the estimated coefficient. On the other hand, if we assume the estimated coefficient is unity, then the maximum obtained correlation between two variables is one geometric mean of the two reliability coefficients:

$$\text{Max} \quad r_{xy} = \sqrt{r_{xx} r_{yy}} \qquad (15.17)$$

From our prior illustration the maximum coefficient would be:

$$\text{Max} \quad r_{xy} = \sqrt{(0.80)(0.90)}$$

$$= \sqrt{0.72}$$

$$= 0.85$$

It is important to note that the reliability of our measures sets limits upon the magnitude of the obtained coefficient, and that this coefficient is in part a function of two reliability coefficients.

The Standard Error of Measurement. The reliability of a set of measurements is highly associated with the concept of the standard error of measurement or the standard error of a score. The standard error of measurement is an estimation of the variability of the errors of measurement, in standard deviation units, that we may obtain over repeated sampling. In theory, if we took repeated measurements of a group of individuals' behavior, holding everything constant, we would find some variability in the individuals' scores due to random errors. However, rather than taking repeated measurements, we can estimate the errors from a large sample of subjects. The standard error of measurement is given by Formula 15.18.

$$S_{e\,of\,m} = S\sqrt{1 - r_{xx}} \qquad (15.18)$$

where S = total standard deviation

r_{xx} = reliability of the measures

As an example, let us assume the following data

$$X = 80 \qquad \bar{X} = 100 \qquad S = 15 \qquad r_{xx} = 0.96$$

From Formula 15.18

$$S_{e\,of\,m} = 15\sqrt{1 - 0.96}$$

$$= 3$$

Our best prediction of an individual's future score is his past performance of 80. However, due to random sampling errors we would expect some variability over repeated sampling. The obtained standard error of measurement is expressed in terms of standard deviation test score units. Therefore, the range of $\pm S_{e\,of\,m}$ would be 77 to 83 or $\pm 2S_{e\,of\,m}$ from 74 to 86. It is most important in the interpretation of an individual score to fully realize that the value is not a true value, but rather an index that is subject to variability in repeated measurement. The standard error of measurement then, is perhaps best used in the determination of confidence limits of a true score from a single estimate.

This index is highly suited for the interpretation of an individual's test score and perhaps provides more useful and appropriate information than does the reliability coefficient. Many psychological tests make the assumption that the error variance of the measures is equal throughout the range of scores. Thus, we would have a single index. On the other hand, many tests do not meet this assumption. Thus, test manuals often report various standard errors of measurement associated with different test scores and sample levels.

Summary of Terms

constant errors
correction of attenuation
internal consistency
Kuder-Richardson formula
observed measure

Spearman-Brown formulas
split-half
standard error of measurement
systematic errors
true score

odd-even
parallel forms
random errors
reliability
reliability coefficient

Summary of Symbols

X $\overline{X}_t$ $S_{e \text{ of } m}$
X_t S_t^2
X_k r_{xx}
X_e Max r_{xy}

Problems

1. John received a score of 89 on a test of creativity. Given the following information, what is the probability that a true measure of John's creativity lies between 85 and 93?

    $$\overline{X} = 80, S = 12, r_{xx} = 0.79$$

2. Assume that the correlation between reading speed and IQ is 0.74, and the reliability of the IQ measure is 0.94 while the reliability of the reading speed measure is only 0.66. What is the attenuated correlation coefficient between reading speed and IQ?

Answers to Problems

The answers given may differ at the third or fourth decimal place as a function of rounding and of the way various machines compute.

Chapter 2

1. a. Only that the two objects differ in some manner.

    b. That object "three" has or is more of something than object "one."

    c. That object "three" has or is three more standard units of something than object "one."

    d. That object "three" has or is three times more of something than object "one."

2. a. Nominal

    b. Interval

    c. Ratio

    d. Ordinal

    e. Ratio (using the wave-length of the electromagnetic energy reflected)

Chapter 3

1. a. .0868   8.68%

    b. .0364   3.64%

    c. .0448   4.48%

    d. .2191   21.91%

        $N = 356$ $1/N = .0028$

2. Check the following things about your graphs:

    a. (1) Although the bar widths have no mathematical mean-
        ing they are (by convention) made identical.
        (2) The nominal level of measurement assumes a discrete
        or discontinuous distribution, thus there should be a
        space between each of the bars in graph A.

    b. (1) On this level of measurement the distribution is
        assumed to be continuous, and thus there should be
        no spaces between the bars of graph B. (This bar
        graph is actually a histogram.)
        (2) The categories must be arranged in order (1-4 or 4-1).

3.

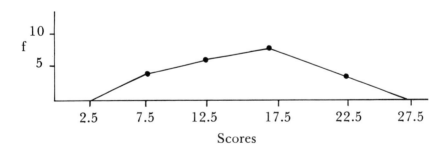

        $N = 20$
        $1/N = .05$

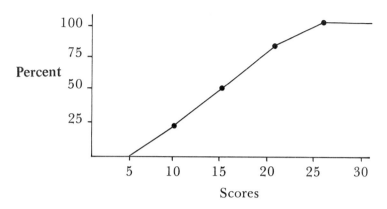

Chapter 4

1. In terms of frequencies, more people viewed program W than the other shows.

   Because the data were best described as frequency within the various categories. Thus the most appropriate scale of measurement is nominal.

2. (10 mice)(20 trials) = 200 (sum of scores)
   (12 mice)(9 trials) = 108 (sum of scores)

   $$\overline{X} = \frac{308}{22} = 14$$

3. 7

4. mean = 4.5
   median = 4
   mode = 2

5. a. 28

   b. 35.5

6. a. Below

   b. Above

   c. Below

   d. Below

7.　a.　$\overline{X} = 6.5$　　$\overline{G} = 6$

　　b.　$\overline{X} = 2.3$　　$\overline{G} = 2$

Chapter 5

1.　.4808

2.　$R = 80.5 - 10.5 = 70$

$$Q_3 = 50.5 + \left[\frac{45 - 29}{20} \right] 10 = 58.5$$

$$Q_1 = 30.5 + \left[\frac{15 - 8}{9} \right] 10 = 38.3$$

$$\text{Mdn} = 50.5 + \left[\frac{30 - 29}{20} \right] 10 = 51$$

$$\frac{Q_3 - Q_1}{2} = \frac{20.2}{2} = 10.1$$

Since: Q_3 – Mdn $<$ Mdn – Q_1 the distribution is negatively skewed, this means that the bulk of the students did relatively well. This would suggest that the students found the test to be relatively easy.

3.　$N = 20$
$\Sigma X = 96$
$\Sigma X^2 = 586$

$$S = \sqrt{\frac{\Sigma X^2 - \dfrac{(\Sigma X^2)}{N}}{N - 1}}$$

$$= \sqrt{\frac{586 - \dfrac{(96)^2}{20}}{19}}$$

$$= 2.5669$$

4.　a.　.4332

　　b.　.1915

　　c.　.8385

　　d.　.0035

    e. .9918

    f. .0394

5.   a. .5000

    b. .1587

    c. .9750

Chapter 6

1.   a. Ranks or percentile ranks. This measure of dominance is based on the ordinal level of measurement; it cannot be said that the distance between the intervals is equal.

    b. $\text{Score} = 19.5 + \left[\dfrac{(.40)(50) - 8}{12} \right] 5 = 24.5$

    c. $\% \text{ rank} = \left[\dfrac{(36 - 34.5)\left(\frac{12}{5}\right)}{50} \right] + \dfrac{34}{50} = .75 = 75\%$

2.   a. $\overline{X} = 7.9, \ S = 7.2$

    b.

Score	z	% rank
25	+2.375	99.18
20	+1.680	95.54
15	+ .986	84.13
10	+ .291	61.79
5	− .402	34.46

    c.

Score	Z
25	73.75
20	66.80
15	59.86
10	52.91
5	45.98

    d.

Score	% rank	Score	f	cf	P	cp
25	99.5	21-25	1	20	.05	1.00
20	93.5	16-20	3	19	.15	.95
15	79.0	11-15	2	16	.10	.80
10	67.5	6-10	5	14	.25	.70
5	40.5	1-5	9	9	.45	.45

e. | Score | T |
    |-------|-----|
    | 25 | 80 (approx.) |
    | 20 | 66 " |
    | 15 | 58 " |
    | 10 | 55 " |
    | 5 | 49 " |

f. The distribution given in this problem is positively skewed. The percentile ranks computed in "b" assumed that the distribution was normally distributed, while the percentile ranks computed by formula 6.1 were based on the actual distribution given.

Chapter 8

1. a. .2

    b. .8

    c. .8

    d. .25

    e. .02

    f. .5

    g. .67

2. a. .8

    b. .6

    c. 1.0

    d. .033

3. a. 120

    b. 20

4. a. 1

    b. 10

    c. 45

    d. 120

    e. 210

    f. 252

g. 210

h. 120

i. 45

j. 10

k. 1

5. a. .2461

b. .1641

c. .0703

d. .0176

e. .0020

f. .2540

6. $P = .2$
$Q = .8$
Expanding the binomial, $P^5 = 0.0003$ and $5P^4 Q = 0.0064$, thus the probability of 4 or more art critics selecting the original is $0.0003 + 0.0064 = 0.0067$.

Chapter 9

1. a. The amount of time spent on the two end grids is a function of chance. Since the grids are equal in size and the end grids make up 40% (2/5) of the floor, the mean amount of time spent on the two end grids is equal to two fifths of the toal amount of time spent in the apparatus.

b. $N = 1200$
$P = .4$
$Q = .6$
$\mu = 480$
$(X = 613)$
$X > \mu, - 0.5$
$= 16.9$
$z = 7.84$
Since a z value equal to or greater than 7.84 occurs less than 5% of the time, we can reject the null hypothesis and accept the research hypothesis. Thus it can be concluded that mice spend a greater amount of time at the

ends of the apparatus than would be expected by the basis of chance alone.

2. $x^2 = 7.33$, $df = 2$, $p < 0.05$. Thus the null hypothesis is rejected and the research hypothesis is accepted, the frequency of freezing increases as anxiety level increases.

3.   a. $x^2 = 13.6$, $df = 1$

b.   No. The professor's research hypothesis was directional, and the difference was not in the right direction to support his hypothesis.

Chapter 10

1.

	1 16-oz.	2 8-oz.	4 4-oz.	Total
Above Mdn	0	3	8	11
Below Mdn	5	4	0	9
Total	5	7	8	20

$x^2 = 13.07$
$df = 2$
$p < 0.05$
When the total weight of the reinforcer is held constant, increasing the number of pieces (1, 2, 4) of the reinforcer increases hoop jumping behavior in lions.

2. $n_1 = 24$ (fall)
$n_2 = 22$ (spring)
$\mu = 264$
$\sigma_u = 45.47$
$U = 211.5$
$R_1 = 616.5$
$Z_u = -1.15$
$p > .05$
Since the probability of a Z_u of -1.15 is far greater than .05 the null hypothesis must be retained and the research hypothesis must be rejected.

3.

	f	cf	f	cf	D
21–25	5	20	3	20	0
16–20	5	15	3	17	2
11–15	3	10	4	14	4
6–10	4	7	3	10	3
1–5	3	3	7	7	4

$n_1 = n_2 = N = 20$
Max $D = 4$
$P < .01$

4. The sign test.

$X = 8$
$N = 11$
$p = .5$
$\mu = 5.5$
$\sigma = 1.65$
$z_{(sign)} = 1.21$
$p > .05$

The null hypothesis cannot be rejected, thus the research hypothesis cannot be supported.

Chapter 11

1. $\overline{X} = 3.75$
$\mu = 3.00$
$t = 6.0970$
$df = 19$
$p < .01$

2. Homogeneity of variance test:

$$F = \frac{S_1^2}{S_2^2} = 2.19 \quad p < .05$$

The assumption of homogeneity of variance must be rejected, and the t test for heterogeneous variances with equal N's must be used.

t test:
$t = 2.912, df = 19, p < .05$

$$t_{(.05)} = \frac{(.2875)(2.09) + (.6299)(2.09)}{(.2875) + (.6299)} = 2.09$$

3. $\overline{X}_1 = 73.2$
$\overline{X}_2 = 47.2$
$t = 4.9771$
$p < .05$

4.

	Low	Medium	High	Total
X	1057	815	678	2550
X^2	147857	88433	65058	301348
$\overline{X}$	132.1250	101.8750	84.7500	106.2500
ΣX_w^2	8200.8750	5404.8750	7597.5000	21203.2500
S_w^2	1171.5535	772.1250	1085.3571	
F_{max}	= 1171.5535/772.1250 = 1.5173 $p > .05$			
ΣX_B^2	5356.1250	153.1250	3698.0000	9207.2500

Source	SS	df	MS	F	p
Total	30410.5000	23	- - - - - -	- - - -	- - - -
Between	9207.2500	2	4603.6250	4.5594	.05
Within	21203.2500	21	1009.6785	- - - -	- - - -

Group 1 & 2: $N\text{-}K = 2.69$, $r = 2$, $p > .05$ Tabled $_{(N-K)} = 2.95$

Group 1 & 3: $N\text{-}K = 4.21$, $r = 3$, $p < .05$ Tabled $_{(N-K)} = 3.58$

Group 2 & 3: $N\text{-}K = 1.52$, $r = 2$, $p > .05$ Tabled $_{(N-K)} = 2.95$

						Totals
5.	ΣX	1496	1142	969	707	4314
	ΣX^2	305708	226422	159673	75443	767246
	$\overline{X}$	187.000	142.750	121.125	88.375	

Source	SS	df	MS	F	p
Total	185664.875	31	- - - - - -	- - - -	- - - -
Days	41042.625	3	13680.8750	6.1213	<.05
Subjects	97688.375	7	- - - - - -	- - - -	- - - -
Residual	46933.875	21	2234.9464	- - - -	- - - -

						Total
6.	ΣX	165	528	837	589	2119
	ΣX^2	3125	28984	70285	36009	138403
	$\overline{X}$	16.5	52.8	83.7	58.9	

Source	SS	df	MS	F	p
Total	26148.975	39	- - - - - -	- - - - -	- - - -
Magazine	13432.225	1	13432.225	158.3833	<.001
Picture	330.625	1	330.625	3.8984	>.001
(Mag.) x					
(Pict.)	9333.025	1	9333.025	110.0484	>.001
Within	3050.100	36	84.8083	- - - - -	- - - -

Chapter 12

1. $\chi^2 = 46.6021$, $df = 1$, $p < .01$
    $C = .4089$
    There is a significant (at the .01 alpha level) degree of associa-
    tion between the number of speeches given and the number of
    votes received. The fewer the speeches given, the more votes
    are received.

2. $\phi = -.3628$
 $\chi^2 = 29.7469$
 $p < .05$
 Herman's hypothesis was directional, unfortunately, it was in the wrong direction and even though the degree of association was significant at the .05 alpha level he cannot reject his null hypothesis of no association.

3. Uncertainty of the effect (U_e)

		P	$-p \log_2 P$
No effect	10/40	.25	.5000
Successful	16/40	.40	.5288
Fatal	14/40	.35	.5301

Conditional Uncertainty $(U_{e|d})$

.4644	.2161	.0000	.0000
.2161	.4105	.4105	.2161
.0000	.2161	.3322	.4644
Totals .6805	.8427	.7427	.6805

$U_{e|d} = (.6805 + .8427 + .7427 + .6805) (.25) = .7366$

Contingent Uncertainty $= 1.5589 - .7366 = .8223$ bits
$\chi^2 = (1.3863) (40) (.8223) = 45.5981,$
$\quad df = (r-1) (k-1) = (2) (3) = 6$
$\quad \underline{p} < .001$

Chapter 13

1.

Ranked Exploration Scores	Ranked Learning Scores
1	6
2	18
5.5	1
5.5	19.5
5.5	15.5
5.5	4
5.5	7.5
5.5	9
9.5	7.5
9.5	17
11.5	3
11.5	19.5
13.5	13.5
13.5	5
15.5	10
15.5	13.5

17.5	2
17.5	11.5
19	15.5
20	11.5

$Rho = +.0379$, $df = 18$, $p > .05$
$Tau = +.0315$
   $z = .1942$, $p > .05$

2. | R | 13 | 18 | 14 | 16 | 32 | 35 |
    |---|----|----|----|----|----|----|
    | R | 16 | 45 | 40 | 46 | Total — 275 | |

$R-\bar{R}$	-14.5	-9.5	-13.5	-11.5	4.5	7.5
$R-\bar{R}$	-11.5	17.5	12.5	18.5 Total — 00.0		

$(R-\bar{R})^2$	210.25	90.25	182.25	132.25	20.25	56.25
$(R-\bar{R})^2$	132.25	306.25	156.25	342.25		

$\Sigma (R - R)^2 = 1,628.5$

$\bar{R} = 27.5$

$S_0 = 1,628.5$

$S_{pa} = 2,062.5$

$W = 0.79$

$\chi^2 = 35.53$, $df = 9$, $p < .01$

3. $Tau_{(DA.W)} = 0.64$

Chapter 14

1. $N = 15$
       $\bar{X} = 25.67$ $\bar{Y} = 44.07$
       $\Sigma X = 385$ $\Sigma Y = 661$
       $\Sigma X^2 = 10497$ $\Sigma Y^2 = 30435$
                       $\Sigma XY = 17776$
                       $r_{yx} = +.9036$
                       $a_{yx} = 10.27$
                       $b_{yx} = 1.3168$
                       $S_{yx} = 3.9985$
                       $\tilde{Y} = 76.11 \pm 3.9985 = (72.1115 - 80.1085)$

2.   eta = .517
     Test for linearity:
     $F = 7.345$, $df = 3/70$, $p < .05$

3.

	Number of Relatives (3)	Average Income (2)	Years of Marriage (1)
$\overline{X}$	8.4	11.44	33.7
ΣX	84	114.4	337
ΣX^2	1616	1477.66	17171.0
S_x	9.5414	4.1100	24.1124

$r_{1.23} = .6925$

$B_{12.3} = .789$

$B_{13.2} = -.2.397$

$b_{12.3} = 4.628$ $b_{13.2} = 5.407$ $a_{1.23} = 26.175$

$Z_{(99\%)} = 2.326$ $S_{1.23} = 17.395$

$\tilde{X}_1 = 60.770 \pm 40.461$

4. $\Sigma Y_1 = 23.40$ $\Sigma Y_2 = 24.28$
    $Y_1 = 2.34$ $Y_2 = 2.428$
    $p = .5$ $q = .5$

$\Sigma Y = 47.68$
$Y^2 = 124.027$
$st = 0.72$

$r_{pb} = -.611$
$t = 3.278$
$df = 8$
$p < .05$

5. $r_b = -.6114 \left(\dfrac{\sqrt{(.5)\,(.5)}}{.3989} \right) = -.7663$

The large discrepancy indicates that the value of the population coefficient is large.

6. The values in the cells are not independent as their sum is $(\underset{2}{N})$ rather than N. The chi-square is meaningful only with independent observations.

Chapter 15

1. $S_{e\ of\ m} = 5.52$

Z of 85 = .72 $p = 0.2642$
Z of 93 = .72 $p = \underline{0.2642}$
                 $p = 0.5284$

2. $r_{x'y'} = .94$

References and Suggested Readings

Attneave, F. *Applications of information theory to psychology: A summary of basic concepts, methods, and results.* New York: Holt, Rinehart and Winston, 1959.

Auble, D. Extended tables for the Mann-Whitney statistic. *Bulletin of the Institute of Educational Research at Indiana University,* 1953, **1**, No. 2.

Bakan, D. The test of significance in psychological research. *Psychological Bulletin,* 1966, **66**, 433-437.

Bergman, G., & Spence, K. W. The logic of psychological measurement. *Psychological Review,* 1944, **51**, 1-24.

Binder, A. Further considerations on testing the null hypothesis and the strategy and tactics of investigating theoretical models. *Psychological Review,* 1963, **70**, 107-115.

Binder, A. Statistical theory. In P. Farnsworth (Ed.), *Annual review of psychology.* Palo Alto, Calif.: Annual Reviews, 1964.

Blum, J. R. & Fatter, N. A. Nonparametric methods. *Review of of Educational Research,* 1954, **24**, 467-487.

Bruning, J. L., & Kintz, B. L. *Computational handbook of statistics.* Glenview, Ill.: Scott, Foresman, 1968.

Carlborg, F. W. *Introduction to statistics.* Glenview, Ill.: Scott, Foresman, 1968.

Churchman, C. W., & Ratoosh, P. *Measurement: Definition and theories.* New York: Wiley, 1959.

Clark, C. A. Hypothesis testing in relation to statistical methodology. *Review of Educational Research,* 1963, **33**, 455-457.

Cochran, W. G. The χ^2 test of goodness of it. *Annals of Mathematical Statistics,* 1952, **23**, 315-345.

Cochran, W. G. Some methods for strengthening the common χ^2 tests. *Biometrics,* 1954, **10**, 417-451.

Cochran, W. G., & Cox, G. M. *Experimental design*. New York: Wiley, 1957

Coombs, C. H. Psychological scaling without a unit of measurement. *Psychological Review*, 1950, **57**, 145-158.

Davidoff, M. D., & Goheen, H. W. A table for the rapid determination of the tetrachoric correlation coefficient. *Psychometrika*, 1953, **18**, 115-121.

Dixon, W. J. Power under normality of several nonparametric tests. *Annals of Mathematical Statistics*, 1954, **25**, 610-614.

Dixon, W. J., & Massey, F. J. *Introduction to statistical analysis*. McGraw-Hill, 1957.

Dixon, W. J. & Mood, A. M. The statistical sign test. *Journal of the American Statistical Association*, 1946, **41**, 557-566.

Edwards, A. L. *Experimental design in psychological research*. New York: Holt, Rinehart and Winston, 1960.

Edwards, W. Tactical note on the relation between scientific and statistical hypotheses. *Psychological Bulletin*, 1965, **63**, 400-402.

Eisenhart, C., Hastoy, M. W., & Wallis, W. T. *Techniques of Statistical Analysis*. New York: McGraw-Hill, 1947.

Feller, W. *An Introduction to probability theory and its application*. Vol. 1. New York: Wiley, 1960.

Fisher, R. A. *Statistical methods for research workers*. Edinburgh: Oliver and Boyd, 1936.

Fisher, R. A. *The design of experiments*. Edinburgh: Oliver and Boyd, 1942.

Fisher, R. A., & Yates, F. *Statistical tables for biological, agricultural and medical research*. New York: Hafner, 1948.

Fraser, D. A. S. *Nonparametric methods in statistics*. New York: Wiley, 1957.

Friedman, M. A comparison of alternative tests of significance for the problem of *m* rankings. *Annals of Mathematical Statistics*, 1940, **11**. 86-92.

Goodman, L. A. Kolmogorov-Smirnov tests for psychological research. *Psychological Bulletin,* 1954, **51**, 160-168.

Guthrie, E. R. Psychological facts and psychological theory. *Psychological bulletin,* 1946, **43**, 1-20.

Hays, W. L. *Statistics for psychologists.* New York: Holt, Rinehart and Winston, 1963.

Hick, W. E. A note on one-tailed and two-tailed tests. *Psychological Review,* 1952, **59**, 316-317.

Hopkins, K. D., & Chadbourn, R. A. A schema for proper utilization of multiple comparisons in research and a case study. *American Educational Research Journal,* 1967, **4**, 407-412.

Horst, P. *Psychological measurement and prediction.* Belmont, Calif.: Wadsworth, 1966.

Hotelling, H. The statistical method and the philosophy of science. *American Statistician,* 1958, **12**, 9-14.

Jones, L. V. Tests of hypotheses: one-sided vs. two-sided alternatives. *Psychological Bulletin,* 1952, **49**, 43-46.

Kendall, M. G. *The advanced theory of statistics.* Vol. II. London: Charles Griffin, 1948.

Kendall, M. G. *Rank correlation methods.* London: Charles Griffin, 1948.

Kirk, G. E. *Experimental design: Procedures for the behavioral sciences.* Belmont, Calif.: Brooks/Cole, 1968.

Lewis, D. *Quantitative methods in psychology.* New York: McGraw-Hill, 1960.

Lewis, D., & Burke, C. J. The use and misuse of the chi-square test. *Psychological Bulletin,* 1949, **46**, 433-489.

Linquist, E. F. *Design and analysis of experiments in psychology and education.* Boston: Houghton Mifflin, 1953.

Mann, H. B., & Whitney, D. R. On a test of whether one of two random variables is stochastically larger than the other. *Annals of Mathematical Statistics,* 1947, **18**, 50-60.

Massey, F. J., Jr. The distribution of the maximum deviation between two sample cumulative step functions. *Annals of Mathematical Statistics,* 1951, **22,** 125-128.

Massey, F. J., Jr. The Kolmogorov-Smirnov test for goodness of fit. *Journal of the American Statistical Association,* 1951, **46,** 68-78.

McNemar, Q. *Psychological Statistics.* New York: Wiley, 1962.

Mendenhall, W. *Introduction to probability and statistics.* Belmont, Calif.: Wadsworth, 1967.

Meredith, W. M. *Basic mathematical and statistical tables for psychology and education.* New York: McGraw-Hill, 1967.

Michael, W. B. Selected contributions to parametric and nonparametric statistics. *Review of Educational Research,* 1963, **33,** 474-489.

Michael, W. B., & Hanka, S. Research tools: statistical methods. *Review of Educational Research,* 1960, **30,** 440-486.

Moonan, W. J., & Wolfe, J. H. Regression and correlation. *Review of Educational Research,* 1963, **33,** 501-509.

Morrison, D. F. *Multivariate statistical methods.* New York: McGraw-Hill, 1967.

Noether, G. E. *Elements of nonparametric statistics.* New York: Wiley, 1967.

Olds, E. G. The 5% significance levels for sum of squares of rank difference and a correction. *Annals of Mathematical Statistics,* 1949, **20,** 117-118.

Pearson, S. S., & Hartley, H. O. (Eds.) *Biometrika tables for statisticians.* New York: Cambridge, 1958.

Scheffé, H. *The analysis of variance.* New York: Wiley, 1959.

Siegel, S. *Nonparametric statistics for the behavioral sciences.* New York: McGraw-Hill, 1956.

Smirnov, N. Tables for estimating the goodness of fit of empirical distributions. *Annals of Mathematical Statistics,* 1948, **19,** 279-281.

Smith, D. E., Reeve, W. D., & Morss, E. L. *Elementary mathematical tables.* Boston: Ginn, 1928.

Stevens, S. S. Mathematics, measurement and psychophysics. In S. S. Stevens (Ed.), *Handbook of experimental psychology.* New York: Wiley, 1951, pp. 1-49.

Stevens, S. S. Measurement, statistics and the schemapiric view. *Science,* 1968, **161,** 849-856.

Swed, F. S., & Eisenhart, C. Tables for testing randomness of grouping in a sequence of alternatives. *Annals of Mathematical Statistics,* 1943, **14,** 83-86.

Tatsuaka, M. M., & Tiedeman, D. O. Statistics as an aspect of scientific method in research on teaching. In Gage, N. L. (Ed.), *Handbook of research on teaching.* New York: Rand McNally, 1963.

Walsh, J. E. *Handbook of nonparametric statistics.* Princeton, N. J.: Van Nostrand, 1962, 1965.

Whitney, D. R. A bivariate extension of the U test. *Annals of Mathematical Statistics,* 1951, **22,** 274-282.

Wilcoxon, F. *Some rapid approximate statistical procedures.* Stamford, Conn.: American Cyanamid, 1949.

Wilson, W. A note on the inconsistency inherent in the necessity to perform multiple comparisons. *Psychological Bulletin,* 1962, **59,** 296-300.

Winer, B. J. *Statistical principles in experimental design.* New York: McGraw-Hill, 1962.

Glossary of Symbols

$+$	addition of
α	alpha, the level of significance, probability of a Type I error
H_1	an alternative or research hypotheses
z^2	approximately equals x^2
$\bar{r}_S$	average of rhos
β	beta, the power of a test of significance, probability of a Type II error
$\beta_{12.3}$	beta coefficients, see multiple regression
Σx_b^2	between sum of squares: the analysis of variance
$\binom{n}{r}$	binomial coefficient, combination of n things taken r at a time
r_b	biserial correlation coefficient
χ^2	chi square statistical test
r^2	coefficient of determination
$1\text{-}r^2$	coefficient of non-determination
V	coefficient of variation

$_nC_r$	combination of n things taken r at a time
$\binom{n}{r}$	combination of n things taken r at a time, binomial coefficient
X_k	constant error
C^2	constant in Scheffé's method for subsequent analysis
e	constant of 2.7183
π	constant of 3.1416, pi
C	the contingency coefficient
U_{xy}	contingent uncertainty
cf	cumulative frequency
$c\%$	cumulative percentage
cp	cumulative proportion
df	degrees of freedom
z	a deviation score from a distribution with a mean of 0 and a standard deviation of 1; a theoretical distribution of deviation scores
z_n	a deviation score from a normal distribution with a mean of 0 and a standard deviation of 1
T	a deviation score from a normal distribution with a mean of 50 and a standard deviation of 10
Z	a deviation score with a mean of 50 and a standard deviation of 10
d_i	difference between two scores in values or ranks
$=$	equal to
η	eta, population correlation ratio
F	F test for the analysis of variance; testing for homogeneity variance
F'	F' for subsequent analysis: the analysis of variance
F_{max}	F_{max} test for determining the homogeneity of variance
$!$	factorial, product of numbers from 1 to N
Q_2	50th percentile or the median

f_w	frequencies within class interval
f	frequency of cases
f_i	frequency of cases within the ith category
i	generalized case
$\overline{G}$	geometric mean
$>$	greater than
∞	infinity
$A \times B$	interaction between the A and B variables: analysis of variance
a_{xy}	intercept of the regression line of X and Y
a_{yx}	intercept of the regression line of Y and X
W	Kendall's coefficient of concordance
$\tau_{12.3}$	Kendall's partial rank correlation
τ	Kendall's rank correlation coefficient, tau
$<$	less than
α	the level of significance, probability of a Type I error, alpha
$_rL_1$	lower real limits
U	Mann-Whitney statistical test
z_u	Mann-Whitney test for large N's
D	maximum difference statistical test
S_{max}	maximum values in tau
$\overline{X}$	mean of a sample
$M.S._b$	mean square between groups: the analysis of variance
$M.S._e$	mean square error: the analysis of variance
$M.S._{A \times B}$	mean square for the interaction effect: analysis of variance
$M.S._w$	mean square within groups: the analysis of variance
Mdn	median of a sample
μ	mu, population mean

$r_{1 \cdot 23}$	multiple correlation coefficient
$\neq$	not equal to
$\ngtr$	not greater than
$\nless$	not less than
H_o	a null hypothesis
$n(A)$	the number of a particular class
N	number of cases
K	number of equally likely choices
o_{ij}	observed frequency of cases in the ith row and jth column
X	an observed score
y	ordinate of the normal curve
$r_{12 \cdot 3}$	partial correlation coefficient
$b_{12 \cdot 3}$	partial regression coefficient
r	Pearson's product-moment correlation coefficient
$\%$	percent of
$_nP_n$	permutations of n things taken n at a time
ϕ	the phi coefficient
π	pi, constant of 3.1416
r_{pb}	point biserial correlation coefficient
ρ	population correlation coefficient, rho
η	population correlation ratio, eta
μ	population mean, mu
μ_T	population mean estimate for tau
μ_r	population mean estimate of the sampling distribution of the runs test
μ_T	population mean estimate of the sampling distribution of the sign rank test
μ_u	population mean estimate of the sampling distributed of U
σ	population standard deviation, sigma

$\sigma_{\bar{x}}$	population standard error of the mean
σ^2	population variance
β	the power of a test of significance, probability of a Type II error, beta
$\tilde{X}_y$	predicted value of X from a regression equation of X on Y
$\tilde{Y}_x$	predicted value of Y from a regression equation of Y on X
$P(\Lambda)$	probability of an outcome A
$Q(A)$	probability of an outcome that is not A
α	probability of a Type I error, alpha, the level of significance
β	probability of a Type II error, beta, the power of a test of significance
!	product of numbers from 1 to N, factorial
X_e	random error
R	range of scores
b_{xy}	regression coefficient of X on Y
b_{yx}	regression coefficient of Y on X
M.S.$_{res.}$	residual mean square: the analysis of variance
$\Sigma(X - \tilde{X})^2$	residual sum of squares of X on Y
$\Sigma(x - \tilde{x})^2$	residual sum of squares of X on Y (deviation form)
$\Sigma(Y - \tilde{Y})^2$	residual sum of squares of Y on X
$\Sigma(y - \tilde{y})^2$	residual sum of squares of Y on X (deviation form)
S^2_{xy}	residual variance of X on Y
S^2_{yx}	residual variance of Y on X
ρ	rho, population correlation coefficient
z_r	runs test for large Ns
E_{yx}	sample correlation ratio
Q	semi-interquartile range
Q_3	75th percentile
Σ	sigma, summation of

σ	sigma, population standard deviation
$z_{\text{sign-rank}}$	sign rank test for large Ns
z_{sign}	sign test for large Ns
T	smaller sum of two ranks
r_{xx}	Spearman-Brown Formula
$r_{s12.3}$	Spearman's partial rank correlation
r_s	Spearman's rank correlation coefficient (rho)
$\sqrt{}$	square root
S	the standard deviation of a sample
$\overline{S}_{xy}$	standard error of estimate of X on Y
$\overline{S}_{yx}$	Standard error of estimate of Y on X
$S_{e\text{ of }m}$	standard error of measurement
$S'z$	standard error of r
σ_{τ}	standard error for tau
$S_{\bar{x}_1 - \bar{x}_2}$	standard error of the difference between means
$S_{\bar{x}}$	standard error of the mean for a sample
σ_r	standard error of the runs test sampling distribution
σ_T	standard error of the sign rank test sampling distribution
σ_u	standard error of the U sampling distribution
z-test	a statistical test utilizing the theoretical normal curve
$\overline{S}$	subject
Ss	subjects
Σxy	sum of cross products
s_o	sum of negative and positive values for all pairs, see tau
R_1	sum of ranks in one group, Mann-Whitney test
R_2	sum of ranks in the other group, Mann-Whitney test
ΣX^2	sum of the squared scores
Σx^2	sum of squares of the deviations from the mean
Σd^2	sum of squares of the difference between two scores

Σx	sum of the deviation scores
Σfb	sum of the frequencies below
Σ	summation of, sigma
$\sum_{1}^{N}$	summation of scores from 1 to the Nth case
τ	tau, Kendell's rank correlation coefficient
r_t	tetrachoric correlation coefficient
e_{ij}	theoretical or expected frequency of cases in the ith row and jth column
T_j	total frequency for significant changes
Σx_t^2	total sum of squares: the analysis of variance
$z'r$	transformed r
$z'\rho$	transformed ρ
$\overline{X}_t$	true mean of a sample
X_t	true score value or measure
S_t^2	true variance of a sample
Q_1	25th percentile
U	uncertainty
U_x	uncertainty of a variable
$_rU_l$	upper real limits
$S_{\overline{x}}^2$	variance of the mean for a sample
S^2	the variance of a sample
Σx_w^2	within sum of squares: the analysis of variance

Tables

Table A.1.   *Table of Four-Place Logarithms*

N	0	1	2	3	4	5	6	7	8	9	1 2 3	4 5 6	7 8 9
1.0	.0000	.0043	.0086	.0128	.0170	.0212	.0253	.0294	.0334	.0374	4 8 12	17 21 25	29 33 37
1.1	.0414	.0453	.0492	.0531	.0569	.0607	.0645	.0682	.0719	.0755	4 8 11	15 19 23	26 30 34
1.2	.0792	.0828	.0864	.0899	.0934	.0969	.1004	.1038	.1072	.1106	3 7 10	14 17 21	24 28 31
1.3	.1139	.1173	.1206	.1239	.1271	.1303	.1335	.1367	.1399	.1430	3 6 10	13 16 19	23 26 29
1.4	.1461	.1492	.1523	.1553	.1584	.1614	.1644	.1673	.1703	.1732	3 6 9	12 15 18	21 24 27
1.5	.1761	.1790	.1818	.1847	.1875	.1903	.1931	.1959	.1987	.2014	3 6 8	11 14 17	20 22 25
1.6	.2041	.2068	.2095	.2122	.2148	.2175	.2201	.2227	.2253	.2279	3 5 8	11 13 16	18 21 24
1.7	.2304	.2330	.2355	.2380	.2405	.2430	.2455	.2480	.2504	.2529	2 5 7	10 12 15	17 20 22
1.8	.2553	.2577	.2601	.2625	.2648	.2672	.2695	.2718	.2742	.2765	2 5 7	9 12 14	16 19 21
1.9	.2788	.2810	.2833	.2856	.2878	.2900	.2923	.2945	.2967	.2989	2 4 7	9 11 13	16 18 20
2.0	.3010	.3032	.3054	.3075	.3096	.3118	.3139	.3160	.3181	.3201	2 4 6	8 11 13	15 17 19
2.1	.3222	.3243	.3263	.3284	.3304	.3324	.3345	.3365	.3385	.3404	2 4 6	8 10 12	14 16 18
2.2	.3424	.3444	.3464	.3483	.3502	.3522	.3541	.3560	.3579	.3598	2 4 6	8 10 12	14 15 17
2.3	.3617	.3636	.3655	.3674	.3692	.3711	.3729	.3747	.3766	.3784	2 4 6	7 9 11	13 15 17
2.4	.3802	.3820	.3838	.3856	.3874	.3892	.3909	.3927	.3945	.3962	2 4 5	7 9 11	12 14 16
2.5	.3979	.3997	.4014	.4031	.4048	.4065	.4082	.4099	.4116	.4133	2 3 5	7 9 10	12 14 15
2.6	.4150	.4166	.4183	.4200	.4216	.4232	.4249	.4265	.4281	.4298	2 3 5	7 8 10	11 13 15
2.7	.4314	.4330	.4346	.4362	.4378	.4393	.4409	.4425	.4440	.4456	2 3 5	6 8 9	11 13 14
2.8	.4472	.4487	.4502	.4518	.4533	.4548	.4564	.4579	.4594	.4609	2 3 5	6 8 9	11 12 14
2.9	.4624	.4639	.4654	.4669	.4683	.4698	.4713	.4728	.4742	.4757	1 3 4	6 7 9	10 12 13
3.0	.4771	.4786	.4800	.4814	.4829	.4843	.4857	.4871	.4886	.4900	1 3 4	6 7 9	10 11 13
3.1	.4914	.4928	.4942	.4955	.4969	.4983	.4997	.5011	.5024	.5038	1 3 4	6 7 8	10 11 12
3.2	.5051	.5065	.5079	.5092	.5105	.5119	.5132	.5145	.5159	.5172	1 3 4	5 7 8	9 11 12
3.3	.5185	.5198	.5211	.5224	.5237	.5250	.5263	.5276	.5289	.5302	1 3 4	5 6 8	9 10 12
3.4	.5315	.5328	.5340	.5353	.5366	.5378	.5391	.5403	.5416	.5428	1 3 4	5 6 8	9 10 11
3.5	.5441	.5453	.5465	.5478	.5490	.5502	.5514	.5527	.5539	.5551	1 2 4	5 6 7	9 10 11
3.6	.5563	.5575	.5587	.5599	.5611	.5623	.5635	.5647	.5658	.5670	1 2 4	5 6 7	8 10 11
3.7	.5682	.5694	.5705	.5717	.5729	.5740	.5752	.5763	.5775	.5786	1 2 3	5 6 7	8 9 10
3.8	.5798	.5809	.5821	.5832	.5843	.5855	.5866	.5877	.5888	.5899	1 2 3	5 6 7	8 9 10
3.9	.5911	.5922	.5933	.5944	.5955	.5966	.5977	.5988	.5999	.6010	1 2 3	4 5 7	8 9 10
4.0	.6021	.6031	.6042	.6053	.6064	.6075	.6085	.6096	.6107	.6117	1 2 3	4 5 6	8 9 10
4.1	.6128	.6138	.6149	.6160	.6170	.6180	.6191	.6201	.6212	.6222	1 2 3	4 5 6	7 8 9
4.2	.6232	.6243	.6253	.6263	.6274	.6284	.6294	.6304	.6314	.6325	1 2 3	4 5 6	7 8 9
4.3	.6335	.6345	.6355	.6365	.6375	.6385	.6395	.6405	.6415	.6425	1 2 3	4 5 6	7 8 9
4.4	.6435	.6444	.6454	.6464	.6474	.6484	.6493	.6503	.6513	.6522	1 2 3	4 5 6	7 8 9
4.5	.6532	.6542	.6551	.6561	.6571	.6580	.6590	.6599	.6609	.6618	1 2 3	4 5 6	7 8 9
4.6	.6628	.6637	.6646	.6656	.6665	.6675	.6684	.6693	.6702	.6712	1 2 3	4 5 6	7 7 8
4.7	.6721	.6730	.6739	.6749	.6758	.6767	.6776	.6785	.6794	.6803	1 2 3	4 5 5	6 7 8
4.8	.6812	.6821	.6830	.6839	.6848	.6857	.6866	.6875	.6884	.6893	1 2 3	4 4 5	6 7 8
4.9	.6902	.6911	.6920	.6928	.6937	.6946	.6955	.6964	.6972	.6981	1 2 3	4 4 5	6 7 8
5.0	.6990	.6998	.7007	.7016	.7024	.7033	.7042	.7050	.7059	.7067	1 2 3	3 4 5	6 7 8
5.1	.7076	.7084	.7093	.7101	.7110	.7118	.7126	.7135	.7143	.7152	1 2 3	3 4 5	6 7 8
5.2	.7160	.7168	.7177	.7185	.7193	.7202	.7210	.7218	.7226	.7235	1 2 2	3 4 5	6 7 7
5.3	.7243	.7251	.7259	.7267	.7275	.7284	.7292	.7300	.7308	.7316	1 2 2	3 4 5	6 6 7
5.4	.7324	.7332	.7340	.7348	.7356	.7364	.7372	.7380	.7388	.7396	1 2 2	3 4 5	6 6 7

*From *Essentials of Trigonometry* by D. E. Smith, W. D. Reeve, and E. L. Morss; Copyright 1928 by D. E. Smith, W. D. Reeve, and E. L. Morss; Copyright renewed, 1955, by W. D. Reeve and E. L. Morss. Published by Ginn and Company. Used with permission.

To obtain the mantissa for a four-digit number, find in the body of the table the mantissa for the first three digits and then, neglecting the decimal point temporarily, add the number in the proportional-parts table at the right which is on the same line as the mantissa already obtained and in the column corresponding to the fourth digit.

Table A.2.   *Table of Four-Place Logarithms*–Continued

N	0	1	2	3	4	5	6	7	8	9	1 2 3	4 5 6	7 8 9
5.5	.7404	.7412	.7419	.7427	.7435	.7443	.7451	.7459	.7466	.7474	1 2 2	3 4 5	5 6 7
5.6	.7482	.7490	.7497	.7505	.7513	.7520	.7528	.7536	.7543	.7551	1 2 2	3 4 5	5 6 7
5.7	.7559	.7566	.7574	.7582	.7589	.7597	.7604	.7612	.7619	.7627	1 2 2	3 4 5	5 6 7
5.8	.7634	.7642	.7649	.7657	.7664	.7672	.7679	.7686	.7694	.7701	1 1 2	3 4 4	5 6 7
5.9	.7709	.7716	.7723	.7731	.7738	.7745	.7752	.7760	.7767	.7774	1 1 2	3 4 4	5 6 7
6.0	.7782	.7789	.7796	.7803	.7810	.7818	.7825	.7832	.7839	.7846	1 1 2	3 4 4	5 6 6
6.1	.7853	.7860	.7868	.7875	.7882	.7889	.7896	.7903	.7910	.7917	1 1 2	3 4 4	5 6 6
6.2	.7924	.7931	.7938	.7945	.7952	.7959	.7966	.7973	.7980	.7987	1 1 2	3 3 4	5 6 6
6.3	.7993	.8000	.8007	.8014	.8021	.8028	.8035	.8041	.8048	.8055	1 1 2	3 3 4	5 5 6
6.4	.8062	.8069	.8075	.8082	.8089	.8096	.8102	.8109	.8116	.8122	1 1 2	3 3 4	5 5 6
6.5	.8129	.8136	.8142	.8149	.8156	.8162	.8169	.8176	.8182	.8189	1 1 2	3 3 4	5 5 6
6.6	.8195	.8202	.8209	.8215	.8222	.8228	.8235	.8241	.8248	.8254	1 1 2	3 3 4	5 5 6
6.7	.8261	.8267	.8274	.8280	.8287	.8293	.8299	.8306	.8312	.8319	1 1 2	3 3 4	5 5 6
6.8	.8325	.8331	.8338	.8344	.8351	.8357	.8363	.8370	.8376	.8382	1 1 2	3 3 4	4 5 6
6.9	.8388	.8395	.8401	.8407	.8414	.8420	.8426	.8432	.8439	.8445	1 1 2	2 3 4	4 5 6
7.0	.8451	.8457	.8463	.8470	.8476	.8482	.8488	.8494	.8500	.8506	1 1 2	2 3 4	4 5 6
7.1	.8513	.8519	.8525	.8531	.8537	.8543	.8549	.8555	.8561	.8567	1 1 2	2 3 4	4 5 5
7.2	.8573	.8579	.8585	.8591	.8597	.8603	.8609	.8615	.8621	.8627	1 1 2	2 3 4	4 5 5
7.3	.8633	.8639	.8645	.8651	.8657	.8663	.8669	.8675	.8681	.8686	1 1 2	2 3 4	4 5 5
7.4	.8692	.8698	.8704	.8710	.8716	.8722	.8727	.8733	.8739	.8745	1 1 2	2 3 4	4 5 5
7.5	.8751	.8756	.8762	.8768	.8774	.8779	.8785	.8791	.8797	.8802	1 1 2	2 3 3	4 5 5
7.6	.8808	.8814	.8820	.8825	.8831	.8837	.8842	.8848	.8854	.8859	1 1 2	2 3 3	4 5 5
7.7	.8865	.8871	.8876	.8882	.8887	.8893	.8899	.8904	.8910	.8915	1 1 2	2 3 3	4 4 5
7.8	.8921	.8927	.8932	.8938	.8943	.8949	.8954	.8960	.8965	.8971	1 1 2	2 3 3	4 4 5
7.9	.8976	.8982	.8987	.8993	.8998	.9004	.9009	.9015	.9020	.9025	1 1 2	2 3 3	4 4 5
8.0	.9031	.9036	.9042	.9047	.9053	.9058	.9063	.9069	.9074	.9079	1 1 2	2 3 3	4 4 5
8.1	.9085	.9090	.9096	.9101	.9106	.9112	.9117	.9122	.9128	.9133	1 1 2	2 3 3	4 4 5
8.2	.9138	.9143	.9149	.9154	.9159	.9165	.9170	.9175	.9180	.9186	1 1 2	2 3 3	4 4 5
8.3	.9191	.9196	.9201	.9206	.9212	.9217	.9222	.9227	.9232	.9238	1 1 2	2 3 3	4 4 5
8.4	.9243	.9248	.9253	.9258	.9263	.9269	.9274	.9279	.9284	.9289	1 1 2	2 3 3	4 4 5
8.5	.9294	.9299	.9304	.9309	.9315	.9320	.9325	.9330	.9335	.9340	1 1 2	2 3 3	4 4 5
8.6	.9345	.9350	.9355	.9360	.9365	.9370	.9375	.9380	.9385	.9390	1 1 2	2 3 3	4 4 5
8.7	.9395	.9400	.9405	.9410	.9415	.9420	.9425	.9430	.9435	.9440	0 1 1	2 2 3	3 4 4
8.8	.9445	.9450	.9455	.9460	.9465	.9469	.9474	.9479	.9484	.9489	0 1 1	2 2·3	3 4 4
8.9	.9494	.9499	.9504	.9509	.9513	.9518	.9523	.9528	.9533	.9538	0 1 1	2 2 3	3 4 4
9.0	.9542	.9547	.9552	.9557	.9562	.9566	.9571	.9576	.9581	.9586	0 1 1	2 2 3	3 4 4
9.1	.9590	.9595	.9600	.9605	.9609	.9614	.9619	.9624	.9628	.9633	0 1 1	2 2 3	3 4 4
9.2	.9638	.9643	.9647	.9652	.9657	.9661	.9666	.9671	.9675	.9680	0 1 1	2 2 3	3 4 4
9.3	.9685	.9689	.9694	.9699	.9703	.9708	.9713	.9717	.9722	.9727	0 1 1	2 2 3	3 4 4
9.4	.9731	.9736	.9741	.9745	.9750	.9754	.9759	.9763	.9768	.9773	0 1 1	2 2 3	3 4 4
9.5	.9777	.9782	.9786	.9791	.9795	.9800	.9805	.9809	.9814	.9818	0 1 1	2 2 3	3 4 4
9.6	.9823	.9827	.9832	.9836	.9841	.9845	.9850	.9854	.9859	.9863	0 1 1	2 2 3	3 4 4
9.7	.9868	.9872	.9877	.9881	.9886	.9890	.9894	.9899	.9903	.9908	0 1 1	2 2 3	3 4 4
9.8	.9912	.9917	.9921	.9926	.9930	.9934	.9939	.9943	.9948	.9952	0 1 1	2 2 3	3 4 4
9.9	.9956	.9961	.9965	.9969	.9974	.9978	.9983	.9987	.9991	.9996	0 1 1	2 2 3	3 3 4

Table B.1. *Table for Values of* $\log_2 N$ *and* $-p \log_2 P$

Values of $\log_2 n$ and $-p \log_2 p$. The entry is either n or p, depending on which column is read out.

n or p	$\log_2 n$	$-p \log_2 p$	n or p	$\log_2 n$	$-p \log_2 p$
1	0.000	.0664	51	5.672	.4954
2	1.000	.1129	52	5.700	.4906
3	1.585	.1518	53	5.728	.4854
4	2.000	.1858	54	5.755	.4800
5	2.322	.2161	55	5.781	.4744
6	2.585	.2435	56	5.807	.4684
7	2.807	.2686	57	5.833	.4623
8	3.000	.2915	58	5.858	.4558
9	3.170	.3127	59	5.883	.4491
10	3.322	.3322	60	5.907	.4422
11	3.459	.3503	61	5.931	.4350
12	3.585	.3671	62	5.954	.4276
13	3.700	.3826	63	5.977	.4199
14	3.807	.3971	64	6.000	.4121
15	3.907	.4105	65	6.022	.4040
16	4.000	.4230	66	6.044	.3957
17	4.087	.4346	67	6.066	.3871
18	4.170	.4453	68	6.087	.3784
19	4.248	.4552	69	6.109	.3694
20	4.322	.4644	70	6.129	.3602
21	4.392	.4728	71	6.150	.3508
22	4.459	.4806	72	6.170	.3412
23	4.524	.4877	73	6.190	.3314
24	4.585	.4941	74	6.209	.3215
25	4.644	.5000	75	6.229	.3113
26	4.700	.5053	76	6.248	.3009
27	4.755	.5100	77	6.267	.2903
28	4.807	.5142	78	6.285	.2796
29	4.858	.5179	79	6.304	.2687
30	4.907	.5211	80	6.322	.2575
31	4.954	.5238	81	6.340	.2462
32	5.000	.5260	82	6.358	.2348
33	5.044	.5278	83	6.375	.2231
34	5.087	.5292	84	6.392	.2113
35	5.129	.5301	85	6.409	.1993
36	5.170	.5306	86	6.426	.1871
37	5.209	.5307	87	6.443	.1748
38	5.248	.5304	88	6.459	.1623
39	5.285	.5298	89	6.476	.1496
40	5.322	.5288	90	6.492	.1368
41	5.358	.5274	91	6.508	.1238
42	5.392	.5256	92	6.524	.1107
43	5.426	.5236	93	6.539	.0974
44	5.459	.5211	94	6.555	.0839
45	5.492	.5184	95	6.570	.0703
46	5.524	.5153	96	6.585	.0565
47	5.555	.5120	97	6.600	.0426
48	5.585	.5083	98	6.615	.0286
49	5.615	.5043	99	6.629	.0140
50	5.644	.5000	100	6.644	.0000

These values were originally prepared at the Operational Applications Laboratory. Complete tables are available in Air Force Cambridge Research Center, Technical Report 54-50.

Table C.1.   *Areas and Ordinates of the Normal Curve in Terms of* x/σ

(1) z STANDARD SCORE $\left(\dfrac{x}{\sigma}\right)$	(2) A AREA FROM MEAN TO $\dfrac{x}{\sigma}$	(3) B AREA IN LARGER PORTION	(4) C AREA IN SMALLER PORTION	(5) y ORDINATE AT $\dfrac{x}{\sigma}$
0.00	.0000	.5000	.5000	.3989
0.01	.0040	.5040	.4960	.3989
0.02	.0080	.5080	.4920	.3989
0.03	.0120	.5120	.4880	.3988
0.04	.0160	.5160	.4840	.3986
0.05	.0199	.5199	.4801	.3984
0.06	.0239	.5239	.4761	.3982
0.07	.0279	.5279	.4721	.3980
0.08	.0319	.5319	.4681	.3977
0.09	.0359	.5359	.4641	.3973
0.10	.0398	.5398	.4602	.3970
0.11	.0438	.5438	.4562	.3965
0.12	.0478	.5478	.4522	.3961
0.13	.0517	.5517	.4483	.3956
0.14	.0557	.5557	.4443	.3951
0.15	.0596	.5596	.4404	.3945
0.16	.0636	.5636	.4364	.3939
0.17	.0675	.5675	.4325	.3932
0.18	.0714	.5714	.4286	.3925
0.19	.0753	.5753	.4247	.3918
0.20	.0793	.5793	.4207	.3910
0.21	.0832	.5832	.4168	.3902
0.22	.0871	.5871	.4129	.3894
0.23	.0910	.5910	.4090	.3885
0.24	.0948	.5948	.4052	.3876
0.25	.0987	.5987	.4013	.3867
0.26	.1026	.6026	.3974	.3857
0.27	.1064	.6064	.3936	.3847
0.28	.1103	.6103	.3897	.3836
0.29	.1141	.6141	.3859	.3825
0.30	.1179	.6179	.3821	.3814
0.31	.1217	.6217	.3783	.3802
0.32	.1255	.6255	.3745	.3790
0.33	.1293	.6293	.3707	.3778
0.34	.1331	.6331	.3669	.3765

Table C.2.   *Areas and Ordinates of the Normal Curve in Terms of x /σ*–Continued

(1) z STANDARD SCORE $\left(\dfrac{x}{\sigma}\right)$	(2) A AREA FROM MEAN TO $\dfrac{x}{\sigma}$	(3) B AREA IN LARGER PORTION	(4) C AREA IN SMALLER PORTION	(5) y ORDINATE AT $\dfrac{x}{\sigma}$
0.35	.1368	.6368	.3632	.3752
0.36	.1406	.6406	.3594	.3739
0.37	.1443	.6443	.3557	.3725
0.38	.1480	.6480	.3520	.3712
0.39	.1517	.6517	.3483	.3697
0.40	.1554	.6554	.3446	.3683
0.41	.1591	.6591	.3409	.3668
0.42	.1628	.6628	.3372	.3653
0.43	.1664	.6664	.3336	.3637
0.44	.1700	.6700	.3300	.3621
				.3605
0.45	.1736	.6736	.3264	
0.46	.1772	.6772	.3228	.3589
0.47	.1808	.6808	.3192	.3572
0.48	.1844	.6844	.3156	.3555
0.49	.1879	.6879	.3121	.3538
0.50	.1915	.6915	.3085	.3521
0.51	.1950	.6950	.3050	.3503
0.52	.1985	.6985	.3015	.3485
0.53	.2019	.7019	.2981	.3467
0.54	.2054	.7054	.2946	.3448
0.55	.2088	.7088	.2912	.3429
0.56	.2123	.7123	.2877	.3410
0.57	.2157	.7157	.2843	.3391
0.58	.2190	.7190	.2810	.3372
0.59	.2224	.7224	.2776	.3352
0.60	.2257	.7257	.2743	.3332
0.61	.2291	.7291	.2709	.3312
0.62	.2324	.7324	.2676	.3292
0.63	.2357	.7357	.2643	.3271
0.64	.2389	.7389	.2611	.3251
0.65	.2422	.7422	.2578	.3230
0.66	.2454	.7454	.2546	.3209
0.67	.2486	.7486	.2514	.3187
0.68	.2517	.7517	.2483	.3166
0.69	.2549	.7549	.2451	.3144

Table C.3.   *Areas and Ordinates of the Normal Curve in Terms of* x/σ–Continued

(1) z STANDARD SCORE $\left(\frac{x}{\sigma}\right)$	(2) A AREA FROM MEAN TO $\frac{x}{\sigma}$	(3) B AREA IN LARGER PORTION	(4) C AREA IN SMALLER PORTION	(5) y ORDINATE AT $\frac{x}{\sigma}$
0.70	.2580	.7580	.2420	.3123
0.71	.2611	.7611	.2389	.3101
0.72	.2642	.7642	.2358	.3079
0.73	.2673	.7673	.2327	.3056
0.74	.2704	.7704	.2296	.3034
0.75	.2734	.7734	.2266	.3011
0.76	.2764	.7764	.2236	.2989
0.77	.2794	.7794	.2206	.2966
0.78	.2823	.7823	.2177	.2943
0.79	.2852	.7852	.2148	.2920
0.80	.2881	.7881	.2119	.2897
0.81	.2910	.7910	.2090	.2874
0.82	.2939	.7939	.2061	.2850
0.83	.2967	.7967	.2033	.2827
0.84	.2995	.7995	.2005	.2803
0.85	.3023	.8023	.1977	.2780
0.86	.3051	.8051	.1949	.2756
0.87	.3078	.8078	.1922	.2732
0.88	.3106	.8106	.1894	.2709
0.89	.3133	.8133	.1867	.2685
0.90	.3159	.8159	.1841	.2661
0.91	.3186	.8186	.1814	.2637
0.92	.3212	.8212	.1788	.2613
0.93	.3238	.8238	.1762	.2589
0.94	.3264	.8264	.1736	.2565
0.95	.3289	.8289	.1711	.2541
0.96	.3315	.8315	.1685	.2516
0.97	.3340	.8340	.1660	.2492
0.98	.3365	.8365	.1635	.2468
0.99	.3389	.8389	.1611	.2444
1.00	.3413	.8413	.1587	.2420
1.01	.3438	.8438	.1562	.2396
1.02	.3461	.8461	.1539	.2371
1.03	.3485	.8485	.1515	.2347
1.04	.3508	.8508	.1492	.2323

Table C.4.   *Areas and Ordinates of the Normal Curve in Terms of* x/σ–Continued

(1) z STANDARD SCORE $\left(\frac{x}{\sigma}\right)$	(2) A AREA FROM MEAN TO $\frac{x}{\sigma}$	(3) B AREA IN LARGER PORTION	(4) C AREA IN SMALLER PORTION	(5) y ORDINATE AT $\frac{x}{\sigma}$
1.05	.3531	.8531	.1469	.2299
1.06	.3554	.8554	.1446	.2275
1.07	.3577	.8577	.1423	.2251
1.08	.3599	.8599	.1401	.2227
1.09	.3621	.8621	.1379	.2203
1.10	.3643	.8643	.1357	.2179
1.11	.3665	.8665	.1335	.2155
1.12	.3686	.8686	.1314	.2131
1.13	.3708	.8708	.1292	.2107
1.14	.3729	.8729	.1271	.2083
1.15	.3749	.8749	.1251	.2059
1.16	.3770	.8770	.1230	.2036
1.17	.3790	.8790	.1210	.2012
1.18	.3810	.8810	.1190	.1989
1.19	.3830	.8830	.1170	.1965
1.20	.3849	.8849	.1151	.1942
1.21	.3869	.8869	.1131	.1919
1.22	.3888	.8888	.1112	.1895
1.23	.3907	.8907	.1093	.1872
1.24	.3925	.8925	.1075	.1849
1.25	.3944	.8944	.1056	.1826
1.26	.3962	.8962	.1038	.1804
1.27	.3980	.8980	.1020	.1781
1.28	.3997	.8997	.1003	.1758
1.29	.4015	.9015	.0985	.1736
1.30	.4032	.9032	.0968	.1714
1.31	.4049	.9049	.0951	.1691
1.32	.4066	.9066	.0934	.1669
1.33	.4082	.9082	.0918	.1647
1.34	.4099	.9099	.0901	.1626
1.35	.4115	.9115	.0885	.1604
1.36	.4131	.9131	.0869	.1582
1.37	.4147	.9147	.0853	.1561
1.38	.4162	.9162	.0838	.1539
1.39	.4177	.9177	.0823	.1518

Table C.5.   *Areas and Ordinates of the Normal Curve in Terms of x/σ*–Continued

(1) z STANDARD SCORE $\left(\frac{x}{\sigma}\right)$	(2) A AREA FROM MEAN TO $\frac{x}{\sigma}$	(3) B AREA IN LARGER PORTION	(4) C AREA IN SMALLER PORTION	(5) y ORDINATE AT $\frac{x}{\sigma}$
1.40	.4192	.9192	.0808	.1497
1.41	.4207	.9207	.0793	.1476
1.42	.4222	.9222	.0778	.1456
1.43	.4236	.9236	.0764	.1435
1.44	.4251	.9251	.0749	.1415
1.45	.4265	.9265	.0735	.1394
1.46	.4279	.9279	.0721	.1374
1.47	.4292	.9292	.0708	.1354
1.48	.4306	.9306	.0694	.1334
1.49	.4319	.9319	.0681	.1315
1.50	.4332	.9332	.0668	.1295
1.51	.4345	.9345	.0655	.1276
1.52	.4357	.9357	.0643	.1257
1.53	.4370	.9370	.0630	.1238
1.54	.4382	.9382	.0618	.1219
1.55	.4394	.9394	.0606	.1200
1.56	.4406	.9406	.0594	.1182
1.57	.4418	.9418	.0582	.1163
1.58	.4429	.9429	.0571	.1145
1.59	.4441	.9441	.0559	.1127
1.60	.4452	.9452	.0548	.1109
1.61	.4463	.9463	.0537	.1092
1.62	.4474	.9474	.0526	.1074
1.63	.4484	.9484	.0516	.1057
1.64	.4495	.9495	.0505	.1040
1.65	.4505	.9505	.0495	.1023
1.66	.4515	.9515	.0485	.1006
1.67	.4525	.9525	.0475	.0989
1.68	.4535	.9535	.0465	.0973
1.69	.4545	.9545	.0455	.0957
1.70	.4554	.9554	.0446	.0940
1.71	.4564	.9564	.0436	.0925
1.72	.4573	.9573	.0427	.0909
1.73	.4582	.9582	.0418	.0893
1.74	.4591	.9591	.0409	.0878

Table C.6.   *Areas and Ordinates of the Normal Curve in Terms of* x/σ–Continued

(1) z STANDARD SCORE $\left(\dfrac{x}{\sigma}\right)$	(2) A AREA FROM MEAN TO $\dfrac{x}{\sigma}$	(3) B AREA IN LARGER PORTION	(4) C AREA IN SMALLER PORTION	(5) y ORDINATE AT $\dfrac{x}{\sigma}$
1.75	.4599	.9599	.0401	.0863
1.76	.4608	.9608	.0392	.0848
1.77	.4616	.9616	.0384	.0833
1.78	.4625	.9625	.0375	.0818
1.79	.4633	.9633	.0367	.0804
1.80	.4641	.9641	.0359	.0790
1.81	.4649	.9649	.0351	.0775
1.82	.4656	.9656	.0344	.0761
1.83	.4664	.9664	.0336	.0748
1.84	.4671	.9671	.0329	.0734
1.85	.4678	.9678	.0322	.0721
1.86	.4686	.9686	.0314	.0707
1.87	.4693	.9693	.0307	.0694
1.88	.4699	.9699	.0301	.0681
1.89	.4706	.9706	.0294	.0669
1.90	.4713	.9713	.0287	.0656
1.91	.4719	.9719	.0281	.0644
1.92	.4726	.9726	.0274	.0632
1.93	.4732	.9732	.0268	.0620
1.94	.4738	.9738	.0262	.0608
1.95	.4744	.9744	.0256	.0596
1.96	.4750	.9750	.0250	.0584
1.97	.4756	.9756	.0244	.0573
1.98	.4761	.9761	.0239	.0562
1.99	.4767	.9767	.0233	.0551
2.00	.4772	.9772	.0228	.0540
2.01	.4778	.9778	.0222	.0529
2.02	.4783	.9783	.0217	.0519
2.03	.4788	.9788	.0212	.0508
2.04	.4793	.9793	.0207	.0498
2.05	.4798	.9798	.0202	.0488
2.06	.4803	.9803	.0197	.0478
2.07	.4808	.9808	.0192	.0468
2.08	.4812	.9812	.0188	.0459
2.09	.4817	.9817	.0183	.0449

Table C.7.   *Areas and Ordinates of the Normal Curve in Terms of x/σ*–Continued

(1) z STANDARD SCORE $\left(\dfrac{x}{\sigma}\right)$	(2) A AREA FROM MEAN TO $\dfrac{x}{\sigma}$	(3) B AREA IN LARGER PORTION	(4) C AREA IN SMALLER PORTION	(5) y ORDINATE AT $\dfrac{x}{\sigma}$
2.10	.4821	.9821	.0179	.0440
2.11	.4826	.9826	.0174	.0431
2.12	.4830	.9830	.0170	.0422
2.13	.4834	.9834	.0166	.0413
2.14	.4838	.9838	.0162	.0404
2.15	.4842	.9842	.0158	.0396
2.16	.4846	.9846	.0154	.0387
2.17	.4850	.9850	.0150	.0379
2.18	.4854	.9854	.0146	.0371
2.19	.4857	.9857	.0143	.0363
2.20	.4861	.9861	.0139	.0355
2.21	.4864	.9864	.0136	.0347
2.22	.4868	.9868	.0132	.0339
2.23	.4871	.9871	.0129	.0332
2.24	.4875	.9875	.0125	.0325
2.25	.4878	.9878	.0122	.0317
2.26	.4881	.9881	.0119	.0310
2.27	.4884	.9884	.0116	.0303
2.28	.4887	.9887	.0113	.0297
2.29	.4890	.9890	.0110	.0290
2.30	.4893	.9893	.0107	.0283
2.31	.4896	.9896	.0104	.0277
2.32	.4898	.9898	.0102	.0270
2.33	.4901	.9901	.0099	.0264
2.34	.4904	.9904	.0096	.0258
2.35	.4906	.9906	.0094	.0252
2.36	.4909	.9909	.0091	.0246
2.37	.4911	.9911	.0089	.0241
2.38	.4913	.9913	.0087	.0235
2.39	.4916	.9916	.0084	.0229
2.40	.4918	.9918	.0082	.0224
2.41	.4920	.9920	.0080	.0219
2.42	.4922	.9922	.0078	.0213
2.43	.4925	.9925	.0075	.0208
2.44	.4927	.9927	.0073	.0203

Table C.8.   *Areas and Ordinates of the Normal Curve in Terms of x/σ*–Continued

(1) z STANDARD SCORE $\left(\frac{x}{\sigma}\right)$	(2) A AREA FROM MEAN TO $\frac{x}{\sigma}$	(3) B AREA IN LARGER PORTION	(4) C AREA IN SMALLER PORTION	(5) y ORDINATE AT $\frac{x}{\sigma}$
2.45	.4929	.9929	.0071	.0198
2.46	.4931	.9931	.0069	.0194
2.47	.4932	.9932	.0068	.0189
2.48	.4934	.9934	.0066	.0184
2.49	.4936	.9936	.0064	.0180
2.50	.4938	.9938	.0062	.0175
2.51	.4940	.9940	.0060	.0171
2.52	.4941	.9941	.0059	.0167
2.53	.4943	.9943	.0057	.0163
2.54	.4945	.9945	.0055	.0158
2.55	.4946	.9946	.0054	.0154
2.56	.4948	.9948	.0052	.0151
2.57	.4949	.9949	.0051	.0147
2.58	.4951	.9951	.0049	.0143
2.59	.4952	.9952	.0048	.0139
2.60	.4953	.9953	.0047	.0136
2.61	.4955	.9955	.0045	.0132
2.62	.4956	.9956	.0044	.0129
2.63	.4957	.9957	.0043	.0126
2.64	.4959	.9959	.0041	.0122
2.65	.4960	.9960	.0040	.0119
2.66	.4961	.9961	.0039	.0116
2.67	.4962	.9962	.0038	.0113
2.68	.4963	.9963	.0037	.0110
2.69	.4964	.9964	.0036	.0107
2.70	.4965	.9965	.0035	.0104
2.71	.4966	.9966	.0034	.0101
2.72	.4967	.9967	.0033	.0099
2.73	.4968	.9968	.0032	.0096
2.74	.4969	.9969	.0031	.0093
2.75	.4970	.9970	.0030	.0091
2.76	.4971	.9971	.0029	.0088
2.77	.4972	.9972	.0028	.0086
2.78	.4973	.9973	.0027	.0084
2.79	.4974	.9974	.0026	.0081

Table C.9. *Areas and Ordinates of the Normal Curve in Terms of x/σ*–Continued

(1) *z* STANDARD SCORE $\left(\dfrac{x}{\sigma}\right)$	(2) *A* AREA FROM MEAN TO $\dfrac{x}{\sigma}$	(3) *B* AREA IN LARGER PORTION	(4) *C* AREA IN SMALLER PORTION	(5) *y* ORDINATE AT $\dfrac{x}{\sigma}$
2.80	.4974	.9974	.0026	.0079
2.81	.4975	.9975	.0025	.0077
2.82	.4976	.9976	.0024	.0075
2.83	.4977	.9977	.0023	.0073
2.84	.4977	.9977	.0023	.0071
2.85	.4978	.9978	.0022	.0069
2.86	.4979	.9979	.0021	.0067
2.87	.4979	.9979	.0021	.0065
2.88	.4980	.9980	.0020	.0063
2.89	.4981	.9981	.0019	.0061
2.90	.4981	.9981	.0019	.0060
2.91	.4982	.9982	.0018	.0058
2.92	.4982	.9982	.0018	.0056
2.93	.4983	.9983	.0017	.0055
2.94	.4984	.9984	.0016	.0053
2.95	.4984	.9984	.0016	.0051
2.96	.4985	.9985	.0015	.0050
2.97	.4985	.9985	.0015	.0048
2.98	.4986	.9986	.0014	.0047
2.99	.4986	.9986	.0014	.0046
3.00	.4987	.9987	.0013	.0044
3.01	.4987	.9987	.0013	.0043
3.02	.4987	.9987	.0013	.0042
3.03	.4988	.9988	.0012	.0040
3.04	.4988	.9988	.0012	.0039
3.05	.4989	.9989	.0011	.0038
3.06	.4989	.9989	.0011	.0037
3.07	.4989	.9989	.0011	.0036
3.08	.4990	.9990	.0010	.0035
3.09	.4990	.9990	.0010	.0034
3.10	.4990	.9990	.0010	.0033
3.11	.4991	.9991	.0009	.0032
3.12	.4991	.9991	.0009	.0031
3.13	.4991	.9991	.0009	.0030
3.14	.4992	.9992	.0008	.0029

Table C.10. *Areas and Ordinates of the Normal Curve in Terms of x/σ*–Continued

(1) z STANDARD SCORE $\left(\frac{x}{\sigma}\right)$	(2) A AREA FROM MEAN TO $\frac{x}{\sigma}$	(3) B AREA IN LARGER PORTION	(4) C AREA IN SMALLER PORTION	(5) y ORDINATE AT $\frac{x}{\sigma}$
3.15	.4992	.9992	.0008	.0028
3.16	.4992	.9992	.0008	.0027
3.17	.4992	.9992	.0008	.0026
3.18	.4993	.9993	.0007	.0025
3.19	.4993	.9993	.0007	.0025
3.20	.4993	.9993	.0007	.0024
3.21	.4993	.9993	.0007	.0023
3.22	.4994	.9994	.0006	.0022
3.23	.4994	.9994	.0006	.0022
3.24	.4994	.9994	.0006	.0021
3.30	.4995	.9995	.0005	.0017
3.40	.4997	.9997	.0003	.0012
3.50	.4998	.9998	.0002	.0009
3.60	.4998	.9998	.0002	.0006
3.70	.4999	.9999	.0001	.0004

Table D. T *Scores Corresponding to Ranks* *

NUMBER OF PERSONS OR OBJECTS RANKED

Rank	5	6	7	8	9	10	11	12	13	14	15	16	17	18	19	20	21	22	23	24	25	26	27	28	29	30	31	32	33	34	35	36	37	38	39	40	41	42	43	44	45	Rank
1	63	64	65	65	66	66	67	67	68	68	68	69	69	69	69	70	70	70	70	70	71	71	71	71	71	71	71	72	72	72	72	72	72	72	72	72	72	73	73	73	73	1
2	55	57	58	59	60	60	61	62	62	62	63	63	64	64	64	64	65	65	65	65	66	66	66	66	66	66	67	67	67	67	67	67	67	68	68	68	68	68	68	68	68	2
3	50	52	54	55	56	57	57	58	59	59	60	60	60	61	61	62	62	62	62	63	63	63	63	63	64	64	64	64	64	65	65	65	65	65	65	65	65	66	66	66	66	3
4	45	48	50	52	53	54	55	55	56	57	57	58	58	59	59	59	60	60	60	61	61	61	61	62	62	62	62	62	62	63	63	63	63	63	63	64	64	64	64	64	64	4
5	37	43	46	48	50	51	52	53	54	55	55	56	56	57	57	58	58	58	59	59	59	59	60	60	60	60	61	61	61	61	61	62	62	62	62	62	62	62	63	63	63	5
6		36	42	45	47	49	50	51	52	53	53	54	55	55	56	56	56	57	57	57	58	58	58	59	59	59	59	59	60	60	60	60	60	61	61	61	61	61	61	62	62	6
7			35	41	44	46	48	49	50	51	52	52	53	54	54	55	55	55	56	56	56	57	57	57	58	58	58	58	59	59	59	59	59	59	60	60	60	60	60	60	61	7
8				35	40	43	45	47	48	49	50	51	51	52	53	53	54	54	55	55	55	56	56	56	56	57	57	57	57	58	58	58	58	59	59	59	59	59	59	60	60	8
9					34	40	43	45	46	47	48	49	50	51	51	52	52	53	53	54	54	54	55	55	55	56	56	56	57	57	57	57	57	58	58	58	58	58	58	59	59	9
10						34	39	42	44	45	47	48	49	49	50	51	51	52	52	53	53	53	54	54	54	55	55	55	56	56	56	56	57	57	57	57	57	58	58	58	58	10
11							33	38	41	43	45	46	47	48	49	49	50	51	51	52	52	52	53	53	54	54	54	54	55	55	55	55	56	56	56	56	57	57	57	57	57	11
12								33	38	41	43	44	45	46	47	48	49	49	50	51	51	51	52	52	53	53	53	54	54	54	54	55	55	55	55	56	56	56	56	56	57	12
13									32	38	40	42	44	45	46	47	48	48	49	49	50	50	51	51	52	52	52	53	53	53	54	54	54	54	55	55	55	55	56	56	56	13
14										32	37	40	42	43	44	45	46	47	48	48	49	50	50	50	51	51	52	52	52	53	53	53	53	54	54	54	54	55	55	55	55	14
15											32	37	40	41	43	44	45	46	47	47	48	49	49	50	50	50	51	51	52	52	52	52	53	53	53	54	54	54	54	54	55	15
16												31	36	39	41	42	44	45	45	46	47	48	48	49	49	50	50	50	51	51	51	52	52	52	53	53	53	53	54	54	54	16
17													31	36	39	41	42	43	44	45	46	47	47	48	48	49	49	50	50	50	51	51	51	52	52	52	52	53	53	53	53	17
18														31	36	38	40	42	43	44	45	46	46	47	47	48	48	49	49	50	50	50	51	51	51	52	52	52	52	53	53	18
19															31	36	38	40	41	43	44	44	45	46	46	47	48	48	48	49	49	49	49	50	51	51	51	51	52	52	52	19
20																30	35	38	40	41	42	43	44	45	46	46	47	47	48	48	49	49	49	50	50	50	51	51	51	51	52	20
21																	30	35	38	39	41	42	43	44	45	45	46	46	47	47	48	48	49	49	49	50	50	50	51	51	51	21
22																		30	35	37	39	41	42	43	44	44	45	46	46	47	47	48	48	48	49	49	49	50	50	50	51	22
23																			30	35	37	39	40	41	42	43	44	45	45	46	46	47	47	48	48	48	49	49	49	50	50	23
24																				30	34	37	39	40	41	42	43	44	44	45	46	46	47	47	47	48	48	48	49	49	49	24
25																					29	34	37	38	40	41	42	43	43	44	45	45	46	46	47	47	48	48	48	49	49	25
26																						29	34	37	38	40	41	42	42	43	44	45	45	46	46	46	47	47	48	48	48	26
27																							29	34	36	38	39	41	41	42	43	44	44	45	45	46	46	47	47	47	48	27
28																								29	34	36	38	39	40	41	42	43	43	44	45	45	46	46	46	47	47	28
29																									29	34	36	38	39	40	41	42	43	43	44	44	45	45	46	46	47	29
30																										29	33	36	38	39	40	41	42	42	43	44	44	45	45	46	46	30
31																											29	33	36	37	39	40	41	41	42	43	43	44	44	45	45	31
32																												28	33	35	37	38	40	41	41	42	43	43	44	44	45	32
33																													28	33	35	37	38	39	40	41	42	42	43	44	44	33
34																														28	33	35	37	38	39	40	41	42	42	43	43	34
35																															28	33	35	37	38	39	40	41	42	42	43	35
36																																28	33	35	37	38	39	40	41	41	42	36
37																																	28	32	35	36	38	39	40	40	41	37
38																																		28	32	35	36	38	39	40	40	38
39																																			28	32	35	36	37	38	39	39
40																																				28	32	34	36	37	38	40
41																																					28	32	34	36	37	41
42																																						27	32	34	36	42
43																																							27	32	34	43
44																																								27	32	44
45																																									27	45

This table converts rankings to a normalized standard score scale with a mean of 50 and a standard deviation of 10. To use the table, first determine the number of persons or objects ranked. Then, enter the table with the rank of the individual or object. (A rank of 3 indicates a person who is third from the top.) At the intersection of the row indicating rank, and the column indicating number of persons or objects ranked will be found the standard score. For example, the 4th person in a group of 22 would have a score of 60. While the 17th person in a group of 30 would have a score of 49.

Reprinted from a table published by the Air Training Command in ATRC Manual 50-900-9 and prepared under the direction of J. R. Berkshire.

Table E.1. *Table of T Scores*

PROPORTION	T SCORE	PROPORTION	T SCORE
.001	20	.540	51
.002	21	.579	52
.003	22	.618	53
.004	23	.655	54
.005	24	.692	55
.006	25	.726	56
.008	26	.758	57
.011	27	.788	58
.014	28	.816	59
.018	29	.841	60
.023	30	.864	61
.029	31	.885	62
.036	32	.903	63
.045	33	.919	64
.055	34	.933	65
.067	35	.945	66
.081	36	.955	67
.097	37	.964	68
.115	38	.971	69
.136	39	.977	70
.159	40	.982	71
.184	41	.986	72
.212	42	.989	73
.242	43	.992	74
.274	44	.994	75
.308	45	.995	76
.345	46	.996	77
.382	47	.997	78
.421	48	.998	79
.460	49	.999	80
.500	50		

Modified from a table published by the Air Training Command in ATRC Manual 50-900-9 prepared under the direction of J. R. Berkshire.

The proportions refer to the proportion of the total frequency below a given score plus ½ the frequency of that score. *T* scores are read directly from the given proportions.

Table F.1. *Table of Random Numbers*

	1	2	3	4	5	6	7	8	9	10	11	12	13	14	15	16	17	18	19	20	21	22	23	24	25
1	10	27	53	96	23	71	50	54	36	23	54	31	04	82	98	04	14	12	15	09	26	78	25	47	47
2	28	41	50	61	88	64	85	27	20	18	83	36	36	05	56	39	71	65	09	62	94	76	62	11	89
3	34	21	42	57	02	59	19	18	97	48	80	30	03	30	98	05	24	67	70	07	84	97	50	87	46
4	61	81	77	23	23	82	82	11	54	08	53	28	70	58	96	44	07	39	55	43	42	34	43	39	28
5	61	15	18	13	54	16	86	20	26	88	90	74	80	55	09	14	53	90	51	17	52	01	63	01	59
6	91	76	21	64	64	44	91	13	32	97	75	31	62	66	54	84	80	32	75	77	56	08	25	70	29
7	00	97	79	08	06	37	30	28	59	85	53	56	68	53	40	01	74	39	59	73	30	19	99	85	48
8	36	46	18	34	94	75	20	80	27	77	78	91	69	16	00	08	43	18	73	68	67	69	61	34	25
9	88	98	99	60	50	65	95	79	42	94	93	62	40	89	96	43	56	47	71	66	46	76	29	67	02
10	04	37	59	87	21	05	02	03	24	17	47	97	81	56	51	92	34	86	01	82	55	51	33	12	91
11	63	62	06	34	41	94	21	78	55	09	72	76	45	16	94	29	95	81	83	83	79	88	01	97	30
12	78	47	23	53	90	34	41	92	45	71	09	23	70	70	07	12	38	92	79	43	14	85	11	47	23
13	87	68	62	15	43	53	14	36	59	25	54	47	33	70	15	59	24	48	40	35	50	03	42	99	36
14	47	60	92	10	77	88	59	53	11	52	66	25	69	07	04	48	68	64	71	06	61	65	70	22	12
15	56	88	87	59	41	65	28	04	67	53	95	79	88	37	31	50	41	06	94	76	81	83	17	16	33
16	02	57	45	86	67	73	43	07	34	48	44	26	87	93	29	77	09	61	67	84	06	69	44	77	75
17	31	54	14	13	17	48	62	11	90	60	68	12	93	64	28	46	24	79	16	76	14	60	25	51	01
18	28	50	16	43	36	28	97	85	58	99	67	22	52	76	23	24	70	36	54	54	59	28	61	71	96
19	63	29	62	66	50	02	63	45	52	38	67	63	47	54	75	83	24	78	43	20	92	63	13	47	48
20	45	65	58	26	51	76	96	59	38	72	86	57	45	71	46	44	67	76	14	55	44	88	01	62	12
21	39	65	36	63	70	77	45	85	50	51	74	13	39	35	22	30	53	36	02	95	49	34	88	73	61
22	73	71	98	16	04	29	18	94	51	23	76	51	94	84	86	79	93	96	38	63	08	58	25	58	94
23	72	20	56	20	11	72	65	71	08	86	79	57	95	13	91	97	48	72	66	48	09	71	17	24	89
24	75	17	26	99	76	89	37	20	70	01	77	31	61	95	46	26	97	05	73	51	53	33	18	72	87
25	37	48	60	82	29	81	30	15	39	14	48	38	75	93	29	06	87	37	78	48	45	56	00	84	47
26	68	08	02	80	72	83	71	46	30	49	89	17	95	88	29	02	39	56	03	46	97	74	06	56	17
27	14	23	98	61	67	70	52	85	01	50	01	84	02	78	43	10	62	98	19	41	18	83	99	47	99
28	49	08	96	21	44	25	27	99	41	28	07	41	08	34	66	19	42	74	39	91	41	96	53	78	72
29	78	37	06	08	43	63	61	62	42	29	39	68	95	10	96	09	24	23	00	62	56	12	80	73	16
30	37	21	34	17	68	68	96	83	23	56	32	84	60	15	31	44	73	67	34	77	91	15	79	74	58
31	14	29	09	34	04	87	83	07	55	07	76	58	30	83	64	87	29	25	58	84	86	50	60	00	25
32	58	43	28	06	36	49	52	83	51	14	47	56	91	29	34	05	87	31	06	95	12	45	57	09	09
33	10	43	67	29	70	80	62	80	03	42	10	80	21	38	84	90	56	35	03	09	43	12	74	49	14
34	44	38	88	39	54	86	97	37	44	22	00	95	01	31	76	17	16	29	56	63	38	78	94	49	81
35	90	69	59	19	51	85	39	52	85	13	07	28	37	07	61	11	16	36	27	03	78	86	72	04	95
36	41	47	10	25	62	97	05	31	03	61	20	26	36	31	62	68	69	86	95	44	84	95	48	46	45
37	91	94	14	63	19	75	89	11	47	11	31	56	34	19	09	79	57	92	36	59	14	93	87	81	40
38	80	06	54	18	66	09	18	94	06	19	98	40	07	17	81	22	45	44	84	11	24	62	20	42	31
39	67	72	77	63	48	84	08	31	55	58	24	33	45	77	58	80	45	67	93	82	75	70	16	08	24
40	59	40	24	13	27	79	26	88	86	30	01	31	60	10	39	53	58	47	70	93	85	81	56	39	38
41	05	90	35	89	95	01	61	16	96	94	50	78	13	69	36	37	68	53	37	31	71	26	35	03	71
42	44	43	80	69	98	46	68	05	14	82	90	78	50	05	62	77	79	13	57	44	59	60	10	39	66
43	61	81	31	96	82	00	57	25	60	59	46	72	60	18	77	55	66	12	62	11	08	99	55	64	57
44	42	88	07	10	05	24	98	65	63	21	47	21	61	88	32	27	80	30	21	60	10	92	35	36	12
45	77	94	30	05	39	28	10	99	00	27	12	73	73	99	12	49	99	57	94	82	96	88	57	17	91
46	78	83	19	76	16	94	11	68	84	26	23	54	20	86	85	23	86	66	99	07	36	37	34	92	09
47	87	76	59	61	81	43	63	64	61	61	65	76	36	95	90	18	48	27	45	68	27	23	65	30	72
48	91	43	05	96	47	55	78	99	95	24	37	55	85	78	78	01	48	41	19	10	35	19	54	07	73
49	84	97	77	72	73	09	62	06	65	7.	87	12	49	03	60	41	15	20	76	27	50	47	02	29	16
50	87	41	60	76	83	44	88	96	07	80	83	05	83	38	96	73	70	66	81	90	30	56	10	48	59

Table F. is taken from Table 33 of Fisher and Yates, *Statistical Tables for Biological, Agricultural and Medical Research,* published by Oliver and Boyd Ltd., Edinburgh, by permission of the authors and publishers.

Table F.2.   *Table of Random Numbers*—Continued

	1 2 3 4 5	6 7 8 9 10	11 12 13 14 15	16 17 18 19 20	21 22 23 24 25
1	22 17 68 65 84	68 95 23 92 35	87 02 22 57 51	61 09 43 95 06	58 24 82 03 47
2	19 36 27 59 46	13 79 93 37 55	39 77 32 77 09	85 52 05 30 62	47 83 51 62 74
3	16 77 23 02 77	09 61 87 25 21	28 06 24 25 93	16 71 13 59 78	23 05 47 47 25
4	78 43 76 71 61	20 44 90 32 64	97 67 63 99 61	46 38 03 93 22	69 81 21 99 21
5	03 28 28 26 08	73 37 32 04 05	69 30 16 09 05	88 69 58 28 99	35 07 44 75 47
6	93 22 53 64 39	07 10 63 76 35	87 03 04 79 88	08 13 13 85 51	55 34 57 72 69
7	78 76 58 54 74	92 38 70 96 92	52 06 79 79 45	82 63 18 27 44	69 66 92 19 09
8	23 68 35 26 00	99 53 93 61 28	52 70 05 48 34	56 65 05 61 86	90 92 10 70 80
9	15 39 25 70 99	93 86 52 77 65	15 33 59 05 28	22 87 26 07 47	86 96 98 29 06
10	58 71 96 30 24	18 46 23 34 27	85 13 99 24 44	49 18 09 79 49	74 16 32 23 02
11	57 35 27 33 72	24 53 63 94 09	41 10 76 47 91	44 04 95 49 66	39 60 04 59 81
12	48 50 86 54 48	22 06 34 72 52	82 21 15 65 20	33 29 94 71 11	15 91 29 12 03
13	61 96 48 95 03	07 16 39 33 66	98 56 10 56 79	77 21 30 27 12	90 49 22 23 62
14	36 93 89 41 26	29 70 83 63 51	99 74 20 52 36	87 09 41 15 09	98 60 16 03 03
15	18 87 00 42 31	57 90 12 02 07	23 47 37 17 31	54 08 01 88 63	39 41 88 92 10
16	88 56 53 27 59	33 35 72 67 47	77 34 55 45 70	08 18 27 38 90	16 95 86 70 75
17	09 72 95 84 29	49 41 31 06 70	42 38 06 45 18	64 84 73 31 65	52 53 37 97 15
18	12 96 88 17 31	65 19 69 02 83	60 75 86 90 68	24 64 19 35 51	56 61 87 39 12
19	85 94 57 24 16	92 09 84 38 76	22 00 27 69 85	29 81 94 78 70	21 94 47 90 12
20	38 64 43 59 98	98 77 87 68 07	91 51 67 62 44	40 98 05 93 78	23 32 65 41 18
21	53 44 09 42 72	00 41 86 79 79	68 47 22 00 20	35 55 31 51 51	00 83 63 22 55
22	40 76 66 26 84	57 99 99 90 37	36 63 32 08 58	37 40 13 68 97	87 64 81 07 83
23	02 17 79 18 05	12 59 52 57 02	22 07 90 47 03	28 14 11 30 79	20 69 22 40 98
24	95 17 82 06 53	31 51 10 96 46	92 06 88 07 77	56 11 50 81 69	40 23 72 51 39
25	35 76 22 42 92	96 11 83 44 80	34 68 35 48 77	33 42 40 90 60	73 96 53 97 86
26	26 29 13 56 41	85 47 04 66 08	34 72 57 59 13	82 43 80 46 15	38 26 61 70 04
27	77 80 20 75 82	72 82 32 99 90	63 95 73 76 63	89 73 44 99 05	48 67 26 43 18
28	46 40 66 44 52	91 36 74 43 53	30 82 13 54 00	78 45 63 98 35	55 03 36 67 68
29	37 56 08 18 09	77 53 84 46 47	31 91 18 95 58	24 16 74 11 53	44 10 13 85 57
30	61 65 61 68 66	37 27 47 39 19	84 83 70 07 48	53 21 40 06 71	95 06 79 88 54
31	93 43 69 64 07	34 18 04 52 35	56 27 09 24 86	61 85 53 83 45	19 90 70 99 00
32	21 96 60 12 99	11 20 99 45 18	48 13 93 55 34	18 37 79 49 90	65 97 38 20 46
33	95 20 47 97 97	27 37 83 28 71	00 06 41 41 74	45 89 09 39 84	51 67 11 52 49
34	97 86 21 78 73	10 65 81 92 59	58 76 17 14 97	04 76 62 16 17	17 95 70 45 80
35	69 92 06 34 13	59 71 74 17 32	27 55 10 24 19	23 71 82 13 74	63 52 52 01 41
36	04 31 17 21 56	33 73 99 19 87	26 72 39 27 67	53 77 57 68 93	60 61 97 22 61
37	61 06 98 03 91	87 14 77 43 96	43 00 65 98 50	45 60 33 01 07	98 99 46 50 47
38	85 93 85 86 88	72 87 08 62 40	16 06 10 89 20	23 21 34 74 97	76 38 03 29 63
39	21 74 32 47 45	73 96 07 94 52	09 65 90 77 47	25 76 16 19 33	53 05 70 53 30
40	15 69 53 82 80	79 96 23 53 10	65 39 07 16 29	45 33 02 43 70	02 87 40 41 45
41	02 89 08 04 49	20 21 14 68 86	87 63 93 95 17	11 29 01 95 80	35 14 97 35 33
42	87 18 15 89 79	85 43 01 72 73	08 61 74 51 69	89 74 39 82 15	94 51 33 41 67
43	98 83 71 94 22	59 97 50 99 52	08 52 85 08 40	87 80 61 65 31	91 51 80 32 44
44	10 08 58 21 66	72 68 49 29 31	89 85 84 46 06	59 73 19 85 23	65 09 29 75 63
45	47 90 56 10 08	88 02 84 27 83	42 29 72 23 19	66 56 45 65 79	20 71 53 20 25
46	22 85 61 68 90	49 64 92 85 44	16 40 12 89 88	50 14 49 81 06	01 82 77 45 12
47	67 80 43 79 33	12 83 11 41 16	25 58 19 68 70	77 02 54 00 52	53 43 37 15 26
48	27 62 50 96 72	79 44 61 40 15	14 53 40 65 39	27 31 58 50 28	11 39 03 34 25
49	33 78 80 87 15	38 30 06 38 21	14 47 47 07 26	54 96 87 53 32	40 36 40 96 76
50	13 13 92 66 99	47 24 49 57 74	32 25 43 62 17	10 97 11 69 84	99 63 22 32 98

Table G.1. *Table of Pascal's Triangle and Binomial Coefficients*

N	$\binom{N}{0}$	$\binom{N}{1}$	$\binom{N}{2}$	$\binom{N}{3}$	$\binom{N}{4}$	$\binom{N}{5}$	$\binom{N}{6}$	$\binom{N}{7}$	$\binom{N}{8}$	$\binom{N}{9}$	$\binom{N}{10}$
0	1										
1	1	1									
2	1	2	1								
3	1	3	3	1							
4	1	4	6	4	1						
5	1	5	10	10	5	1					
6	1	6	15	20	15	6	1				
7	1	7	21	35	35	21	7	1			
8	1	8	28	56	70	56	28	8	1		
9	1	9	36	84	126	126	84	36	9	1	
10	1	10	45	120	210	252	210	120	45	10	1
11	1	11	55	165	330	462	462	330	165	55	11
12	1	12	66	220	495	792	924	792	495	220	66
13	1	13	78	286	715	1287	1716	1716	1287	715	286
14	1	14	91	364	1001	2002	3003	3432	3003	2002	1001
15	1	15	105	455	1365	3003	5005	6435	6435	5005	3003
16	1	16	120	560	1820	4368	8008	11440	12870	11440	8008
17	1	17	136	680	2380	6188	12376	19448	24310	24310	19448
18	1	18	153	816	3060	8568	18564	31824	43758	48620	43758
19	1	19	171	969	3876	11628	27132	50388	75582	92378	92378
20	1	20	190	1140	4845	15504	38760	77520	125970	167960	184756

Table G is taken from S. Siegel, *Nonparametric Statistics for the Behavioral Sciences,* published by McGraw-Hill, New York, by permission of the author and publishers.

Table H.   *Table of Critical Values of Chi Square*

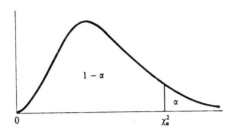

df	.99	.98	.95	.90	.80	.70	.50	.30	.20	.10	.05	.02	.01	.001
1	$.0^3157$	$.0^3628$	.00393	.0158	.0642	.148	.455	1.074	1.642	2.706	3.841	5.412	6.635	10.827
2	.0201	.0404	.103	.211	.446	.713	1.386	2.408	3.219	4.605	5.991	7.824	9.210	13.815
3	.115	.185	.352	.584	1.005	1.424	2.366	3.665	4.642	6.251	7.815	9.837	11.345	16.266
4	.297	.429	.711	1.064	1.649	2.195	3.357	4.878	5.989	7.779	9.488	11.668	13.277	18.467
5	.554	.752	1.145	1.610	2.343	3.000	4.351	6.064	7.289	9.236	11.070	13.388	15.086	20.515
6	.872	1.134	1.635	2.204	3.070	3.828	5.348	7.231	8.558	10.645	12.592	15.033	16.812	22.457
7	1.239	1.564	2.167	2.833	3.822	4.671	6.346	8.383	9.803	12.017	14.067	16.622	18.475	24.322
8	1.646	2.032	2.733	3.490	4.594	5.527	7.344	9.524	11.030	13.362	15.507	18.168	20.090	26.125
9	2.088	2.532	3.325	4.168	5.380	6.393	8.343	10.656	12.242	14.684	16.919	19.679	21.666	27.877
10	2.558	3.059	3.940	4.865	6.179	7.267	9.342	11.781	13.442	15.987	18.307	21.161	23.209	29.588
11	3.053	3.609	4.575	5.578	6.989	8.148	10.341	12.899	14.631	17.275	19.675	22.618	24.725	31.264
12	3.571	4.178	5.226	6.304	7.807	9.034	11.340	14.011	15.812	18.549	21.026	24.054	26.217	32.909
13	4.107	4.765	5.892	7.042	8.634	9.926	12.340	15.119	16.985	19.812	22.362	25.472	27.688	34.528
14	4.660	5.368	6.571	7.790	9.467	10.821	13.339	16.222	18.151	21.064	23.685	26.873	29.141	36.123
15	5.229	5.985	7.261	8.547	10.307	11.721	14.339	17.322	19.311	22.307	24.996	28.259	30.578	37.697
16	5.812	6.614	7.962	9.312	11.152	12.624	15.338	18.418	20.465	23.542	26.296	29.633	32.000	39.252
17	6.408	7.255	8.672	10.085	12.002	13.531	16.338	19.511	21.615	24.769	27.587	30.995	33.409	40.790
18	7.015	7.906	9.390	10.865	12.857	14.440	17.338	20.601	22.760	25.989	28.869	32.346	34.805	42.312
19	7.633	8.567	10.117	11.651	13.716	15.352	18.338	21.689	23.900	27.204	30.144	33.687	36.191	43.820
20	8.260	9.237	10.851	12.443	14.578	16.266	19.337	22.775	25.038	28.412	31.410	35.020	37.566	45.315
21	8.897	9.915	11.591	13.240	15.445	17.182	20.337	23.858	26.171	29.615	32.671	36.343	38.932	46.797
22	9.542	10.600	12.338	14.041	16.314	18.101	21.337	24.939	27.301	30.813	33.924	37.659	40.289	48.268
23	10.196	11.293	13.091	14.848	17.187	19.021	22.337	26.018	28.429	32.007	35.172	38.968	41.638	49.728
24	10.856	11.992	13.848	15.659	18.062	19.943	23.337	27.096	29.553	33.196	36.415	40.270	42.980	51.179
25	11.524	12.697	14.611	16.473	18.940	20.867	24.337	28.172	30.675	34.382	37.652	41.566	44.314	52.620
26	12.198	13.409	15.379	17.292	19.820	21.792	25.336	29.246	31.795	35.563	38.885	42.856	45.642	54.052
27	12.879	14.125	16.151	18.114	20.703	22.719	26.336	30.319	32.912	36.741	40.113	44.140	46.963	55.476
28	13.565	14.847	16.928	18.939	21.588	23.647	27.336	31.391	34.027	37.916	41.337	45.419	48.278	56.893
29	14.256	15.574	17.708	19.768	22.475	24.577	28.336	32.461	35.139	39.087	42.557	46.693	49.588	58.302
30	14.953	16.306	18.493	20.599	23.364	25.508	29.336	33.530	36.250	40.256	43.773	47.962	50.892	59.703

For $v > 30$, the expression $\sqrt{2_x^2} - \sqrt{2v - 1}$ may be used as a normal deviate with unit variance.

Table H is taken from Table 4 of Fisher and Yates, *Statistical Tables for Biological, Agricultural and Medical Research,* published by Oliver and Boyd Ltd., Edinburgh, by permission of the authors and publishers.

Table I.1. *Table of Critical Values for Mann-Whitney U-Test*

n = 3

U \ n	1	2	3
0	.250	.100	.050
1	.500	.200	.100
2	.750	.400	.200
3		.600	.350
4			.500
5			.650

n = 4

U \ n	1	2	3	4
0	.200	.067	.028	.014
1	.400	.133	.057	.029
2	.600	.267	.114	.057
3		.400	.200	.100
4		.600	.314	.171
5			.429	.243
6			.571	.343
7				.443
8				.557

n = 5

U \ n	1	2	3	4	5
0	.167	.047	.018	.008	.004
1	.333	.095	.036	.016	.008
2	.500	.190	.071	.032	.016
3	.667	.286	.125	.056	.028
4		.429	.196	.095	.048
5		.571	.286	.143	.075
6			.393	.206	.111
7			.500	.278	.155
8			.607	.365	.210
9				.452	.274
10				.548	.345
11					.421
12					.500
13					.579

n = 6

U \ n	1	2	3	4	5	6
0	.143	.036	.012	.005	.002	.001
1	.286	.071	.024	.010	.004	.002
2	.428	.143	.048	.019	.009	.004
3	.571	.214	.083	.033	.015	.008
4		.321	.131	.057	.026	.013
5		.429	.190	.086	.041	.021
6		.571	.274	.129	.063	.032
7			.357	.176	.089	.047
8			.452	.238	.123	.066
9			.548	.305	.165	.090
10				.381	.214	.120
11				.457	.268	.155
12				.545	.331	.197
13					.396	.242
14					.465	.294
15					.535	.350
16						.409
17						.469
18						.531

Table reproduced from "On a test of whether one of two random variables is stochastically larger than the other," *Annals of Mathematical Statistics,* 1947, **18**, 50-60, with permission of the authors, H. B. Mann and D. R. Whitney, and the editor.

Table I.2.   *Table of Critical Values for Mann-Whitney U-Test*—Continued

$n = 7$

U \ n	1	2	3	4	5	6	7
0	.125	.028	.008	.003	.001	.001	.000
1	.250	.056	.017	.006	.003	.001	.001
2	.375	.111	.033	.012	.005	.002	.001
3	.500	.167	.058	.021	.009	.004	.002
4	.625	.250	.092	.036	.015	.007	.003
5		.333	.133	.055	.024	.011	.006
6		.444	.192	.082	.037	.017	.009
7		.556	.258	.115	.053	.026	.013
8			.333	.158	.074	.037	.019
9			.417	.206	.101	.051	.027
10			.500	.264	.134	.069	.036
11			.583	.324	.172	.090	.049
12				.394	.216	.117	.064
13				.464	.265	.147	.082
14				.538	.319	.183	.104
15					.378	.223	.130
16					.438	.267	.159
17					.500	.314	.191
18					.562	.365	.228
19						.418	.267
20						.473	.310
21						.527	.355
22							.402
23							.451
24							.500
25							.549

Table I.3. *Table of Critical Values for Mann-Whitney U-Test*—Continued

$n = 8$

U \ n	1	2	3	4	5	6	7	8
0	.111	.022	.006	.002	.001	.000	.000	.000
1	.222	.044	.012	.004	.002	.001	.000	.000
2	.333	.089	.024	.008	.003	.001	.001	.000
3	.444	.133	.042	.014	.005	.002	.001	.001
4	.556	.200	.067	.024	.009	.004	.002	.001
5		.267	.097	.036	.015	.006	.003	.001
6		.356	.139	.055	.023	.010	.005	.002
7		.444	.188	.077	.033	.015	.007	.003
8		.556	.248	.107	.047	.021	.010	.005
9			.315	.141	.064	.030	.014	.007
10			.387	.184	.085	.041	.020	.010
11			.461	.230	.111	.054	.027	.014
12			.539	.285	.142	.071	.036	.019
13				.341	.177	.091	.047	.025
14				.404	.217	.114	.060	.032
15				.467	.262	.141	.076	.041
16				.533	.311	.172	.095	.052
17					.362	.207	.116	.065
18					.416	.245	.140	.080
19					.472	.286	.168	.097
20					.528	.331	.198	.117
21						.377	.232	.139
22						.426	.268	.164
23						.475	.306	.191
24						.525	.347	.221
25							.389	.253
26							.433	.287
27							.478	.323
28							.522	.360
29								.399
30								.439
31								.480
32								.520

Table I.4.   *Table of Critical Values for Mann-Whitney U-Tests*

For a one-tailed test at $\alpha = .01$ *or two-tailed test at* $\alpha = .02$

n_1 \ n_2	9	10	11	12	13	14	15	16	17	18	19	20
1												
2												
3									0	0	0	0
4		0	0	0	1	1	1	2	2	3	3	3
5	1	1	2	2	3	3	4	5	5	6	7	7
6	2	3	4	4	5	6	7	8	9	10	11	12
7	3	5	6	7	8	9	10	11	13	14	15	16
8	5	6	8	9	11	12	14	15	17	18	20	21
9	7	8	10	12	14	15	17	19	21	23	25	26
10	8	10	12	14	17	19	21	23	25	27	29	32
11	10	12	15	17	20	22	24	27	29	32	34	37
12	12	14	17	20	23	25	28	31	34	37	40	42
13	14	17	20	23	26	29	32	35	38	42	45	48
14	15	19	22	25	29	32	36	39	43	46	50	54
15	17	21	24	28	32	36	40	43	47	51	55	59
16	19	23	27	31	35	39	43	48	52	56	60	65
17	21	25	29	34	38	43	47	52	57	61	66	70
18	23	27	32	37	42	46	51	56	61	66	71	76
19	25	29	34	40	45	50	55	60	66	71	77	82
20	26	32	37	42	48	54	59	65	70	76	82	88

Table I.5.   *Table of Critical Values for Mann-Whitney U-Test*—Continued

n_1 \ n_2	9	10	11	12	13	14	15	16	17	18	19	20
1												
2					0	0	0	0	0	0	1	1
3	1	1	1	2	2	2	3	3	4	4	4	5
4	3	3	4	5	5	6	7	7	8	9	9	10
5	5	6	7	8	9	10	11	12	13	14	15	16
6	7	8	9	11	12	13	15	16	18	19	20	22
7	9	11	12	14	16	17	19	21	23	24	26	28
8	11	13	15	17	20	22	24	26	28	30	32	34
9	14	16	18	21	23	26	28	31	33	36	38	40
10	16	19	22	24	27	30	33	36	38	41	44	47
11	18	22	25	28	31	34	37	41	44	47	50	53
12	21	24	28	31	35	38	42	46	49	53	56	60
13	23	27	31	35	39	43	47	51	55	59	63	67
14	26	30	34	38	43	47	51	56	60	65	69	73
15	28	33	37	42	47	51	56	61	66	70	75	80
16	31	36	41	46	51	56	61	66	71	76	82	87
17	33	38	44	49	55	60	66	71	77	82	88	93
18	36	41	47	53	59	65	70	76	82	88	94	100
19	38	44	50	56	63	69	75	82	88	94	101	107
20	40	47	53	60	67	73	80	87	93	100	107	114

Adapted and abridged from Tables 1, 3, 5, and 7 of Auble, D. 1953. Extended tables for the Mann-Whitney statistic. *Bulletin of the Institute of Educational Research at Indiana University,* **1,** No. 2, with the permission of the author and the publisher.

Table I.6. *Table of Critical Values for Mann-Whitney U-Test*—Continued

For a one-tailed test at α = *.025 or two-tailed test at* α = *.05*

n_1 \ n_2	9	10	11	12	13	14	15	16	17	18	19	20
1												
2	0	0	0	1	1	1	1	1	2	2	2	2
3	2	3	3	4	4	5	5	6	6	7	7	8
4	4	5	6	7	8	9	10	11	11	12	13	13
5	7	8	9	11	12	13	14	15	17	18	19	20
6	10	11	13	14	16	17	19	21	22	24	25	27
7	12	14	16	18	20	22	24	26	28	30	32	34
8	15	17	19	22	24	26	29	31	34	36	38	41
9	17	20	23	26	28	31	34	37	39	42	45	48
10	20	23	26	29	33	36	39	42	45	48	52	55
11	23	26	30	33	37	40	44	47	51	55	58	62
12	26	29	33	37	41	45	49	53	57	61	65	69
13	28	33	37	41	45	50	54	59	63	67	72	76
14	31	36	40	45	50	55	59	64	67	74	78	83
15	34	39	44	49	54	59	64	70	75	80	85	90
16	37	42	47	53	59	64	70	75	81	86	92	98
17	39	45	51	57	63	67	75	81	87	93	99	105
18	42	48	55	61	67	74	80	86	93	99	106	112
19	45	52	58	65	72	78	85	92	99	106	113	119
20	48	55	62	69	76	83	90	98	105	112	119	127

Table I.7. *Table of Critical Values for Mann-Whitney U-Test*–Continued

For a one-tailed test at α = *.05 or two-tailed test at* α = *.10*

n_1 / n_2	9	10	11	12	13	14	15	16	17	18	19	20
1											0	0
2	1	1	1	2	2	2	3	3	3	4	4	4
3	3	4	5	5	6	7	7	8	9	9	10	11
4	6	7	8	9	10	11	12	14	15	16	17	18
5	9	11	12	13	15	16	18	19	20	22	23	25
6	12	14	16	17	19	21	23	25	26	28	30	32
7	15	17	19	21	24	26	28	30	33	35	37	39
8	18	20	23	26	28	31	33	36	39	41	44	47
9	21	24	27	30	33	36	39	42	45	48	51	54
10	24	27	31	34	37	41	44	48	51	55	58	62
11	27	31	34	38	42	46	50	54	57	61	65	69
12	30	34	38	42	47	51	55	60	64	68	72	77
13	33	37	42	47	51	56	61	65	70	75	80	84
14	36	41	46	51	56	61	66	71	77	82	87	92
15	39	44	50	55	61	66	72	77	83	88	94	100
16	42	48	54	60	65	71	77	83	89	95	101	107
17	45	51	57	64	70	77	83	89	96	102	109	115
18	48	55	61	68	75	82	88	95	102	109	116	123
19	51	58	65	72	80	87	94	101	109	116	123	130
20	54	62	69	77	84	92	100	107	115	123	130	138

Table J.1.   *Table of Critical Values for Maximum Difference Test.*
Critical value of D for one-sample test

Sample size (N)	Level of significance for $D = \text{maximum } |F_0(X) - S_N(X)|$				
	.20	.15	.10	.05	.01
1	.900	.925	.950	.975	.995
2	.684	.726	.776	.842	.929
3	.565	.597	.642	.708	.828
4	.494	.525	.564	.624	.733
5	.446	.474	.510	.565	.669
6	.410	.436	.470	.521	.618
7	.381	.405	.438	.486	.577
8	.358	.381	.411	.457	.543
9	.339	.360	.388	.432	.514
10	.322	.342	.368	.410	.490
11	.307	.326	.352	.391	.468
12	.295	.313	.338	.375	.450
13	.284	.302	.325	.361	.433
14	.274	.292	.314	.349	.418
15	.266	.283	.304	.338	.404
16	.258	.274	.295	.328	.392
17	.250	.266	.286	.318	.381
18	.244	.259	.278	.309	.371
19	.237	.252	.272	.301	.363
20	.231	.246	.264	.294	.356
25	:21	.22	.24	.27	.32
30	.19	.20	.22	.24	.29
35	.18	.19	.21	.23	.27
Over 35	$\dfrac{1.07}{\sqrt{N}}$	$\dfrac{1.14}{\sqrt{N}}$	$\dfrac{1.22}{\sqrt{N}}$	$\dfrac{1.36}{\sqrt{N}}$	$\dfrac{1.63}{\sqrt{N}}$

Adapted from Massey, F. J., Jr. 1951. The Kolmogorov-Smirnov test for goodness of fit. *J. Amer. Statist. Ass.*, **46**, 70, with the permission of the author and publisher.

Table J.2.   *Table of Critical Values for Maximum Difference Test*
Critical values in two-sample case: Small N's. *†*

N	One-tailed test*		Two-tailed test†	
	$\alpha = .05$	$\alpha = .01$	$\alpha = .05$	$\alpha = .01$
3	3	—	—	—
4	4	—	4	—
5	4	5	5	5
6	5	6	5	6
7	5	6	6	6
8	5	6	6	7
9	6	7	6	7
10	6	7	7	8
11	6	8	7	8
12	6	8	7	8
13	7	8	7	9
14	7	8	8	9
15	7	9	8	9
16	7	9	8	10
17	8	9	8	10
18	8	10	9	10
19	8	10	9	10
20	8	10	9	11
21	8	10	9	11
22	9	11	9	11
23	9	11	10	11
24	9	11	10	12
25	9	11	10	12
26	9	11	10	12
27	9	12	10	12
28	10	12	11	13
29	10	12	11	13
30	10	12	11	13
35	11	13	12	
40	11	14	13	

*Abridged from Goodman, L. A. 1954. Kolmogorov-Smirnov tests for psychological research. *Psychol. Bull.*, **51**, 167, with the permission of the author and the American Psychological Association.

†Derived from Table 1 of Massey, F. J., Jr. 1951. The distribution of the maximum deviation between two sample cumulative step functions. *Ann. Math. Statist.*, **22**, 126-127, with the permission of the author and the publisher.

Table J.3.   *Table of Critical Values for Maximum Difference Test*
             Critical values in two-sample case: Large N's two-tailed test. [*]

Level of significance	Value of D so large as to call for rejection of H_0 at the indicated level of significance, wnere $D = \text{maximum} \left\| S_{n_1}(X) - S_{n_2}(X) \right\|$
.10	$1.22 \sqrt{\dfrac{n_1 + n_2}{n_1 n_2}}$
.05	$1.36 \sqrt{\dfrac{n_1 + n_2}{n_1 n_2}}$
.025	$1.48 \sqrt{\dfrac{n_1 + n_2}{n_1 n_2}}$
.01	$1.63 \sqrt{\dfrac{n_1 + n_2}{n_1 n_2}}$
.005	$1.73 \sqrt{\dfrac{n_1 + n_2}{n_1 n_2}}$
.001	$1.95 \sqrt{\dfrac{n_1 + n_2}{n_1 n_2}}$

Adapted from Smirnov, N. 1948. Tables for estimating the goodness of fit of empirical distributions. *Ann. Math. Statist.*, **19**, 280-281, with the permission of the publisher.

Table K.1.   *Table of Critical Values for the Runs Test**
For the one-sample case, any r that is equal to or less than that of the K.l.a Table or, that is equal to or greater than the K.l.b, Table is significant at =.05. With a two sample runs test any r that is equal to or less than that shown in rhw K.l.a Table is significant at = .05.

Table K.l.a.

n_1 \ n_2	2	3	4	5	6	7	8	9	10	11	12	13	14	15	16	17	18	19	20
2											2	2	2	2	2	2	2	2	2
3				2	2	2	2	2	2	2	2	2	3	3	3	3	3	3	
4			2	2	2	3	3	3	3	3	3	3	3	4	4	4	4	4	
5			2	2	3	3	3	3	3	4	4	4	4	4	4	4	5	5	5
6		2	2	3	3	3	3	4	4	4	4	5	5	5	5	5	5	6	6
7		2	2	3	3	3	4	4	5	5	5	5	5	6	6	6	6	6	6
8		2	3	3	3	4	4	5	5	5	6	6	6	6	6	7	7	7	7
9		2	3	3	4	4	5	5	5	6	6	6	7	7	7	7	8	8	8
10		2	3	3	4	5	5	5	6	6	7	7	7	7	8	8	8	8	9
11		2	3	4	4	5	5	6	6	7	7	7	8	8	8	9	9	9	9
12	2	2	3	4	4	5	6	6	7	7	7	8	8	8	9	9	9	10	10
13	2	2	3	4	5	5	6	6	7	7	8	8	9	9	9	10	10	10	10
14	2	2	3	4	5	5	6	7	7	8	8	9	9	9	10	10	10	11	11
15	2	3	3	4	5	6	6	7	7	8	8	9	9	10	10	11	11	11	12
16	2	3	4	4	5	6	6	7	8	8	9	9	10	10	11	11	11	12	12
17	2	3	4	4	5	6	7	7	8	9	9	10	10	11	11	11	12	12	13
18	2	3	4	5	5	6	7	8	8	9	9	10	10	11	11	12	12	13	13
19	2	3	4	5	6	6	7	8	8	9	10	10	11	11	12	12	13	13	13
20	2	3	4	5	6	6	7	8	9	9	10	10	11	12	12	13	13	13	14

Table K.l.b.

n_1 \ n_2	2	3	4	5	6	7	8	9	10	11	12	13	14	15	16	17	18	19	20
2																			
3																			
4				9	9														
5			9	10	10	11	11												
6			9	10	11	12	12	13	13	13	13								
7				11	12	13	13	14	14	14	14	15	15	15					
8				11	12	13	14	14	15	15	16	16	16	16	17	17	17	17	17
9					13	14	14	15	16	16	16	17	17	18	18	18	18	18	18
10					13	14	15	16	16	17	17	18	18	18	19	19	19	20	20
11					13	14	15	16	17	17	18	19	19	19	20	20	20	21	21
12					13	14	16	16	17	18	19	19	20	20	21	21	21	22	22
13						15	16	17	18	19	19	20	20	21	21	22	22	23	23
14						15	16	17	18	19	20	20	21	22	22	23	23	23	24
15						15	16	18	18	19	20	21	22	22	23	23	24	24	25
16							17	18	19	20	21	21	22	23	23	24	25	25	25
17							17	18	19	20	21	22	23	23	24	25	25	26	26
18							17	18	19	20	21	22	23	24	25	25	26	26	27
19							17	18	20	21	22	23	23	24	25	26	26	27	27
20							17	18	20	21	22	23	24	25	25	26	27	27	28

*Adapted from Swed, Frieda S., and Eisenhart, C. 1943. Tables for testing randomness of grouping in a sequence of alternatives. *Ann. Math. Statist.*, **14**, 83-86, with the permission of the authors and publisher.

Table L.1.   *Table of Critical Values for the Rank-Sign Test*

N	Level of significance for one-tailed test		
	.025	.01	.005
	Level of significance for two-tailed test		
	.05	.02	.01
6	0	—	—
7	2	0	—
8	4	2	0
9	6	3	2
10	8	5	3
11	11	7	5
12	14	10	7
13	17	13	10
14	21	16	13
15	25	20	16
16	30	24	20
17	35	28	23
18	40	33	28
19	46	38	32
20	52	43	38
21	59	49	43
22	66	56	49
23	73	62	55
24	81	69	61
25	89	77	68

Adapted from Table 2 of Wilcoxon, F. 1949. *Some rapid approximate statistical procedures.* New York: American Cyanamid Company, p. 13, with the permission of Mrs. Wilcoxon.

Table M.   Table of Critical Values for the t-Test

df	α .25 2α .50	.20 .40	.15 .30	.10 .20	.05 .10	.025 .05	.01 .02	.005 .01	.0005 .001
1	1.000	1.376	1.963	3.078	6.314	12.706	31.821	63.657	636.619
2	.816	1.061	1.386	1.886	2.920	4.303	6.965	9.925	31.598
3	.765	.978	1.250	1.638	2.353	3.182	4.541	5.841	12.924
4	.741	.941	1.190	1.533	2.132	2.776	3.747	4.604	8.610
5	.727	.920	1.156	1.476	2.015	2.571	3.365	4.032	6.869
6	.718	.906	1.134	1.440	1.943	2.447	3.143	3.707	5.959
7	.711	.896	1.119	1.415	1.895	2.365	2.998	3.499	5.408
8	.706	.889	1.108	1.397	1.860	2.306	2.896	3.355	5.041
9	.703	.883	1.100	1.383	1.833	2.262	2.821	3.250	4.781
10	.700	.879	1.093	1.372	1.812	2.228	2.764	3.169	4.587
11	.697	.876	1.088	1.363	1.796	2.201	2.718	3.106	4.437
12	.695	.873	1.083	1.356	1.782	2.179	2.681	3.055	4.318
13	.694	.870	1.079	1.350	1.771	2.160	2.650	3.012	4.221
14	.692	.868	1.076	1.345	1.761	2.145	2.624	2.977	4.140
15	.691	.866	1.074	1.341	1.753	2.131	2.602	2.947	4.073
16	.690	.865	1.071	1.337	1.746	2.120	2.583	2.921	4.015
17	.689	.863	1.069	1.333	1.740	2.110	2.567	2.898	3.965
18	.688	.862	1.067	1.330	1.734	2.101	2.552	2.878	3.922
19	.688	.861	1.066	1.328	1.729	2.093	2.539	2.861	3.883
20	.687	.860	1.064	1.325	1.725	2.086	2.528	2.845	3.850
21	.686	.859	1.063	1.323	1.721	2.080	2.518	2.831	3.819
22	.686	.858	1.061	1.321	1.717	2.074	2.508	2.819	3.792
23	.685	.858	1.060	1.319	1.714	2.069	2.500	2.807	3.767
24	.685	.857	1.059	1.318	1.711	2.064	2.492	2.797	3.745
25	.684	.856	1.058	1.316	1.708	2.060	2.485	2.787	3.725
26	.684	.856	1.058	1.315	1.706	2.056	2.479	2.779	3.707
27	.684	.855	1.057	1.314	1.703	2.052	2.473	2.771	3.690
28	.683	.855	1.056	1.313	1.701	2.048	2.467	2.763	3.674
29	.683	.854	1.055	1.311	1.699	2.045	2.462	2.756	3.659
30	.683	.854	1.055	1.310	1.697	2.042	2.457	2.750	3.646
40	.681	.851	1.050	1.303	1.684	2.021	2.423	2.704	3.551
60	.679	.848	1.046	1.296	1.671	2.000	2.390	2.660	3.460
120	.677	.845	1.041	1.289	1.658	1.980	2.358	2.617	3.373
∞	.674	.842	1.036	1.282	1.645	1.960	2.326	2.576	3.291

Table M is taken from Table 3 of Fisher and Yates, *Statistical Tables for Biological, Agricultural and Medical Research,* published by Oliver and Boyd Ltd., Edinburgh, by permission of the authors and publishers.

Table N.1.   *Table of Critical Values of the F Distribution*

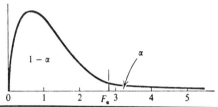

df for de-nomi-nator	α	df for numerator											
		1	2	3	4	5	6	7	8	9	10	11	12
1	.25	5.83	7.50	8.20	8.58	8.82	8.98	9.10	9.19	9.26	9.32	9.36	9.41
	.10	39.9	49.5	53.6	55.8	57.2	58.2	58.9	59.4	59.9	60.2	60.5	60.7
	.05	161	200	216	225	230	234	237	239	241	242	243	244
2	.25	2.57	3.00	3.15	3.23	3.28	3.31	3.34	3.35	3.37	3.38	3.39	3.39
	.10	8.53	9.00	9.16	9.24	9.29	9.33	9.35	9.37	9.38	9.39	9.40	9.41
	.05	18.5	19.0	19.2	19.2	19.3	19.3	19.4	19.4	19.4	19.4	19.4	19.4
	.01	98.5	99.0	99.2	99.2	99.3	99.3	99.4	99.4	99.4	99.4	99.4	99.4
3	.25	2.02	2.28	2.36	2.39	2.41	2.42	2.43	2.44	2.44	2.44	2.45	2.45
	.10	5.54	5.46	5.39	5.34	5.31	5.28	5.27	5.25	5.24	5.23	5.22	5.22
	.05	10.1	9.55	9.28	9.12	9.01	8.94	8.89	8.85	8.81	8.79	8.76	8.74
	.01	34.1	30.8	29.5	28.7	28.2	27.9	27.7	27.5	27.3	27.2	27.1	27.1
4	.25	1.81	2.00	2.05	2.06	2.07	2.08	2.08	2.08	2.08	2.08	2.08	2.08
	.10	4.54	4.32	4.19	4.11	4.05	4.01	3.98	3.95	3.94	3.92	3.91	3.90
	.05	7.71	6.94	6.59	6.39	6.26	6.16	6.09	6.04	6.00	5.96	5.94	5.91
	.01	21.2	18.0	16.7	16.0	15.5	15.2	15.0	14.8	14.7	14.5	14.4	14.4
5	.25	1.69	1.85	1.88	1.89	1.89	1.89	1.89	1.89	1.89	1.89	1.89	1.89
	.10	4.06	3.78	3.62	3.52	3.45	3.40	3.37	3.34	3.32	3.30	3.28	3.27
	.05	6.61	5.79	5.41	5.19	5.05	4.95	4.88	4.82	4.77	4.74	4.71	4.68
	.01	16.3	13.3	12.1	11.4	11.0	10.7	10.5	10.3	10.2	10.1	9.96	9.89
6	.25	1.62	1.76	1.78	1.79	1.79	1.78	1.78	1.78	1.77	1.77	1.77	1.77
	.10	3.78	3.46	3.29	3.18	3.11	3.05	3.01	2.98	2.96	2.94	2.92	2.90
	.05	5.99	5.14	4.76	4.53	4.39	4.28	4.21	4.15	4.10	4.06	4.03	4.00
	.01	13.7	10.9	9.78	9.15	8.75	8.47	8.26	8.10	7.98	7.87	7.79	7.72
7	.25	1.57	1.70	1.72	1.72	1.71	1.71	1.70	1.70	1.69	1.69	1.69	1.68
	.10	3.59	3.26	3.07	2.96	2.88	2.83	2.78	2.75	2.72	2.70	2.68	2.67
	.05	5.59	4.74	4.35	4.12	3.97	3.87	3.79	3.73	3.68	3.64	3.60	3.57
	.01	12.2	9.55	8.45	7.85	7.46	7.19	6.99	6.84	6.72	6.62	6.54	6.47
8	.25	1.54	1.66	1.67	1.66	1.66	1.65	1.64	1.64	1.63	1.63	1.63	1.62
	.10	3.46	3.11	2.92	2.81	2.73	2.67	2.62	2.59	2.56	2.54	2.52	2.50
	.05	5.32	4.46	4.07	3.84	3.69	3.58	3.50	3.44	3.39	3.35	3.31	3.28
	.01	11.3	8.65	7.59	7.01	6.63	6.37	6.18	6.03	5.91	5.81	5.73	5.67
9	.25	1.51	1.62	1.63	1.63	1.62	1.61	1.60	1.60	1.59	1.59	1.58	1.58
	.10	3.36	3.01	2.81	2.69	2.61	2.55	2.51	2.47	2.44	2.42	2.40	2.38
	.05	5.12	4.26	3.86	3.63	3.48	3.37	3.29	3.23	3.18	3.14	3.10	3.07
	.01	10.6	8.02	6.99	6.42	6.06	5.80	5.61	5.47	5.35	5.26	5.18	5.11

Table N.2.   *Table of Critical Values of the F Distribution* – Continued

					df *for numerator*									df *for denominator*
15	20	24	30	40	50	60	100	120	200	500	∞	α	
9.49	9.58	9.63	9.67	9.71	9.74	9.76	9.78	9.80	9.82	9.84	9.85	.25	
61.2	61.7	62.0	62.3	62.5	62.7	62.8	63.0	63.1	63.2	63.3	63.3	.10	1
246	248	249	250	251	252	252	253	253	254	254	254	.05	
3.41	3.43	3.43	3.44	3.45	3.45	3.46	3.47	3.47	3.48	3.48	3.48	.25	
9.42	9.44	9.45	9.46	9.47	9.47	9.47	9.48	9.48	9.49	9.49	9.49	.10	2
19.4	19.4	19.5	19.5	19.5	19.5	19.5	19.5	19.5	19.5	19.5	19.5	.05	
99.4	99.4	99.5	99.5	99.5	99.5	99.5	99.5	99.5	99.5	99.5	99.5	.01	
2.46	2.46	2.46	2.47	2.47	2.47	2.47	2.47	2.47	2.47	2.47	2.47	.25	
5.20	5.18	5.18	5.17	5.16	5.15	5.15	5.14	5.14	5.14	5.14	5.13	.10	3
8.70	8.66	8.64	8.62	8.59	8.58	8.57	8.55	8.55	8.54	8.53	8.53	.05	
26.9	26.7	26.6	26.5	26.4	26.4	26.3	26.2	26.2	26.2	26.1	26.1	.01	
2.08	2.08	2.08	2.08	2.08	2.08	2.08	2.08	2.08	2.08	2.08	2.08	.25	
3.87	3.84	3.83	3.82	3.80	3.80	3.79	3.78	3.78	3.77	3.76	3.76	.10	4
5.86	5.80	5.77	5.75	5.72	5.70	5.69	5.66	5.66	5.65	5.64	5.63	.05	
14.2	14.0	13.9	13.8	13.7	13.7	13.7	13.6	13.6	13.5	13.5	13.5	.01	
1.89	1.88	1.88	1.88	1.88	1.88	1.87	1.87	1.87	1.87	1.87	1.87	.25	
3.24	3.21	3.19	3.17	3.16	3.15	3.14	3.13	3.12	3.12	3.11	3.10	.10	5
4.62	4.56	4.53	4.50	4.46	4.44	4.43	4.41	4.40	4.39	4.37	4.36	.05	
9.72	9.55	9.47	9.38	9.29	9.24	9.20	9.13	9.11	9.08	9.04	9.02	.01	
1.76	1.76	1.75	1.75	1.75	1.75	1.74	1.74	1.74	1.74	1.74	1.74	.25	
2.87	2.84	2.82	2.80	2.78	2.77	2.76	2.75	2.74	2.73	2.73	2.72	.10	6
3.94	3.87	3.84	3.81	3.77	3.75	3.74	3.71	3.70	3.69	3.68	3.67	.05	
7.56	7.40	7.31	7.23	7.14	7.09	7.06	6.99	6.97	6.93	6.90	6.88	.01	
1.68	1.67	1.67	1.66	1.66	1.66	1.65	1.65	1.65	1.65	1.65	1.65	.25	
2.63	2.59	2.58	2.56	2.54	2.52	2.51	2.50	2.49	2.48	2.48	2.47	.10	7
3.51	3.44	3.41	3.38	3.34	3.32	3.30	3.27	3.27	3.25	3.24	3.23	.05	
6.31	6.16	6.07	5.99	5.91	5.86	5.82	5.75	5.74	5.70	5.67	5.65	.10	
1.62	1.61	1.60	1.60	1.59	1.59	1.59	1.58	1.58	1.58	1.58	1.58	.25	
2.46	2.42	2.40	2.38	2.36	2.35	2.34	2.32	2.32	2.31	2.30	2.29	.10	8
3.22	3.15	3.12	3.08	3.04	3.02	3.01	2.97	2.97	2.95	2.94	2.93	.05	
5.52	5.36	5.28	5.20	5.12	5.07	5.03	4.96	4.95	4.91	4.88	4.86	.01	
1.57	1.56	1.56	1.55	1.55	1.54	1.54	1.53	1.53	1.53	1.53	1.53	.25	
2.34	2.30	2.28	2.25	2.23	2.22	2.21	2.19	2.18	2.17	2.17	2.16	.10	9
3.01	2.94	2.90	2.86	2.83	2.80	2.79	2.76	2.75	2.73	2.72	2.71	.05	
4.96	4.81	4.73	4.65	4.57	4.52	4.48	4.42	4.40	4.36	4.33	4.31	.01	

Table N.3.   *Table of Critical Values of the F Distribution*– Continued

| df for denominator | α | \multicolumn{12}{c}{df for numerator} |
		1	2	3	4	5	6	7	8	9	10	11	12
10	.25	1.49	1.60	1.60	1.59	1.59	1.58	1.57	1.56	1.56	1.55	1.55	1.54
	.10	3.29	2.92	2.73	2.61	2.52	2.46	2.41	2.38	2.35	2.32	2.30	2.28
	.05	4.96	4.10	3.71	3.48	3.33	3.22	3.14	3.07	3.02	2.98	2.94	2.91
	.01	10.0	7.56	6.55	5.99	5.64	5.39	5.20	5.06	4.94	4.85	4.77	4.71
11	.25	1.47	1.58	1.58	1.57	1.56	1.55	1.54	1.53	1.53	1.52	1.52	1.51
	.10	3.23	2.86	2.66	2.54	2.45	2.39	2.34	2.30	2.27	2.25	2.23	2.21
	.05	4.84	3.98	3.59	3.36	3.20	3.09	3.01	2.95	2.90	2.85	2.82	2.79
	.01	9.65	7.21	6.22	5.67	5.32	5.07	4.89	4.74	4.63	4.54	4.46	4.40
12	.25	1.46	1.56	1.56	1.55	1.54	1.53	1.52	1.51	1.51	1.50	1.50	1.49
	.10	3.18	2.81	2.61	2.48	2.39	2.33	2.28	2.24	2.21	2.19	2.17	2.15
	.05	4.75	3.89	3.49	3.26	3.11	3.00	2.91	2.85	2.80	2.75	2.72	2.69
	.01	9.33	6.93	5.95	5.41	5.06	4.82	4.64	4.50	4.39	4.30	4.22	4.16
13	.25	1.45	1.55	1.55	1.53	1.52	1.51	1.50	1.49	1.49	1.48	1.47	1.47
	.10	3.14	2.76	2.56	2.43	2.35	2.28	2.23	2.20	2.16	2.14	2.12	2.10
	.05	4.67	3.81	3.41	3.18	3.03	2.92	2.83	2.77	2.71	2.67	2.63	2.60
	.01	9.07	6.70	5.74	5.21	4.86	4.62	4.44	4.30	4.19	4.10	4.02	3.96
14	.25	1.44	1.53	1.53	1.52	1.51	1.50	1.49	1.48	1.47	1.46	1.46	1.45
	.10	3.10	2.73	2.52	2.39	2.31	2.24	2.19	2.15	2.12	2.10	2.08	2.05
	.05	4.60	3.74	3.34	3.11	2.96	2.85	2.76	2.70	2.65	2.60	2.57	2.53
	.01	8.86	6.51	5.56	5.04	4.69	4.46	4.28	4.14	4.03	3.94	3.86	3.80
15	.25	1.43	1.52	1.52	1.51	1.49	1.48	1.47	1.46	1.46	1.45	1.44	1.44
	.10	3.07	2.70	2.49	2.36	2.27	2.21	2.16	2.12	2.09	2.06	2.04	2.02
	.05	4.54	3.68	3.29	3.06	2.90	2.79	2.71	2.64	2.59	2.54	2.51	2.48
	.01	8.68	6.36	5.42	4.89	4.56	4.32	4.14	4.00	3.89	3.80	3.73	3.67
16	.25	1.42	1.51	1.51	1.50	1.48	1.47	1.46	1.45	1.44	1.44	1.44	1.43
	.10	3.05	2.67	2.46	2.33	2.24	2.18	2.13	2.09	2.06	2.03	2.01	1.99
	.05	4.49	3.63	3.24	3.01	2.85	2.74	2.66	2.59	2.54	2.49	2.46	2.42
	.01	8.53	6.23	5.29	4.77	4.44	4.20	4.03	3.89	3.78	3.69	3.62	3.55
17	.25	1.42	1.51	1.50	1.49	1.47	1.46	1.45	1.44	1.43	1.43	1.42	1.41
	.10	3.03	2.64	2.44	2.31	2.22	2.15	2.10	2.06	2.03	2.00	1.98	1.96
	.05	4.45	3.59	3.20	2.96	2.81	2.70	2.61	2.55	2.49	2.45	2.41	2.38
	.01	8.40	6.11	5.18	4.67	4.34	4.10	3.93	3.79	3.68	3.59	3.52	3.46
18	.25	1.41	1.50	1.49	1.48	1.46	1.45	1.44	1.43	1.42	1.42	1.41	1.40
	.10	3.01	2.62	2.42	2.29	2.20	2.13	2.08	2.04	2.00	1.98	1.96	1.93
	.05	4.41	3.55	3.16	2.93	2.77	2.66	2.58	2.51	2.46	2.41	2.37	2.34
	.01	8.29	6.01	5.09	4.58	4.25	4.01	3.84	3.71	3.60	3.51	3.43	3.37
19	.25	1.41	1.49	1.49	1.47	1.46	1.44	1.43	1.42	1.41	1.41	1.40	1.40
	.10	2.99	2.61	2.40	2.27	2.18	2.11	2.06	2.02	1.98	1.96	1.94	1.91
	.05	4.38	3.52	3.13	2.90	2.74	2.63	2.54	2.48	2.42	2.38	2.34	2.31
	.01	8.18	5.93	5.01	4.50	4.17	3.94	3.77	3.63	3.52	3.43	3.36	3.30
20	.25	1.40	1.49	1.48	1.46	1.45	1.44	1.43	1.42	1.41	1.40	1.39	1.39
	.10	2.97	2.59	2.38	2.25	2.16	2.09	2.04	2.00	1.96	1.94	1.92	1.89
	.05	4.35	3.49	3.10	2.87	2.71	2.60	2.51	2.45	2.39	2.35	2.31	2.28
	.01	8.10	5.85	4.94	4.43	4.10	3.87	3.70	3.56	3.46	3.37	3.29	3.23

Table N.4. *Table of Critical Values of the F Distribution*—Continued

				df *for numerator*								α	df *for denominator*
15	20	24	30	40	50	60	100	120	200	500	∞		
1.53	1.52	1.52	1.51	1.51	1.50	1.50	1.49	1.49	1.49	1.48	1.48	.25	
2.24	2.20	2.18	2.16	2.13	2.12	2.11	2.09	2.08	2.07	2.06	2.06	.10	10
2.85	2.77	2.74	2.70	2.66	2.64	2.62	2.59	2.58	2.56	2.55	2.54	.05	
4.56	4.41	4.33	4.25	4.17	4.12	4.08	4.01	4.00	3.96	3.93	3.91	.01	
1.50	1.49	1.49	1.48	1.47	1.47	1.47	1.46	1.46	1.46	1.45	1.45	.25	
2.17	2.12	2.10	2.08	2.05	2.04	2.03	2.00	2.00	1.99	1.98	1.97	.10	11
2.72	2.65	2.61	2.57	2.53	2.51	2.49	2.46	2.45	2.43	2.42	2.40	.05	
4.25	4.10	4.02	3.94	3.86	3.81	3.78	3.71	3.69	3.66	3.62	3.60	.01	
1.48	1.47	1.46	1.45	1.45	1.44	1.44	1.43	1.43	1.43	1.42	1.42	.25	
2.10	2.06	2.04	2.01	1.99	1.97	1.96	1.94	1.93	1.92	1.91	1.90	.10	12
2.62	2.54	2.51	2.47	2.43	2.40	2.38	2.35	2.34	2.32	2.31	2.30	.05	
4.01	3.86	3.78	3.70	3.62	3.57	3.54	3.47	3.45	3.41	3.38	3.36	.01	
1.46	1.45	1.44	1.43	1.42	1.42	1.42	1.41	1.41	1.40	1.40	1.40	.25	
2.05	2.01	1.98	1.96	1.93	1.92	1.90	1.88	1.88	1.86	1.85	1.85	.10	13
2.53	2.46	2.42	2.38	2.34	2.31	2.30	2.26	2.25	2.23	2.22	2.21	.05	
3.82	3.66	3.59	3.51	3.43	3.38	3.34	3.27	3.25	3.22	3.19	3.17	.01	
1.44	1.43	1.42	1.41	1.41	1.40	1.40	1.39	1.39	1.39	1.38	1.38	.25	
2.01	1.96	1.94	1.91	1.89	1.87	1.86	1.83	1.83	1.82	1.80	1.80	.10	14
2.46	2.39	2.35	2.31	2.27	2.24	2.22	2.19	2.18	2.16	2.14	2.13	.05	
3.66	3.51	3.43	3.35	3.27	3.22	3.18	3.11	3.09	3.06	3.03	3.00	.01	
1.43	1.41	1.41	1.40	1.39	1.39	1.38	1.38	1.37	1.37	1.36	1.36	.25	
1.97	1.92	1.90	1.87	1.85	1.83	1.82	1.79	1.79	1.77	1.76	1.76	.10	15
2.40	2.33	2.29	2.25	2.20	2.18	2.16	2.12	2.11	2.10	2.08	2.07	.05	
3.52	3.37	3.29	3.21	3.13	3.08	3.05	2.98	2.96	2.92	2.89	2.87	.01	
1.41	1.40	1.39	1.38	1.37	1.37	1.36	1.36	1.35	1.35	1.34	1.34	.25	
1.94	1.89	1.87	1.84	1.81	1.79	1.78	1.76	1.75	1.74	1.73	1.72	.10	16
2.35	2.28	2.24	2.19	2.15	2.12	2.11	2.07	2.06	2.04	2.02	2.01	.05	
3.41	3.26	3.18	3.10	3.02	2.97	2.93	2.86	2.84	2.81	2.78	2.75	.01	
1.40	1.39	1.38	1.37	1.36	1.35	1.35	1.34	1.34	1.34	1.33	1.33	.25	
1.91	1.86	1.84	1.81	1.78	1.76	1.75	1.73	1.72	1.71	1.69	1.69	.10	17
2.31	2.23	2.19	2.15	2.10	2.08	2.06	2.02	2.01	1.99	1.97	1.96	.05	
3.31	3.16	3.08	3.00	2.92	2.87	2.83	2.76	2.75	2.71	2.68	2.65	.01	
1.39	1.38	1.37	1.36	1.35	1.34	1.34	1.33	1.33	1.32	1.32	1.32	.25	
1.89	1.84	1.81	1.78	1.75	1.74	1.72	1.70	1.69	1.68	1.67	1.66	.10	18
2.27	2.19	2.15	2.11	2.06	2.04	2.02	1.98	1.97	1.95	1.93	1.92	.05	
3.23	3.08	3.00	2.92	2.84	2.78	2.75	2.68	2.66	2.62	2.59	2.57	.01	
1.38	1.37	1.36	1.35	1.34	1.33	1.33	1.32	1.32	1.31	1.31	1.30	.25	
1.86	1.81	1.79	1.76	1.73	1.71	1.70	1.67	1.67	1.65	1.64	1.63	.10	19
2.23	2.16	2.11	2.07	2.03	2.00	1.98	1.94	1.93	1.91	1.89	1.88	.05	
3.15	3.00	2.92	2.84	2.76	2.71	2.67	2.60	2.58	2.55	2.51	2.49	.01	
1.37	1.36	1.35	1.34	1.33	1.33	1.32	1.31	1.31	1.30	1.30	1.29	.25	
1.84	1.79	1.77	1.74	1.71	1.69	1.68	1.65	1.64	1.63	1.62	1.61	.10	20
2.20	2.12	2.08	2.04	1.99	1.97	1.95	1.91	1.90	1.88	1.86	1.84	.05	
3.09	2.94	2.86	2.78	2.69	2.64	2.61	2.54	2.52	2.48	2.44	2.42	.01	

Table N.5.   *Table of Critical Values of the F Distribution* –Continued

df for de-nomi-nator	α	df for numerator											
		1	2	3	4	5	6	7	8	9	10	11	12
22	.25	1.40	1.48	1.47	1.45	1.44	1.42	1.41	1.40	1.39	1.39	1.38	1.37
	.10	2.95	2.56	2.35	2.22	2.13	2.06	2.01	1.97	1.93	1.90	1.88	1.86
	.05	4.30	3.44	3.05	2.82	2.66	2.55	2.46	2.40	2.34	2.30	2.26	2.23
	.01	7.95	5.72	4.82	4.31	3.99	3.76	3.59	3.45	3.35	3.26	3.18	3.12
24	.25	1.39	1.47	1 46	1.44	1.43	1.41	1.40	1.39	1.38	1.38	1.37	1.36
	.10	2.93	2.54	2.33	2.19	2.10	2.04	1.98	1.94	1.91	1.88	1.85	1.83
	.05	4.26	3.40	3.01	2.78	2.62	2.51	2.42	2.36	2.30	2.25	2.21	2.18
	.01	7.82	5.61	4.72	4.22	3.90	3.67	3.50	3.36	3.26	3.17	3.09	3.03
26	.25	1.38	1.46	1.45	1.44	1.42	1.41	1.39	1.38	1.37	1.37	1.36	1.35
	.10	2.91	2.52	2.31	2.17	2.08	2.01	1.96	1.92	1.88	1.86	1.84	1.81
	.05	4.23	3.37	2.98	2.74	2.59	2.47	2.39	2.32	2.27	2.22	2.18	2.15
	.01	7.72	5.53	4.64	4.14	3.82	3.59	3.42	3.29	3.18	3.09	3.02	2.96
28	.25	1.38	1.46	1.45	1.43	1.41	1.40	1.39	1.38	1.37	1.36	1.35	1.34
	.10	2.89	2.50	2.29	2.16	2.06	2.00	1.94	1.90	1.87	1.84	1.81	1.79
	.05	4.20	3.34	2.95	2.71	2.56	2.45	2.36	2.29	2.24	2.19	2.15	2.12
	.01	7.64	5.45	4.57	4.07	3.75	3.53	3.36	3.23	3.12	3.03	2.96	2.90
30	.25	1.38	1.45	1.44	1.42	1.41	1.39	1.38	1.37	1.36	1.35	1.35	1.34
	.10	2.88	2.49	2.28	2.14	2.05	1.98	1.93	1.88	1.85	1.82	1.79	1.77
	.05	4.17	3.32	2.92	2.69	2.53	2.42	2.33	2.27	2.21	2.16	2.13	2.09
	.01	7.56	5.39	4.51	4.02	3.70	3.47	3.30	3.17	3.07	2.98	2.91	2.84
40	.25	1.36	1.44	1.42	1.40	1.39	1.37	1.36	1.35	1.34	1.33	1.32	1.31
	.10	2.84	2.44	2.23	2.09	2.00	1.93	1.87	1.83	1.79	1.76	1.73	1.71
	.05	4.08	3.23	2.84	2.61	2.45	2.34	2.25	2.18	2.12	2.08	2.04	2.00
	.01	7.31	5.18	4.31	3.83	3.51	3.29	3.12	2.99	2.89	2.80	2.73	2.66
60	.25	1.35	1.42	1.41	1.38	1.37	1.35	1.33	1.32	1.31	1.30	1.29	1.29
	.10	2.79	2.39	2.18	2.04	1.95	1.87	1.82	1.77	1.74	1.71	1.68	1.66
	.05	4.00	3.15	2.76	2.53	2.37	2.25	2.17	2.10	2.04	1.99	1.95	1.92
	.01	7.08	4.98	4.13	3.65	3.34	3.12	2.95	2.82	2.72	2.63	2.56	2.50
120	.25	1.34	1.40	1.39	1.37	1.35	1.33	1.31	1.30	1.29	1.28	1.27	1.26
	.10	2.75	2.35	2.13	1.99	1.90	1.82	1.77	1.72	1.68	1.65	1.62	1.60
	.05	3.92	3.07	2.68	2.45	2.29	2.17	2.09	2.02	1.96	1.91	1.87	1.83
	.01	6.85	4.79	3.95	3.48	3.17	2.96	2.79	2.66	2.56	2.47	2.40	2.34
200	.25	1.33	1.39	1.38	1.36	1.34	1.32	1.31	1.29	1.28	1.27	1.26	1.25
	.10	2.73	2.33	2.11	1.97	1.88	1.80	1.75	1.70	1.66	1.63	1.60	1.57
	.05	3.89	3.04	2.65	2.42	2.26	2.14	2.06	1.98	1.93	1.88	1.84	1.80
	.01	6.76	4.71	3.88	3.41	3.11	2.89	2.73	2.60	2.50	2.41	2.34	2.27
∞	.25	1.32	1.39	1.37	1.35	1.33	1.31	1.29	1.28	1.27	1.25	1.24	1.24
	.10	2.71	2.30	2.08	1.94	1.85	1.77	1.72	1.67	1.63	1.60	1.57	1.55
	.05	3.84	3.00	2.60	2.37	2.21	2.10	2.01	1.94	1.88	1.83	1.79	1.75
	.01	6.63	4.61	3.78	3.32	3.02	2.80	2.64	2.51	2.41	2.32	2.25	2.18

Table N.6. *Table of Critical Values of the F Distribution*—Continued

df *for numerator*														df *for de-nomi-nator*
15	20	24	30	40	50	60	100	120	200	500	∞	α	
1.36	1.34	1.33	1.32	1.31	1.31	1.30	1.30	1.30	1.29	1.29	1.28	.25	
1.81	1.76	1.73	1.70	1.67	1.65	1.64	1.61	1.60	1.59	1.58	1.57	.10	22
2.15	2.07	2.03	1.98	1.94	1.91	1.89	1.85	1.84	1.82	1.80	1.78	.05	
2.98	2.83	2.75	2.67	2.58	2.53	2.50	2.42	2.40	2.36	2.33	2.31	.01	
1.35	1.33	1.32	1.31	1.30	1.29	1.29	1.28	1.28	1.27	1.27	1.26	.25	
1.78	1.73	1.70	1.67	1.64	1.62	1.61	1.58	1.57	1.56	1.54	1.53	.10	24
2.11	2.03	1.98	1.94	1.89	1.86	1.84	1.80	1.79	1.77	1.75	1.73	.05	
2.89	2.74	2.66	2.58	2.49	2.44	2.40	2.33	2.31	2.27	2.24	2.21	.01	
1.34	1.32	1.31	1.30	1.29	1.28	1.28	1.26	1.26	1.26	1.25	1.25	.25	
1.76	1.71	1.68	1.65	1.61	1.59	1.58	1.55	1.54	1.53	1.51	1.50	.10	26
2.07	1.99	1.95	1.90	1.85	1.82	1.80	1.76	1.75	1.73	1.71	1.69	.05	
2.81	2.66	2.58	2.50	2.42	2.36	2.33	2.25	2.23	2.19	2.16	2.13	.01	
1.33	1.31	1.30	1.29	1.28	1.27	1.27	1.26	1.25	1.25	1.24	1.24	.25	
1.74	1.69	1.66	1.63	1.59	1.57	1.56	1.53	1.52	1.50	1.49	1.48	.10	28
2.04	1.96	1.91	1.87	1.82	1.79	1.77	1.73	1.71	1.69	1.67	1.65	.05	
2.75	2.60	2.52	2.44	2.35	2.30	2.26	2.19	2.17	2.13	2.09	2.06	.01	
1.32	1.30	1.29	1.28	1.27	1.26	1.26	1.25	1.24	1.24	1.23	1.23	.25	
1.72	1.67	1.64	1.61	1.57	1.55	1.54	1.51	1.50	1.48	1.47	1.46	.10	30
2.01	1.93	1.89	1.84	1.79	1.76	1.74	1.70	1.68	1.66	1.64	1.62	.05	
2.70	2.55	2.47	2.39	2.30	2.25	2.21	2.13	2.11	2.07	2.03	2.01	.01	
1.30	1.28	1.26	1.25	1.24	1.23	1.22	1.21	1.21	1.20	1.19	1.19	.25	
1.66	1.61	1.57	1.54	1.51	1.48	1.47	1.43	1.42	1.41	1.39	1.38	.10	40
1.92	1.84	1.79	1.74	1.69	1.66	1.64	1.59	1.58	1.55	1.53	1.51	.05	
2.52	2.37	2.29	2.20	2.11	2.06	2.02	1.94	1.92	1.87	1.83	1.80	.01	
1.27	1.25	1.24	1.22	1 21	1 20	1.19	1.17	1.17	1.16	1.15	1.15	.25	
1.60	1.54	1.51	1.48	1.44	1.41	1.40	1.36	1.35	1.33	1.31	1.29	.10	60
1.84	1.75	1.70	1.65	1.59	1.56	1.53	1.48	1.47	1.44	1.41	1.39	.05	
2.35	2.20	2.12	2.03	1.94	1.88	1.84	1.75	1.73	1.68	1.63	1.60	.01	
1.24	1.22	1.21	1.19	1.18	1.17	1.16	1.14	1.13	1.12	1.11	1.10	.25	
1.55	1.48	1.45	1.41	1.37	1.34	1.32	1.27	1.26	1.24	1.21	1.19	.10	120
1.75	1.66	1.61	1.55	1.50	1.46	1.43	1.37	1.35	1.32	1.28	1.25	.05	
2.19	2.03	1.95	1.86`	1.76	1.70	1.66	1.56	1.53	1.48	1.42	1.38	.01	
1.23	1.21	1.20	1.18	1.16	1.14	1.12	1.11	1.10	1.09	1.08	1.06	.25	
1.52	1.46	1.42	1.38	1.34	1.31	1.28	1.24	1.22	1.20	1.17	1.14	.10	200
1.72	1.62	1.57	1.52	1.46	1.41	1.39	1.32	1.29	1.26	1.22	1.19	.05	
2.13	1.97	1.89	1.79	1.69	1.63	1.58	1.48	1.44	1.39	1.33	1.28	.01	
1.22	1.19	1.18	1.16	1.14	1.13	1.12	1.09	1.08	1.07	1.04	1.00	.25	
1.49	1.42	1.38	1.34	1.30	1.26	1.24	1.18	1.17	1.13	1.08	1.00	.10	∞
1.67	1.57	1.52	1.46	1.39	1.35	1.32	1.24	1.22	1.17	1.11	1.00	.05	
2.04	1.88	1.79	1.70	1.59	1.52	1.47	1.36	1.32	1.25	1.15	1.00	.01	

Table O.1.   *Table of Critical Values for the Studentized Range Test*

Error df	α	\multicolumn{10}{c}{r = number of means or number of steps between ordered means}
		2	3	4	5	6	7	8	9	10	11
5	.05	3.64	4.60	5.22	5.67	6.03	6.33	6.58	6.80	6.99	7.17
	.01	5.70	6.98	7.80	8.42	8.91	9.32	9.67	9.97	10.24	10.48
6	.05	3.46	4.34	4.90	5.30	5.63	5.90	6.12	6.32	6.49	6.65
	.01	5.24	6.33	7.03	7.56	7.97	8.32	8.61	8.87	9.10	9.30
7	.05	3.34	4.16	4.68	5.06	5.36	5.61	5.82	6.00	6.16	6.30
	.01	4.95	5.92	6.54	7.01	7.37	7.68	7.94	8.17	8.37	8.55
8	.05	3.26	4.04	4.53	4.89	5.17	5.40	5.60	5.77	5.92	6.05
	.01	4.75	5.64	6.20	6.62	6.96	7.24	7.47	7.68	7.86	8.03
9	.05	3.20	3.95	4.41	4.76	5.02	5.24	5.43	5.59	5.74	5.87
	.01	4.60	5.43	5.96	6.35	6.66	6.91	7.13	7.33	7.49	7.65
10	.05	3.15	3.88	4.33	4.65	4.91	5.12	5.30	5.46	5.60	5.72
	.01	4.48	5.27	5.77	6.14	6.43	6.67	6.87	7.05	7.21	7.36
11	.05	3.11	3.82	4.26	4.57	4.82	5.03	5.20	5.35	5.49	5.61
	.01	4.39	5.15	5.62	5.97	6.25	6.48	6.67	6.84	6.99	7.13
12	.05	3.08	3.77	4.20	4.51	4.75	4.95	5.12	5.27	5.39	5.51
	.01	4.32	5.05	5.50	5.84	6.10	6.32	6.51	6.67	6.81	6.94
13	.05	3.06	3.73	4.15	4.45	4.69	4.88	5.05	5.19	5.32	5.43
	.01	4.26	4.96	5.40	5.73	5.98	6.19	6.37	6.53	6.67	6.79
14	.05	3.03	3.70	4.11	4.41	4.64	4.83	4.99	5.13	5.25	5.36
	.01	4.21	4.89	5.32	5.63	5.88	6.08	6.26	6.41	6.54	6.66
15	.05	3.01	3.67	4.08	4.37	4.59	4.78	4.94	5.08	5.20	5.31
	.01	4.17	4.84	5.25	5.56	5.80	5.99	6.16	6.31	6.44	6.55
16	.05	3.00	3.65	4.05	4.33	4.56	4.74	4.90	5.03	5.15	5.26
	.01	4.13	4.79	5.19	5.49	5.72	5.92	6.08	6.22	6.35	6.46
17	.05	2.98	3.63	4.02	4.30	4.52	4.70	4.86	4.99	5.11	5.21
	.01	4.10	4.74	5.14	5.43	5.66	5.85	6.01	6.15	6.27	6.38
18	.05	2.97	3.61	4.00	4.28	4.49	4.67	4.82	4.96	5.07	5.17
	.01	4.07	4.70	5.09	5.38	5.60	5.79	5.94	6.08	6.20	6.31
19	.05	2.96	3.59	3.98	4.25	4.47	4.65	4.79	4.92	5.04	5.14
	.01	4.05	4.67	5.05	5.33	5.55	5.73	5.89	6.02	6.14	6.25
20	.05	2.95	3.58	3.96	4.23	4.45	4.62	4.77	4.90	5.01	5.11
	.01	4.02	4.64	5.02	5.29	5.51	5.69	5.84	5.97	6.09	6.19
24	.05	2.92	3.53	3.90	4.17	4.37	4.54	4.68	4.81	4.92	5.01
	.01	3.96	4.55	4.91	5.17	5.37	5.54	5.69	5.81	5.92	6.02
30	.05	2.89	3.49	3.85	4.10	4.30	4.46	4.60	4.72	4.82	4.92
	.01	3.89	4.45	4.80	5.05	5.24	5.40	5.54	5.65	5.76	5.85
40	.05	2.86	3.44	3.79	4.04	4.23	4.39	4.52	4.63	4.73	4.82
	.01	3.82	4.37	4.70	4.93	5.11	5.26	5.39	5.50	5.60	5.69
60	.05	2.83	3.40	3.74	3.98	4.16	4.31	4.44	4.55	4.65	4.73
	.01	3.76	4.28	4.59	4.82	4.99	5.13	5.25	5.36	5.45	5.53
120	.05	2.80	3.36	3.68	3.92	4.10	4.24	4.36	4.47	4.56	4.64
	.01	3.70	4.20	4.50	4.71	4.87	5.01	5.12	5.21	5.30	5.37
∞	.05	2.77	3.31	3.63	3.86	4.03	4.17	4.29	4.39	4.47	4.55
	.01	3.64	4.12	4.40	4.60	4.76	4.88	4.99	5.08	5.16	5.23

Table O.2. *Table of Critical Values for the Studentized Range Test*—Continued

r = number of means or number of steps between ordered means										Error
12	13	14	15	16	17	18	19	20	α	df
7.32	7.47	7.60	7.72	7.83	7.93	8.03	8.12	8.21	.05	5
10.70	10.89	11.08	11.24	11.40	11.55	11.68	11.81	11.93	.01	
6.79	6.92	7.03	7.14	7.24	7.34	7.43	7.51	7.59	.05	6
9.48	9.65	9.81	9.95	10.08	10.21	10.32	10.43	10.54	.01	
6.43	6.55	6.66	6.76	6.85	6.94	7.02	7.10	7.17	.05	7
8.71	8.86	9.00	9.12	9.24	9.35	9.46	9.55	9.65	.01	
6.18	6.29	6.39	6.48	6.57	6.65	6.73	6.80	6.87	.05	8
8.18	8.31	8.44	8.55	8.66	8.76	8.85	8.94	9.03	.01	
5.98	6.09	6.19	6.28	6.36	6.44	6.51	6.58	6.64	.05	9
7.78	7.91	8.03	8.13	8.23	8.33	8.41	8.49	8.57	.01	
5.83	5.93	6.03	6.11	6.19	6.27	6.34	6.40	6.47	.05	10
7.49	7.60	7.71	7.81	7.91	7.99	8.08	8.15	8.23	.01	
5.71	5.81	5.90	5.98	6.06	6.13	6.20	6.27	6.33	.05	11
7.25	7.36	7.46	7.56	7.65	7.73	7.81	7.88	7.95	.01	
5.61	5.71	5.80	5.88	5.95	6.02	6.09	6.15	6.21	.05	12
7.06	7.17	7.26	7.36	7.44	7.52	7.59	7.66	7.73	.01	
5.53	5.63	5.71	5.79	5.86	5.93	5.99	6.05	6.11	.05	13
6.90	7.01	7.10	7.19	7.27	7.35	7.42	7.48	7.55	.01	
5.46	5.55	5.64	5.71	5.79	5.85	5.91	5.97	6.03	.05	14
6.77	6.87	6.96	7.05	7.13	7.20	7.27	7.33	7.39	.01	
5.40	5.49	5.57	5.65	5.72	5.78	5.85	5.90	5.96	.05	15
6.66	6.76	6.84	6.93	7.00	7.07	7.14	7.20	7.26	.01	
5.35	5.44	5.52	5.59	5.66	5.73	5.79	5.84	5.90	.05	16
6.56	6.66	6.74	6.82	6.90	6.97	7.03	7.09	7.15	.01	
5.31	5.39	5.47	5.54	5.61	5.67	5.73	5.79	5.84	.05	17
6.48	6.57	6.66	6.73	6.81	6.87	6.94	7.00	7.05	.01	
5.27	5.35	5.43	5.50	5.57	5.63	5.69	5.74	5.79	.05	18
6.41	6.50	6.58	6.65	6.73	6.79	6.85	6.91	6.97	.01	
5.23	5.31	5.39	5.46	5.53	5.59	5.65	5.70	5.75	.05	19
6.34	6.43	6.51	6.58	6.65	6.72	6.78	6.84	6.89	.01	
5.20	5.28	5.36	5.43	5.49	5.55	5.61	5.66	5.71	.05	20
6.28	6.37	6.45	6.52	6.59	6.65	6.71	6.77	6.82	.01	
5.10	5.18	5.25	5.32	5.38	5.44	5.49	5.55	5.59	.05	24
6.11	6.19	6.26	6.33	6.39	6.45	6.51	6.56	6.61	.01	
5.00	5.08	5.15	5.21	5.27	5.33	5.38	5.43	5.47	.05	30
5.93	6.01	6.08	6.14	6.20	6.26	6.31	6.36	6.41	.01	
4.90	4.98	5.04	5.11	5.16	5.22	5.27	5.31	5.36	.05	40
5.76	5.83	5.90	5.96	6.02	6.07	6.12	6.16	6.21	.01	
4.81	4.88	4.94	5.00	5.06	5.11	5.15	5.20	5.24	.05	60
5.60	5.67	5.73	5.78	5.84	5.89	5.93	5.97	6.01	.01	
4.71	4.78	4.84	4.90	4.95	5.00	5.04	5.09	5.13	.05	120
5.44	5.50	5.56	5.61	5.66	5.71	5.75	5.79	5.83	.01	
4.62	4.68	4.74	4.80	4.85	4.89	4.93	4.97	5.01	.05	∞
5.29	5.35	5.40	5.45	5.49	5.54	5.57	5.61	5.65	.01	

Table P.   *Table of Critical Values of the F_{max} Statistic*

$$F_{max} = (\hat{\sigma}^2_{largest})/(\hat{\sigma}^2_{smallest})$$

df for $\hat{\sigma}^2_j$	α	\multicolumn{11}{c}{k = number of variances}
		2	3	4	5	6	7	8	9	10	11	12
4	.05	9.60	15.5	20.6	25.2	29.5	33.6	37.5	41.4	44.6	48.0	51.4
	.01	23.2	37.	49.	59.	69.	79.	89.	97.	106.	113.	120.
5	.05	7.15	10.8	13.7	16.3	18.7	20.8	22.9	24.7	26.5	28.2	29.9
	.01	14.9	22.	28.	33.	38.	42.	46.	50.	54.	57.	60.
6	.05	5.82	8.38	10.4	12.1	13.7	15.0	16.3	17.5	18.6	19.7	20.7
	.01	11.1	15.5	19.1	22.	25.	27.	30.	32.	34.	36.	37.
7	.05	4.99	6.94	8.44	9.70	10.8	11.8	12.7	13.5	14.3	15.1	15.8
	.01	8.89	12.1	14.5	16.5	18.4	20.	22.	23.	24.	26.	27.
8	.05	4.43	6.00	7.18	8.12	9.03	9.78	10.5	11.1	11.7	12.2	12.7
	.01	7.50	9.9	11.7	13.2	14.5	15.8	16.9	17.9	18.9	19.8	21.
9	.05	4.03	5.34	6.31	7.11	7.80	8.41	8.95	9.45	9.91	10.3	10.7
	.01	6.54	8.5	9.9	11.1	12.1	13.1	13.9	14.7	15.3	16.0	16.6
10	.05	3.72	4.85	5.67	6.34	6.92	7.42	7.87	8.28	8.66	9.01	9.34
	.01	5.85	7.4	8.6	9.6	10.4	11.1	11.8	12.4	12.9	13.4	13.9
12	.05	3.28	4.16	4.79	5.30	5.72	6.09	6.42	6.72	7.00	7.25	7.48
	.01	4.91	6.1	6.9	7.6	8.2	8.7	9.1	9.5	9.9	10.2	10.6
15	.05	2.86	3.54	4.01	4.37	4.68	4.95	5.19	5.40	5.59	5.77	5.93
	.01	4.07	4.9	5.5	6.0	6.4	6.7	7.1	7.3	7.5	7.8	8.0
20	.05	2.46	2.95	3.29	3.54	3.76	3.94	4.10	4.24	4.37	4.49	4.59
	.01	3.32	3.8	4.3	4.6	4.9	5.1	5.3	5.5	5.6	5.8	5.9
30	.05	2.07	2.40	2.61	2.78	2.91	3.02	3.12	3.21	3.29	3.36	3.39
	.01	2.63	3.0	3.3	3.4	3.6	3.7	3.8	3.9	4.0	4.1	4.2
60	.05	1.67	1.85	1.96	2.04	2.11	2.17	2.22	2.26	2.30	2.33	2.36
	.01	1.96	2.2	2.3	2.4	2.4	2.5	2.5	2.6	2.6	2.7	2.7
∞	.05	1.00	1.00	1.00	1.00	1.00	1.00	1.00	1.00	1.00	1.00	1.00
	.01	1.00	1.00	1.00	1.00	1.00	1.00	1.00	1.00	1.00	1.00	1.00

Table Q.   *Table of Critical Values of Cochran's Test for Homogeneity of Variance*

$$C = \frac{\text{largest } \hat{\sigma}_j^2}{\Sigma \hat{\sigma}_j^2}$$

df for $\hat{\sigma}_j^2$	α	$k = $ number of variances										
		2	3	4	5	6	7	8	9	10	15	20
1	.05	.9985	.9669	.9065	.8412	.7808	.7271	.6798	.6385	.6020	.4709	.3894
	.01	.9999	.9933	.9676	.9279	.8828	.8376	.7945	.7544	.7175	.5747	.4799
2	.05	.9750	.8709	.7679	.6838	.6161	.5612	.5157	.4775	.4450	.3346	.2705
	.01	.9950	.9423	.8643	.7885	.7218	.6644	.6152	.5727	.5358	.4069	.3297
3	.05	.9392	.7977	.6841	.5981	.5321	.4800	.4377	.4027	.3733	.2758	.2205
	.01	.9794	.8831	.7814	.6957	.6258	.5685	.5209	.4810	.4469	.3317	.2654
4	.05	.9057	.7457	.6287	.5441	.4803	.4307	.3910	.3584	.3311	.2419	.1921
	.01	.9586	.8335	.7212	.6329	.5635	.5080	.4627	.4251	.3934	.2882	.2288
5	.05	.8772	.7071	.5895	.5065	.4447	.3974	.3595	.3286	.3029	.2195	.1735
	.01	.9373	.7933	.6761	.5875	.5195	.4659	.4226	.3870	.3572	.2593	.2048
6	.05	.8534	.6771	.5598	.4783	.4184	.3726	.3362	.3067	.2823	.2034	.1602
	.01	.9172	.7606	.6410	.5531	.4866	.4347	.3932	.3592	.3308	.2386	.1877
7	.05	.8332	.6530	.5365	.4564	.3980	.3535	.3185	.2901	.2666	.1911	.1501
	.01	.8988	.7335	.6129	.5259	.4608	.4105	.3704	.3378	.3106	.2228	.1748
8	.05	.8159	.6333	.5175	.4387	.3817	.3384	.3043	.2768	.2541	.1815	.1422
	.01	.8823	.7107	.5897	.5037	.4401	.3911	.3522	.3207	.2945	.2104	.1646
9	.05	.8010	.6167	.5017	.4241	.3682	.3259	.2926	.2659	.2439	.1736	.1357
	.01	.8674	.6912	.5702	.4854	.4229	.3751	.3373	.3067	.2813	.2002	.1567
16	.05	.7341	.5466	.4366	.3645	.3135	.2756	.2462	.2226	.2032	.1429	.1108
	.01	.7949	.6059	.4884	.4094	.3529	.3105	.2779	.2514	.2297	.1612	.1248
36	.05	.6602	.4748	.3720	.3066	.2612	.2278	.2022	.1820	.1655	.1144	.0879
	.01	.7067	.5153	.4057	.3351	.2858	.2494	.2214	.1992	.1811	.1251	.0960
144	.05	.5813	.4031	.3093	.2513	.2119	.1833	.1616	.1446	.1308	.0889	.0675
	.01	.6062	.4230	.3251	.2644	.2229	.1929	.1700	.1521	.1376	.0934	.0709

Adapted from chapter 15 of *Techniques of Statistical Analysis,* edited by C. Eisenhart, M. W. Hastay, and W. A. Wallis, McGraw-Hill Book Company, 1947, with the permission of the editors and publishers.

Table R.   *Table of Critical Values for Spearman's Correlations*

N	Significance level (one-tailed test)	
	.05	.01
4	1.000	
5	.900	1.000
6	.829	.943
7	.714	.893
8	.643	.833
9	.600	.783
10	.564	.746
12	.506	.712
14	.456	.645
16	.425	.601
18	.399	.564
20	.377	.534
22	.359	.508
24	.343	.485
26	.329	.465
28	.317	.448
30	.306	.432

*Adapted from Olds, E. G. 1938. Distributions of sums of squares of rank differences for small numbers of individuals. *Ann. Math. Statist.*, **9**, 133-148, and from Olds, E. G. 1949. The 5% significance levels for sums of squares of rank differences and a correction. *Ann. Math. Statist.*, **20**, 117-118, with the permission of the publisher.

Table S.   *Table of Critical Values for Kendall's Coefficient of Concordance*

k	N				
	3	4	5	6	7
Values at the .05 level of significance					
3			64.4	103.9	157.3
4		49.5	88.4	143.3	217.0
5		62.6	112.3	182.4	276.2
6		75.7	136.1	221.4	335.2
8	48.1	101.7	183.7	299.0	453.1
10	60.0	127.8	231.2	376.7	571.0
15	89.8	192.9	349.8	570.5	864.9
20	119.7	258.0	468.5	764.4	1,158.7
Values at the .01 level of significance					
3			75.6	122.8	185.6
4		61.4	109.3	176.2	265.0
5		80.5	142.8	229.4	343.8
6		99.5	176.1	282.4	422.6
8	66.8	137.4	242.7	388.3	579.9
10	85.1	175.3	309.1	494.0	737.0
15	131.0	269.8	475.2	758.2	1,129.5
20	177.0	364.2	641.2	1,022.2	1,521.9

Adapted from Friedman, M. 1940. A comparison of alternative tests of significance for the problem of *m* rankings. *Ann. Math. Statist.*, **11**, 86-92, with the permission of the author and the publisher.

Table T.   *Table of Critical Values for Pearson's Correlations*

df P =	.050	.025	.010	.005
1	.988	.997	.9995	.9999
2	.900	.950	.980	.990
3	.805	.878	.934	.959
4	.729	.811	.882	.917
5	.669	.754	.833	.874
6	.622	.707	.789	.834
7	.582	.666	.750	.798
8	.549	.632	.716	.765
9	.521	.602	.685	.735
10	.497	.576	.658	.708
11	.476	.553	.634	.684
12	.458	.532	.612	.661
13	.441	.514	.592	.641
14	.426	.497	.574	.623
15	.412	.482	.558	.606
16	.400	.468	.542	.590
17	.389	.456	.528	.575
18	.378	.444	.516	.561
19	.369	.433	.503	.549
20	.360	.423	.492	.537
21	.352	.413	.482	.526
22	.344	.404	.472	.515
23	.337	.396	.462	.505
24	.330	.388	.453	.496
25	.323	.381	.445	.487
26	.317	.374	.437	.479
27	.311	.367	.430	.471
28	.306	.361	.423	.463
29	.301	.355	.416	.456
30	.296	.349	.409	.449
35	.275	.325	.381	.418
40	.257	.304	.358	.393
45	.243	.288	.338	.372
50	.231	.273	.322	.354
60	.211	.250	.295	.325
70	.195	.232	.274	.302
80	.183	.217	.256	.283
90	.173	.205	.242	.267
100	.164	.195	.230	.254

Table T is taken from Table V.A. of R. A. Fisher, *Statistical Methods for Research Workers,* Oliver & Boyd Ltd., Edinburgh, by permission of the author and publishers.

The probabilities given are for a one-sided test.

Table U.   *Table of Z' Transformations of r*

r	z'	r	z'	r	z'	r	z'	r	z'
.000	.000	.200	.203	.400	.424	.600	.693	.800	1.009
.005	.005	.205	.208	.405	.430	.605	.701	.805	1.113
.010	.010	.210	.213	.410	.436	.610	.709	.810	1.127
.015	.015	.215	.218	.415	.442	.615	.717	.815	1.142
.020	.020	.220	.224	.420	.448	.620	.725	.820	1.157
.025	.025	.225	.229	.425	.454	.625	.733	.825	1.172
.030	.030	.230	.234	.430	.460	.630	.741	.830	1.188
.035	.035	.235	.239	.435	.466	.635	.750	.835	1.204
.040	.040	.240	.245	.440	.472	.640	.758	.840	1.221
.045	.045	.245	.250	.445	.478	.645	.767	.845	1.238
.050	.050	.250	.255	.450	.485	.650	.775	.850	1.256
.055	.055	.255	.261	.455	.491	.655	.784	.855	1.274
.060	.060	.260	.266	.460	.497	.660	.793	.860	1.293
.065	.065	.265	.271	.465	.504	.665	.802	.865	1.313
.070	.070	.270	.277	.470	.510	.670	.811	.870	1.333
.075	.075	.275	.282	.475	.517	.675	.820	.875	1.354
.080	.080	.280	.288	.480	.523	.680	.829	.880	1.376
.085	.085	.285	.293	.485	.530	.685	.838	.885	1.398
.090	.090	.290	.299	.490	.536	.690	.848	.890	1.422
.095	.095	.295	.304	.495	.543	.695	.858	.895	1.447
.100	.100	.300	.310	.500	.549	.700	.867	.900	1.472
.105	.105	.305	.315	.505	.556	.705	.877	.905	1.499
.110	.110	.310	.321	.510	.563	.710	.887	.910	1.528
.115	.116	.315	.326	.515	.570	.715	.897	.915	1.557
.120	.121	.320	.332	.520	.576	.720	.908	.920	1.589
.125	.126	.325	.337	.525	.583	.725	.918	.925	1.623
.130	.131	.330	.343	.530	.590	.730	.929	.930	1.658
.135	.136	.335	.348	.535	.597	.735	.940	.935	1.697
.140	.141	.340	.354	.540	.604	.740	.950	.940	1.738
.145	.146	.345	.360	.545	.611	.745	.962	.945	1.783
.150	.151	.350	.365	.550	.618	.750	.973	.950	1.832
.155	.156	.355	.371	.555	.626	.755	.984	.955	1.886
.160	.161	.360	.377	.560	.633	.760	.996	.960	1.946
.165	.167	.365	.383	.565	.640	.765	1.008	.965	2.014
.170	.172	.370	.388	.570	.648	.770	1.020	.970	2.092
.175	.177	.375	.394	.575	.655	.775	1.033	.975	2.185
.180	.182	.380	.400	.580	.662	.780	1.045	.980	2.298
.185	.187	.385	.406	.585	.670	.785	1.058	.985	2.443
.190	.192	.390	.412	.590	.678	.790	1.071	.990	2.647
.195	.198	.395	.418	.595	.685	.795	1.085	.995	2.994

Table V.   Table of Estimated Tetrachoric Coefficients

r_t	$\dfrac{bc}{ad}$	r_t	$\dfrac{bc}{ad}$	r_t	$\dfrac{bc}{ad}$
.00	0–1.00	.35	2.49–2.55	.70	8.50– 8.90
.01	1.01–1.03	.36	2.56–2.63	.71	8.91– 9.35
.02	1.04–1.06	.37	2.64–2.71	.72	9.36– 9.82
.03	1.07–1.08	.38	2.72–2.79	.73	9.83– 10.33
.04	1.09–1.11	.39	2.80–2.87	.74	10.34– 10.90
.05	1.12–1.14	.40	2.88–2.96	.75	10.91– 11.51
.06	1.15–1.17	.41	2.97–3.05	.76	11.52– 12.16
.07	1.18–1.20	.42	3.06–3.14	.77	12.17– 12.89
.08	1.21–1.23	.43	3.15–3.24	.78	12.90– 13.70
.09	1.24–1.27	.44	3.25–3.34	.79	13.71– 14.58
.10	1.28–1.30	.45	3.35–3.45	.80	14.59– 15.57
.11	1.31–1.33	.46	3.46–3.56	.81	15.58– 16.65
.12	1.34–1.37	.47	3.57–3.68	.82	16.66– 17.88
.13	1.38–1.40	.48	3.69–3.80	.83	17.89– 19.28
.14	1.41–1.44	.49	3.81–3.92	.84	19.29– 20.85
.15	1.45–1.48	.50	3.93–4.06	.85	20.86– 22.68
.16	1.49–1.52	.51	4.07–4.20	.86	22.69– 24.76
.17	1.53–1.56	.52	4.21–4.34	.87	24.77– 27.22
.18	1.57–1.60	.53	4.35–4.49	.88	27.23– 30.09
.19	1.61–1.64	.54	4.50–4.66	.89	30.10– 33.60
.20	1.65–1.69	.55	4.67–4.82	.90	33.61– 37.79
.21	1.70–1.73	.56	4.83–4.99	.91	37.80– 43.06
.22	1.74–1.78	.57	5.00–5.18	.92	43.07– 49.83
.23	1.79–1.83	.58	5.19–5.38	.93	49.84– 58.79
.24	1.84–1.88	.59	5.39–5.59	.94	58.80– 70.95
.25	1.89–1.93	.60	5.60–5.80	.95	70.96– 89.01
.26	1.94–1.98	.61	5.81–6.03	.96	89.02–117.54
.27	1.99–2.04	.62	6.04–6.28	.97	117.55–169.67
.28	2.05–2.10	.63	6.29–6.54	.98	169.68–293.12
.29	2.11–2.15	.64	6.55–6.81	.99	293.13–923.97
.30	2.16–2.22	.65	6.82–7.10	1.00	923.98–
.31	2.23–2.28	.66	7.11–7.42		
.32	2.29–2.34	.67	7.43–7.75		
.33	2.35–2.41	.68	7.76–8.11		
.34	2.42–2.48	.69	8.12–8.49		

Reprinted from M. D. Davidoff and H. W. Goheen, "A table for the rapid determination of the tetrachoric correlation coefficient." *Psychometrika,* 1953, **18**, 115-121, by permission of the authors and the editors of *Psychometrika.* See also "A Note on a table for the rapid determination of the tetrachoric correlation coefficient" by Davidoff, *Psychometrika,* Vol. 19, No. 2, June 1954.

To use the table, set the data up in a 2 X 2 table. Enter the table with be/ad or its reciprocal, whichever is the larger, and read the corresponding value of r_t. The accuracy of the values given for r_t does not extend beyond the second decimal, and interpolation between the values listed for be/ad is not recommended.

Table W.   *Table of Squares, Square Roots and Reciprocals*

N	N²	$\sqrt{N}$	$\sqrt{10N}$	1/N
1	1	1.000 000	3.162 278	1.0000000
2	4	1.414 214	4.472 136	.5000000
3	9	1.732 051	5.477 226	.3333333
4	16	2.000 000	6.324 555	.2500000
5	25	2.236 068	7.071 068	.2000000
6	36	2.449 490	7.745 967	.1666667
7	49	2.645 751	8.366 600	.1428571
8	64	2.828 427	8.944 272	.1250000
9	81	3.000 000	9.486 833	.1111111
10	100	3.162 278	10.00000	.1000000
11	121	3.316 625	10.48809	.09090909
12	144	3.464 102	10.95445	.08333333
13	169	3.605 551	11.40175	.07692308
14	196	3.741 657	11.83216	.07142857
15	225	3.872 983	12.24745	.06666667
16	256	4.000 000	12.64911	.06250000
17	289	4.123 106	13.03840	.05882353
18	324	4.242 641	13.41641	.05555556
19	361	4.358 899	13.78405	.05263158
20	400	4.472 136	14.14214	.05000000
21	441	4.582 576	14.49138	.04761905
22	484	4.690 416	14.83240	.04545455
23	529	4.795 832	15.16575	.04347826
24	576	4.898 979	15.49193	.04166667
25	625	5.000 000	15.81139	.04000000
26	676	5.099 020	16.12452	.03846154
27	729	5.196 152	16.43168	.03703704
28	784	5.291 503	16.73320	.03571429
29	841	5.385 165	17.02939	.03448276
30	900	5.477 226	17.32051	.03333333
31	961	5.567 764	17.60682	.03225806
32	1 024	5.656 854	17.88854	.03125000
33	1 089	5.744 563	18.16590	.03030303
34	1 156	5.830 952	18.43909	.02941176
35	1 225	5.916 080	18.70829	.02857143
36	1 296	6.000 000	18.97367	.02777778
37	1 369	6.082 763	19.23538	.02702703
38	1 444	6.164 414	19.49359	.02631579
39	1 521	6.244 998	19.74842	.02564103
40	1 600	6.324 555	20.00000	.02500000
41	1 681	6.403 124	20.24846	.02439024
42	1 764	6.480 741	20.49390	.02380952
43	1 849	6.557 439	20.73644	.02325581
44	1 936	6.633 250	20.97618	.02272727
45	2 025	6.708 204	21.21320	.02222222
46	2 116	6.782 330	21.44761	.02173913
47	2 209	6.855 655	21.67948	.02127660
48	2 304	6.928 203	21.90890	.02083333
49	2 401	7.000 000	22.13594	.02040816
50	2 500	7.071 068	22.36068	.02000000

N	N²	$\sqrt{N}$	$\sqrt{10N}$	1/N .0
50	2 500	7.071 068	22.36068	2000000
51	2 601	7.141 428	22.58318	1960784
52	2 704	7.211 103	22.80351	1923077
53	2 809	7.280 110	23.02173	1886792
54	2 916	7.348 469	23.23790	1851852
55	3 025	7.416 198	23.45208	1818182
56	3 136	7.483 315	23.66432	1785714
57	3 249	7.549 834	23.87467	1754386
58	3 364	7.615 773	24.08319	1724138
59	3 481	7.681 146	24.28992	1694915
60	3 600	7.745 967	24.49490	1666667
61	3 721	7.810 250	24.69818	1639344
62	3 844	7.874 008	24.89980	1612903
63	3 969	7.937 254	25.09980	1587302
64	4 096	8.000 000	25.29822	1562500
65	4 225	8.062 258	25.49510	1538462
66	4 356	8.124 038	25.69047	1515152
67	4 489	8.185 353	25.88436	1492537
68	4 624	8.246 211	26.07681	1470588
69	4 761	8.306 624	26.26785	1449275
70	4 900	8.366 600	26.45751	1428571
71	5 041	8.426 150	26.64583	1408451
72	5 184	8.485 281	26.83282	1388889
73	5 329	8.544 004	27.01851	1369863
74	5 476	8.602 325	27.20294	1351351
75	5 625	8.660 254	27.38613	1333333
76	5 776	8.717 798	27.56810	1315789
77	5 929	8.774 964	27.74887	1298701
78	6 084	8.831 761	27.92848	1282051
79	6 241	8.888 194	28.10694	1265823
80	6 400	8.944 272	28.28427	1250000
81	6 561	9.000 000	28.46050	1234568
82	6 724	9.055 385	28.63564	1219512
83	6 889	9.110 434	28.80972	1204819
84	7 056	9.165 151	28.98275	1190476
85	7 225	9.219 544	29.15476	1176471
86	7 396	9.273 618	29.32576	1162791
87	7 569	9.327 379	29.49576	1149425
88	7 744	9.380 832	29.66479	1136364
89	7 921	9.433 981	29.83287	1123596
90	8 100	9.486 833	30.00000	1111111
91	8 281	9.539 392	30.16621	1098901
92	8 464	9.591 663	30.33150	1086957
93	8 649	9.643 651	30.49590	1075269
94	8 836	9.695 360	30.65942	1063830
95	9 025	9.746 794	30.82207	1052632
96	9 216	9.797 959	30.98387	1041667
97	9 409	9.848 858	31.14482	1030928
98	9 604	9.899 495	31.30495	1020408
99	9 801	9.949 874	31.46427	1010101
100	10 000	10.00000	31.62278	1000000

From *Experimental Design: Procedures for the Behavioral Sciences* by Roger E. Kirk. Copyright 1968 by Wadsworth Publishing Company, Inc. Reprinted by permission of the publisher, Brooks/Cole Publishing Company, Monterey, California.

Index

The Author

Merle E. Meyer (Ph.D, University of Washington) is Professor and Chairman of the Psychology Department and Director of Social and Behavioral Sciences, University of Florida. In addition, he is Professor of Clinical Psychology at that university. Prior to his current post, Dr. Meyer was Chairman of the Psychology Department at Western Washington State College, and prior to that he was Chairman and Major Professor of Psychology at Whitman College.

He is a member of numerous honorary, learned, and professional societies, including the American Psychological Association's Division of Experimental Psychology, Division of the Experimental Analysis of Behavior, and Division of Comparative and Physiological Psychology, as well as the Psychonomic Society, Animal Behavior Society, and Sigma Xi.

Among Dr. Meyer's several honors, he has been recognized as a Danforth Associate and has been awarded a Carnegie Fellowship and a National Science Foundation Faculty Fellowship. He has published over seventy research papers and edited three books within the general areas of statistics-measurement, learning-motivation, physiological-comparative, and developmental psychology.